ARTS
AND
LETTERS

ARTS
AND
LETTERS

by Edmund White

CLEIS
PRESS

Published in the United States by Cleis Press Inc., P.O. Box 14684, San Francisco, California 94114.
Printed in the United States.
Cover design: Scott Idleman
Cover photograph: Marion Ettlinger
Book design: Karen Quigg
Cleis Press logo art: Juana Alicia
First Edition.
10 9 8 7 6 5 4 3 2

List of previously published works appear on page 361.

Library of Congress Cataloging-in-Publication Data

White, Edmund, 1940-
    Arts and letters / by Edmund White.—1st ed.
       p. cm.
    ISBN 1-57344-195-3 (hardcover : alk. paper)
1. Arts, Modern—20th century. 2. Artists—Biography. I. Title.
    NX456.W49 2004
    700'.92'2—dc22
                    2004010166

This book is dedicated to
Troy Hill.

Contents

ARTS

PERSONALITIES

Introduction:
Members of the Clan
and Fellow Travelers

ANY COLLECTION OF ESSAYS reflects the assignments one has received from various newspapers and journals as much as it reveals abiding preoccupations. I've been lucky in the last two decades that I've been free to pick and choose among the book reviews and profiles that have been proposed to me. Certainly no artist or writer discussed in this book has failed to engage my sympathies, and a handful (Nabokov, Merrill, Proust, Isherwood, Genet) have been icons throughout my creative life.

A novelist inevitably has a strategic relationship to anyone he writes an essay about. I am drawn to a writer or photographer or painter because he or she actually was or is a friend and belonged to the same clan (Dowell, Rorem, Foucault, Chatwin, Brainard, Isherwood, Mapplethorpe) or because they count as inspiring antecedents (Proust, Nabokov, Gide, Genet, George Eliot). I've always been intrigued by unjustly forgotten writers (Bunin, Hamsun, Robbe-Grillet) and have written to bring their names back before the public, if only for an instant.

There are three general essays in this book: one on the historical novel (a subject that interested me when I was writing my own first historical novel, *Fanny: A Fiction*), another an autobiographical overview of my career as a gay novelist and biographer, and finally a piece on bisexuality prompted by a reading of Marjorie Garber's influential *Vice Versa: Bisexuality and the Eroticism of Everyday Life.*

Of course most of the essays in this book are about gay men, since I've often been asked to comment on their work—and I've just as naturally felt unusually moved by men like me and their creative achievement. Not all the people in this book are on easy terms with their sexuality and as a consequence I've not always dwelled on it. Others, such as Deneuve, Nabokov, Bunin, Hamsun, Paley, Rebecca Horn and Duchamp, are or were famously straight. Nobody's perfect.

I have rewritten these essays to a greater or lesser extent in preparing them for this collection. Sometimes I've taken bits from three different pieces on Paul Bowles and fashioned a new essay; at other junctures I've not so much updated a portrait as removed from it distractingly dated references. Since I've devoted a long biography to Genet and a short one to Proust, I make no apology for the slightness of these essays about them. Yves Saint Laurent, David Geffen, Catherine Deneuve, and Elton John I've listed as "Personalities" since they are colorful and significant cultural icons or forces but they can't be snuck into the rubrics "Letters" or "Arts."

I would like to thank Patricia Willis at the Beinecke Library of Yale University for unearthing some of these articles and essays from my archives there. Frédérique Delacoste and Felice Newman have helped immensely to see these pages into print at Cleis Press. I want to thank Donald Weise for conceiving of this collection in the first place.

—EDMUND WHITE

LETTERS

Writing Gay

SOME FORTY YEARS AGO I won a college literary award for a play I'd written that was called *The Blueboy in Black*. The prize money I spent buying cases of a terrible sweet fizzy Italian wine named Asti Spumante, which I considered wildly elegant. Though the award money was quickly dissipated, my name and the name of my play were announced in the *New York Times,* which led to an agent contacting me. Through her a production was arranged and two years later my play, starring the black actors Cicely Tyson and Billy Dee Williams, opened off-Broadway. The play, partly because at the time I was out-of-touch with the newest trends, was a bit démodé, a recycling of the Theatre of the Absurd and Jean Genet's *The Blacks,* and I was criticized for being dated. Worse, in 1964 we were at the height of the Civil Rights Movement when the race problem was supposed to have been solved, but I was showing angry blacks on stage who were taking revenge on their white employers. The critic for the *Times,* Bosley Crowther, said, "Negroes in America have enough problems without Mr. White." The most positive review, by Alan Pryce-Jones in *Theatre Arts,* called it one of the two best plays of the year. But when I met Mr. Pryce-Jones twenty years later (and this is the Proustian part) and thanked him for his kindness, he had no recollection of my play.

The play was not only about race but also about homosexuality. When my ultraconservative Republican father came to the opening night with a business associate he asked me privately, "What's it about—the usual?," which was his way of referring to a gay theme. I had to confess that it was a little bit about the usual. Of course for him discussion of race was almost as offensive, so it must have made for a rather uncomfortable evening.

When I was a junior at the University of Michigan I had won a somewhat smaller award for a collection of short stories, and there again "the usual" had been a recurring theme at a time when almost no gay literature existed—and when even the very term was unknown. To be sure, Baldwin had recently published a despairing homosexual-themed novel, his beautiful book *Giovanni's Room,* and Gore Vidal and Paul Bowles and Tennessee Williams were all experimenting with short gay fiction, much of it extremely deft and sophisticated, but none of them became celebrated or successful for their gay fiction. They all had to go on to quite different work in order to achieve their immense fame.

I suppose I never had much of a choice. For some reason I had a burning need to explore my own gay identity in fiction. I'd written my first gay novel when I was just fifteen and a boarding student at Cranbrook boys school in Bloomfield Hills, outside Detroit. Since I didn't play sports I had the long afternoons in which to do my homework and then the official two-hour enforced study hall in the evenings to work on my novel, which I called *The Tower Window.* It was all about a boy much like myself who turns to an adult man, a handsome Mexican, because he's been rejected by a girl his own age. I had a highly developed fantasy that I would sell this novel and make a fortune, which would allow me to escape my dependence on my parents—but even though my mother's secretary typed it up for me I never got around to sending it off. Perhaps I didn't know where to send it.

No matter what I wrote, even at the very beginning, it was bound to have homosexual subject matter. I studied fiction in a creative writing class at the University of Michigan in a workshop conducted by Allan Seager. The one time I had a conference with him he thoroughly frightened me by saying, "The nouns in a paragraph should be arranged like the heads in a painting by Uccello." "Utrillo?" I asked. "Aw, get out of here," he said, fed up and waving me out.

In those years, long before gay liberation, no one could write a proud, self-respecting, self-affirming gay text, since no gay man, no matter how clever, had found a way to like himself—not even Proust, the sovereign intellect of fiction, had managed that one. But a homosexual writer could be impertinent, elusive, camp—and that was a tone I adopted in a novel I submitted to the Hopwood Committee in my senior year, a book called *The Amorous History of Our Youth,* which was quite an arch performance, starting with its title, an allusion to two books—Lermontov's *A Hero of Our Times* and a scandalous character attack of the seventeenth century called *The Amorous History of the Gauls* by Bussy-Rabutin, Mme de Sévigné's cousin. Louis XIV exiled him for his book. I remember that the Hopwood judge, a woman novelist, was quite rightly so irritated by the flipness of this novel—an account of a sexual love between two brothers, one rich and one poor, separated at birth—that she couldn't contain her rage and gave it a severe drubbing (I rather fear I wasn't meant to see this evaluation and pulled strings in order to read it). Of course she was right— the novel must have been appallingly grating. But I suspect that in that period, when no homosexual could defend his identity as anything other than an illness, a sin or a crime, our inexpressible anger came out in bizarre forms—as a hostile and inappropriate superciliousness, for instance.

And though I was a fairly bright student I had almost no skill as a writer. I wrote in a trance, almost unconsciously, because I was writing to stay sane, to conduct my own autoanalysis, to drain off my daily dose of anguish, remorse and hostility. That was the era of the bitchy queen, since there were no available modes of open anger, of self-legitimizing affirmation. I wrote as drag queens bitched at each other on the street corner—to claim attention, to shock, even to horrify the straight people passing by. Later, after gay liberation, we were able as people and as writers to redefine ourselves as members of a minority group who could mount campaigns for our rights and against societal stereotyping, but back then, forty years ago, such a program would have caused us to puff on our cigarettes and to say, "Get *you,* Mary."

This terrible unconsciousness and obsessiveness continued to mark my writing after graduation. I'd found a job in the very bastion of American conservatism, the halls of *Time* and *Life.* I worked in New York for Time-Life Books, writing essays about everything from the giant molecule to the Japanese garden, but every night I grimly returned to my office after a solitary supper and wrote many, many bad plays, which my agent refused even to send out—and a long novel. The novel rather confusingly bore a title, *The Beautiful Room Is Empty,* which I used years later for an entirely different book. This book was confessional, despairing, and all about a hopeless, one-sided love affair with a handsome, brilliant guy my age who became temporarily insane, so guilty was he about being a homosexual at all. This book, which I finished in 1966, three years before the advent of gay liberation, was sent out to some twenty publishing houses, all of which rejected it. Two of the editors who read it were clandestinely gay and were afraid to accept it lest they be labeled as gay themselves and fired—or so they told me years later.

After this defeat I thought I should write a good book—it sounds ludicrous, but it only then occurred to me that I could and should write a book that was obviously impressive. For if I'd never bothered to write well myself, I was a connoisseur of good writing done by others. I loved Firbank and Proust and Colette and Jean Genet and at this time specially Nabokov. I could suddenly imagine what it would be like to bring to the page the same pleasure I took in reading the fiction of these geniuses. Not that I hoped to emulate their art; I just wanted to exercise in my own writing the taste that made me respond to theirs.

The Usual was still part of my new novel, *Forgetting Elena*, except now it was as obscure as the rest of the book. The narrator is an amnesiac who doesn't want to admit he's lost his memory and who struggles to second-guess from other people's reactions what sort of person he must be. He has no idea what sex and love are, and the heterosexual love scene, which must be one of the most peculiar in literature, he construes as something like a dangerous and ultimately painful religious rite. A man named Herbert displays all the signs (at least to our eyes) of being in love with the narrator. The whole thing takes place in an island kingdom (which may or may not be real—or perhaps just a distorted vision of Fire Island), an ambiguity which in some ways recalls the real or unreal kingdom in Nabokov's *Pale Fire*. *Forgetting Elena*, my first book to be published, was not perceived as a gay-themed book at all; three years after it had come out to no acclaim whatsoever, Nabokov singled it out as one of his favorite American novels. By then, of course, most of the first edition had been pulped.

I don't want to recapitulate my writing career, such as it has been; I'd rather focus on two or three aspects of gay writing that have interested me in recent years. Most importantly, I'd like to talk about the writing of biographies of gay men and how that has affected some of my own fiction.

In 1982 I published what has possibly become my best-known book, *A Boy's Own Story*. At the time the craze for memoirs had not yet taken off.

Of course generals who'd won the battle of Iwo Jima might write their memoirs, but the interest in their historical accomplishment was firmly established in advance. Back then few nobodies wrote their memoirs, and I was quite happy to call my piece of autofiction a novel. First of all calling something a novel, at least back then, protected a writer from pesky personal questions of the sort, "Why did you betray your high school teacher when he was so nice to you?"

Second, by calling my book a novel I could take all sorts of liberties with the truth without being held accountable for the discrepancies. I could change around the chronology to make it more dramatic. I could reduce the cast of characters, so messy and redundant in real life. And, in my particular case, I could nudge my own weird case towards the norm, at least the gay norm, and hope to pick up a bit more reader identification along the way. Whereas in real life I had been bizarrely brazen (or perhaps driven) sexually, and just as unpleasantly precocious intellectually, in the fictional derivation from my life I could make my stand-in shy and not outstanding in any way. In short, I could make him much more likable.

In the summer of 1983 I moved to Paris, where I stayed for the next sixteen years except for a few short intervals. When I finally moved back to the States four years ago I was surprised by many things: the institutionalization of identity politics, which had still been struggling to impose itself when I'd left; the concurrent ascendance of a rather Stalinist brand of political correctness; and finally the parallel growth of *Oprah*-style programs and the memoir industry. I suppose all three phenomena—identity politics, political correctness and the memoir (usually linked to a disability or an oppressed minority or a childhood trauma)—could all be labeled aspects of the culture of complaint, though I see them more as parts of a very American tradition of bearing witness and of commandeering that testimony into a political program: the personal as political, which may be America's most salient contribution to the armamentarium of progressive politics.

I followed up *A Boy's Own Story* with two other books in a trilogy—*The Beautiful Room Is Empty* (1987) and *The Farewell Symphony*, ten years later, in 1997. Already, with *The Beautiful Room Is Empty*, I had discovered that whereas there is something eternal about childhood, that the strong nameless moods of that first period of life are undated, there is something highly historical about early adulthood. The sheltered if miserable childhood I had in Cincinnati and Texas as a boy could just as easily have been led in the nineteenth century as in the twentieth. My childhood, at least, was all yearning and brooding, running through woods and fields, and much of it was spent in isolation or with maids who resented all of us. As a result I never indicated when or where the action was taking place in *A Boy's Own Story*. Even the narrator's all-male boarding school has a distinctly nineteenth-century feel to it. The one thing that was undeniably American about the book, as I learned later from talking with European readers, was how free and unsupervised the boy was. But that sort of freedom was something Europeans had noticed about American children already in the nineteenth century

By the time I got to describing my protagonist's early adulthood in *The Beautiful Room Is Empty* I knew it was crucial that I show exactly when and where he came of age. Coming out in New York in the 1960s was obviously something very different from what coming out in London in 2000, say, would be. Moreover, I decided to have my narrator-protagonist enter directly into a major historical turning point—the beginning of gay liberation. That breakthrough occurred in June 1969 at the Stonewall Uprising, the first time gays resisted arrest en masse and rose up against the cops after the raid of a popular gay bar in Greenwich Village. As it happened, I had witnessed this event firsthand and it had had a direct impact on me.

In fact in planning the book I started with the violence that would come at the end, with Stonewall, and decided to construct a book leading up to it that would prompt even the most conservative heterosexual reader to become impatient with the hero's self-hatred and his years spent in therapy seeking in vain to go straight. I wanted that reader to say out loud, "Oh, for crissake, get on with your life and leave us all in peace." I was pleased when the daily *New York Times* critic wrote something almost exactly like that.

In the ten years that intervened between the publication of this second book and that of the third I had devoted seven years to researching and writing my biography of Jean Genet.

I would like to tell you a little bit about that experience and then eventually lead the discussion back to how my Genet affected the shape of *The Farewell Symphony*.

Genet died in 1986 and a year later my editor, Bill Whitehead, asked me if I knew anyone interested in writing his biography. Without much reflection I said, "Me!" I thought the project would take no more than three years of researching and writing. But at the end of three years I'd written not one word and knew almost nothing about my subject. I lied to my new editor (Bill in the meanwhile had died of AIDS) and said it was coming along swimmingly, but in fact I was in a complete panic and considered stepping in front of an oncoming bus just to get out of my contract. I didn't dare admit I didn't even know the name of the village where Genet had been born (no one did). Although I'm considered brash, I could be defeated by the slightest refusal from a stranger, and in the world Genet had left behind everyone was very strange indeed.

Genet was completely unlike most subjects of literary biography, who are middle-class prodigies, adored by their mothers; the mothers save every scrap of their juvenilia and as the little darlings grow up they are surrounded by friends who are also writers or at least highly literate. These other people all keep journals, send letters, now even print up the e-mails they receive from distinguished friends, publish accounts of their own lives and create fictional portraits of one another. The parents and mates of the middle-class writer save every scrap they write and their movements are widely reported in the press.

Writing a biography of someone such as Sartre, for instance, is primarily a question of what to exclude in an overly documented life.

Genet, by contrast, was an orphan, raised in a village—but which one?—and had already entered the French penal system by the time he was an adolescent. He had no literary friends until he was in his early thirties and was briefly taken up by the gay men around Cocteau as well as by Cocteau himself. Even that Parisian literary interlude lasted less then ten years. Throughout most of his life Genet's friends were criminals, fellow soldiers, fellow prisoners, shady boyfriends, thieves for whom he worked as a fence, Black Panthers, Palestinian soldiers—in other words, people hard to identify and locate, people who die young, people who are suspicious of a white American interviewer, people who in any event scarcely know what a biography is. Criminals in particular are people who die young, who can't be found (if they're still alive), who if they're found won't talk, who if they talk are not to be believed and who in any event want to be paid. I knew perfectly well that Genet would have disliked me, since he detested whites, members of the middle-class, Americans, writers and avowed homosexuals—on five counts I was out. Why should his friends and survivors like me any more? Moreover, Genet detested the idea of anyone ever writing his biography, partly because a "real" life would challenge and even overthrow his own account of things in his so-called autobiographical novels such as *A Thief's Journal.*

In addition, Genet had eventually rejected and abandoned all his friends, so each time I met one of them I was dealing with a wounded person, someone who remembered Genet only as a painful episode in his or her life, yet sometimes as the most important one.

After three years of fruitless research I was so obsessed with Genet that I'd virtually forgotten I'd ever written novels of my own. Once in England when I was giving a talk about Genet someone asked me about my own fiction and I blinked, uncomprehending for a moment.

In my ignorance and arrogance I had initially hired a beautiful American boy and girl to help me with my research, though they had no special skills as scholars and had never read Genet's oeuvre (nor did they get around to it now). They had no idea of where to start, no more than I did. Unwittingly we had stumbled onto the most challenging and intransigent of all modern literary biographical subjects. Nevertheless, each of these two beauties provided me with one vital link in the story. The young woman I hired to pretend to take French lessons from Paule Thevenin, someone who had refused to grant me an interview. Paule was an extremely difficult older woman who had befriended Genet in the 1960s and helped him prepare the final version of his great play *The Screens.* Although my young American spoke excellent French she engaged Paule for a year as her coach (all at my expense); at last she'd become sufficiently close to her to be able to ask her to give me an interview, which was finally granted. After an initial coldness Mme Thevenin opened up and shared freely with me hundreds of specific and enlightening memories—and even showed me X-rays of Genet's kidneys! (Her husband had been Genet's doctor and had provided him with the powerful sleeping pills he'd consumed by the handful.)

The young handsome American man also had a find. A friend of his sent him a clipping from *Le Morvandiau,* a newspaper published in Paris for people who'd moved to the capital from the rather primitive district known as the Morvan. In this paper was an article by a certain M. Bruley about "my classmate, Jean Genet." The article itself was a whitewash of Genet's highly questionable character but it did give us the name of the village (Alligny) and M. Bruley eventually led us to a dozen other villagers who'd grown up with Genet and considered him to have been a highly dubious character.

As the years went by I teamed up with the world's leading Genet expert, Albert Dichy, who prepared me a complete chronology of Genet's life and who established Genet's elaborate police record in every town and village in France. He also introduced me to key people in Genet's life including his three heirs (a seven-year-old Moroccan boy, a circus horse trainer and an ex–race car driver). Through Albert I met Genet's literary lawyer and several criminal lawyers who'd worked with his legal dossier as well as Leila Shahid, the Palestinian ambassador to Paris. I interviewed a woman who pointed a pistol at the lion when her husband put his head in the animal's mouth during their circus act.

Genet was as assiduous a traveler as I myself am, so I took some pleasure in following him to Damascus and to Morocco, where I visited his grave, which looks out on the local prison, a bordello and the sea— three of the great tropes of his fiction. I interviewed Jane Fonda, the mother of one of my former students, Vanessa Vadim. She had met Genet at a benefit for the Panthers in the early 1970s in Hollywood. Genet had grabbed onto her because she was one of the few people present who could speak French at the party (for years she'd lived in France when she'd been married to the French film director Roger Vadim). Genet took her phone number and called her the next morning at six. He'd awakened in a strange house, he didn't know where he was and he wanted his coffee. Miss Fonda said, "Okay, I'll come right away but where are you?" Genet didn't know. At last she, who'd grown up in Hollywood and knew every house, said, "Go outside and come back and describe the pool to me." He did so and she said, "Oh, you're at Donald Sutherland's. I'll be right over."

One of the valuable keys to Genet's American period that Albert Dichy tracked down was the testimony of a Swiss woman named Marianne de Pury. Albert had seen that Genet had written her several letters, which she had sold or given to the library at Kent State University. We tracked her down just as she was moving back to Switzerland from Santa Fe, New Mexico, after some twenty-five years in the States. She had been a pretty upper-class Swiss girl with blonde hair and a pearl necklace who'd moved to the States and almost immediately become involved with the Panthers and in particular their minister of information known as Big Man. It was she who had translated for Genet almost everywhere he went in the States—and fortunately she had a good memory.

I read the interviews that Genet had given to Japanese papers and Arab papers and Spanish theatrical magazines and Austrian and Italian magazines—none of them previously collected. I got my hands on some rather stiff and literary love letters Genet had written in his late twenties to Lily Pringsheim, a German leftist living in Czechoslovakia in the mid-1930s, a woman who had harbored him when he was fleeing the authorities after he'd deserted from the army. I interviewed the English journalist who'd interviewed Genet on television—a memorable occasion during which Genet, insisting that every person in the room had as much to say as he did, or more, turned the cameras on the technicians and interrogated them. I went to a garage outside Cannes where one of Genet's lovers now worked in what he called the Garage Saint Genet. His wife spoke freely and interestingly to me, but her husband gunned the motors he was repairing louder and louder to drown out our voices. I interviewed a ghastly racist millionaire who had been one of Genet's first patrons and who spoke insultingly of blacks while his black servants waited on us. I interviewed Sartre's male secretary from the years during which Sartre had known Genet and written his huge tome, his literary psychoanalysis, *Saint Genet*. In the end I spent every penny I earned, and then some, on my research and my travels, but my book did win the National Book Critics Circle Award—and the citation singled out my research as what most impressed the judges.

When at last, after the seven years consecrated to Genet, I came back to my own fiction I found that I had been influenced not so much by Genet (whose work I intensely admire but have never attempted to emulate) as by the experience of writing a biography. And not just any biography but a gay biography which, depending on the subject, is marginally different from a biography of a heterosexual. Of course all lives are different, and nationality or profession or period are factors at least as determining as sexual orientation. But I would like to suggest that there are special problems and considerations touching on gay biography. In Genet's case he usually fell for younger heterosexual men with connections to the underworld. Genet several times in his life built houses for these lovers and reserved a room in each house for himself. He invariably befriended their wives and in disputes usually took their side. Because I'm gay myself and just thirty years younger than Genet, I flatter myself that I knew how to interpret these relationships. From my experience of the world I knew that such relationships between older gay "patrons," if you will, and younger heterosexual studs were quite common in the old Mediterranean world and I knew enough not to make too much of them or too little.

Biographers, to be sure, are no better or worse than their fellow citizens and in treating the lives of lesbians and gay men biographers have been guilty of whitewashing or rewriting or even suppressing their subjects' sexual and romantic lives.

Perhaps the prejudices against homosexuals can be said to begin with ignoring many gay writers or relegating them to playing minor roles in the lives of supposedly more important heterosexuals. A figure like Oscar Wilde was always too influential to ignore—too scandalous, too quotable— though at first he was turned into a tragic fop, a witty, epigrammatic Pagliacci, and few biographers were prepared to take him as seriously as everyone took even such an incompetent heterosexual as Nietzsche, for instance, though the parallels are striking (a love of paradox, argumentation through apothegms, hatred of the bourgeoisie, little concern about self-contradiction, an exhortation of readers towards the transvaluation of all values). Only Richard Ellmann's *Oscar Wilde* redressed this balance; moreover, it took another gay man, Neil Bartlett in *Who Was That Man?*, to speculate about the exact nature of Wilde's sexuality. Of course the question is far from being settled and Wilde's grandson, Merlin Holland, whom I've met, is campaigning for Wilde-as-bisexual.

Just as homosexuals themselves were (and often still are) shrugged off as minor retainers at life's banquet, uninitiated in the mysteries of childbirth, adultery and divorce, in the same way an elusive but major gay novelist such as the late Edwardian Ronald Firbank has been largely ignored by biographers, despite the fact that writers as different from one another as Hemingway and Evelyn Waugh all claimed they'd been influenced by him, Hemingway by the practice of representing a crowd scene through unassigned bits of dialogue and Waugh through the exquisite timing of his humor. Brigid Brophy did write a massive biography of Firbank, *Prancing Novelist,* but it is so subjective, capricious and unreliable as to be anything but a standard life. Brophy refused to conduct any original research of her own. She relied on the only other biographer, Miriam Benkowitz, an American librarian, who approached Firbank primarily as a bibliographical problem. Never was a biographer more ill-suited to her subject. Only now is an English gay man, Richard Canning, at last writing Firbank's life, reopening long-closed archives, revisiting all the places Firbank knew, including Rome and North Africa, and studying the effect of Jamaican Creole in Firbank's novel *Sorrow in Sunlight*. Canning has also uncovered the comedy of errors that surrounded the author's burial and reburial in Rome. Such painstaking scholarship is lavished on a writer only when the biographer is convinced of his first-rank value.

In the past sometimes all trace of homosexuality in a statesman or military officer, say, would simply be erased. Cambacarès, for instance, was Napoleon's prime minister and so openly gay that he convinced the emperor to decriminalize homosexuality. Thanks to Cambacarès France had no laws against homosexuals until the pro-Nazi Vichy government came to power during World War II. But when I picked up a French biography of Cambacarès written in the 1950s, there was no mention of his sexuality nor of his influence on France's laws. A misplaced prudishness, in other words, had led the biographer to ignore altogether the legislation for which his subject is most likely to be remembered.

When I was working on my life of Genet the French publisher was worried that I would turn him into a "gay writer." (I had made the mistake in an interview in the French press of calling Rimbaud a homosexual poet.) The French are strenuously opposed to all minority designations of writers, past or present; it's part of the legacy of their universalism dating back to the Enlightenment and the Revolution and it is one of the main cultural differences with the values of the United States, the home of identity politics. Gallimard, the French publisher, was relieved when my Genet manuscript came in and seemed devoid of any special pleading for Genet as a gay hero.

When I wrote my Penguin life of Proust I decided to discuss his homosexuality—how else could I make my book different from the hundreds that had preceded it?—but I was attacked for this approach in the *New York Times Book Review* and in the *New York Review*. The *Times* critic, the English novelist and biographer Peter Ackroyd, took me to task for reducing Proust to his sexuality. Similarly, Roger Shattuck in the *New York Review* struck a blow for Proust's universality against my supposedly narrowing view. And the Egyptian memoirist André Aciman announced that Proust had been a masturbator and not homosexual at all.

I think anyone who has read my book will attest to at least the density and inclusiveness of my brief biography and to my discussion of everything from Proust's crippling asthma to his youthful social-climbing, from his liberating translations of Ruskin into French to his various and prolonged struggles to become a writer, from his dark vision of love and friendship to his strenuous efforts to court prize committees, but I refuse to apologize for my treatment of his sexuality, especially since it presented him with complex literary problems.

Proust himself recognized that homosexuality was a key theme—and a thoroughly original one—in his book and worried that his friend Lucien Daudet had beat him to the punch in his early novel. Only when Proust had examined Daudet's book was he reassured that it was a trivial and inexplicit treatment of the theme and no threat to his own primacy in the field. Proust had promised his publisher, Gallimard, early on that his book might be judged "obscene" since it treated a "pedophile." Indeed many of the female characters turn out to be lesbians and nearly all of the male characters are queer—except "Marcel," the narrator and the stand-in for Proust himself. Since, as Proust told André Gide, all of his sexual experiences had been with men and none with women, he was obliged to transpose his homosexual experiences into heterosexual terms in order to flesh out those scenes, characters and situations. This transposition, I'd claim, was in fact the most creative part of his book, the very area where he had to combine memory of real experiences with objective observations of real women he'd studied in the world and their heterosexual male lovers. In his treatment of Albertine, the great love of Marcel's life and the name that appears most frequently in the book, Proust drew on his affair with Agostinelli, his chauffeur, who met an early death during a flying lesson as a pilot, and with Henri Rochat, a handsome Swiss waiter at the Ritz who eventually moved in with Proust.

When I call these Proustian transpositions of men into women "creative," I'm remembering my own experiences when I was in Ann Arbor as a student between 1958 and 1962. I belonged to the Sigma Nu fraternity but I was also cruising guys in the Union and less reputable places. One of my best friends was arrested for doing what I was constantly doing—and he had to report to a parole officer once a week for the next seven years. Not surprisingly, he became a prison psychologist not long afterwards.

In that period it was impossible to speak openly of one's homosexual adventures. One had to translate them into heterosexual terms, and one had to have a detailed and capacious memory to keep track of all the lies one had invented, often on the spur of the moment. One also needed to be resourceful in finding plausible female activities (sewing, dancing) that would be a counterpart to the real-life male activities of one's partners (sewing, cruising).

I feel that Proust's elaborate transposition of male friends into female characters was an example of the same sort of obsessive and creative mendacity. The transpositions were precisely the most artistic part of Proust's conception of his book, and to ignore them is to miss out on a true literary value peculiarly suited to be analyzed by a biographer.

Just to finish my little disquisition on homosexuality and biography, I'd say that gay lives are not like straight lives. One must know them intimately from the inside in order to place the right emphasis on the facts. For instance, those heterosexual biographers and critics who have attacked Michel Foucault for infecting people even after he knew he was positive for AIDS are ignoring several crucial things. First, Foucault was a sadomasochistic bottom, a slave, unlikely to have infected anyone, since a slave does not transmit his sperm. Second, Foucault certainly didn't know he was positive, since there was no test to determine one's HIV status in Europe until 1984, after Foucault's death. Finally, since he was a friend of mine I can attest that he guessed at his diagnosis only five months before his death. He worried that he might have infected his lover, Daniel Defert, but he knew perfectly well that he'd never infected any of those leather guys in San Francisco. But of course my approach would not please the muckrakers. I'm afraid that all too often biography is the revenge of little people on big people.

Or take another issue, not at all technical or medical but just as telling. Those critics who attacked Brad Gooch's *City Poet,* the biography of the New York poet of the '50s, Frank O'Hara, complained that Gooch had talked too much about his sex life and not enough about the poetry. But in fact O'Hara, the founder of "Personalism," wrote poems to his tricks and had such an active sex life, one might be tempted to say, in order to generate his poems, which are often dedicated to real tricks (who were all also his friends) or imaginary crushes. When Joan Accocela in the *New Yorker* complained that *City Poet* was too "gossipy," she missed the point. O'Hara's grinding social schedule and hundreds of sexual encounters offend people who want his life to be like a straight man's of the same period. If O'Hara had had one or two gay marriages and had made his domestic life more important than his friendships, then he would have seemed like a reassur ing translation of straight experience into gay terms. But O'Hara's real life was messy and episodic in the retelling, even picaresque—it doesn't add up to a simple, shapely narrative. It's all day after day of drinks with X, dinner with Y and sex with Z—not what we expect in the usual literary biography. Biographies were originally meant to be exemplary lives, whether they were written as the *Lives of the Saints* or Plutarch's *Lives,* whereas the lives of most gay men, especially those before gay liberation, were furtive, fragmented, submerged—half-erased tales that need special tools if they are to be rendered in glowing colors.

When I turned to *The Farewell Symphony,* the last volume of my autobiographical trilogy, I had just come out of the experience of researching and writing the Genet biography. I was now both a biographer and a novelist, I could tell myself. People often speak of fictional techniques—suspense, shapeliness, narrative flow—influencing the form of biographies, but in my case biographical techniques influenced my new understanding of the novel. Writing Genet's life—which led from his childhood as a peasant foster child in the Morvan into a life of petty crime, prostitution and begging to a flight across Eastern Europe in the 1930s into French prisons under the Nazis and the threat of extermination in the death camps—from such a marginal existence to the consecration of success as a published novelist and produced playwright and the subject of a massive psychoanalytic study by Sartre, the greatest philosopher of the day, and later to contacts with the leading European sculptor, Giacometti, and two other prominent philosophers, Foucault and Derrida, finally to a posthumous masterpiece, *Prisoner of Love,* dedicated to the Black Panthers and the Palestinians—writing this amazing story, with its completely unexpected developments, convinced me that no matter how scattered and multifarious a person's activities might be, the fact that they all have happened to one individual moving chronologically through time lends the story a surprising coherence. Having written Genet's life I took on the subject of my own life in the 1970s and '80s in a novel, *The Farewell Symphony,* with a new willingness to discuss subjects I had downplayed or excluded altogether in the previous two books—subjects such as friendships, intellectual projects, artistic career and family relationships, sexual peccadilloes and romantic one-night stands—a multitude of subjects I had soft-pedaled in my earlier volumes of autobiographical fiction.

The novel as a genre is essentially a nineteenth century bourgeois con-coction. In a Jane Austen novel a small cast of characters, all members of the gentry or nobility, revolve around each other in a village until two or four get married. The mother's bad values, the father's incapacitating eccentricity, the young women's vanity or virtue—everything is properly redressed or punished or rewarded by the last page. As in a Haydn trio the simplest themes are fully exploited and thoroughly developed. For better or worse *Emma* remains our ideal of the novel, the Ur-novel.

There is no way modern gay life could be shoved into this Procrustean bed. Often the most intense and memorable moments in a gay life are with-out foreshadowing or consequence. A moment ago I deliberately used the expression "romantic one-night stands" for its shock value, for straight people often imagine that sex at the sauna must be cold and impersonal pre-cisely because it is out of all social context and may never be repeated. Outsiders assume that "anonymous sex" is somehow unfeeling or mechani-cal or merely lust-driven; neither Emma nor Elizabeth would know what to make of it. And yet, as André Gide recalled at the end of his life in his book *Ainsi Soit-Il,* the most meaningful moment of his eventful life had been sex with two beautiful Arab teenagers who'd been assigned to his caravan when he crossed Tunisia at the beginning of the twentieth century. Another French thinker, Michel Foucault, once remarked that if courtship was the most romantic moment for the heterosexual couple, for a gay lover the most romantic moment was after sex and after one had put one's brand-new partner in a taxi. Straight love is all about anticipation, whereas gay love is all aftermath. In straight life love, friendship and sex are ideally all joined in the same person, whereas in gay life these drives can be separated out.

Perhaps assimilation and the safe-sex years have caused gay life in the '90s and in our decade to resemble straight life, but in the period I wanted to cover in *The Farewell Symphony,* the time between the beginning of gay liberation and the onset of AIDS, this period that Brad Gooch has called The Golden Age of Promiscuity, gay life was radically different from any-thing novelists had ever written about before unless we go back to *The Satyricon* of Petronius. In *The Farewell Symphony* I stretched the bound-ary of coherence to the breaking point but I had the courage to do so because I'd written a long biography of a man who could not be totalized, whose evolution was always surprising and certainly unpredictable and whose affairs were always messy.

If I had begun my autobiographical series with a cool distance between my adult self as narrator and myself as teenage protagonist, if I had reshaped my life in the first two volumes towards telling a good story and structuring a pleasing narrative, in the last volume, *The Farewell Symphony,* I decided to narrow the distance between narrator and protagonist, even as the story in real time was catching up with the moment in which I was writing the book. It was all a bit like the end of *A Hundred Years of Solitude* in which the last member of the Buendia family, as the allotted century comes to an end, is reading about himself reading before the book and the village catch fire and go up in flames in a great synthesis of conflagration.

Before I began the Genet biography I had imagined I'd turn my autobiographical series into a tetralogy, one volume devoted to the '70s and the heyday of promiscuity and one to the '80s and the tragedy of AIDS. But after the decade that went by following the publication of the second volume I realized that in the late '90s it would be intolerable to read one book about everyone having a great time sexually and even more painful to read another volume about everyone dying. Accordingly I decided to collapse the two books into one and to weave my way back and forth from the '80s into the '70s. The inevitable gloomy trajectory of a strict chronology I would avoid, just as a temporal fluidity would mitigate both the tragic aftermath and the preceding hedonism.

I have not mentioned in these pages many of the issues that have affected my career as a gay author. I have not talked about the gay writing group, The Violet Quill, which I belonged to at the time I took my own leap forward and wrote *A Boy's Own Story*. I could have pointed out how this group was revolutionary because it did not address in its fiction an apology for gay life to a straight reader, as all previous gay writing had done, even Genet's. I could have argued that the gay writing that emerged in the late '70s and throughout the '80s plunged the reader into the midst of gay urban experience. No longer were we writing about lonely and tortured gay men nor about gay couples living in the forest or on a deserted coast. Now for the first time we were showing the gay ghetto and gay friendships as well as gay romances. Nor were we presenting just a few anguished and ever-so-sensitive esthetes; no, we wanted to show the full range of the gay typology, as anthological as that of any society.

I could have written about how this moment in gay writing is now coming to an end and is spawning mindless gay genre writing (murder mysteries and dog stories and teen dating tales) or something more serious, something one could call post-gay writing, in which one or two characters might be gay but in which they are inserted into a more general society. I'm thinking of post-gay writers such as Michael Cunningham or Allan Gurganus or Peter Cameron.

I could have touched on many subjects but I have tried to concentrate on just two or three things, drawing on a career I know well, my own. I've hoped to show how my own writing has evolved away from a traditional conception of the novel towards something broader, more episodic, even picaresque, and how the reach of *The Farewell Symphony* also owes something to a new, more daring conception of gay biography.

The New Historical Novel

DICKENS AND GEORGE ELIOT almost never invoke the products of their day. It's remarkable how few footnotes are required to clarify the text of a first-rate nineteenth-century author. Perhaps for that very reason social historians, in search of information about material culture, prefer the novels of a Gissing to a Robert Louis Stevenson, of a Eugène Sue to a Flaubert. If you want to know about the factory conditions of the period you must read Mrs. Gaskell's *North and South*, just as if you want to know about the suffering of the London poor you must read Mrs. Humphrey Ward (or Mayhew).

Perhaps one could even be tempted to say that a classic novelist re-creates an era from the inside out and concentrates on rendering rather than discussing the great social and political and intellectual currents of a particular period, whereas a lesser novelist attempts to make up for an insufficient grasp of the soul of an epoch by devoting himself or herself to its upholstery. This rule, probably not by coincidence, works against, for instance, the enduring reputation of engagé novels of the 1930s about social problems whereas it honors and preserves novels of a moral or psychological density like those of Henry James in an earlier period.

Writing need not have a clear political message or erupt into slogans in order to exert a subtle political power over us. One could imagine, for instance, a bad or weak novel that shows the plight of a lone Native

American lost in the big city and comments on his condition in a heavy-handed, programmatic way. Such a book might be ultimately less effective politically or ethically than one that has no explicit message but that represents without commentary the complex group life of a reservation, say. In other words it is more progressive to show the functioning of a reservation than to tell the reader any number of high-sounding messages about Native Americans. The life that is imagined, especially in a historical novel, can prompt a rethinking of prejudices, a new understanding of a community that is more thorough than a weakly imagined but more explicitly political bit of sloganeering. When we read historical fiction (or fiction of any sort) we are in search of an experience, not a paraphrasable idea.

We can only laugh when we read in a recent bad historical novel about the encounter between the schoolgirl Fanny Skynner and William Wordsworth. When Wordsworth announces he wants to write poetry in a contemporary idiom, Fanny says,

> "You'll do it.... I know, you'll do it. A complete renewal of poetry in England. You've got to overthrow all the worn-out, dated models of your forebears. You've got to carry out a revolution!"
>
> William seized her hand and kissed it. "If more readers of poetry were like you, Miss Skynner, the future of literature would be secure. Poets need encouragement to persevere and carry out the deepest longings of their hearts. Your words are like rain falling on my parched earth. Thank you."

This dialogue commits what Hollywood calls the mistake of being "on the money," that is, it is too eager to communicate exactly what the Cliff Notes version of the novel would want the characters to say. There is no indirection, nothing accidental, nothing at cross-purposes.

Walter Benjamin even goes so far as to say that classic storytelling, which is close to the oral tradition, sticks in the mind longer precisely because it is devoid of information, which is more characteristic of the printed word and the modern novel.

Permit me to quote one long paragraph from Benjamin's essay "The Storyteller": "The first storyteller of the Greeks was Herodotus. In the fourteenth chapter of the third book of his *Histories*, there is a story from which much can be learned. It deals with Psammenitus. After the Egyptian king Psammenitus had been vanquished and captured by the Persian king Cambyses, Cambyses was bent on humbling his prisoner. He ordered that Psammenitus be placed on the road that the Persian triumphal procession was to take. And he further arranged that the prisoner should see his daughter pass by as a maid going to the well with her pitcher. While all the Egyptians were lamenting and bewailing this spectacle, Psammenitus stood alone, mute and motionless, his eyes fixed on the ground, and when presently he saw his son, who was being taken along in the procession to be executed, he likewise remained unmoved. But when he subsequently recognized one of his servants, an old impoverished man, in the ranks of the prisoners, he beat his fists against his head and gave all the signs of deepest mourning.

"This tale shows what true storytelling is. The value of information does not survive the moment in which it was new. It lives only at that moment, it has to surrender to it completely and explain itself to it without losing any time. A Story is different. It does not expend itself. It preserves and concentrates its energy and is capable of releasing it even after a long time. Accordingly, Montaigne referred to this Egyptian king and asked himself why he mourned only when he caught sight of his servant. Montaigne answered: 'Since he was already over-full of griefs, it took only the smallest increase for it to burst thorough its dams.' Thus Montaigne. But one could also say: The king is not moved by the fate of those of royal blood, for it is his own fate. Or: We are moved by much on the stage that does not move us in life; to the king, this servant is only an actor. Or: Great grief is pent up and breaks forth only with relaxation; seeing this servant was the relaxation. Herodotus offers no explanations. His report is utterly dry. That is why, after thousands of years, this story from ancient Egypt is still capable of provoking astonishment and reflection. It is like those seeds of grain that have lain for centuries in the airtight chamber of the pyramids and have retained their germinative power to this day."

Of course there is the greatest of historical novelists, Tolstoy in *War and Peace,* who discusses at length his little-man theory of history, but these discussions, subtle and interesting as they are, would not suffice to make us keep reading his long book. What we remember afterwards are the little Princess's slight down on her lip or Natasha singing out one clear high note in an empty ballroom out of the sheer exuberance of existing or Pierre's confusion during the Battle of Borodino as to who is on which side as he bobs through the different ranks wearing his high white hat. Or we remember Prince Andrei's gradual indifference to life as he prepares to die, as he turns his face to the wall. These are the piquant and irreducible details that glow in our memories years later when we have long since forgotten Tolstoy's pronouncements on the unpredictability of future events.

Sometimes Tolstoy even imagines his details so brilliantly that they derail the message he was setting out to demonstrate. In *Anna Karenina*, for instance, he was hoping to denounce the heroine as a man-devouring, lascivious she-devil, but he abandoned an early version of the book that did just that because he sensed it was shallow and unconvincing esthetically. When he returned to the book much later it grew under his pen into the living, contradictory, hard-to-parse book it was to become in which Anna is a tragic figure and not an allegorical one.

I may sound as if I'm endorsing the unconscious storyteller while denigrating the intellectual and constantly questioning writer. Nothing could be farther from my intention. Perhaps explicit discussion, or what Benjamin dismisses as "information," may be ephemeral, but the presentation of historical action in a novel can and should follow a highly cunning design. The historical novelist must be something of a philosopher, even if he or she does not spell out his thinking. For instance, the historical novelist should decide that what counts is history, not nature. Like a good Marxist he or she should see human nature as malleable, not as fixed for all eternity. To be sure, such an approach will contradict the spirit of much of our popular culture, including our popular fiction (what Roland Barthes refers to dismissively as "myth"). Barthes has shown us how the function of bourgeois literature in general and of modern myth in particular is to depoliticize speech, or at least to disguise its reactionary drift, to empty out the human and the historical and to replace it with something incontrovertible and universal—with NATURE written in all caps. As Barthes writes, "…myth is constituted by the loss of the historical quality of things: in myth, things lose the memory that they were made…. A conjuring trick has taken place; it has turned reality inside out, it has emptied it of history and has filled it with Nature…."

If Barthes is right, then the corrective function of the new, serious historical novelist is to reverse the process followed by the modern myths of advertising and entertainment and genre fiction. The progressive historical novelist must banish nature and re-create history. For instance, we must not suggest that boys will be boys, regardless of their period and place, or that love obeys eternal laws irrespective of the particular social and economic circumstances of the characters. In fact, as we know, love changes constantly. The high aristocratic passion of Racine's *Phèdre* or even of *Romeo and Juliet* is the destructive, impractical, overbred sentiment characteristic of a privileged caste descended from hotheaded warriors but now evolved into a court society with a nostalgia for the violence and cruel caprice of the past. The tragic hopelessness of high passion struck court audiences of the seventeenth century as admirable: noble, as proof of the characters' high birth, as a form of emotional conspicuous consumption. Those characters were placed in a historical setting in faraway Italy or Greece in order to free the author's fantasy from the restraints of realism.

By the same token the cunning love strategies indulged in by the characters in *Les Liaisons dangereuses* are typical of a bored society in the late eighteenth century that has a traditional bride-price esteem for virginity and fidelity yet practices nothing now but licentiousness and calculated seduction. By contrast, *Madame Bovary*, written almost a hundred years later, is a thoroughly modern novel because the heroine betrays what was then the recently created institution of companionate marriage; she even betrays it in a highly conventional way—through pathetic acts of adultery.

If as historical novelists we do not show these ever-changing practices and definitions of love then we are guilty of replacing history with nature. We mislead our readers into believing that nothing has ever been different from right now. We have embraced an extremely conservative and pessimistic worldview. We begin to coo those unhelpful platitudes—"Oh, I guess love is the same the world over" or "Mother love is always the same powerful force" or "Blood is thicker than water" or "There's nothing new under the sun." The job of the enlightened historical novelist is to show that the sun never rises twice on the same human sentiments. Each period has its own character, and no sentiment is natural, a tabula rasa uninscribed by the prevailing social forces. If we could be airlifted into eighteenth-century France, say, we would find everything utterly foreign, starting with the humor.

Many books of fiction, even most books, are historical novels, whether we call them that or not. The usual mode of narrative, of course, is the storytelling past tense, which suggests that this story belongs to that special fairy tale temporal zone of "once upon a time."

For instance, when I wrote in the 1980s about the 1950s I not only had to describe the fashions and automobiles of the time but I also needed to re-create the moral atmosphere. Since *A Boy's Own Story* is the first volume in a trilogy about evolving attitudes toward homosexuality in the second half of the twentieth century, I needed to create a base line of oppression, something against which to measure the subsequent advances of later decades. In that first volume I wanted to show the power of psychiatry over gays, who had willingly internalized their own oppression. I wanted to show that the only allies gays had were bohemians, a small, embattled community of artists who were too cool and cosmopolitan to mistreat homosexuals, although there were notable exceptions; the Abstract Expressionists in New York at that time were sometimes dangerously homophobic. I wanted to show the total and unexamined suppression and exploitation of blacks in the white America of the 1950s, something that the teenage narrator is sensitive to precisely because he is also oppressed to a lesser extent and for quite different reasons. The parallel struggles of blacks and gays represent a repeating sub-theme in my trilogy (which includes *The Beautiful Room Is Empty* and *The Farewell Symphony*).

I also wanted to indicate how the all-male homosocial world of the boys' boarding school, far from being the erotic funfest that it's shown to be in most gay pornography, actually institutionalizes homosexual dread. Like the army barracks or the athletes' locker room, the all-male dormitory is easily destabilized by any whisper of homosexual desire—not that any such whispers were ever heard back then. Homosexuality was feared precisely because it was surrounded by silence, and the silence was proof of the fear. One could watch television for a year back then without ever hearing the word pronounced; now, by contrast, homosexuality has become the main source of humor on television, replacing black and Jewish themes.

Finally, at the end of my novel I wanted to show my young self-hating homosexual protagonist betraying the only adult man who had ever reciprocated his desire. When the young hero turns in the part-time music teacher to the school authorities, he accuses him, accurately enough, of offering drugs to the other kids rather than of sleeping with the narrator, which had also happened but mustn't be mentioned. This accusation functions as the trap door beside the bed and as an expression of the boy's self-hatred. As the next to the last paragraph reads: "Sometimes I think I seduced and betrayed Mr. Beattie because neither one action nor the other alone but the complete cycle allowed me to have sex with a man and then to disown him and it; this sequence was the ideal formulation of my impossible desire to love a man but not to be a homosexual. Sometimes I think I liked bringing pleasure to a heterosexual man...at the same time I was able to punish him for not loving me."

This passage was the most unpopular in the whole book since up till the last page the hero looked something like a victim, a nice guy if only given the chance to come out and enjoy some affection or at least action. Now, given the chance, he destroys the man who has responded to his advances. A film producer once told me that this tough, unpleasant conclusion was what had turned off several people who'd been tempted to adapt the book to the cinema. Despite the regrettable loss of revenue and celebrity, I remained committed to my goal; I felt I had to show how a deforming period deforms people. I didn't want my lad to be a positive role model, an appealing oleograph of a victim; I wanted to show how he had internalized the general homophobia of the era and become somewhat monstrous as a result. I was writing a historical novel about my own past.

For if I disapprove of too many brand names in lieu of a genuine re-creation of the moral and political tension of an epoch, by the same token I dislike characters who are flat ideals, made up of attractive posturing and rendered by describing their clothes and stylish possessions rather than presented as rounded human beings forged out of hard moral choices, some of them choices for evil. Perhaps the whole matter can be traced back to Aristotle and adjudicated by him. In the *Poetics* Aristotle chooses action over mere secondary qualities as the chief dynamic source of energy in a drama. As he writes: "Tragedy is essentially an imitation not of persons but of action and life, of happiness and misery. All human happiness or misery takes the form of action; the end for which we live is a certain kind of activity, not a quality. Character gives us qualities, but it is in our actions—what we do—that we are happy or the reverse."

This distinction between defining action and accessory qualities is relevant to a serious discussion of historical fiction since no other genre has at its most meretricious invited more vapid scene-painting and sentimental fakery. If we are to give historical fiction the same weight we admire in the best tales of modern life then we must forego the picturesque and trace out the consequences of moral choices, but only those that were genuine options in their period. We must set aside any up-to-date notions of fairness and erotic appeal, of well-functioning small families and happy marriages between sharing and loving partners of the same age and station. On the contrary—we must uncover the buried shapes of long-forgotten values and social arrangements. We must remember that until the twentieth century the condescension of the upper class and the submissiveness of the working class were considered normal and even admirable; Beryl Bainbridge's excellent recent novel, *Master Georgie,* works so well because it accurately re-creates these class distinctions in the mid-nineteenth century—and shows that they did not preclude genuine affection. We must recognize that in certain periods women were prized for their robustness—in Maupassant's story "Boule de Suif" a Prussian officer occupying a town in Normandy will not let a group of French nuns and notables travel on until the roly-poly prostitute in their midst agrees to sleep with him. If we were writing about the same period we would be making a mistake if we transferred to the France of 1870 our own ideal of anorexic women. Just as we would be in error if we showed the typical married couple in Victorian England as consisting of a man and woman of the same age; the usual arrangement was for the groom to be thirty-five and the bride eighteen or nineteen, an age difference that made somewhat more plausible the idea that the man was wiser than his wife (at least he was older).

This is a good moment to discuss the importance of unearthing historical facts—little true facts as the French call them, *les petits faits vrais*— which will make a narrative come to life in a convincing way; these facts are both psychological and material, and they derive from the inner world as well as the outer, to such a degree that we can talk about an archeology of feelings. In order to excavate these facts and feelings we must sometimes ignore the imperatives of political correctness. If we are to think ourselves, for instance, into the mind of not just a nineteenth-century slaveowner but even a nineteenth-century American abolitionist, we must emphasize values and preconceptions and a worldview utterly foreign to our own, ideas we are uncomfortable ascribing to our enemies and especially to our heroes.

There was a time when the historical novel suffered from very low prestige. Readers laughed at it, as if it were a shameful form of entertainment to read on a train or in the bath (or the boudoir). I can remember the historical novels of my youth, bodice-rippers like *Forever Amber* or *Désirée* or Taylor Caldwell's novel about Genghis Khan full of quailing captive women and cruel lascivious tartars! In France the historical novel continues to make serious people smile when it is mentioned, but then again the French have the same scorn for literary biography and travel books, two genres that rate very high in the English-speaking world. I suppose we could characterize the old bad historical novel as very, very long, a sustained exotic dream in which thoroughly modern men and women are decked out in suitably exotic costumes and placed against a quaint gazebo or in a well-polished phaeton. Think of *Gone with the Wind* and you'll have the idea—a production starring a spitfire of a heroine who needs to be brought down a peg and a Rhett Butler who is just the sort of sexy beast to do the job. Conventional readers and movie-goers have always been able to lend themselves to these drag shows—modern people in old-fashioned clothes— because the costumes and props are sufficiently distancing to grant the audience permission to indulge in exciting fantasies they might not otherwise permit themselves to conjure up.

Today the historical novel has been rehabilitated because it has radically changed its ways. The new historical novel is shorter or at least more densely written, full of unexpected twists and turns in language, certainly more crisply written than ever before, and rich in those "little true facts." Let me return to Bainbridge's *Master Georgie*. It is the story of a woman photographer who follows her master into the Crimean War in the 1850s in order to document the military action—and to stay near her beloved Master Georgie. He is a doctor treating the wounded in the field and she assists him when she isn't taking photos. One day she hopes to accompany him for a moment into his tent, just to be near him, but he dismisses her. "Five minutes later Dr. Potter joined him, and I could hear the murmur of their voices. I do understand that Georgie prefers the companionship of his own sex, men being so afraid of women, but sometimes I almost wish he'd fall sick so that I could look after him." Here the writing is simple, efficient but not anachronistic— and it is clean, which is characteristic of the new historical novel. The throw-away observation that men are afraid of women is immediately striking—and strikes us as true to the period.

A few pages later the female narrator describes riding out one day in the countryside near Istanbul with another woman. They pass a country boy sitting with his back to a tree, eating, his lap full of cherries and his cheeks bright red. When the narrator comes back the same way much later she sees another soldier in her path. "He stood with arms wrapped about himself, as though he was cold, and stared past us. Following the direction of his petrified gaze, I swivelled in the saddle and looked behind. The country boy still sat with his back to the tree, only now the pink had quite gone from his cheeks and his skin was mottled, like meat lain too long on the slab. He hadn't eaten all the cherries; flies crawled along his fingers and buzzed at his mouth."

This description of random death during war is original and vivid in a manner that Tolstoy first worked out in his war reportage, *The Sebastopol Sketches*, about the very same conflict. In describing the surgeon's tent Tolstoy pictures the stack of sawed-off legs and the blood quietly flowing into a drain. He too used crisp, short sentences and few adjectives and underplayed emotion. This is war writing entirely at odds with the overdrawn horror of James Jones' *From Here to Eternity*, a book in which the bombast begins with the title.

My own favorite author of historical fiction is the French novelist Jean Giono. Although he was admired by André Gide and considered one of the great French authors in the period between the two wars, later he was relegated to obscurity because he made two bad career choices—in 1939 he announced he was a pacifist at the very moment the French were resisting the German invasion, a position which led to his arrest, and in 1945 he announced he was anti-Communist at a time when every French intellectual had embraced Marxism in some form or other, which led to a blackout on all publication of his work for five years.

These bad choices may explain why Giono has been forgotten everywhere except in his native country, where the sheer force of his genius has always won him a few readers. His greatest book, *The Horseman on the Roof*, he wrote between 1934 and 1951 (it was recently made into an excellent movie). In this novel Giono wrote about his native Provence during the 1820s when the region was besieged by a cholera epidemic that killed almost half the population. For Giono this cholera epidemic became a metaphor of the war he was living through—World War II.

In page after page Giono paints the picture of a whole land devastated by the disease but he never deals in broad rhetorical effects or generalities but rather in pointillistic details. Take this description of Provence:

At the bottom of the hill lay the town: a tortoise shell in the grass; the sunlight, now slightly slanting, checkered the scaly roofs with lines of shadow; the wind went in by one street and out by another, trailing columns of straw dust. Shutters were grinding on their hinges and banging, doubling the sadness of the houses.

Beyond the town rose a plain of yellow grass, stained with great patches of rust. These were grain fields from which the harvest had not been gathered in, and would not be, because the owners were dead....

If Giono is remarkable in his simple, nearly adjective-free descriptions of the devastated landscape, he is equally adept at portraying the moral character of the period. The hero is a young dashing Italian aristocrat named Angelo who has come to Provence in order to escape the Austrians, the foreigners ruling his country and against whom he is fighting in an unsuccessful armed rebellion. Giono had a deep understanding of the gay, lighthearted aristocratic code of conduct, a set of beliefs and values and manners he'd learned to admire through his study of Stendhal and especially of Stendhal's Fabrizio del Dongo, the hero of *The Charterhouse of Parma*.

At a certain moment Angelo, who seems to be immune to cholera and who has worked day and night attending to the dying, offers to help two strangers who are aiding a third man, a dying man. His help is rejected: "Learn a little selfishness,' he told himself; 'it's very useful, and keeps you from looking like a fool. Those two have sent you packing, and they're right. They're intent on their own business and doing it the way they want to. They haven't the slightest wish for you to come and meddle in it. Whether this sick man gets better or worse, in a quarter of an hour they won't be weeping any more: they'll only be thinking of what to do next. Do you imagine generosity is always good? Nine times out of ten it's offensive. And it's never manly.' "

Here we have a straightforward-seeming passage that is actually mined with odd attitudes that Giono reconstructed out of the aristocratic past— the cult of manliness, the esthetic evaluation of personal ethics, the pressing fear of appearing a fool. A few pages later Angelo's mother writes him: "The sailor you sent to me told me you were foolhardy. That reassured me. Always be very foolhardy, my dear; it's the only way of getting a little pleasure out of life in this factory age of ours." Here we have the very ring of the old gallantry of the past, not to mention an explicit rejection of the industrial age.

Perhaps the most admired writer of the new historical novel is the late Penelope Fitzgerald and especially for one book, *The Blue Flower,* the story of the German poet Novalis in the days of Goethe. In one scene Novalis— or Fritz as he was called at this point in the tale—is asked to be a second in a student duel.

As they crossed the field one of the duellists cut and ran for it to a gate, in the other direction. His opponent left standing, dropped his Schlager (a sort of student sword), then fell himself, with his right hand masked in blood, perhaps cut off.

"No, only two fingers," said Dietmahlerm urgently bending down to the earth, where weeds and coarse grass were already beginning to sprout. He picked up the fingers, red and wet as if skinned, one of them the top joint only, one with a gold ring.

"Put them in your mouth," said Dietmahler. "If they are kept warm I can perhaps sew them back on our return."

Fritz was not likely to forget the sensation of the one and a half fingers and the heavy ring, smooth and hard while they were yielding, in his mouth. "All Nature is one," he told himself....

In another scene the twenty-four-year-old Fritz sees Sophie in a crowded room for just fifteen minutes but immediately falls in love with the twelve-year-old:

"I am Fritz von Hardenberg," he had said to her. "You are Fraulein Sophie von Kuhn. You are twelve years of age, I heard your gracious mother say so."

Sophie put her hands to her hair. "Up, it should be up."

"In four years' time you will have to consider what man would be fortunate enough to hope to be your husband. Don't tell me that he would have to ask your stepfather! What do you say yourself?"

"In four years time I don't know what I shall be."

"You mean you don't know what you will become."

"I don't want to become. I want to be and not to have to think about it."

"But you must not remain a child."

"I am not a child now."

"Sophie, I am a poet but in four years I shall be an administrative official receiving a salary. That is the time when we shall be married."

"I don't know you!"

"You have seen me. I am what you see."

Sophie laughed.

"Do you always laugh at your guests?"

"No, but at Gruningen we don't talk like this."

"But would you be content to live with me?"

Sophie hesitated and then said:

"Truly, I like you."

How many other contemporary writers would be able to recount this scene without fretting over the age difference and the purely modern notion of child exploitation? To be sure, Novalis isn't trying to seduce the child. He just knows he loves her and always will and he wants her to promise to marry him. His sentiments are unexceptionable for the period, especially among aristocrats like Fritz and Sophie, but I suspect most contemporary writers wouldn't be sufficiently tough-minded to give us this scene without some mitigating comments. We must be brave to be archeologists of the sentiments.

I don't want to suggest, by the way, that I am against political correctness. When I look back at the routinely disgusting and patronizing pictures of women in even the so-called serious fiction of the 1950s (I'm thinking of Lionel Trilling's novel *The Middle of the Journey*) or of gays in even the otherwise beautiful writing of James Salter in the 1970s I can only be grateful for the refinement, the sensitization, that consciousness-raising has brought about. We were all capable of exclusiveness or simple crudeness in the past. I can still remember the day when a deaf friend asked me why I said routinely "deaf and dumb" when only a tiny fraction of the deaf are incapable of speech. I can remember the moment when after living in Europe sixteen years I put together an anthology of gay male fiction and seriously underrepresented blacks, Native Americans and Asian Americans in the mix—which was just pure laziness on my part. As someone seriously out of touch with America who had become virtually European, I hadn't kept up with the times in my own country.

But even if political correctness has sharpened our sensibilities today, it is not something we must apply retrospectively to our own historical fiction nor to the fiction or drama of the past. When Jane Smiley attacks *Huckleberry Finn* for being racist she is just being silly. When we worry about the exact degree of racism in Shakespeare's portraits of Othello or Shylock or of sexism in *The Taming of the Shrew* we are being dangerously ahistorical—and depriving audiences, among other things, of a picture of past attitudes. It's not enough to know vaguely that such attitudes existed; we must also know how they worked.

In my new novel, *Fanny: A Fiction,* I have a scene in which my narrator, an Englishwoman, Frances Trollope, the mother of the prolific novelist, is living in Cincinnati in the 1820s. She had come to the New World in search of fortune or at least security, but she has found only penury and near-starvation for her children and herself. At this point in the book she is waiting for her husband and one of her older sons to arrive from England. At the same time she is becoming closer and closer to her neighbor, a black man named Jupiter Higgins, an escaped slave.

In the scene Mrs. Trollope pretends to be repelled by Mr. Higgins's African features (though she is secretly attracted to him). She refers to the Negro's natural love of inventive language and delights Higgins by reading him a passage from Shakespeare. He tells her in detail about his escape from a cruel master in Kentucky—moments that the real Mrs. Trollope later re-created in her antislavery novel, *Jonathan Jefferson Whitlaw,* which she wrote before *Uncle Tom's Cabin* was published.

I suppose one might find such a chapter offensive with its naïve racism (and genuine affection), and it would have taken no trouble at all to make it politically correct and anodyne. What cost me a lot of effort was to re-create in a plausible way the exact dimensions of Mrs. Trollope's prejudices. Why should anyone bother? you might well ask. My intention is to unearth the past, not as we would have it be but as it truly was. After all, it is a past—shameful, all-too-human, hopeful—that we all share.

George Eliot

EORGE ELIOT IS ABOVE ALL AN INTELLIGENT AUTHOR—as intelligent as Jane Austen, but less resignedly feminine in her preoccupations. She is as intelligent as Robert Browning and George Meredith—more so, since their intelligence is always linked to tiresome verbal prankishness. She is as intelligent as Henry James, but more explicitly so (which was one of his chief complaints about her, her lack of indirection). She speaks to us directly ("Dear Reader"), as Fielding and Thackeray did before her, but she has finer, stranger, more important things to tell us. Trollope advised her to write for the tens of thousands of readers, not just the happy thousands. Luckily she ignored his advice. We are the happy few.

There is not a page of *Daniel Deronda* that is not marked with intelligence, and a few are as queer and perceptive as any I've read. If I use such words as *queer* and *strange* it is because I'm convinced that almost all masterpieces in the English language are characterized by something preposterous, homemade, and all seem too long or too far-fetched or too narrow or too bizarre (I'm thinking of everything from *The Faerie Queene* to *Gravity's Rainbow,* from *Moby-Dick* to *Our Mutual Friend*).

Take this sentence, which is both wise and odd, which comes towards the end of *Daniel Deronda:*

The beings closest to us, whether in love or hate, are virtually our interpreters of the world, and some feather-headed gentleman or lady whom in passing we regret to take as legal tender for a human being may be acting as a melancholy theory of life in the minds of those who live with them—like a piece of yellow and wavy glass that distorts form and makes color an affliction. Their trivial sentences, their petty standards, their low suspicions, their loveless ennui, may be making somebody else's life no better than a promenade through a pantheon of ugly idols. Gwendolen had that kind of window before her, affecting the distant equally with the near.

Everything in this passage is splendid—and striking (the "feather-headed gentleman or lady" and the "melancholy theory of life," especially if we remember that the Greek verb at the origin of *theory* means "to look at or contemplate").

Daniel Deronda is intelligent in every word though its overall design and intent seem confused or at least wavering. There are two almost unrelated plots. One of them is the story of the young, spirited Gwendolen Harleth and her disastrous marriage; the other is of Daniel Deronda's discovery of his true identity as a Jew and his decision to marry a poor Jewish girl he has saved following her attempt to drown herself in the Thames. After their marriage they travel to Palestine. Eliot must have been aware of the incongruity of playing off a spoiled, undereducated girl (Gwendolen) against great world events (the politicization of Jewish identity). She writes rather lamely: "What in the midst of that mighty drama are girls and their blind visions? They are the Yea or Nay of that good for which men are enduring and fighting. In these delicate vessels is borne onward through the ages the treasure of human affections."

The two stories scarcely overlap. In the beginning Deronda sees Gwendolen gambling recklessly at a continental spa (this scene was inspired by George Eliot's trip to the German spa of Bad Homburg in 1872, where she saw Byron's great-niece losing heavily). Deronda is saddened by the spectacle of Gwendolen's recklessness (for Eliot Jews came to represent the eternal moral judges of human failings). Then the charismatic Deronda vanishes for a hundred pages, only to reemerge in an entirely distinct story line as he searches for his origins and befriends Mirah and her brother Mordecai, a dying Jewish sage. Whereas the pages devoted to Gwendolen are complex in tone, shifting from satire of the English gentry to a clear-eyed but not always compassionate look at Gwendolen's maneuvering, the Deronda chapters are very high-toned, bordering on the melodramatic, when they aren't slightly condescending to the dear, picturesque Jews.

There are efforts to stitch the stories together—Deronda appears at a musical party where Mirah sings in her small, fragile voice and the unhappily married Gwendolen attempts to establish contact with him. Toward the end of the book (which doesn't know how to close and keeps staggering on), Gwendolen and Deronda meet in Genoa. Less obviously, there are psychological and thematic echoes. Gwendolen and Deronda both suffer from egotistical mothers, though Gwendolen's is fearful and helpless and ignorant, whereas Deronda's is a famous opera singer free of all hypocrisy and is anything but helpless. Gwendolen and Deronda have both known hugely self-satisfied Englishmen of prominence, though Deronda's guardian, Sir Hugo Mallinger, is a thoroughly decent, well-educated sort, whereas the most important man in Gwendolen's life is the rather fatuous and hyper-conventional rector, her uncle Mr. Gascoigne. Both stories are quests—Gwendolen's for security and then for forgiveness and a higher meaning, Deronda's for a resolution to the mystery of his identity and then for a political purpose and higher meaning. The higher meaning part is the Victorian note.

Not only are the plots poorly joined but also the Gwendolen half is so superior to the Deronda half that the twentieth-century British critic F. R. Leavis seriously suggested the book be split in half and the good part be published separately under the title *Gwendolen Harleth*. Such an arrangement would rob the reader, however, of some of George Eliot's most intriguing if least successful explorations.

Eliot was fascinated by the fate of the Jews—their history, their status, their trials, their culture. She suggested something like Zionism two decades before Theodor Herzl came up with the idea in his book *The Jewish State* (1896). She based her portrait of the assimilationist German Jewish musician Klesmer on the Russian composer and pianist Anton Rubinstein, whom she met in 1854 and again at a concert in 1876. Her interest in Jewish questions became all the more concrete when she came to know the Talmudic scholar Emanuel Deutsch (the model for Mordecai in

Daniel Deronda). Eliot seems to have been specially close with him in the last years of his life, between 1867 and his death from cancer in 1873.

Born in Prussian Silesia, Deutsch came to London in 1855, found a job at the British Museum and wrote influential articles on Jewish culture and the Bible for British reference works. He had visited the Holy Land in 1869 and set out again just before his death; he died en route. He not only answered Eliot's questions about the Talmud (an essay he wrote on the Talmud for *The Quarterly Review* was so admired that that issue of the magazine had to be republished six times), he also gave Eliot Hebrew lessons. Mordecai's bad health, passion for Jewish culture and yearning for the promised land are all based on similar traits and feelings in Deutsch. Like Disraeli, the novelist and statesman, Eliot was opposed to the idea of Jewish assimilation.

As a pious, highly educated Christian, Eliot when she was a girl had already been intrigued by the Old Testament and Christianity's links with Judaism. Much later, in her book-length volume of notes jotted down in preparation for writing *Daniel Deronda*, Eliot devotes many pages to the Kabbalah, the Mishnah, to Hebrew names and phrases, to "the inner life of Judaism," German Jews in the Middle Ages, Biblical interpretation, Alexandrian Jewish literature, the Jewish liturgy, the Jewish year, Hebrew literature, Jewish festivals, books on Jewish subjects, Yiddish proverbs and so on.

Such an interest was highly unusual in Victorian England, but Eliot's far-ranging curiosity was only one more sign that she was as much a European writer as an English one. Moreover, once she'd lost her faith (though she retained her interest in religion as an intellectual and cultural discourse), Judaism took on an added allure for her.

Daniel Deronda had an immediate impact on the Jewish community. The chief rabbi of London wrote Eliot soon after publication and thanked her for depicting so faithfully some of the best qualities of the Jewish character (most portraits of Jews in Victorian fiction were malicious or mocking—think of Fagin in Dickens's *Oliver Twist*). A scion of a Moroccan Jewish family was so moved by Eliot's proto-Zionism that he offered to retire an immense debt owed by the Turkish government in return for the property rights of Erez Israel, then a possession of the Turkish Empire. Nothing, alas, came of the scheme. In Germany a professor wrote a pamphlet called "George Eliot and Judaism," which was quickly translated into English. When cynics criticized Eliot's call to build a Jewish state in Israel, she replied, "Columbus had some impressions about himself which we call superstitious," but he also had "the passionate patience of genius.... The world has made up its mind rather contemptuously about those who were deaf to Columbus." Freud, as he wrote in his letters to his fiancée, was astonished by the accuracy and intimacy of Eliot's grasp of the Jewish character; he felt she understood Jews better than any other gentile.

The Jewish theme—so unexpected in Eliot's work and imperfectly dramatized—nevertheless is an inexhaustible subject of study and meditation. It marks the point where the mythic and the historical merge and where a meticulous and masterful study of English Christian country life gives way to an exalted (if not entirely convincing) evocation of Judaism and its aspirations. Here the past joins the future, the timeless bursts into the present.

If Jews throughout the world were grateful to Eliot, most gentiles seem to have laughed at her ardent partisanship. Henry James wrote "A Conversation," which was published in *The Atlantic Monthly* in December 1876, in which three gentiles discuss *Daniel Deronda*—the hostile Pulcheria, the enthusiastic Theodora and the equivocating Constantius. In the very first paragraph Pulcheria, playing with her dog, speculates about what happened after the end of the book when Deronda went to the Near East with his new Jewish wife:

> Oh, they had tea-parties at Jerusalem,—exclusively of ladies,—and he sat in the midst and stirred his tea and made high-toned remarks. And then Mirah sang a little, just a little, on account of her voice being so weak. "Sit still, Fido," she continued, addressing the little dog, "and keep your nose out of my face. But it's a nice little nose, all the same," she pursued, "a nice little short snub nose, and not a horrid big Jewish nose. Oh, my dear, when I think what a collection of noses there must have been at that wedding!"

Pulcheria wonders why the author failed to describe Deronda's nose and why Jews in general are so dirty—in fact the level of casual anti-Semitic insult is so vile that the modern reader reels with disbelief.

If Pulcheria is frivolous and intolerable, Constantius seems to speak for James himself:

Roughly speaking, all the Jewish burden of the story tended to weary me; it is this part that produced the small illusion which I agree with Pulcheria in finding. Gwendolen and Grandcourt are admirable. Gwendolen is a masterpiece. She is known, felt, and presented, psychologically, altogether in the grand manner. Beside her and beside her husband—a consummate picture of English brutality refined and distilled (for Grandcourt is before all things brutal)—Deronda, Mordecai, and Mirah are hardly more than shadows. They and their fortunes are all improvisation. I don't say anything against improvisation. When it succeeds it has a surpassing charm. But it must succeed. With George Eliot it seems to me to succeed only partially, less than one would expect of her talent. The story of Deronda's life, his mother's story, Mirah's story, are quite the sort of thing one finds in George Sand. But they are really not so good as they would be in George Sand. George Sand would have carried it off with a lighter hand.

(Incidentally, James put his admiration of Gwendolen and Grandcourt to good use in his portraits of Isabel Archer and her monstrously cold, refined husband in *Portrait of a Lady,* arguably his best book.)

Theodora, the enthusiast, will not stand for such carping, much less for Pulcheria's terrible racism. Theodora praises *Daniel Deronda* for its ambitious conception of what the novel can be: "It shows a large conception of what one may do in a novel. I heard you say, the other day, that most novels were so trivial—that they had no general idea. Here is a general idea, the idea interpreted by Deronda. I have never disliked the Jews, as some people do; I am not like Pulcheria, who sees a Jew in every bush. I wish there were one: I would cultivate shrubbery! I have known too many clever and charming Jews; I have known none that were not clever...."

What's symptomatic is that the book is obviously so complicated—and it elicits such complex responses—that the only way James can account for his full reaction is to stage a debate among three conflicting opinions. But it's equally symptomatic that such refined, sophisticated people could express such ghastly anti-Semitism so lightheartedly in the 1870s—this is Victorian brutality refined and distilled. In this world anti-Semitism is presented as an amusing option.

George Eliot—like just a handful of other writers—transcended and surpassed her background and education and became someone almost unrecognizably broad-spirited by the time she reached her maturity. She was born as Mary Anne Evans on November 22, 1819, the same year as Queen Victoria. Her father was the manager of the large estate of the Newdigate family in Warwickshire (as a child Mary Anne was given access to the family's well-stocked private library at Arbury Hall). She, unlike Gwendolen, grew up in a fixed abode in a region she knew thoroughly and in a social position that was solid and unambiguous. As the youngest child of a large family and as the daughter of an estate manager, she had the ideal vantage point on family life and on the gentry.

In 1828 at the age of nine she was sent off to a boarding school, where she came under the spell of an evangelical teacher, Maria Lewis. Four years later she was sent to a school in Coventry run by the two daughters of a Baptist minister. At school and at home Mary Anne came into contact with religious dissent of every variety—Congregationalist, Quaker, Baptist, Unitarian and evangelical Anglicanism.

After her mother's death in 1836, when Mary Ann (she'd dropped the *e* from her name) was seventeen, the girl became her father's housekeeper. Undoubtedly her father was looking for a suitable husband for her, but none was to be found. Mary Ann was neither attractive nor appealing; in fact she was quite forbiddingly intellectual. And she was at this time in her life austerely pious.

The piety, at least, did not last. By 1841, when her father retired and they moved to a new house on the outskirts of Coventry, Mary Ann was reading widely in non-religious literature—Shakespeare, Cervantes, Walter Scott, Schiller, Carlyle. She also became friendly with Charles Bray, a wealthy manufacturer and a progressive in politics. Bray and his circle introduced Mary Ann to German biblical historians who threw doubt on the miracles and the supernatural elements in the life of Christ. Soon she had renounced her faith—and she refused to go to church with her father. He threatened to turn her out. After a difficult period Mary Ann finally agreed to accompany her father to church so long as he accepted that she could believe what she pleased. She nursed her father until his death in 1849. In the meanwhile she'd begun translating difficult German books that aimed to demystify scripture.

Mary Ann moved to London in 1851. Through Charles Bray, Mary Ann (who now changed her name to the more dignified Marian) had contacts in the world of radical journalism and politics. She became friendly with the publisher John Chapman and through him met both the philosopher Herbert Spencer and the critic and novelist G. H. Lewes, both of whom she was to fall in love with. She also flirted with Chapman, but when his wife caught them holding hands she was excommunicated from their circle. Eventually, however, Mrs. Chapman relented and Marian Evans was hired as the de facto editorial director of the *Westminster Review* (Chapman retained the official title). Marian reviewed books on everything from German philosophy to English literature, from science to evangelical sermons.

For a while Spencer seemed to reciprocate Marian's passion, but soon he backed away. She next turned her affections towards G. H. Lewes, who fortunately reciprocated them. They became lovers, though they were never able to marry; Lewes was already married in an open marriage and, because he had condoned his wife's adultery and even registered her children by another man as his own, he had foregone his right to sue for divorce (adultery was at the time the only legitimate grounds). Living out of wedlock with Lewes placed Marian in a delicate position; throughout her life respectable women refused to be introduced to her.

By 1857 Marian had reinvented herself again, this time as George Eliot, the name under which she published her first book, the highly successful *Scenes of Clerical Life*. These stories did so well she next undertook her first novel, *Adam Bede,* which made her famous. It was followed by *The Mill on the Floss, Silas Marner* and her more difficult and controversial later novels, *Romola, Felix Holt, Middlemarch* and *Daniel Deronda*.

Two years after Lewes died of cancer in 1878 at the age of sixty-one, the deeply grieving Marian married her financial advisor, the banker John Walter Cross, her junior by some twenty years. During their honeymoon in Venice Cross attempted suicide by throwing himself from the balcony of their hotel room into the Grand Canal. He survived but soon she was ailing from a failing kidney. She died in 1880—and Cross became her first (and most pious) biographer. A hundred years after her death a memorial stone was finally installed in Westminster Abbey in the Poet's Corner, though as an adulteress and an unbeliever, she had been unwelcome in holy ground for a century.

Henry James writes of George Eliot's "deep, strenuous, much-considering mind, of which the leading mark is the capacity for a sort of luminous brooding." His assessment does justice to one side of her genius (the side to which he owes the larger debt), but one would never suspect that this was the same person whom Virginia Woolf's father, Leslie Stephens, praised for her "charm."

Although Eliot did not leave behind a vast oeuvre (she didn't begin writing fiction till she was in her late thirties and published only nine books in her lifetime), nevertheless she wrote enough to have both an early and a late period. Leslie Stephens was the critic who admired the early works such as *Adam Bede* and *The Mill on the Floss* (precisely for their good-naturedness and their depiction of quiet English country life) and deplored the late works such as *Felix Holt* and *Daniel Deronda,* her last book, though even he was quick to acknowledge that in the ten-year period during which Eliot outlived Dickens she reigned as the greatest English author.

For Stephens the problem with the late books was that they betrayed a tendency "to substitute elaborate analysis for direct presentation." Perhaps as an essayist himself Stephens wanted to keep novelists off his turf; it is certainly true that George Eliot began her literary life as an essayist and translator of serious philosophical works. A year before she published her first bit of fiction in a magazine, she wrote a sort of manifesto for the novelist of the future in the guise of a book review. The essay is called "The Natural History of German Life," a review of the "natural history" of his people written by a pioneering German social historian, Wilhelm Heinrich von Riehl. Eliot singles out for praise Riehl's objective and minutely descriptive method, which she proposes should be adopted by novelists.

"The greatest benefit we owe to the artist, whether painter, poet, or novelist, is the extension of our sympathies," she declares. The novelist, by presenting the thoughts and customs and actions and values of the working "masses," bridges the social gap between the middle-class reader and the working-class subject more effectively than any preacher or politician might do. And she states, as a sort of credo, "Art is the nearest thing to life; it is a mode of amplifying experience and extending our contact with our fellow men beyond the bounds of our personal lot."

But Eliot is not simply a universalist, seeking to break down all boundaries, even national and political ones. She might be in favor of an international exchange of ideas amongst the nations, but like her beloved Goethe, whom she translated, she believes that climate and geography determine the character of the clan and the individual clan member (this is an idea that in France Maurice Barrès was espousing and that Gertrude Stein recycled in the twentieth century, as did many fascists). As she writes in *Daniel Deronda,* "A human life, I think, should be well rooted in some spot of native land, where it may get the love of a tender kinship for the face of the earth." One of the lacunae behind Gwendolen's misguided values is that she was never raised in one single place, a geography and a milieu that might have nurtured her spirit. Already in "The Natural History of German Life" Eliot is deploring not only a faceless culture but also the idea of a universal language, one that would erase life-giving poetical differences of expression. She is against a rational sort of Esperanto "which has no uncertainty, no whims of idiom, no cumbrous forms, no fitful shimmer of many-hued significance, no hoary archaisms."

Deronda himself discovers in the course of the novel that he is not the illegitimate son of an English gentleman, as he has always believed, but rather the child of a continental Jewish couple—and is most importantly the descendant of a grandfather who fiercely defended Jewish culture. Deronda, at the end of the book, has become a Zionist before there was such a thing. As he announces, "I am going to the East to become better acquainted with the condition of my race in various countries there.... The idea that I am possessed with is that of restoring a political existence to my people, making them a nation again, giving them a national center, such as the English have, though they too are scattered over the face of the globe." Deronda is doing for the Jewish people what someone failed to do for Gwendolen—give her roots in an authentic place and its culture.

This kind of nationalism, especially when proposed before the death camps made the idea of Israel a necessity, was consistent with Eliot's brand of enlightened conservatism. Ironically the Jews, who seemed the most "cosmopolitan" of all peoples, are promised a political existence (their rights as full-fledged British citizens had been guaranteed only some forty years earlier) and, of all things, British colonialism is compared to the Jewish diaspora, probably mainly for rhetorical effect.

Eliot was always fed up with English xenophobia and in particular its anti-Semitism. She wrote to Harriet Beecher Stowe, the American author of *Uncle Tom's Cabin,* a book Eliot vastly admired for its role in defending another oppressed people: "...precisely because I felt that the usual attitudes of Christians towards Jews is—I hardly know whether to say more impious or more stupid when viewed in the light of their professed principles, I therefore felt urged to treat Jews with such sympathy and understanding as my nature and knowledge could attain to. Moreover, not only towards the Jews, but towards all oriental peoples with whom we English come in contact, a spirit of arrogance and contemptuous dictatorialness is observable, which has become a national disgrace to us. There is nothing I should care more to do, if it were possible, than to rouse the imagination of men and women to a vision of human claims in those races of fellow-men who most differ from them in customs and beliefs. But towards the Hebrews we western people who have been reared in Christianity have a peculiar debt and, whether we acknowledge it or not, a peculiar thoroughness of fellowship in religious and moral sentiment. Can anything be more disgusting than to hear people called 'educated' making small jokes about eating ham?... They hardly know that Christ was a Jew. And I find men educated at Rugby supposing the Christ spoke Greek." Such absurdities, she averred, were possible only among members of a nation dead to history.

Eliot's intelligence is a peculiarly novelistic one. If the novel is "the nearest thing to life" and is superior to life in its power to broaden our sympathies, then it reigns supreme because it dramatizes moral dilemmas or at least moral close choices. For instance, after Gwendolen discovers that her fiance, Grandcourt, has a mistress and four children by her, she is morally obligated not to marry him (in fact she's promised the mistress she won't marry him). But on the other hand, as a penniless and proud spinster she, Gwendolen, will be forced to work as a governess for an arrogant rich family. She will occupy a position midway between social equal and hired help, genteel but poor. And if she doesn't marry she won't be in a position to help her destitute mother and sisters. By marrying Grandcourt, Gwendolen will be breaking her promise to the other woman, Lydia Glasher, and silently endorsing Grandcourt's caddish behavior, since he should marry Lydia now that her husband is dead; but if Gwendolen does marry him her pride will be gratified (she'll be rich and respected) and she'll be able to provide lavishly for her family. What she doesn't realize until much later is that Grandcourt is aware of her meeting with Lydia. He knows that she has broken her promise to Mrs. Glasher. This knowledge puts him in a position of strength in his systematic campaign to break Gwendolen's will. He married her because she was high-spirited, but throughout the second half of the novel he works in his dandified, cold-hearted way to trample her pride.

Eliot reports on every movement of Gwendolen's inner and outer drama with a keen sense of how these states of being progress and link up. This fine intermeshing of feelings and ideas is the novelist's most challenging task. It places the biggest demand on the writer's emotional memory of similar real-life moments and on his or her sense of presence, that you-are-there gift that only rare authors possess. Eliot's skills at envisioning the interplay between outer staging and inner response, her total recall of emotional progression (the exact route traced from one mood to another) and her powers of expression in rapidly notating feelings (as the critic F. R. Leavis first observed) and rendering them through transforming metaphors—all of these skills wonderfully exercised are what place her in the company of the Tolstoy of *Anna Karenina* and the Flaubert of *Madame Bovary,* at the height of the novelistic art.

Flaubert, in a letter to his mistress and fellow author Louise Colet, written at the time (1852) when he was struggling with *Madame Bovary,* points to this cluster of skills: "I'm working well, that is with some heart, but it's difficult to express clearly what one has never felt: it requires long preparations and digging deep into the brain in order not to overshoot the mark and at the same time to hit it exactly. The linking of feelings costs me endless effort, and everything depends on that in this novel; for I maintain that one can interest the reader as much with ideas as with facts, but for that to happen they must flow one into the other like one cascade into another; that's how to draw the leader on in the midst of shimmering sentences and bubbling metaphors...." Here, in these dashed-off notes, Flaubert evokes the quasi-scientific goal of transcribing accurately the movement from one thought to another, or from one conscious feeling to the next, a delicate exercise in observation and invention that every working novelist knows about but few can emulate.

In a turning point of *Daniel Deronda*, Gwendolen receives from the housekeeper a package, which she suspects might contain the heirloom diamonds her new husband, Grandcourt, has promised her.

> Gwendolen, yielding up her hat and mantle, threw herself into a chair by the glowing hearth, and saw herself repeated in glass panels with all her faint-green satin surroundings.... Within all the sealed paper coverings was a box, but within the box there was a jewel-case; and now she felt no doubt that she had the diamonds. But on opening the case, in the same instant that she saw their gleam she saw a letter lying above them.

She reads a letter from Lydia Glasher that tells her that Grandcourt once gave her these jewels. Now that Gwendolen has broken her promise to Lydia and married him, these jewels will place a curse on her.

> It seemed at first as if Gwendolen's eyes were spellbound in reading the horrible words of the letter over and over again as a doom of penance; but suddenly a new spasm of terror made her lean forward and stretch the paper towards the fire, lest accusation and proof at once should meet all eyes. It flew like a feather from her trembling fingers and was caught up in the great draught of flame. In her movement the casket fell on the floor and the diamonds rolled out. She took no notice, but fell back in her chair again helpless. She could not see the reflections of herself then: they were like so many women petrified white.... Grandcourt entered, dressed for dinner. The sight of him brought a new nervous shock, and Gwendolen screamed again and again with hysterical violence. He had expected to see her dressed and smiling, ready to be led down. He saw her pallid, shrieking as it seemed with terror, the jewels scattered around her on the floor.

The hypnotic repetition of words ("saw herself repeated," "saw the gleam," "saw the letter," "see," "sight," "expected to see her," "he saw her") in one short passage beats on the ear with urgency. The natural but scarcely developed figures ("like a feather" or "women petrified white") and the telegraphed descriptions ("faint-green satin surroundings") allow us to see everything, first from Gwendolen's point of view, then from an omniscient one and finally from Grandcourt's. The weight of the letter's contents is neatly contrasted with the lightness of the "feather." This scene is strategically placed at the end of a long section and before a turning aside to the other plot about Deronda. It is meant to function as a summary and an intensification of the action—and of what's at stake. That it proceeds through a display of brilliantly seen suffering only adds to its power, for this is the one moment every reader of *Daniel Deronda* remembers even years later.

Although hostile critics of *Daniel Deronda* have accused it of being overly analytical, in fact Eliot always clung to the novel as a form because at its best it could engage in theory without giving up the detail of sensuous particularity. As the critic George Levine has written, "She sought always to bring together intellect and feeling. In the days in which she renounced Christianity and thereby offended her father—the 'Holy Wars,' she called them in a letter—she retreated from the apparently necessary consequences of her intellectual rejection, for what mattered in the end was what she called the 'truth of feeling,' a truth that allowed her to return to church without believing in its doctrine, for the sake of her love of her father." She was against the heartless imposition of moral judgments against living (or fictional) human beings, and more than any other novelist she is open and ambiguous in her interpretation of her characters' doings. Perhaps because she had suffered from her morally ambiguous position as a woman "living in sin," Eliot was slow to judge Gwendolen or even her overly worldly uncle, Mr. Gascoigne. For her such shading was a cardinal principle of Realism, the only approach to art she believed in.

Although George Eliot professed to be interested in ordinary people— and in her first four books managed to discipline herself to write about them—in fact she was fascinated by people who were morally or intellectually or even socially superior. In *Daniel Deronda* Gwendolen is her hostage to the ordinary, though even she is given exceptional beauty, wit and sinfully high self-esteem.

The actions of all the characters in the book seem both allegorical and concrete—allegorical in that they stand for larger moral dilemmas or social questions or just social realities, and concrete in that we become more and more convinced by the living, breathing existence of Gwendolen and

Grandcourt. The allegorical resides in Eliot's elevated use of language (phrases such as "a melancholy theory of life" or Grandcourt's cold elegance made up of "refined negations") and in her hushed, heightened seriousness in the face of her most dramatic scenes.

The concrete is conveyed by Eliot's pictorial use of detail. Fiction of the eighteenth century is scanty on visual detail—often *Tom Jones* or *Moll Flanders* seems all plot, though moralizing is invariably in full flow. By contrast, twentieth-century minimalist fiction is cloudy about what it means, even morally, yet like the writing of the eighteenth century it is also scanty on visual and psychological detail. In addition, it is also nearly plotless. An anecdote, never interpreted, is presented in an objective and subjective brownout. Minimalist fiction, instead of seeming robust and propelled forward, is stuttering, becalmed.

Victorian fiction, which comes between these two extremes, is still heavily plotted, even sensationalistic. The dialogue is not naturalistic as in twentieth-century fiction, but rather stilted, rehearsed, as in eighteenth-century novels. In great Victorian fiction, however, there is an unprecedented density and convergence of psychological, moral and visual detail. Eliot's masterpiece, *Daniel Deronda,* is subtler, richer, more rapidly notated and more challenging intellectually than anything that preceded or followed it.

If her early novels are praised for their charm, it is because in them she suppressed her urge to interpret and remained true to her goal to present— the goal she had first set herself in "The Natural History of German Life." In *Middlemarch* and *Daniel Deronda,* however, she came to be accused of formal confusion and human coldness precisely because she had at last begun to deal with the great issues—and the exceptional people—she'd been thinking about all her life.

Ivan Bunin

VAN BUNIN MAY HAVE WON THE NOBEL PRIZE for literature in 1933 but today he is nearly entirely forgotten. Even my most erudite friends either have never heard of him or vaguely associate his name with a single short story, "The Gentleman from San Francisco," an atypical work. Strangely enough, at the time of his death in 1953 he was widely regarded as the best—and most celebrated—Russian émigré author.

What happened? Why have most of his many collections of stories and poems been allowed to fall out of print, in English at least? Why has his name been so utterly forgotten? Other than a Northwestern University Press paperback of his autobiographical novel, *The Life of Arseniev,* and a Penguin, *The Gentleman from San Francisco and Other Stories,* nothing is readily available.

Not because of any lack of talent, even genius. Bunin has a style that conveys better than any other I know the hush and serenity of the Russian landscape as well as the squalor and desperation of the typical village. Whereas Chekhov is casual and general (he once advised Maxim Gorky never to write a nature description more specific than "It grew dark" or "It was raining"), Bunin renders all the poetic specificity of woods and steppes, or of muddy paths and huts without chimneys, of derelict manor houses glimmering with candles in front of soot-smudged icons.

Bunin's world is the countryside after the liberation of the serfs, of Russia at the end of the nineteenth century and the beginning of the twentieth. His 1910 story, "The Village," gives glimpses of peasant uprisings, of burning farms and workers on strike. Bunin left Russia in 1920 and lived in France until his death; everyone who read him in the later years was amazed by his total recall of his homeland. Like Nabokov, he was determined not to give up a single recollection. Perhaps the fact he had been trained originally as a painter sharpened his visual observations and memories.

Not that his descriptions are strained or modernist in the Nabokov mode. Whereas Nabokov is almost always witty (of a street he writes, "beginning with a post office and ending with a church, like an epistolary novel"), Bunin is both more serious and more relaxed. Typically he'll write: "When the horses forded the rivulet and climbed the hill, a woman in a man's light overcoat with sagging pockets was driving some turkeys through the burdock. The façade of the house was thoroughly featureless; it had very few windows and those that existed were small and set deep in the thick walls. Yet the gloomy porches were enormous. From one of these a young man wearing a gray school shirt belted with a broad strap was watching the approaching travelers. He was dark, had handsome eyes and was very personable, though his face was pale and bright with freckles, like a bird's egg."

If Maupassant and Chekhov were not still so famous, one might imagine that Bunin had dropped into obscurity because he wrote short stories. Bunin's stories, however, are as good as any ever written—as original and varied in subject and composition, as distinctive from those of other writers, as fully realized and as concisely composed. And we live in an era, inaugurated by Raymond Carver, when new collections of stories (those by Nathan Englander and Anthony Doerr, just to name the most recent examples) are being discussed and praised more than the newest novels. Moreover, Chekhov's own stories have just been reissued in several new anthologies (devoted to "the unknown" or "the comic" stories, for instance, and Richard Ford has edited a collection of his own favorites).

Perhaps Bunin has been forgotten because he struck his non-Russian contemporaries as politically irrelevant. He was neither a reluctant spokesman for the Communist regime like Gorky nor a quiet dissenter like Pasternak. Nor was he driven out of his country for his opinions like

Solzhenitsyn and Joseph Brodsky. No, Bunin left Russia of his own volition and openly denounced Lenin and later Stalin, though in interviews rather than in poetry or fiction, in which he almost always looked to the pre-Soviet past. At the time of his emigration most intellectuals in Europe and America were still pro-Communist; they denounced Bunin as passéist and an aristocratic counter-revolutionary. Right-wingers of the period in Europe blamed Russians for having withdrawn from the First World War before a victory was secured. Nabokov had the good luck to emerge to the general public in Europe and America much later, in the 1950s, after the Cold War had begun. He also wrote plots set in France, Germany and the United States—and during the 1940s he switched to English. Just as important, Nabokov was a scathingly funny satirist who became famous (even infamous) due to a humorous and scandalous novel about a thoroughly American nymphet.

Bunin was thirty years older and a good deal stodgier. His writing is almost never funny. Worse, he was badly served by his translators, with only a few exceptions. And his was not an alluring personality. Although he lived in the south of France, in the perfume capital of Grasse, he had no desire to cultivate French writers and critics and remained hermetically sealed within the Russian émigré community. His only efforts outside his little world were directed towards winning the Nobel, which kept eluding him year after year—until he finally hit gold. Not that the prize money was a huge sum in those days; Bunin and his wife died in extreme poverty, saved from hunger only by handouts from Russian friends.

Someone should bring out a collection of Bunin's greatest stories and novellas, starting with "The Village" and going on to "The Elaghin Affair," "At Sea, At Night," "Dry Valley," "The Gentleman from San Francisco," "Gentle Breathing" and ending with "Mitya's Love."

"The Gentleman from San Francisco," an intimidating American millionaire, dies suddenly of apoplexy in a luxurious Capri hotel; instantly he passes from the status of feared guest to that of shameful refuse. In "At Sea, At Night," two ancient men meet by chance on shipboard and discuss the woman they both loved, though she has long been dead and neither man feels anything for her now. In "Mitya's Love" an idle young man loses Katya, his love, to the lure of the theater. She takes a trip with her enamored acting coach and he returns to his family's estate. There he becomes more and more despondent as he waits for a letter from Katya. After a meaningless sexual encounter with a hired peasant girl, he shoots himself in the mouth.

When he first contemplates suicide, the writing ecstatically argues for all the best reasons to stay alive:

> Even Mitya understood perfectly well that it was impossible to imagine anything more absurd than that—to shoot oneself, shatter one's skull, immediately halt the beating of a strong young heart, halt thought and feeling, lose hearing and sight, disappear from that inexpressibly beautiful world which had only just revealed itself fully to him for the first time, deprive himself instantly and forever of any participation in that life which embraced Katya and the advancing summer, the sky, the clouds, the sun, the warm wind, the corn in the fields, the villages, the countryside, the village girls, Mama, the estate, Anya, Kostya, the poems in the old magazines and, further off, Sebastopol, the Baydar Pass, the sultry mauve hills with their pine and beech forests, the blindingly white, stifling highway, the gardens at Livadia and Alupka, the burning sand by the shining sea, sun-tanned children, sun-tanned beauties—and again Katya in a white dress, under a parasol, sitting on the pebbles at the edge of the waves which were blindingly brilliant and evoked an irrepressible smile of sheer happiness....

The great Russian thinker Lev Vygotsky attempts to explain in *The Psychology of Art* the mysterious appeal of such writing. Why should an essentially dreary anecdote induce in us a feeling of lightness and excitement? Vygotsky analyzes Bunin's story "Gentle Breathing," the depressing tale of a middle-aged officer who shoots a young woman after reading her journal and discovering she despises him. The psychologist notices that all the figurative and descriptive language runs counter to the downward tendency of the story. Boldly, Vygotsky decides that Aristotle was wrong, that the language of a literary masterpiece (whether it be *Hamlet* or "Gentle Breathing") does not reinforce the mood of the action but actually contradicts it. Similarly, the passage in which Mitya contemplates suicide beautifully illustrates this seldom mentioned but convincing principle of dynamic tension.

A collection of Bunin's best writing might include not only his fiction but also three of his vivid portraits of famous friends, "Leo Tolstoy,"

"Chekhov" and "Chaliapin." In all these works the language and especially the descriptive powers are of an unparalleled force.

His description, for example, of meeting the ancient Tolstoy on a frosty night in Moscow when he, Bunin, was only an adolescent is unforgettable. The timid boy is shown into a dim ballroom. Suddenly a bandy-legged old giant in queer clothes comes rushing up to him: "The smile was enchanting, tender and at the same time somewhat sorrowful, almost pathetic, and I saw now that the small eyes were neither frightening nor sharp but just alert like an animal's." The great man asks many questions and gives bits of wisdom in his staccato voice: "A young writer, are you? Well, certainly, go on writing if you feel like it, but remember that it can never be the aim of life.... Don't expect too much from life, you'll never have a better time than you are having now. There is no happiness in life, there are only occasional flares of it." When the old man learns that Bunin is a pacifist "Tolstoyan" living close to the soil, he says, "You wish to lead a simple life and work on the land? That's a very good thing but don't force yourself, don't make a uniform of it, one can be a good man in any kind of life...."

Singular guru, exceptional follower. Fortunately for us, the happy few, Bunin ignored Tolstoy's advice and did go on to make writing the aim of his long, unhappy life. If you're like me, a reader in search of his own sort of canon, a library of books both beautiful and honest, one that contains Hawthorne and Fitzgerald, George Eliot and Proust, Stendhal and Pushkin, then you will be eager to add Ivan Bunin to your list—if you can find him.

Knut Hamsun

KNUT HAMSUN IS ONE OF MY FAVORITE NOVELISTS although my affection for him troubles me. Politically he was deplorable and as a sensibility he can be maddening, more a difficult adolescent than a satisfying mature mind. And yet he remains for me a touchstone of lyric beauty and of fidelity to the irrational patterns the spirit can describe. And I know of no one who writes better than he about passion—the sting of physical desire, the fear of rejection, the tragicomedy of courtship.

Although he is considered one of the pioneers of the twentieth-century novel, he was born in 1859 and his most admired works were all written in the nineteenth century—*Hunger* (1890), *Mysteries* (1892), *Pan* (1894) and *Victoria* (1898). Just as his books are extraordinarily original and point to few precedents, his life seems entirely self-invented. Named Knut Pedersen, the fourth in a family of seven children, he was raised in extreme poverty, first in central south Norway, then in Hameroy, 200 miles north of the polar circle. Although he had little schooling and worked a series of odd jobs, by the time he was eighteen he had already published his first novella, which appeared in 1877. Thirteen years would have to elapse before he would publish his first genuine work of art, *Hunger,* but even as a teenager his ambition to be a writer seems as powerful as it was inexplicable.

Before he could write *Hunger* at age thirty Hamsun (who named himself after a village he'd lived in) had to accumulate experiences and find a tone of voice. Like so many other Norwegians of that period, he traveled to America, first in 1882 and again in 1886. He didn't much like the new country and wrote a clumsy satire on American cultural life, which he later disowned. During the first trip he coughed blood and was told he would die in a few months of galloping tuberculosis. On his way back to Norway Hamsun took the train from Minnesota to New York and climbed onto the roof of the speeding carriage, where he gulped in fresh air hour after hour—his unorthodox cure. Which worked since, as it later turned out, he'd been misdiagnosed and was suffering only from severe bronchitis. During his second trip, he worked as a laborer laying cable for a tramway line in Chicago. Eventually he became a tramway conductor.

Only after his return to Norway in 1888 did he have his first breakthrough with the publication of *Hunger*. As Robert Ferguson speculates in his magisterial biography, *Enigma,* the young writer curiously enough had been impressed by Mark Twain's joking self-satire, a tone that Hamsun was able to translate into his own mordant and unsparing (and unfunny) self-presentation.

Hamsun also discovered how to record the vagaries of moment-by-moment consciousness, without James Joyce's later formal innovations but with a more genuine conviction that no one thought leads naturally into another. I have no idea whether Hamsun knew the work of David Hume, but the Norwegian novelist came to provide the best concrete example possible of the Scottish philosopher's argument that no unified and continuous self exists and that our mental life is composed only of one flash of consciousness after another, each state entirely independent of the one that precedes or follows it.

What Hamsun was deliberately reacting against was the school of Naturalism, especially the doctrine of the salient characteristic. As a very old man Hamsun said of Emile Zola, the leading Naturalist of his youth, "The so-called 'Naturalists,' Zola and his period, wrote about people with dominant characteristics. They had no use for the more subtle psychology, people all had this 'dominant characteristic' which ordained their actions.

"Dostoevsky and others taught us all something different about human beings. From the time I began I do not think that in my entire output you will find a character with a single dominant characteristic. They are all without so-called 'character.' They are split and fragmented, not good and not bad, but both at once, subtle, and changeable in their attitudes and in their deeds. No doubt I am like this myself." Curiously, Proust also singled out this queasy instability in Dostoevsky's characters.

In *Hunger* the full extent of his achievement isn't entirely clear since the fact that the narrator is starving and delirious appears to explain why his thoughts are so incoherent. But if the first readers were not alerted to this dimension of the book, they were struck by all its other masterful qualities, enduring values that make it seem so modern that only the presence of horses and carriages remind us that it was not written yesterday.

Like André Breton's later *Nadja* or like Strindberg's nearly contemporaneous novels *Alone* and *Inferno,* though without their mystical trappings, *Hunger* is one of the major aleatory novels of city life. Baudelaire had invented the notion that the random stroll through urban chaos is the true vocation of the poet, but Hamsun was one of the first writers to adapt this theme to fiction and with a startling increase in urgency.

No longer is the wanderer a dandy on the lookout for impressions; now he's a starving man—desperately searching for a few coins to buy a loaf of bread. We know nothing about him. Hamsun fills in no family or personal background, offers no explanations of how he hit bottom, draws no conclusions about social injustice. What he does provide is a day-by-day, sometimes second-by-second account of every visit to the pawnshop or the newspaper office where he hopes to be paid for one of the farfetched articles he's written on cultural or philosophical subjects. He sells off his vest and tries unsuccessfully to pawn his glasses, even some worthless buttons he's found in the street, finally a dirty blanket he's borrowed from a friend.

No one has ever better described the effects of hunger on a sensitive mind:

> As I stared at my shoes, I felt as if I had met an old friend, or got back some part of me that had been torn off: a feeling of recognition went through me, tears came to my eyes, and I experienced my shoes as a soft whispering sound coming up toward me. "Getting weak!" I said fiercely to myself and I closed my fists and said, "Getting weak." I was furious with myself for these ridiculous sensations, which had overpowered me even though I was fully conscious of them.... Something of my own being had gone over into these shoes, they struck me as being the ghost of my "I," a breathing part of myself.

I used to give my creative writing students a list of the "lies" on which conventional fiction is based. I don't remember them all, but Hamsun is certainly not guilty of those I do recall. He doesn't show individuals as always acting in character. He doesn't believe in the recognition scene during which everything comes clear to the protagonist (and reader). Nor does he believe in the crisis, in which the hero or villain reveals his true colors. The Aristotelian poetic principles of the primacy of action over character and of character over language he reverses in a truly modern way.

Hamsun is purely psychological, never sociological, and his psychology is as shifting, sometimes as queasy-making, as Dostoevsky's. His range (like Beckett's) is narrow but deep; both men write about the pain of being down and out, though Beckett is much funnier and more abstract. Hamsun confounds autobiography and fiction, again in a way that would become the hallmark of the twentieth century. His "autofictions," as the French would call them, enjoy the prestige of confession and the freedom of the novel.

His early books, the good ones, are difficult to keep straight in the memory. One blends into another. In that way they are like the autofictions of Jean Rhys or Colette. In Hamsun's novels the hero is a loner who arrives in a village, where he falls in love with a local young woman, usually above him in station, sometimes already engaged to someone else. She is frequently frightened by his eccentricities but never indifferent to his appeal (Hamsun was a handsome giant of a man and his protagonists are always physically magnetic).

Hamsun's second significant novel is appropriately titled *Mysteries*, and mysteries do indeed quickly accumulate around Johan Nagel. He wears a loud yellow suit yet seems refined. He has no visible source of income and yet carries a bulging wallet. He explains away his good deeds and acts of heroism as cynical bits of self-promotion, yet circumstances prove them genuine. He carries a violin case though it turns out to be full of dirty laundry. Nevertheless, at a town fair he picks up someone's violin and plays plausibly, even brilliantly. He helps the poor and downtrodden people in the village but ends up by terrorizing them.

In *Pan* Lieutenant Thomas Glahn arrives in a coastal village with his gun and his dog, Aesop. He lives off the land and mixes fitfully with the local gentry. One day he goes rowing out to an island with a group of friends. He's in love with Edvarda, who ignores him. "Then I did something that

I regret and have not yet forgotten. Her shoe slipped off; I seized it and hurled it far out over the water—whether from joy at her nearness or from some urge to assert myself and remind her of my existence, I do not know. It all happened so quickly; I did not think, I just acted on an impulse. A cry went up from the ladies. I was as if paralyzed by what I had done; but what good was that?"

Spurned by the notables for his eccentric behavior, he takes consolation in nature. Hamsun is one of the most ardent nature writers I know of, but he never strains after effects. A typical nature passage, unemphatic but ecstatically pantheistic, reads:

> About midday I rowed out and landed on a little island, out beyond the harbor. There were lilac-colored flowers on long stalks that reached to my knees; I waded through strange vegetation, through raspberry bushes and coarse grasses; there were no animals there, perhaps no man had been there either. The sea foamed gently against the rocks, muffling me in a veil of sound; far up by the nesting rocks all the birds of the coast were flying and screaming. Blessed be life and earth and sky, blessed be my enemies, in this hour I want to be merciful to my bitterest enemy, and tie the bands of his shoes.

Hamsun's most original theme was his treatment of the war between the sexes. Whereas Strindberg's misogyny now seems programmatic and ludicrous (a play such as *The Pelican* is so full of hate towards women that to modern audiences it comes off as either ridiculous or lunatic), Hamsun's lovers are equal partners and equally guilty of edginess, excessive pride and tyrannical desire. Each lover is always out of phase with the other. Glahn irritates Edvarda, who cruelly rejects him. He finds someone else, which makes her jealous. She humbly comes to him to avow her quite genuine love for him, but he no longer believes her and brutally mocks her. In the end Glahn commits suicide.

Love is also doomed in *Victoria* but for concrete reasons, not simply out of reciprocal sadism. The baker's son, Johannes, leaves the village and becomes a celebrated writer in the capital, but he is always haunted by the memory of Victoria, the local aristocrat. She, however, must save the sagging family fortunes by becoming engaged to a rich man. In spite of her resolutions, she is powerfully drawn to Johannes. Yet so conflicted are her feelings that when her fiancé, Otto, dies in a hunting accident, she rushes up to Johannes: " 'Otto is dead,' she said harshly, her eyes blazing. 'You don't say a word, you're so superior. He was a hundred thousand times better than you, do you hear? Do you know how he died? He was shot, the whole of his head was blown to pieces, the whole of his silly little head. He was a hundred thousand....' "

Irrational, alienated, headstrong—these are the words that describe the unforgettable novels Hamsun wrote in his youth. They are stunning improvisations, pages torn out of a romantic egotist's heart, spurs jabbing into the side of a raw sensibility. But once his inspiration waned he was left with no wisdom, little technique and no general fund of humanity. Only twice more did he sound his youthful note—in *Under the Autumn Star* (1906) and in his very last book, *On Overgrown Paths* (1949), written when he was going on ninety. And yet he was condemned to write twenty-three more books after *Victoria* and to win the Nobel Prize in 1920 for one of the most tedious, *The Growth of the Soil*. Because his second wife found his confessional first-person novels embarrassing, he traded in his lyric style for one of epic dullness. Worse, in the 1930s and during the war years he was one of the few prominent writers anywhere in the world to defend the Nazi Party. By now he was a deaf, arrogant old man living on a Norwegian farm in nearly total isolation. He espoused the Nazi cause because the Germans had been his most dedicated early fans, because he had an irrational hatred of the English, because he disliked Norwegian Leftists and because Hitler had promised Norway a key role in the Aryan empire of the North. Yet when Hamsun met with Hitler during the war he infuriated the German dictator by questioning him closely about the future of Norway and by demanding that an impossibly cruel German civil leader be withdrawn and all political executions stopped. Hitler was in a rage and still fuming days later; he gave strict instructions never to be introduced again to "people like that."

At the end of the war Hamsun, still true to his bizarre principles, wrote an obituary for Hitler, whom he personally detested. The new peacetime government in Norway, embarrassed that the most famous living Norwegian writer was a traitor, imprisoned his wife and sons, vigorous collaborators, but dropped charges against Hamsun after two psychiatrists declared he was of "permanently impaired mental faculties." He and his wife had to pay huge fines that wiped out their small fortune. Worse for a writer, sales of his books plummeted throughout the world .

A profound obscurity descended on this writer whom Henry Miller had once declared "the Dickens of my generation," whom Hermann Hesse had called "my favorite author" and of whom Thomas Mann had said in 1929, "Never has the Nobel Prize been awarded to someone worthier." In America he'd been admired and imitated by Ernest Hemingway (who'd recommended his work to Fitzgerald) and in Russia, despite ideological differences, he'd been praised by Maxim Gorky. In England Rebecca West had said, "Hamsun has the qualities that belong to the very great, the completest omniscience about human nature."

When I first read Hamsun in the 1960s, I knew nothing of his disastrous flirtation with Nazism and acknowledged but did not read the introduction to *Hunger* by the most important Jewish writer in the States at that time, Isaac Bashevis Singer. At first glance (or even second or third) nothing revealed Hamsun's nefarious politics, though quite recently, after reading about his life, I came to agree with Thomas Mann, who found that any close student of his work would have had to recognize the inevitability of his conduct during the Nazi era. As Mann put it, the habit of shocking decent people, which had been "an interesting point of view, esthetically speaking, a literary paradox" in the 1890s, hardened into moral paralysis in the 1930s.

When I read Robert Ferguson's biography of Hamsun to prepare this essay, I must admit that I became so disgusted by the great writer that his excellence as an artist suddenly seemed trivial, even irrelevant. His history poses the same problem as the cases of Louis Ferdinand Céline and Ezra Pound. People who are indifferent to art have no problem dismissing them out of hand. Esthetes without a conscience enjoy them without a second thought. The rest of us have to face the unresolvable paradox that these key figures in twentieth-century literature are morally intolerable and artistically indispensable.

Marcel Proust

I N THE 1950s, WHEN I WAS A STUDENT at Cranbrook, a boy's school outside Detroit, Michigan, I first discovered Proust. In those days I'd decided that whatever books were listed on the inside cover of a Modern Library book jacket were good—classics, worth reading, nourishing, impressive. Growing up the son of non-readers I was clueless about which books to concentrate on until I realized that the Modern Library list was reliable.

I was a serious, self-improving guy who never read merely for pleasure (no mysteries, no science-fiction, no adventure stories—in fact, no kids' books, either). I was convinced I was preparing myself for something, perhaps the ultimate trivia quiz or a white-and-gold Paris salon, maybe even a life as a writer.

Proust appealed to me, once I'd sorted out that all these volumes constituted one very long novel, precisely because he had been so ambitious, so all-encompassing. Reading him helped me to see my own dull life as a potential novel, even though the people I was meeting in Detroit shared none of the highly colored eccentricities of Proust's characters. At a time when I was just discovering my homosexuality (and struggling to "cure" it with a weird psychiatrist), Proust revealed to me a society in which homosexuality played a major role, rather than being an extremely rare pathology. Not that Proust had much good to say about homosexuality, but at least he did picture it as a fact of life, something no one would have admitted in the Midwest during the Eisenhower years.

While at Cranbrook I wrote a paper in senior English class on the Madame de Sévigné theme in Proust. Proust himself had shown how this great seventeenth-century letter writer shared with Dostoevsky a method of exposition and scene-painting based on impressions rather than logical analysis; I tried to find examples of her method in Proust's prose—not because I was given to lit. crit. specially but rather because I'd been deeply moved by Sévigné's passionate love letters to her own daughter (a theme that fascinated another gay writer, Thornton Wilder, who made her unreciprocated love a major theme in *The Bridge of San Luis Rey*).

I came back to Proust in my late twenties when I was suffering from hepatitis and was required to stay in bed a month. For a few weeks I was removed from the thrilling sexual paradise of Manhattan in the 1970s. Proust's disillusioned view of society fit perfectly with my own dyspeptic convalescence—particularly since I'd just come back from my first trip to Paris where I'd felt unbearably gauche. Whereas Proust's influence had only encouraged my latent snobbishness when I was an adolescent, now, in my first maturity, I realized that the whole book must be read as a condemnation of snobbism.

When I first moved to Paris in 1983 I read Proust yet again. I realized that the world he described had not completely vanished but that in fact there were still reduced versions of literary salons in Paris, that the descendants of the same noble families he'd known were still on the scene. I even met a few of them, which made his portraits of their great-grandparents all the more vivid for me.

By the time I came to write my short life of Proust in 1997 and 1998 (and to reread his seven volumes, this time in French), I'd decided to leave Paris for Princeton, where I now teach creative writing. I'd witnessed the death from AIDS of my French lover, Hubert Sorin, who died in Morocco in 1994. My literary ambitions had been appeased and I'd seen homosexuals begin to assume their rightful place in society. Proust now made a more somber impression on me. He, too, had outlived the great love of his life, his chauffeur Agostinelli; he had won literary distinction but realized it had no power to compensate him for his losses; he had written more candidly about homosexuality than any writer before him, even though he could never bring himself to acknowledge his own homosexuality in print.

As franker biographies were being published every year, I realized that many of the greatest French writers of this waning century had been gay—Proust, Gide, Genet, not to mention Montherlant, Mauriac, Hervé Guibert and countless others. Homosexuality and the grandeur of French literature, two of the most important preoccupations of my life, now came together with intense clarity in the magisterial figure of Proust, just as I must have sensed they were already lurking there when I first opened *Swann's Way* in 1955.

André Gide

ANDRÉ GIDE MADE HIS LIFE the very core of his art. In that way he was very different from Oscar Wilde, who was fifteen years his senior and, for a brief but crucial period, a friend. Oscar Wilde may have said he put his genius into his life and merely his talent into his art; what is indisputable is that he was careful to keep them well apart. Nothing Wilde wrote is directly autobiographical except *De Profundis,* whereas Gide published his indiscreet journals in installments throughout his long life, brought out his tell-all autobiography, *If It Die...,* in 1926, and left a short confession about his marriage, *Et nunc manet in te,* which he wrote after his wife's death in 1938 and arranged to have published after his own in 1951.

Gay men like me who came of age in the 1950s and '60s knew the details of Gide's personal life better than the details of the lives of many of their own friends—his Protestant beginnings, his sexless marriage to his cousin Madeleine, his espousal of Catholicism, then Communism, and his subsequent renunciations of each system, his affair with Marc Allégret, thirty-one years younger than he, his year-long trip to Africa with Marc, his fathering a child with Elizabeth van Rysselberghe after what appears to have been his unique sexual experience with a woman.

Today, of course, many if not most up-and-coming writers in the English-speaking world are routinely confessional, but whereas they are focused on childhood in which they invariably discover the same pathetic blights (parental alcoholism and abuse, family dysfunctionalism, even incest), Gide never saw himself as wounded, never complained about his fate nor sought to assign blame. And he wasn't much interested in the past. On the contrary, Gide was eager to attune himself to each new generation. And he was quick to assess his own exact degree of responsibility for Madeleine's unhappiness, for instance, just as he was unusually receptive to criticism directed at him or his work by his friends. He was more anguished than complaining. When the arch-Catholic poet and playwright Paul Claudel begged him not to publish an overtly gay passage in his 1914 novel *Lafcadio's Adventures,* Gide corresponded with him at length (and agreed to the publication of their complete correspondence). Gide did not drop the offending passage (in fact he and Claudel ended by dropping each other), but at least, unlike the literary feuds of today, those that Gide engaged in were usually substantial, about ideas and issues.

Gide obviously regarded his life as exemplary and, as an open pedophile, he frequently invoked the didactic Greek model of man–boy love. Today adult sex with adolescents is universally condemned. I suppose if people are going to find the definitive moment of their lives to have been the abuse they suffered while young, the act must necessarily be branded as invariably criminal. In the 1990s an American woman teacher was put in prison for seven years after she became pregnant for the second time by her teenage student; the second baby was born behind bars and is being raised alongside the first child by the very young father's mother. But as Alan Sheridan writes of Gide in his comprehensive biography, *André Gide: A Life in the Present,* "Surprisingly, no complaint was ever made against him, either by a boy or by his parents. He was, of course, protected by the innocence of the time. But he never forced his attentions on anyone...."

His circle was sophisticated and indulgent, with the exception of his French Reformed wife and the Catholic converts. He was lucky enough to count among his most intimate friends the writer (and Protestant) Jean Schlumberger and the novelist and Nobel Prize–winner Roger Martin du Gard, both of whom were bisexual, though less conspicuously so. They accompanied him on his adventures or exchanged letters with him about his encounters with adolescents, and they almost never reproached him. More often, they encouraged him and took a vicarious pleasure in his frequent conquests. Even less judgmental was his best female friend, Maria van Rysselberghe, whom Gide called "La Petite Dame." She was a painter's wife and the bohemian companion who shared an apartment with Gide for years on the rue Vaneau in Paris and who judged Gide's affairs only by whether they made him happier, more productive or, as she put it, "younger." She observed his moods in a journal that she kept for some sixty years.

In pursuing youth (and youths), Gide was capable of leaning out a train window while en route and stroking the extended arm of the kid in the next compartment, or of following a troop of sheep for hours on the chance that a shepherd boy might be found at the end of the trail—and he was seldom disappointed. Just as he was able to domesticate wild animals, young men seemed, as the French would say, *tétanisés* by him.

Alan Sheridan in his biography of Gide correctly observes that one of the advantages of "those linguistically innocent days" was that people could perform homosexual acts without naming them and they "therefore regarded them as quite normal." By contrast, one of the unexpected results of the widespread and noisy debate over homosexuality in our day is that only those people who feel powerfully drawn to same-sex love are sufficiently motivated to indulge in it at all; now all those casual bisexual encounters of the past have disappeared, especially since the growing wealth of Europe and America and the collapse of religion have meant that heterosexual "dating" now starts at puberty and no one (except prisoners) has recourse to homosexuality merely because nothing else is on tap. Similarly, working-class boys no longer have an automatic respect for "gentlemen" like Gide nor do they unquestioningly submit to their whims.

Certainly Gide would never be considered a great "moralist" today. Yet his reputation lingers on; in France the *idée reçue* about Gide even now is that he was a "Puritan" or a "preacher," foolishly fussing over his own conscience, and those French readers who dismiss him without having read him say, typically, "His scruples seem so naïve to us now." Alan Sheridan's biography should make them reexamine their assumptions. For instance, the great love of Gide's life was Marc Allégret, a boy of sixteen when the forty-eight-year-old Gide seduced him in 1917. The boy's father, the Pastor Elie Allégret, who had been Gide's best man and was an old family friend, had confided the care of his four young sons to "Uncle" André when he, Elie, was sent off during the war to serve as an army chaplain in the Cameroons. He did not return to France until 1919—by which time Marc and André had already been lovers for two years. Even Gide's wife suspected that something was up; she wrote her husband, "Don't devote yourself too excessively to the Allégrets. I think there is some danger there."

The danger she sensed was that for the first time Gide was madly, profoundly in love. He'd never been so besotted before, though he'd had a short, intense affair with Jean Schlumberger's young brother Maurice a few years earlier. Nevertheless most of his earlier sexual dalliances had been with working boys, usually in North Africa, boys with whom he had had nothing in common. Now he was enamored of a boy of his own class, someone who had a claim not only on his body but also on his mind and soul. In the last three months of 1917 Gide traveled from his house in Normandy to Paris eight times to see Marc and he spent a week each time at the Allégret's house in Passy. As he confided to his journal, "Never have I aspired less to rest, never have I felt more uplifted by that excess of passion that Bossuet regards as the privilege of youth.... Age is unable to empty sensual pleasure of its attraction or the whole world of its charm."

The affair with Marc had a disastrous effect on Gide's marriage. Madeleine and André (he was two years younger than she) had known each other since childhood. He had staged a long campaign to marry her, even though they were first cousins and, as he acknowledged from the very beginning, he was never remotely attracted to her sexually. Madeleine agreed to marry André with deep misgivings; she was especially afraid she would not be up to his constant call to adventure. On their honeymoon in North Africa Gide left her alone for hours on end as he compulsively cruised (something of this situation is reflected in *The Immoralist*). Madeleine had quickly come to understand that her husband would pursue his own life apart from her, but later she came to treasure their shared moments at their Norman house in Cuverville.

When she realized that Gide was going off with Marc Allégret to England for three and a half months (a bit like the married Verlaine and the much younger Rimbaud), she begged him not to leave her. Gide wrote her an unforgivable letter in which he said he had to leave since he was rotting with her. While Gide was with Marc in Cambridge, Madeleine destroyed all of Gide's letters to her—as many as two thousand, written over a thirty-year period. As she later told Gide, "At first I thought that my heart had stopped beating, that I was dying. I had suffered so much.... I burned your letters in order to have something to do. Before I destroyed them I read them all over, one by one...." She confided that they had been her most precious possession. When Gide discovered what she had done, he was inconsolable. He wept for a week, waiting for Madeleine to come to him to comfort him, but she went about her household chores and pretended not to notice his misery. She was waiting—fruitlessly—for his return to the Protestant faith of their childhood; that was where he should seek consolation for his loss. He was convinced that his collected letters to his wife would have been his best book, a warm, human, spiritual testament that would have corrected the much cruder image given by his other work. "An incomplete, inexact, caricatured, grimacing image is now all that will endure of me. My authentic reflection has been wiped out, forever.... All that was purest, noblest in my life, all that could best have survived, and shone, and spread warmth and beauty, all is destroyed. And no effort of mine will ever be able to replace it."

Gide and Marc seem to have remained lovers from 1917 to 1927 and friends until the end of Gide's life. For the first time in his life he experienced jealousy—especially against Cocteau, who enjoyed teasing Gide by flirting with the boy. I had always been puzzled about Gide's antipathy to Cocteau, especially his repeated bitchy denunciations of Cocteau's work. If in France Cocteau was always regarded as something of a charlatan and *un petit touche-à-tout* until his revival in the 1980s, the responsibility lay largely with Gide's attacks in print. Now it turns out that Gide was as irked by Cocteau's behavior as he was by his style. As Sheridan puts it,

> For Gide, with his cult of sincerity, Cocteau represented cultivated insincerity, outward show, showing-off, parade. It was morally dangerous in life as well as in art. It was not to be confused with the kind of "immoralism" that he had himself entertained (without entirely adopting): such a post-Protestant, Nietzschean "immoralism" was, effectively, a "higher" morality, one that must be preached with all the ardor of the Protestant missionary. Gide was afraid that Cocteau might give Marc Allégret something that he himself could not give him, something, moreover, that would be corrupting, that would undermine all the patient Socratic education that he had lavished on the boy.

According to a mutual friend, Gide confessed that "my hatred for C... derived from C...'s moral influence, his brio, which had dazzled, spellbound a still childish mind.... I was like Pygmalion finding his statue damaged, his work vandalized; all my effort, all that care that I had expended as an educator...had been sullied by someone else, the 'nice' C...." Cocteau himself suspected Gide of wanting to kill him.

If Marc Allégret was Gide's great love, then his greatest gay friend was the novelist and doctor Henri Ghéon. From 1898 on throughout the next fifteen years Gide and Ghéon cruised Paris together, frequenting the saunas and having sex in the pissotières. Their correspondence is full of coded references to news about the young men they met in such places. As Ghéon said afterwards, "I think Gide looked to me for what was lacking in himself: a certain drive, exuberance, strength, health, frankness and, I admit, boldness in satisfying my desires." The two men, during the years that led up to World War I, usually went to North Africa together every year as sexual tourists, though they would not have thought of their travels in such disparaging terms; for them they were not exploiting impoverished Arabs but exploring their own erotic depths, thereby liberating their creativity and defying bourgeois conventionality. Nevertheless Gide declared at age seventy, "I like a country only if it offers many opportunities for fornication." Madeleine Gide accompanied Gide to Algeria once and said, after Gide tried to seduce three schoolboys in the next compartment, "You looked like a criminal or a madman."

Gide was so used to sharing his gay experience with Ghéon that when he, Gide, fell in love with the adolescent Maurice Schlumberger in 1904, Gide couldn't wait to share the boy's favors with Ghéon. Maurice obligingly began to sleep with both of the older men, which excited them into a furious correspondence about the youth. This was perhaps the ultimate example of René Girard's "triangulation" in love—the notion that one can experience love only if it is mediated through a third person, an observer-participant. As Sheridan puts it, "The letters are not only a record of the three-sided relationship, an attempt to salvage the details, the words without this adventure could not become a story, a narrative that could endure long after the adventure itself; they also feed back into it." Soon Maurice himself was asked to read the correspondence. After he'd perused the letters he said, with Jamesian elegance, "Yes, everything in our story is marvellous; yes, every chapter, from the beginning; there's no falling-off of interest at any point."

Schlumberger soon enough dropped both men and went on to a long, exclusively heterosexual life (he died in 1976 at age ninety-one as the immensely wealthy founder of the Banque Schlumberger). But the "story" that this adventure was struggling to become was *The Counterfeiters,* Gide's greatest novel (he would have said his only novel, since he called the others either *récits* or *soties). The Counterfeiters* was not published until 1926 and the actual writing of it was inspired by (and addressed to) Marc Allégret, but the Ghéon–Gide–Schlumberger triangle and the "intertextuality" of their correspondence some twenty years before are clearly the background of this brilliant novel, Gide's most "modernist" work.

Ghéon, after years of ecstatically pursuing a bit of trouser with Gide, finally succumbed to the prevailing Catholicism, renounced his old life and came to "pity" Gide's appetites. Ghéon is what American evangelists would today proudly call an "ex-gay." Gide himself was dangerously close to converting, at least if we are to believe one volume of his journals written in 1916. Ghéon's conversion at that time, the horrors of the war and his remorse about his continuous and furious sessions of masturbating all made the consolations of faith seem momentarily appealing. Perhaps Claudel's flattering efforts to convert him, a true military campaign in itself, also swayed him. But soon Gide's own scepticism reasserted itself—and he met Marc Allégret, obviously a god cut closer to Gide's measure. In fact, after this single temptation towards religiosity Gide became quite testy with his pious friends on the spiritual make. When Jacques Maritain, France's most famous theologian, asked Gide in 1924 not to publish *Corydon,* an essay that would later become the founding text of gay liberation, Gide flatly refused. As a parting shot Maritain begged Gide to ask Christ "directly" if he was doing the right thing; Gide said testily, "No. I have lived too long, too intimately, with the thought of Christ, to agree to call him today as one might call someone on the telephone."

All of Gide's friends were horrified by Gide's determination to publish *Corydon* in 1924. The book was the first attempt by a celebrated homosexual to defend his orientation before the general public. They didn't object to Gide's pederasty; they just didn't want to see it discussed in print. They thought *Corydon* would "marginalize" him, to use our word. This little book, a defense of homosexuality, was something he had been working on for years; he had begun it in 1908 and had even published a few copies of part of it (the first two dialogues) in 1911 and locked them away in a drawer; as he had confided in a hasty note to his journal, "The fear that someone else might get there before me; it seems to me that the subject is in the air." It certainly was, as an aftermath of the Wilde trial and of the trial of Philipp von Eulenburg in 1907 (Eulenburg was the former German ambassador to Vienna); the trial had revealed the homosexual activities of several high-ranking German officials and a French diplomat. In 1918 Gide had published twenty-one anonymous copies and distributed them to friends. At that point he was still trying not to offend Madeleine, but after she burned his letters he no longer felt bound to protect her reputation and sensibilities. Accordingly, *Corydon* was at last published under his own name in 1924; within a few months some 13,000 copies had sold, Gide's largest print run to date.

Much later, in 1942, Gide wrote, "*Corydon* is still, for me, the most important of my books," even though he acknowledged it was also his least successful and the one he would most willingly rewrite. Certainly its arguments today seem spurious or absurd; Gide even suggests in it that male homosexuality is the best way to preserve female virtue. There is a lot of rubbish about homosexuality among the monkeys, an old defense that has recently been taken up with much more scientific detail. No matter that there's something fishy about this book or that it defends pedophiles while condemning what Gide calls "sodomites" (those males who sleep with men their age) and "inverts" (which Gide defines as those men who play the female role in bed). Gide even goes so far as to say of inverts, "It has always seemed to me that they alone deserved the reproach of moral and intellectual defamation, and were guilty of some of the accusations leveled at all homosexuals." (Gide can be tedious with his definitions. Much sprightlier is Proust, who once wrote with perfect accuracy, "A homosexual is not a man who loves homosexuals, but a man who, seeing a soldier, immediately wants to have him for a friend.") Despite his Protestant heavy-handedness, Gide must be commended for his courage in defending pederasty against all comers; almost the only friend who saluted his action was the quietly discreet seventy-five-year-old Edmund Gosse, who said, "No doubt, in fifty years, this particular subject will cease to surprise anyone, and how many people in the past might wish to have lived in 1974."

Gide's moral campaigning didn't end there. He traveled to Equatorial Africa in 1925–26 with Marc Allégret, who filmed the expedition; Gide in the two books he wrote about the trip denounced the exploitation of African labor by European rubber monopolies—which led to a reform in French government policy.

More dramatically, Gide visited the Soviet Union in the mid-1930s and, after a painful inner debate and again against the counsel of all his friends, ended by denouncing Stalin's regime. As late as 1933 Gide was extraordinarily naïve about the prevailing mood of the Soviet Union; he wrote a friend, "I'd like them to have *Corydon* translated. It seems to me to have been written for them...." After the Nazis' burning of the Reichstag, Gide published a protest (typically weakened by qualifications and second thoughts) in the Communist paper *L'Humanité*. For quite a while he justified Soviet censorship and lack of civil rights (he didn't know about the terrorism) as necessary and somehow different from Nazi tactics; the Communists represented the "future," whereas the Nazis stood for the "past." Of course Gide was specially drawn to Communist youth summer camps in France and their scantily clad boys. Gide's adherence to Communism became so celebrated, though he was never a party member nor a Marxist, that it caused the Royal Society of Literature in Britain to "revoke" the honorary membership it had conferred on Gide in 1924.

Slowly and against his will Gide was weaned away from his endorsement of the Soviet Union. He learned that the apparently easygoing attitude in Russia towards sexual morality had changed into a new puritanism; homosexuality was now declared illegal. Stalin's Great Purge had also begun, a reign of terror that would eventually result in the death of some ten million victims. In 1936 Gide made plans to visit Russia and ascertain the situation for himself; he told the suave Soviet diplomat Ilya Ehrenburg of his plans to speak directly to Stalin about the legal position of homosexuals. The Soviet government prepared for his visit by printing up 300,000 postcards bearing his photograph; Gide, no doubt anticipating anonymous adventures, was dismayed and said, "But everyone will recognize me!"

For nine weeks, from June 17, 1936, to the end of August, Gide traveled through the Soviet Union. Maxim Gorky died about the time of his arrival (some people said he'd been killed by Stalin); Gide spoke at his funeral on June 20 in Red Square, standing on the podium beside Bulganin, Molotov, Stalin and Zhdanov, the cultural commissar who had put in place the hateful doctrine of "Socialist Realism," which Gide was quick to denounce. Gide was shocked by the statues to Stalin everywhere, the privilege enjoyed by party members, the censorship applied even to his own speeches, the deadening state control of the arts and journalism, the elaborate etiquette forced on Gide even in his own telegrams to Stalin, the farcical show trials that made a mockery of justice. Gide was determined to reveal this situation to the Western world, even though his leftist friends, including the Dutch proletariat writer Jef Last, urged him to wait. After all, the Left was under fire, not only from Hitler but also from Franco. Perhaps because Gide had gained confidence in his fights against equally persuasive Catholic friends, not to mention less subtle if more virulent homophobes, he did not shrink from his new mission.

By November 1936 Gide had rushed into print his *Return from the U.S.S.R.*, which almost instantly sold some 146,000 copies and was quickly translated into several languages. The world's Communist press treated him as a lackey of imperialism and a fascist counter-agent. When the Second International Congress of Intellectuals for the Defence of Culture took place in Madrid in 1937, Stephen Spender recalled that the unstated theme of the meeting was the Stalinists versus André Gide.

Although Alan Sheridan modestly asserts, "I have no theory about André Gide," he does render him with a wealth of telling detail as a fearless crusader and as a major literary innovator. Sheridan, for instance, draws attention to Gide's 1895 novel *Paludes,* which in the lightest, most Parisian way foreshadows the preoccupation in the twentieth century with intertextuality, books-within-books, perilously shifting levels of reality and the blurring between genres—between autobiography and fiction, for instance, or essay and *récit.* The splendidly detailed picture of Paris gay life before World War I that emerges from Sheridan's pages never obscures the account of Gide's growing mastery as an artist, which culminates in *The Counterfeiters,* a book that today has a peculiarly post-modernist ring to it.

Until his last breath Gide remained a convinced atheist. As he told the young Claude Mauriac, who grew weary of his Catholic father's hairsplitting with Gide over dogma, the essential remained: "I don't believe; I know there is no reason to believe; that's a certainty for me." Gide replaced his Protestant biological family with a select "family" of friends he saw constantly and to whom he remained fiercely faithful. His pedophilia accompanied and reinforced his sympathy for the young, who he declared were always right. After World War I the youth of France, even the cantankerous, homophobic Surrealists, embraced him and his books; he was suddenly famous. His trademark *"inquiétude"* kept him constantly in motion. Even if Sheridan's day-by-day account of his comings and goings sometimes becomes tedious, it at least drives home exactly how restless Gide was. He seldom spent more than a week or two in the same place, and the reader becomes exhausted just reading his itinerary during sixty years of château-hopping. Gide inhabited a world of rich bohemians who migrated from one week-long stay at someone's country house to another in a ceaseless, lifelong villeggiatura.

Compared to the mendacious Proust, Gide was of an exemplary honesty about his sexual nature. In fact, no one was as provocatively open, even exhibitionistic, as Gide. His style was simple, nervous, pared-down—minimalist *avant la lettre;* no wonder he didn't at first recognize the importance of *Swann's Way* and even initially refused to publish it. Not only was Proust considered society's pet flatterer, a chronicler of *mondan-ités* for the newspapers, his style also looked heavy and elaborate and insincere to the young editors of the newly founded *Nouvelle Revue Française.*

Proust, of course, has had the last laugh. The French have never set much store by Gide's cult of "sincerity," and they far prefer Proust's multiple disguises. But Gide is certainly overdue for a major comeback, especially because long before anyone else he explored the ambiguities of autofiction, one of the most fertile genres of our day.

Oscar Wilde

A CARELESS OR NAÏVE READER, especially during the Victorian period, could have entirely missed that *The Picture of Dorian Gray* is a gay book. After all, the protagonist, Dorian, himself is guilty of, among other things, destroying previously respectable women's reputations. When Basil Hallward, the painter who has executed the fatal portrait, finally confronts Dorian with his sins, he says, "When you met Lady Gwendolen, not a breath of scandal had ever touched her. Is there a single decent woman in London now who would drive with her in the Park? Why, even her children are not allowed to live with her.... Lord Gloucester was one of my greatest friends at Oxford. He showed me a letter that his wife had written to him when she was dying alone in her villa at Mentone. Your name was implicated in the most terrible confession I ever read." Through his cruelty and faithlessness, Dorian causes the young actress, Sibyl Vane, to commit suicide, just as towards the end of the book he is involved with an aristocratic woman and a peasant girl, both of whom he renders intensely unhappy.

Similarly, Lord Henry Wotton, the man who infects Dorian with the longing to be above morality and eternally young, is married, even if his wife reveals she is jealous of Dorian—no wonder, since her husband has seventeen photos of the beautiful Dorian around the house and neglects her utterly. Moreover, Henry is a decided misogynist and strongly opposed to marriage: "You seem to forget that I am married, and the one charm of marriage is that it makes a life of deception absolutely necessary for both parties." Later he adds: "Never marry at all, Dorian. Men marry because they are tired; women, because they are curious; both are disappointed." Naturally, by the end of the novel Wotton's wife has divorced him.

Of the three main characters, the most candidly homosexual is the painter, who acknowledges that he worships Dorian's beauty. (Wilde had said: "Basil Hallward is what I think I am: Lord Henry what the world thinks me: Dorian is what I would like to be—in other ages, perhaps.") To be sure, there is never a question of any sexual act between Basil and Dorian, but their first encounter sounds very much like love at first sight— or at least cruising. As Basil explains to Lord Henry, he'd met Dorian at a crush filled with "huge, overdressed dowagers and tedious Academicians." He continues: "I suddenly became conscious that someone was looking at me. I turned halfway round, and saw Dorian Gray for the first time. When our eyes met, I felt I was growing pale. A curious sensation of terror came over me. I knew that I had come face to face with someone whose mere personality was so fascinating that, if I allowed it to do so, it would absorb my whole nature, my whole soul, my very art itself.... I have always been my own master; had at least always been so, till I met Dorian Gray.... I had a strange feeling that Fate had in store for me exquisite joys and exquisite sorrows.... We would have spoken to each other without any introduction. I am sure of that. Dorian told me so afterwards. He, too, felt that we were destined to know each other." Walter Pater had convinced Wilde to delete the only explicitly homosexual passage about Hallward's love for Dorian.

The book enjoyed an immense success when it was published in 1891. As Richard Ellmann in his definitive biography has remarked, "No novel had commanded so much attention for years, or awakened sentiments so contradictory in its readers." W. H. Smith (which recently sold me my latest copy) originally refused to carry it on the grounds that it was "filthy." Wilde's wife, Constance, complained, "Since Oscar wrote *Dorian Gray,* no one will speak to us." One paper said that *Dorian Gray* was a matter for the police, not the critic. Perhaps the most tragic consequence of the book's notoriety was that it attracted the attention of the young man who would be the cause of Wilde's downfall. Lord Alfred Douglas read it nine times and begged to be introduced to the author—an encounter that would lead four years later to Wilde's trial and imprisonment.

If *Dorian Gray* created such a furor, it was not just because of its general estheticism but also because of its specific homosexual subtext. The word "curious" is Wilde's usual substitution for the more explicit "queer," and indeed "curious" is surely the most frequently used adjective in the entire book.

When Hallward paints Dorian he has in mind Antinous, the Emperor Hadrian's lover; Dorian is pictured as "crowned with heavy lotus-blossoms... on the prow of Adrian's barge." Dorian dresses up as Anne de Joyeuse, the French admiral who was one of Henri III's mignons, just as Galveston was Edward II's beloved. Wilde believed that this new (if veiled) content contributed to the force of the book's impact: "Any attempt to extend the subject-matter of art is extremely distasteful to the public; and yet the vitality and progress of art depend in a large measure on the continual extension of the subject-matter."

Those readers who were sophisticated knew perfectly well what to make of the references to the "Hellenic ideal," and with a bit more effort they could have decoded this sentence about Hallward's affection for Dorian: "It was such love as Michael Angelo had known, and Montaigne, and Winckelmann, and Shakespeare himself." Michelangelo (whose sonnets had been mentioned earlier in the novel) wrote tormented love poems to the young heterosexual aristocrat Tommaso Cavalieri. Montaigne was the intimate friend of Etienne de La Boétie and, as Wilde put it in an essay, in Montaigne's meditation on friendship "he ranks it higher than the love of brother for brother, or the love of man for woman." Johann Joachim Winckelmann, the eighteenth-century German art historian and one of the founders of neoclassicism in the eighteenth century, was notoriously homosexual; and Wilde had once written that "a romantic friendship with a young Roman of his day initiated Winckelmann into the secret of Greek art, taught him the mystery of its beauty and the meaning of its form."

Wilde had devoted a notorious text (partially published originally in 1889 in Blackwood's *Edinburgh Magazine* but not printed in full until two decades after Wilde's death) to the theory that Shakespeare's sonnets had been addressed to a boy actor, a certain Willie Hughes, their "onlie begetter," who, like Dorian, possesses the secret of eternal youth. The story-essay, "The Portrait of Mr. W. H.," already adumbrates several other themes that show up later in *Dorian Gray*—including a portrait (forged, in this case) and endless eulogies to the boy's white and rose and gold beauty. In the frame tale of the story, the nineteenth-century inventor of the theory about Willie Hughes is a certain Cyril Graham who played Shakespeare's girls at Eton and Trinity and who, like Dorian, inherited his mother's beauty, became an orphan while still a child and was raised by a rough, disapproving grandfather (most of Wilde's heroes are orphans, as though freedom from the family is the necessary condition for spiritual—and sexual—liberty).

An echo of that boy in Shakespeare can be heard in *Dorian Gray* when Dorian himself falls in love with Sibyl Vane on the night she is dressed in male attire and is playing Rosalind in *As You Like It* (the role in which Cyril Graham shone and which, according to the theory, was one of the handful that Shakespeare wrote for his beloved, Willie Hughes). "When she came on in her boy's clothes," Dorian tells Lord Henry and Hallward, "she was perfectly wonderful. She wore a moss-colored velvet jerkin with cinnamon sleeves, slim brown cross-gartered hose, a dainty little green cap with a hawk's feather caught in a jewel, and a hooded cloak lined with dull red. She had never seemed to me more exquisite."

Rosalind, of course, is disguised in the play as the boy Ganymede ("I'll have no worse a name than Jove's own page"). When she encounters the man she loves, Orlando, she tells him that she will cure him of his love: "I would cure you, if you would but call me Rosalind, and come every day to my cote, and woo me." Although Orlando thinks he is speaking to a boy, he readily agrees to accept this "cure." Rosalind, disguised as Ganymede, teaches Orlando the arts of love and the understanding of a woman's nature, and even acts out a mock (or is it a real?) engagement ceremony.

Perhaps the most striking scene occurs when "Ganymede" sees a blood-soaked handkerchief and learns that Orlando has fought a lioness to save his brother's life and now lies gravely wounded in a cave. "Ganymede" faints, recovers and is chided for a lack of manliness by Orlando's brother Oliver.

> ROSALIND: I do so, I confess it.... Ah, sirrah, a body would think this was well counterfeited. I pray you, tell your brother how well I counterfeited....Heigh-ho!

OLIVER: This was not counterfeit, there is too great testimony in your complexion that it was a passion in earnest.

ROSALIND: Counterfeit, I assure you.

OLIVER: Well then, take a good heart, and counterfeit to be a man.

ROSALIND: So I do: but, i'faith, I should have been a woman by right.

Of course what gives substance to these allusions to a counterfeit gender is not just that Rosalind is playing a gay boy, Ganymede, who instructs a man in how to make love to a woman, but also that on Shakespeare's stage the woman was acted by a real-life boy and the enthusiastic audience was in on the joke.

The androgyny of this situation stirs the ambiguous Dorian Gray to his first great passion. But the night he invites Lord Henry and Basil to see Sibyl Vane play Juliet (another role, according to the theory, that Shakespeare had written for Willie Hughes), she bitterly disappoints him with her listless, unconvincing performance. Her problem is that she has fallen in love with a real flesh-and-blood human being, Dorian (though, paradoxically and unbelievably, she doesn't know his real name and calls him simply "Prince Charming"). As she tearfully explains to him after his scalding reproaches, "You taught me what reality really is. Tonight, for the first time in my life, I saw through the hollowness, the sham, the silliness of the empty pageant in which I had always played."

Dorian refuses to understand, abandons her with a curse—and she kills herself. At this point the portrait begins to change; there is a new touch of cruelty to the mouth. Sibyl's life has ended tragically because she had given up the mask of art for the face of reality. In "The Portrait of Mr. W. H." Wilde had already argued that inspired deception or counterfeiting is essential to the actor's art, especially the travestied actor's.

The dangerous ideas presented in both "The Portrait of Mr. W.H." and in *The Picture of Dorian Gray* came back to haunt Wilde during his trial. Here's an excerpt in the cross-examination by Edward Carson on April 3, 1895:

A perverted novel might be a good book?

—I don't know what you mean by a "perverted" novel.

Then I will suggest *Dorian Gray* as open to the interpretation of being such a novel?

—That could only be to brutes and illiterates. The views of Philistines on art are incalculably stupid.

An illiterate person reading *Dorian Gray* might consider it such a novel?

—The views of illiterates on art are unaccountable. I am concerned only with my view of art. I don't care twopence what other people think of it.

The majority of persons would come under your definition of Philistines and illiterates?

—I have found wonderful exceptions.

Do you think that the majority of people live up to the position you are giving us?

—I am afraid they are not cultivated enough.

Not cultivated enough to draw the distinction between a good book and a bad book?

—Certainly not.

The affection and love of the artist of *Dorian Gray* might lead an ordinary individual to believe that it might have a certain tendency?

—I have no knowledge of the views of ordinary individuals.

You did not prevent the ordinary individual from buying your book?

—I have never discouraged him.

The curious truth is that if *Dorian Gray* is about the double life of a Victorian gentleman, it is also, in its very construction, an example of formal and thematic doubling. It is on one level an archetypal parable, comparable to *Dr Jekyll and Mr Hyde*—that is, a story that everyone knows but that few people have read, or not reread since adolescence. Wilde started out as a writer of fairy tales, an essentially oral form of art; indeed, as André Gide tells us in his little essay "In Memoriam," "Wilde didn't converse: he recounted." Gide remembers an evening in Paris in 1891 when, after dinner, Wilde told his French friends the story of the river in which Narcissus drowned because the boy was trying to embrace his own reflection. " 'But if I loved him,' responded the river, 'it was because when he bent over my waters I saw the reflection of my waters in his eyes.'"

Even when he wasn't telling a tale, Wilde was reciting, as it were, the dialogue from his fiction and plays. To the astonished, puritanical Gide, longing to be tempted by Wilde in his guise as Lord Henry, the Irish writer said: "I don't like your lips; they're straight like the lips of someone who has never lied. I want to teach you how to lie so that your lips will become as beautiful and twisted as those of an ancient mask."

Wilde's working method was to start with a collection of quips and clever sayings and gradually build up scenes in which such remarks could be set off; he constructed the broach around his precious gems. As a writer in the Gaelic tradition (his father, Sir William Wilde, had put together a collection of Irish folk tales that the son later drew on), Oscar was alive to wit, paradox, puns, repetition, melodic language and all the other oral, bardic strategies of literature—and he understood the importance of a gripping legend as he "recounted" his story to a spellbound audience.

But if *Dorian Gray* contains some of the most brilliant dialogue in English fiction, full of epigrams that the author would recycle in his plays, it is also a melodrama of the most conventional Victorian sort. I'm referring specially to the revenge that Sibyl Vane's brother James has sworn to take on Dorian—a plot element that Wilde built up when he changed the text from a magazine story into a proper book. There's the ruined prostitute's denunciation of "Prince Charming," the near escape outside the opium den, the accidental murder during the hunting season in the country—all the excitement that Wilkie Collins had trained contemporary readers to expect.

This double nature of the writing—creaky plot and oiled dialogue—corresponds to what the French critic Roland Barthes has identified as two different rates of reading: a fast scanning for plot appropriate to nineteenth-century potboilers and a close study suitable to modernist works. As Barthes puts it in *The Pleasure of the Text,* "Read slowly, read all of a novel by Zola, and the book will drop from your hands; read fast, in snatches, some modern text, and it becomes opaque, inaccessible to your pleasure: you want something to happen and nothing does, for what happens to the language does not happen to the plot...." Wilde, oddly enough, tempts us through suspense to read as fast as possible, whereas at the same time his epigrams, his mini-essays on jewels, embroideries and ecclesiastical vestments as well as his intricate philosophical speculations on conventional virtue versus hedonism all demand that we peruse those passages as slowly as possible. *The Picture of Dorian Gray* is a book to be read at two speeds; in its very form it is ambiguous. In French someone who lives *à deux vitesses* is leading a double life, or at least a contradictory one.

Morally, *Dorian Gray* is just as complex, especially when it's compared to a book that must have partially inspired it. Although uncanny and unsettling, Robert Louis Stevenson's *Dr Jekyll and Mr Hyde* is about the asymmetrical relationship between two men inhabiting the same body; the monster, Hyde, is the respectable Jekyll's "son," in a sense, and Stevenson even writes, "Jekyll had more than a father's interest; Hyde had more than a son's indifference." The repressed Jekyll relishes the crimes that the bestial Hyde commits. But when Jekyll discovers that he keeps turning into Hyde, even without swallowing the transforming chemical draught, he realizes that soon Hyde will entirely supplant him. At the moment the demonic Hyde is about to be caught by the law, he commits suicide.

Jekyll never exactly repents, but he does become increasingly aware that Hyde's infamy expresses his own lust for evil. This awareness, however, does not come at once. As Jekyll himself writes, weirdly discussing himself in the third-person: "Henry Jekyll stood at times aghast before the acts of Edward Hyde; but the situation was apart from ordinary laws, and insidiously relaxed the grasp of conscience. It was Hyde, after all, and Hyde alone, who was guilty. Jekyll was no worse; he woke again to his good qualities seemingly unimpaired; he would even make haste, when it was possible, to undo the evil done by Hyde. And thus his conscience slumbered."

Jekyll's conscience, however, does finally awaken, whereas Dorian's never rises above self-pity and petulance. After he has murdered Hallward, Dorian "for a moment felt keenly the terrible pleasure of a double life." He rather wanly regrets that he's lost all ability to bestow affection on others; as he tells Lord Henry, "I wish I could love.... But I seem to have lost the passion, and forgotten the desire." When he recalls Hallward, rather than feeling repentance for having killed him, he merely experiences all over again his original vexation. And when he slashes the picture it's only to destroy the evidence of his evil—certainly not to end his own life.

Even if Dorian does not repent, the reader is never left in any doubt that Lord Henry's philosophy of self-indulgence and of the ultimate value of physical beauty and eternal youth has led the younger man astray. Indeed, Dorian's terrible immorality—his nasty rejection of Sibyl, his disastrous, reputation-destroying influence on the lives of many of the men and women he comes into contact with, his murder of Hallward and his provocation of Alan Campbell's suicide—are all the direct result of his estheticism and hedonism. In the legal cross-examination quoted earlier Wilde, if he'd only been willing to humble his pride, could easily have justified his novel as a stern, dramatic demonstration of the consequences of evil ideas. He certainly had neither served his own cause (nor accurately presented his own work of fiction, which clearly solicits the reader's indignation) by having written to a Scottish newspaper editor, in defense of his novel, "An artist, sir, has no ethical sympathies at all. Virtue and wickedness are to him simply what the colors on his palette are to the painter." Wilde obviously enjoyed posing as the apostle of art for art's sake before the shocked public, but in truth he had carefully (and more mundanely) constructed his plot to demonstrate the tares that wickedness reaps.

Of course his opponents could quite rightly have pointed out that *The Picture of Dorian Gray* does not tell the whole tale. As Richard Ellmann puts it, "If *Dorian Gray* presented aestheticism in an almost negative way, his essays 'The Critic as Artist' and 'The Soul of Man Under Socialism' gave it affirmation." These long texts were published almost simultaneously with *Dorian;* the first essay came out in 1890, the second in 1891. Walter Pater, the philosopher of estheticism who reviewed *Dorian* at Wilde's request, had objected that Lord Henry's hedonism left no place for the higher pleasures of generosity and renunciation. For long-range hedonism, as everyone knows, can be perfectly consistent with goodness; to be good is a pleasure. Now, in his essays, Wilde corrected the distorted image he'd projected in his novel. In "The Critic as Artist" Wilde rejects the Romantic idea of art as a primitive excess of unconscious sentiment ("All bad poetry comes from genuine feeling") and defends the notion that the critical faculty is crucial for generating fresh and beautiful forms.

In "The Soul of Man Under Socialism," Wilde argues that a just division of goods and the abolition of private property would handle the problems of material existence and set the stage for the flourishing of art, a highly idiosyncratic business. According to Wilde, under socialism the community will supply the useful things, and "the beautiful things will be made by the individual." In italics Wilde emphasizes: "*Art is the most intense mode of individualism that the world has known.*" Through this clever division of labor, Wilde imagines he has reconciled public justice with individual freedom of expression. These two faces of the same coin are, to be sure, less exciting and melodramatic than the contrast between Dorian's flawless, unchanging face and the grotesque portrait.

For Wilde was torn not only by conflicting ideas of morality but also by contradictory styles of conceptualizing such problems. On one side Wilde was a Decadent, very much inspired by J. K. Huysmans's *Against Nature* (in French *A Rebours*), published in 1884. This is the very book that Lord Henry gives to Dorian and that "poisons" his life; in his novel Wilde never gives the title, but in his trial he did identify it as the damaging fiction.

Like a combination of Lord Henry and Dorian, Des Esseintes, the hero of *Against Nature*, lives surrounded by beautiful furniture, reads curious old books, is hostile to marriage, smokes opium and tries to corrupt young people. Des Esseintes, for instance, introduces an innocent working-class young man to the pleasures of a bordello, which the older man pays for at first. He then cuts the boy off financially—and hopes that the youngster will now be tempted to steal and even murder to pay for his visits (the plan comes to nothing, however). Like Dorian, Des Esseintes ends up disgusted and disillusioned by his amoral, single-minded pursuit of pleasure.

If Huysmans, virtually the founder of the Decadent movement, inspired Wilde, nevertheless the Irish master was a far better writer—and a more modern spirit—than the French novelist. Huysmans smells today of opium and mothballs, and certainly his veering between blasphemy and piety in alternating gusts of brimstone and incense can only make a modern reader smile.

Although *Dorian* has its period side, especially in the way Wilde's high-born rebels obediently attend tedious society events and never consider absenting themselves, nevertheless it is a far more contemporary novel than Huysmans's. This fresh quality might be called Wilde's Nietzschian side, even though neither man was aware of the other's existence despite the fact they were contemporaries (they both died in 1900). Nietzsche attacked the "slave morality" of Christianity and denounced the materialism and pessimism of his century. If Huysmans was the inventor of Decadence, Nietzsche was its great enemy. Thomas Mann had been the first writer to make the parallel between Wilde and Nietzsche; both men, Mann pointed out, were waging a "furious war on morality" and calling for the transvaluation of moral into esthetic values. Whereas Decadence actually reinforced traditional morality (Huysmans, unsurprisingly, ended up converting back to Catholicism), Wilde and Nietzsche posed a serious threat to establishment conventions. Wilde wanted society to give up its hypocrisy and admit the existence of homosexuality, for instance. Lord Henry sounds very Nietzschian indeed when he says, "I believe that if one man were to live out his life fully and completely, were to give form to every feeling, expression to every thought, reality to every dream—I believe that the world would gain such a fresh impulse of joy that we would forget all the maladies of medievalism, and return to the Hellenic ideal—to something finer, richer, than the Hellenic ideal." Lord Henry concludes: "The only way to get rid of a temptation is to yield to it."

We are only a step away from Nietzsche's praise of the healthiness of paganism and his condemnation of the sickness of Christianity. We hear Wilde's voice when Nietzsche writes: "Books for everybody are always malodorous books; the smell of petty people clings to them." Both writers sound like elitists not because they respect the actual aristocracy but because they reject leveling small-mindedness.

Of course there were differences. Wilde was a showman who put all his arrogance on display, whereas Nietzsche wrote in a riddling style and firmly believed in the difference between esoteric and exoteric wisdom ("Our supreme insights must—and should!—sound like follies, in certain cases like crimes," he wrote, "when they come impermissibly to the ears of those who are not predisposed and predestined for them"). Wilde was not cautious, and he was so foolish that he thought he could bluff Mrs. Grundy into acknowledging his talented work as much as his genial life. When he entered into a correspondence with the *St. James's Gazette* in defense of *The Picture of Dorian Gray,* he concluded his last letter with this remark: "As you assailed me first, I have a right to the last word. Let the last word be the present letter, and leave my book, I beg you, to the immortality it deserves."

Joe Orton

JOE ORTON'S LIFE SOMETIMES RECALLS Oscar Wilde's. Of course Wilde was always going on about beauty, whereas with Orton it's all "bum and hashish," but there are curious parallels nonetheless. When Wilde went with Lord Alfred Douglas to Algeria in 1893, he appeared to the timid André Gide (who was only just then discovering his homosexuality) as the "Lord of Life"— reckless, immoral, royally insouciant, brimming over with vitality. Similarly, Orton was riding high when he went to Tangier in 1967.

He was traveling with his unhappy lover, who, like "Bosie," was usually a nag and a layabout. But on this trip, for once, Halliwell was reasonably content.

As Orton records in his diary, "We sat talking how happy we both felt and of how it couldn't, surely, last. We'd have to pay for it. Or we'd be struck down from afar by disaster because we were, perhaps, too happy. To be young, good-looking, healthy, famous, comparatively rich and happy is surely going against nature."

Like Wilde, Orton was not the usual dim writer who only sparkles on the page or stage. Both men were proud of their looks, their physicality, and both were determined to choose life *and* art. Of course it would be absurd to push the parallels too far, since Wilde was worldly and upper-middle-class, whereas Orton was working-class and curiously naïve. In one diary entry Orton is reluctant to lay out cash for the new Beatles album until he's heard it first (despite the fact the group was his favorite and he'd just written a film-script for them and he'd just been paid 100,000 pounds for the film rights to *Loot*). Elsewhere he dutifully notes in his diary having seen his first butler (this from the man who was at that very moment writing *What the Butler Saw*).

Despite his inexperience, Orton radiates constant awareness of his personal magnetism. He also has a Wildean eye for English moral hypocrisy. Of course Wilde was concerned with philistinism and undoubtedly would have considered Joe Orton to be a philistine, whereas Orton is on the lookout for the pretensions of the despised middle class. In Tangier he wants to murder English tourists whom he overhears saying the best holiday they have had was in Plymouth. And he never ceases taking notes: "We went to Nino's. It was almost empty except for a party of Englishmen who were busy wondering whether it was oeuf or boeuf which meant 'beef.' 'Because if it's beef, I've been warned,' one of them said."

His notes on working-class people are far more amused and amiable. He is specially keen on genteelisms about sex and body functions. "A combination of elegance and crudity is always ridiculous," he remarks. And indeed so much of the humor of his plays is based on just this combination as well as a sublime sense of silliness and a gift for dialogue collage, both derived from the novels of Ronald Firbank.

In the diaries Orton seldom talks about his play-in-progress beyond mentioning that he worked all morning on *What the Butler Saw*. He seems sunnily untroubled by his prodigious talent, and simply tosses off, without comment, the fact that he's seen *The Desert Song* and the "plot gave me the idea for my next play."

What he does talk about are his constant sexual adventures in public toilets ("cottages") with ugly people, odd people, a dwarf, the passing handsome postal worker. He never seems particularly anguished by his homosexuality whereas his lover, Kenneth, is frequently quoted saying, "I'm disgusted by all this immorality" and "Homosexuals disgust me." To Orton, homosexuality breaks down into anonymous and satisfying if unemotional physical encounters and, in a quite different vein, as hilarious conversations with Big Camps. Orton dutifully records many of the funny lines: "England is America's poodle"; "No good deed ever goes unpunished"; "Some of the dirtiest eaters I've seen have graduated from stately homes"; and "We went to Malaga. Not a hotel room to be had. All these old norms, darling. All norming about. 'Come along, Millicent, we'll sit over here. Where we can catch the warmth.' "

The diaries, which cover the period from December 1966 until Orton's murder in August 1967 at the age of thirty-four, put us on the most intimate terms with a boisterous talent at its zenith. Here we have the thoughts of a man acutely observant of the hilarious tics of passers-by and strangely oblivious to the hysteria and hatred boiling up in his lover-murderer, Halliwell.

Kenneth Halliwell had first met Orton at the Royal Academy of Dramatic Arts where they were both studying acting. Halliwell was twenty-five; he had a flat, a car and a classical education. Orton, by contrast, was just seventeen and had never been away from Leicester for longer than two weeks. The moody, already balding and ambitious but untalented Halliwell teamed up with the poor but brilliant, uneducated Orton. Halliwell and Orton lived in a single room, named each other in their wills as their sole heirs, shunned society and devoted themselves to reading, studying, writing. They even wrote a novel together, *The Boy Hairdresser*.

But Halliwell couldn't keep up. After Orton became famous Halliwell turned to making frightening collages of body parts and dead babies. Halliwell registered every social slight and resented Orton's promiscuity as well as his good looks and obvious virility. By turns he would lament his lot ("Kenneth, quel moan," Orton notes tersely) and threatens to take his own life or attack Joe. As their friend Penelope Gilliatt remarked later, "Halliwell was the wife who doesn't notice that her husband is coming up in the world and changing. Halliwell didn't change and had no capacity for change and no vision of it at all."

In the end, Halliwell battered in Orton's head with a hammer and then killed himself by swallowing Nembutals. If Wilde was destroyed by the English horror of homosexuality, so was Orton in a way, for Halliwell had turned public contempt into self-loathing. One of the last recorded conversations between them was about this very subject. Halliwell said, "I'm basically guilty about being a homosexual, you see." To which Orton replied: "Reject all the values of society. And enjoy sex. When you're dead you'll regret not having fun with your genital organs." Certainly Orton can have no regret on that score in the afterlife.

And one can imagine him saying to Halliwell the same words that Wilde addressed to Alfred Douglas: "Your terrible lack of imagination, the one really fatal defect of your character, was entirely the result of the hate that lived in you."

Paul Bowles

I HAVE A THEORY THAT THE WAY TO BECOME FAMOUS is to be the one celebrity in a city that everyone wants to visit. Paul Bowles in Tangier, Peggy Guggenheim in Venice, Pessoa in Lisbon, Cavafy in Alexandria, Tennessee Williams in Key West.... In reading Millicent Dillon's biography of Paul Bowles I recalled my own single effort in the late 1980s when I went to interview him for *Vogue*. So many other journalists had made the unrewarding pilgrimage because they needed an excuse to write off their Tangier jaunt. In Dillon's descriptions I recognized the same dirty little apartment in the ugly modern building, the dusty plants everywhere, the eternal smell of kif, the noisy histrionics of Bowles's illiterate lover/friend Mohammed Mrabet who, when I asked him if he was going to "write" or rather dictate to Bowles a sequel to *A Life Full of Holes,* said, unsmilingly, "No, I don't like to write anymore. I make more money from my sheep." The comings and goings (that day it was Patricia Highsmith and the English novelist and screenwriter Gavin Lambert), the stoned jokes and silences, the rehashing of old hash anecdotes, Bowles's impeccable, dandi-fied appearance in the midst of the squalor—oh, it all came flooding back and I didn't envy Dillon her assignment one bit.

I had sought out Bowles because I felt certain he must have known Jean Genet, whose biography I was writing. Bowles didn't have a phone but he did receive every day about five-thirty. His apartment was just across the street from the U.S. consulate. Although the neighborhood was considered smart, sheep were grazing on an empty lot. When I found Bowles's apartment he was still out but I spoke with Mrabet, who told me that someday he planned to write a biography of both Paul and Jane Bowles, but only after Paul's death ("I have things to say that Paul wouldn't like"). At last Bowles showed up—smiling, unforthcoming, stoned.

One of Bowles's friends said to me recently, "Paul was as passive as some of his characters." An observation that gains credibility when one reads that Bowles refused to encourage or discourage a woman who was courting him after Jane's death. "I never said anything," Dillon quotes Bowles as saying. "Well, I never do. I don't know why you have to say something. You just have to go on living. People can guess for themselves whether it's yes or no." Elsewhere, when Dillon asks him if his feelings were hurt when one of his Moroccan lovers left him for a rich woman, Bowles says in his best Zen or extraterrestrial manner, "I don't know. I don't know what it feels like to have your feelings hurt." And in his most troubling short story, "Pages from Cold Point," the father who has just slept with his son says, "Destiny, when one perceives it clearly from very near, has no qualities at all."

Bowles accepted everything, including cruelty, including the idea of black magic, including the stoned, senseless monologues of the men who populated his life. He didn't want to choose one thing over another, not even one person over another. On an amateur tape made in the early 1960s Jane Bowles is talking to Paul and a friend. Soon Paul can be heard closing the door behind him. Jane says, "There's a disconnection. Even if he's on the same floor, he's in another room."

Paul Bowles first visited Morocco in 1931 at Gertrude Stein's suggestion. He was just twenty, an American in Paris and having a hard time deciding whether he was a poet, a composer or perhaps even a short story writer. He was also easily distracted and, according to his friend the soon-to-be-eminent composer Aaron Copland, somewhat lazy. Both young men were studying musical composition in Paris. As Copland pointed out to Bowles: "If you don't work now when you're twenty, nobody will love you when you are thirty."

Stein told Bowles to go to Tangier. She said, ruling out two French sea-side resorts, "You don't want to go to Villefranche. Everybody's there. And

St. Jean-de-Luz is empty and with an awful climate. The place you should go is Tangier." When Bowles accepted her advice and set off for the Moroccan port (with Aaron Copland), he had no idea that Tangier would prove to be much more than "a rest, a lark, a one-summer stand." Eventually it would turn out to be the city where he would spend most of his adult life. And Moroccan culture would provide him with the material and inspiration that his admirers associate with his name.

During that first summer in Tangier, Copland was distracted by the constant, menacing beat of distant drums, the dirt and flies, the lack of "civilization" and of other "civilized" people with the exception of a Danish painter, Kristians Tonny, and his American girlfriend. But Bowles took to the place, which he described in his 1972 memoir, *Without Stopping,* as "a dream city." He wrote: "Its topography was rich in proto-typical dream scenes: covered streets like corridors with doors opening into rooms on each side, hidden terraces high above the sea, streets consisting only of steps, dark impasses, small squares built on sloping terrain so that they looked like ballet sets designed in false perspective, with alleys leading off in several directions: as well as the classical dream equipment of tunnels, ramparts, ruins, dungeons and cliffs...."

The dreamlike dissolves of Tangier, its lively mix of cultures, its anomalous and wide-open status at that time as an international free port, its schizophrenic layout as a new European city above the ancient Moroccan city below, the ready availability of drugs and boys, its flirtatious Arab and Berber populations, so unlike the more dour Muslims of the Middle East, the country's position then as a French possession and the universal use of the French language—all these elements made Tangier at once exotic and accessible, bewildering and familiar, frightening and delightful. Over the years, Tangier's reputation as an affordable sin city would attract writers as diverse as Joe Orton, Tennessee Williams, William Burroughs and Jean Genet. All of them came for the boys and a few for the drugs, fewer still for the culture.

Bowles had a few affairs with women and married the talented writer Jane Bowles (herself a lesbian). His physical Puritanism was coherent with the elegant distance he maintained from other people. This very remoteness, paradoxically, made a traditional society strangely attractive to him, one in which few people prized privacy and conformism was more esteemed than individuality. Perhaps as an American, renowned for his aristocratic good looks, provided with a small income and a small degree of international celebrity, he experienced his solitude all the more markedly in contrast with the poor Moroccan herd. To be sure, as the years went by and he made Moroccan friends and learned to speak (and even translate from) Maghrebi, the local form of Arabic, Bowles came to see his Tangier acquaintances as highly nuanced individuals, but the initial impression had been one of faceless, interchangeable people. As he—the consummate loner— surprisingly wrote of Morocco: "Here for the first time I was made aware that a human being is not an entity and that his interpretation of exterior phenomena is meaningless unless it is shared by the other members of his cultural group." Bowles, who'd always prided himself on his independent spirit, suddenly saw the attraction of sinking into the collective culture.

After 1947 Tangier became Bowles's permanent home for the next half century until his death in 1999. From time to time he would travel to Europe or to Southeast Asia, where he owned an island, but seldom to the United States. Perhaps his very lack of visibility in America accounts for his having been forgotten for so long in the land of his birth. Only shortly before his death did Bertolucci's film of his first novel, *The Sheltering Sky,* and a concert in New York of his most substantial music, bring his name back to the attention of the American public.

He may have made Tangier his home but his attitude towards it wavered. In letters to his friend, the American writer-composer Ned Rorem, Bowles takes a lightly disparaging but resigned tone in referring to his adopted city. In 1973, when he is sixty-three, Bowles writes Rorem: "What I want is not tranquillity, as you put it, and not happiness—merely survival. That seems enough to hope for. (Too much, at times.) The attitude of a nonagenarian, of course, but no less valid for that. Life needn't be pleasurable or amusing; it need only continue playing its program. Everything goes well here in the vacuum of Tangier." To be sure he had a reason to take a bleak outlook; his wife, Jane, had just died in pain and mental collapse in a clinic in Malaga, Spain.

At other times he seems to glory in the sinister side of Tangier. He writes: "I relish the idea that in the night, all around me in my sleep, sorcery is burrowing its invisible tunnels in every direction, from thousands of senders to thousands of unsuspecting recipients. Spells are being cast, poison is running its course.... There is a drumming out there most nights.

It never awakens me; I hear the drums and incorporate them into my dream, like the nightly call of the muezzins. Even if in the dream I am in New York, the first *Allah akbar!* effaces the backdrop and carries whatever comes next to North Africa, and the dream goes on." Like a child longing to be scared, Bowles delights in the weird and unsettling aspects of Tangier, but whereas a child feels an excess of excitement and then seeks a reason to be frightened, one has the impression that Bowles truly is a dreamer—detached, almost numb, dimly registering outside signals but incorporating them into his dream narrative—"and the dream goes on." Bowles seems to take a ghoulish relish in how bad things can get. He is an esthete of the Baudelaire school with a pronounced "nostalgia for the mud."

In his 1955 novel, *The Spider's House,* one of his characters prizes above all his sense of detachment and his conviction that everything in the Moroccan city is insubstantial: "If he should ever for an instant cease doubting, accept wholly the truth of what his senses conveyed to him, he would be dislodged from the solid ground to which he clung...." The passage is difficult to decipher since it runs so counter to what most people think.

In 1961, when he was fifty-one, Bowles collected his magazine articles and essays and published them in *Their Heads Are Green and Their Hands Are Blue.* These are travel pieces, mostly, and they emphasize the exoticism of their subjects, in accord with the Edward Lear epigraph ("Their heads are green, and their hands are blue, / And they went to sea in a Sieve"). In his "Foreword" Bowles announces that he seeks diversity, not similarity, when he travels; moreover, he comes out strongly against the homogenizing force of Westernization. As he puts it: "My own belief is that the people of the alien cultures are being ravaged not so much by the by-products of our civilization, as by the irrational longing on the part of members of their own educated minorities to cease being themselves and become Westerners." Implicitly, I suppose, this is a criticism of the Marxist elite of most developing countries in the 1950s, a group that has been swept away by Muslim fundamentalism in our own era.

Concluding an essay about southern India, "Notes Mailed at Nagercoil," Bowles articulates sentiments he also applied to the Muslims of North Africa: "The younger generation in India is intent on forgetting a good many things, including some that it might do better to remember. There would seem to be no good reason for getting rid of the country's most ancient heritage, the religion of Hinduism, or of its most recent acquisition, the tradition of independence." Bowles tells us that young Indian intellectuals "have returned again and again to the attack against Gandhi as a betrayer of the Indian people." When Bowles believes or at least seriously entertains an old man's claim that his brother is suffering from a spell that has been cast on him, Bowles's young intellectual friends are appalled that the American should lend credence to such superstitious nonsense.

In the most important essay in this book, "The Rif, to Music," Bowles goes on to denounce "the partially educated young Moroccan for whom material progress has become such an important symbol that he would be willing to sacrifice the religion, culture, happiness, and even the lives of his compatriots in order to achieve even a modicum of it."

By the time he wrote *The Spider's House,* Bowles had an expatriate character in Morocco denounce Westernization: "When I first came here it was a pure country. There was music and dancing and magic every day in the streets. Now it's finished, everything. Even the religion. In a few more years the whole country will be like all the other Muslim countries, just a huge European slum, full of poverty and hatred." Of course, as Edward Said has pointed out in *Orientalism,* Westerners invariably fail to see the tensions and the developments in a so-called "traditional" culture even in its pre-colonial past. We insist on the static, non-historical nature of an "Oriental" country (all of North Africa and anywhere east of Suez). We will not allow it to have a changing economy and a developing culture or evolving social institutions. Moreover, Bowles misread the future; he did not foresee the rise of Muslim fundamentalism.

Perhaps the most dubious essay in this collection for us in our politically correct epoch is "Mustapha and His Friends," which at times sounds so racist that we are tempted to sympathize with the unnamed French woman whom Bowles ridicules in his foreword for having distributed it among "Moslem politicians to illustrate the typical reactionary attitude of Americans toward oppressed peoples." In fact the essay does seem highly reactionary, starting with the decision to create a generic illiterate city-dweller to be named Mustapha. A "spontaneity" and "innocence" are ascribed to him, as white Americans used to attribute such dubious virtues to their black compatriots.

This generic and composite Mustapha is shown to be forgivably hypo-critical about the rigors of Islam. We are put on earth to pray, not to work, he assures us, but he doesn't pray, either, since it is only worth praying if one does it properly, five times a day.... He "juggles" his conscience in order to slip between the moral strictures of his religion. He steals, for instance, by telling himself that "an object inadvertently left on a windowsill or outside a door for a moment no longer falls into the category of private property...." For Mustapha bargaining is a sport, even when he has no intention to buy (and no money). Cut off from the purity of his own culture and its esthetic canons, he is no longer sure of his taste. His moral judgments are also confused ("that is inevitable when Moslems have been subjected to the rule of a foreign nation whose laws, not being based on Koranic precepts, they neither understand nor respect"). Mustapha is devious, prevaricating, foolhardy, disrespectful to women, etc.

What is significant—and speaks of the superiority of the imagination to everyday moral reflexes—is that when Bowles writes about Muslims in *fiction* he creates individuals, not types, and these individuals do not always conform to his preconceptions. In *The Spider's House,* for instance, the young Arab Amar saves the life of a dragonfly that has flown too close to the water and drenched its wings. Amar gently puts the creature beside the pool and lets the sun dry out its wings. This, despite Bowles's claim elsewhere that Arabs are invariably cruel to animals. At the same time the Christian characters, Stenham and Polly, are capable of recycling the same tired, insulting speculations about the Arab character that we encountered in "Mustapha and His Friends." Stenham even tells Polly, "...in their minds one thing doesn't come from another thing. Nothing is a result of anything. Everything merely *is,* and no questions asked. Even the language they speak is constructed around that."

Paradoxically, Bowles is not only a purveyor of cultural stereotypes but also a careful scholar of Morocco's real culture. For whatever political reasons, conservative or progressive, he is willing to study the music of his adopted country—a tradition that the Moroccan elite of that epoch despised. "The Rif, to Music" attests to the patience and zeal and admiration that Bowles brought to recording traditional Moroccan music in many regions and styles. His recordings have preserved what he calls "the most important single element in Morocco's folk culture: music." The literature of Morocco may be negligible, Bowles asserts, but its music and dance are its chief glories—arts that the half-Westernized rulers of the country are embarrassed by. Again and again, as Bowles writes, his efforts to record

Moroccan musicians were blocked by uncooperative Moroccan bureau-crats. One young official in Fez told him, "I detest all folk music, and particularly ours here in Morocco. It sounds like the noises made by sav-ages. Why should I help you to export a thing which we are trying to destroy? You are looking for tribal music. There are no more tribes. We have dissolved them. So the word means nothing. And there never was any tribal music anyway—only noise." Fortunately, Bowles succeeded despite official hostility to his project; his recordings remain as a precious record of a legacy that has now largely disappeared.

In an essay about the Sahara, "Baptism of Solitude," Bowles tells us many interesting things about oasis towns (where the fertility of cultivated plants is all-important and birds are hated as seed-stealers), about the desert-dwelling tribe of the Touareg, whose name in Arabic means "lost souls" but who call themselves *imochagh*, the "free ones." But what Bowles prizes most about the desert is its absolute solitude. "Why go?" he asks. "The answer is that when a man has been there and undergone the baptism of solitude he can't help himself. Once he has been under the spell of the vast, luminous, silent country, no other place is quite strong enough for him, no other surroundings can provide the supremely satisfying sensation of exist-ing in the midst of something that is absolute. He will go back, whatever the cost in comfort or money, for the absolute has no price."

As *The Sheltering Sky* proved, this absolute solitude of the desert may exert a strong appeal, but that magnetism is not necessarily salutary. Kit and her husband, Port, head farther and farther into the desert, even though he is seriously ill and will soon enough die of typhoid (or is it meningitis?). As they are heading there Kit looks out the bus window at the desert and imagines a cube-shaped planet: "The light would be hard and unreal as it was here, the air would be of the same taut dryness, the contours of the landscape would lack the comforting terrestrial curves, just as they did all through this vast region. And the silence would be of the ultimate degree, leaving room only for the sound of the air as it moved past." When they finally arrive at a remote outpost, Kit observes that at last there is no "visi-ble sign of European influence, so that the scene had a purity which had been lacking in the other towns, an unexpected quality of being complete which dissipated the feeling of chaos." Here Port dies and Kit enters into her own slow abjection and self-destruction. "Purity" is the quality his characters cherish, but this is a purity that sometimes destroys them.

Bowles, one of the four or five best writers in English in the second half of the twentieth century, embraced the desert as a Christian saint embraces his martyrdom. His self-abnegation and his love of traditional culture made him one of the keenest observers of other civilizations we have ever had in America. Unlike his countrymen he did not brashly set out to improve the rest of the world. For Bowles, Americanization was the problem, not the solution.

Allen Ginsberg

OR ALLEN GINSBERG, GRANTING AN INTERVIEW was a creative act. He came up with new thoughts on the wing and made new combinations of feelings and concepts to suit the occasion. As anyone knows who has ever been in a political campaign—or on a book tour—most interviewers ask the same three questions and most interviewees have memorized the same three sound bites. Indeed, mastering those sound bites and selling points is even called being "media-trained."

But Ginsberg chewed over his thoughts and more often than not was listening to his own mind at work. We overhear him actually thinking, which is rare enough, and he wanted to preserve the integrity of his complete thought. He relished rather than dreaded long interviews and once reprimanded an interviewer for cutting his answers. He didn't mind eliminating whole responses, but within a given answer he didn't want any editing.

He decided that giving an interview was a way of teaching and he was grateful to journalists for disseminating his ideas. Even hostility could serve his purposes. One of his best interviews is a dramatic confrontation with a born-again Christian named John Lofton. Ginsberg is patient and mannerly but also quite firm about not answering tendentious questions. He is equally supple and true to himself in his courtroom testimony at the Chicago Seven trial in December 1969 during which he was constantly harassed by the prosecutor, Thomas Foran, whose objections were constantly sustained by Judge Julius Hoffman.

His mannerliness even in adversity can be ascribed to one of his religious beliefs. As he wrote in 1978, "An early impulse to treat scholars, newsmen, agents, reporters, interviewers and inquirers as sentient beings equal in Buddha-nature to fellow poets turned me on to answer questions as frankly as possible," though he also admitted he came to understand that such openness might "lead to a hell of media self-hood...."

Quite obviously Ginsberg patterned his responses to the expectations and experience of his interlocutors. He can be observed patiently starting at the beginning in order to explain the fundamentals of American literary life to a Czech interviewer, or citing the familiar names of Céline, Henri Barbusse, Rimbaud and Artaud to a French interviewer and giving as reassuring examples Ungaretti and Marinetti to an Italian woman, Fernanda Pivano.

Not that Ginsberg ever betrayed his ideas in order to flatter his listener's preconceptions. He routinely pointed out in interviews that *Beat* was a facile label invented by journalists. With Ms. Pivano, for instance, he was building on her own literary references in order to bridge into a demanding technical discussion of American prosody in the work of Ezra Pound, Marianne Moore and William Carlos Williams, among others.

I knew Ginsberg only slightly, but I can attest that his essential qualities come through in transcribed interviews: his great personal sweetness and charm; his wide-ranging intellectual curiosity; his teacher-like clarity and patience, always devoid of pedantry; his utter lack of pretension, which permitted him to make his point with the simple words and humble examples at hand; his almost technological fascination with spiritual techniques; and his frank eroticism, free from boasting and the exploitation of others.

I had met him socially over the years in the 1970s and 1980s, but always in large crowds. I was initially surprised to see him in a coat and tie on these occasions, usually sporting the gold-and-purple rosette of the American Academy of Arts and Letters in his lapel—hardly the image of the Wild Man of American Poetry. In the 1970s I had a casual sexual friendship with a handsome Native American from Colorado, a wrestler and writer, who'd run away from home at age sixteen and been taken in by Allen

Ginsberg. Although the guy was badly crippled by an unusually fertile and impervious form of paranoia, Ginsberg was always kind to him and always gave him a place to crash. Other drifters I met over the years had made pit stops at the Ginsberg Home for Wayward Boys in the East Village.

When I was researching my biography of Jean Genet I phoned Ginsberg from Paris sometime in 1991. Ginsberg and Genet had spent time together at the Chicago Democratic Convention in 1968, and I wanted to know what had transpired between them. After all, Genet had been an essential part of Ginsberg's prose pantheon, along with Dostoyevsky, Céline, Henry Miller, Artaud, Huxley and Kerouac.

When I phoned, Ginsberg had only recently had a bout of congestive heart failure and had been instructed by his doctor to rest and refuse all demands on his time—but his life-loving and knowledge-fostering generosity got the better of him. He talked to me for an hour. He quoted verses by heart from Genet's "The Man Sentenced to Death" as well as prose passages from the opening pages of *Our Lady of the Flowers*. After giving me all the political details of the tumultuous events in Chicago, Ginsberg mentioned that he and Genet had gone to bed. As I wrote in my biography, "One night Genet invited Ginsberg to his room and got in bed with him. Ginsberg was offering warmth and affection that might possibly lead to sex, but Genet matter-of-factly felt for his crotch and when he found out that Ginsberg didn't even have an erection, he briskly got out of bed and went about his business." The contrast between Genet's unsentimental, Gallic realism and Ginsberg's Whitmanian adhesiveness could not be more telling.

Ginsberg's ceremonial sense of sex turns up several times in interviews. For instance, as Ginsberg points out to Allen Young, he had slept with Neal Cassady (the model for Kerouac's "Dean Moriarty"), who'd slept with Gavin Arthur (President Chester Arthur's grandson), who'd slept with Edward Carpenter (the English Victorian champion of homosexual love), who'd slept with Walt Whitman, from whom he "received the Whispered Transmission, capital W, capital T, of that love."

Two or three years after the phone interview about Genet, Ginsberg called me in Paris and asked if he could drop in on me right away. I said sure, though I was surprised: why would he want to see me?

He showed up with an attractive young man. Soon I put it together— the young man was a fan of mine and had asked Ginsberg to arrange to meet me. Apparently this guy, a budding American writer living in Paris, had attended Allen's reading at Shakespeare and Company and slipped Allen a nude photo of himself with his phone number scrawled on the back. Allen called him, naturally, and they'd spent the week together.

When I said earlier that Allen didn't exploit these guys, I might have added that at this time in his life he was virtually impotent, due to diabetes, and that his sexual attention was almost a form of courtesy extended to all these runaways, layabouts and unpublished poets, as if he were reassuring them that they did, after all, have something to offer him in exchange for the advice, help, introductions, pocket money and shelter he gave them.

A handsome straight poet once told me that the only man he'd ever slept with was Allen Ginsberg. "Why him?" I asked. The poet looked astonished, as if the answer was self-evident: "Because he was fuckin' Allen Ginsberg, man."

Now, with me, Allen talked in a precise, melodious, well-modulated voice about his works, his travels, his health, Genet, William Burroughs (whom I knew slightly).... The young man fell asleep, perhaps because our attention wasn't focused on him. The tea turned cold in our cups and night fell, but I didn't turn on the lamps. Allen recited part of the Diamond Sutra from memory. It was the sort of unfettered talk that busy grown-ups seldom have a chance to enjoy. Later I heard someone complain of Ginsberg's "egotism." True, he spoke only of his own interests and activities but he shared those with such generosity and spontaneity that only a cold heart could label such artesian kindness "egotism."

When the young man was aroused to leave, he asked me if he could come later in the week to lunch, after Allen's departure. On the appointed day he rang the bell and was standing there in the hallway completely nude (he'd hidden his clothes in the corner). I felt my life was being touched just this once by the sort of lyrical good luck that Ginsberg must have enjoyed every day.

The interviews, in *Spontaneous Mind*, which cover a forty-year period from the 1950s to the 1990s, show the evolution of Ginsberg's mind from a be-bop talking excitement to a calm connoisseurship of world culture of all sorts from all periods. In an early interview Ginsberg refers to "jazz prayer" and tells us that kids today "have a sexual awareness, openness and tolerance and compassionate tenderness that is absolutely ravishing." He was soon to abandon this sort of naïve counterculture utopianism in favor of a

sober scepticism about drugs, the New Left and the avant-garde. In 1978 he
admitted:

> Certain errors of judgment emerge by hindsight: advocacy of LSD
> legislation would now be accompanied by prescription for medita-
> tion practice to qualify its use. I would extend my selfhood less
> widely in sympathy with "movement" contemporaries whose sub-
> conscious belief in confrontation, conflict or violence encouraged
> public confusion and enabled police agents to infiltrate and pro-
> voke further violence and greater confusion. We were finding
> "new reasons for spitefulness," Kerouac explained.

But Ginsberg kept certain enthusiasms all his life—for Jack Kerouac as
an artist, a poet, even a thinker, for instance. Again and again Ginsberg
insists on Kerouac's position as the prime mover and chief inspiration to
the entire Beat movement. Nor does he permit other people to condescend
to Kerouac's late writing or political conservatism. He always finds a justification for remarks that seem indefensible, so great was Ginsberg's
unswerving loyalty to his friends. (He proposed William Burroughs for the
Nobel Prize, incidentally.)

Throughout these interviews Ginsberg returns to his high praise of
William Blake and Walt Whitman. Ginsberg obviously loves Blake the
visionary and Whitman the democratic sensualist, and indeed Ginsberg's
own literary personality can be construed as a union of these two forces.
Even the idea of being a legendary poet, of having "a large persona," is
something he admitted he got from Whitman.

Ginsberg's intense relationship to Blake can be traced to a seemingly
mystical experience he had during the summer of 1948. The twenty-two-
year-old Ginsberg was working a desultory job as a filing clerk and living
in a stifling sublet in Harlem. He'd recently been rejected by Neal Cassady
as a lover, who had just gotten married. Ginsberg had few opportunities to
see Jack Kerouac, who was obsessed with his own writing and who'd just
completed a 1,000-page manuscript. Ginsberg was lonely and frustrated,
artistically and sexually. He had yet to find his own distinctive style as a poet.
His mother, Naomi Ginsberg, had gone mad and been confined to Pilgrim
State Hospital in New Jersey. She wrote Allen constantly, begging him to
help her get out of the asylum, but in fact it was Allen who eventually

signed papers permitting the hospital to perform a prefrontal lobotomy on her.

In the midst of so much unhappiness, as Ginsberg recounts in his *Paris Review* interview, he was reading Blake and masturbating one evening. After his orgasm he heard a deep voice, which he described as "a very deep earthen grave voice in the room, which I immediately assumed, I didn't think twice, was Blake's voice." This auditory hallucination (if that's what it was) changed Ginsberg entirely.

> Anyway, my first thought was this was what I was born for, and second thought, never forget—never forget, never renege, never deny. Never deny the voice—no, never forget it, don't get lost mentally wandering in other spirit worlds or American or job worlds or advertising worlds or war worlds or earth worlds. But the spirit of the universe was what I was born to realize....

If a commitment to poetic mysticism remains central to Ginsberg's thought, other recurring themes in the interviews (and in his life) are ecology (Ginsberg warned of global warming two decades before a general alarm was sounded), mind-expansion through drugs and later yoga, a commitment to pacifism and interpersonal kindness, homosexuality and the key role of spontaneity in making art. Each of these themes, however, received a special twist in Ginsberg's hands.

Take homosexuality. Ginsberg admitted that he was more attracted to young heterosexual men than to homosexuals, and homosexuals themselves he divided into those he liked ("heartfelt, populist, humanist, quasi heterosexual, Whitmanic, bohemian, free-love") and the sort he avoided ("the privileged, exaggeratedly effeminate, gossipy, moneyed, money-style-clothing-conscious, near hysterical"). Basically, what people in the '60s called Downtown Guys and pissy East Side Queens.

True to his cult of Whitmanic democracy and frankness, Ginsberg solicited honesty and openness among homosexuals; he deplored the fearful, closed atmosphere of the usual uptight gay bar. Characteristically, when he met the bisexual Peter Orlovsky in 1954, the man with whom he would spend most of his life, they made a pledge of mutual "ownership" to each other, as if only such extreme terms of possession, such a violent commitment, might allay their deep insecurities.

We made a vow to each other that he could own me, my mind and everything I knew, and my body, and I could own him and all he knew and all his body; and that we would give each other ourselves, so that we possessed each other as property, to do everything we wanted to, sexually or intellectually, and in a sense explore each other until we reached the mystical "X" together, emerging two merged souls.

Probably no couple ever swore such desperate, literal marriage vows.

Ginsberg bore the traces of the general homosexual oppression of his epoch, but he did more than anyone else of his generation to overcome his gay self-hatred and to take a pro-gay militant stand. He was an apostle of tenderness among men. He never allowed his political and spiritual energies, however, to confine themselves to a gay ghetto. Like other big spirits of his time—Pasolini, Juan Goytisolo, Genet—Ginsberg was interested in the fate of the oppressed everywhere.

In 1965, four years before the beginning of gay liberation, Ginsberg visited Cuba and almost instantly became aware that Castro was consigning homosexuals to work camps, denouncing and outlawing homosexuality and censoring pro-gay statements in the press. Ginsberg responded fearlessly by criticizing the policy—and was hustled out of Havana on a plane bound to Prague. There he was crowned King of the May by Czech students, and again forced by worried authorities to leave the country. By staying true to his personal values of sexual and artistic freedom, Ginsberg confronted Communist authoritarianism a full decade before most other intellectuals in the west.

Ginsberg did not believe in revision. On the contrary, he'd learned from his guru the slogan "First thought, best thought." No wonder he was attracted to the Chinese and Japanese arts of calligraphy, ink-and-brush painting and the composition of haiku, all of which require years of preparation but only seconds to execute. He proclaimed the "bardic function" to be a form of meditation. He called for the "frank revelation of the heart." Writing, for him, was not a slow, agonizing process but rather a "natural expressive function" as automatic as breathing. He refused to censor his thoughts in order to isolate those suitable for poetry; no, he declared the whole spectrum of feeling to be the proper subject matter of art. He said that knowing how to walk across the street was the same thing as learning how to write. And he believed that if one wrote directly from personal experience one did not need to fear a loss of poetic power; as he put it, "any point on an autobiographical curve is interesting."

More than many American writers, Ginsberg had a sense of history— and the grace to see his cohorts as instant historical personages. His attitude reminds me of someone entirely different in a different country. Boris Kochno, Diaghilev's last secretary, once told me at the end of his life that he could still vividly recall a moment in the 1920s when Picasso had just left a café on the Rond-Point des Champs-Elysées where he'd spent a moment with Stravinsky, Diaghilev and Kochno. Diaghilev had suddenly said to the others, "Look hard at Picasso—it's as if you were seeing da Vinci on the streets of Florence."

Ginsberg had the same precocious awareness of the significance of his fellow Beats and of himself. In one interview he said that for Columbia to have expelled Kerouac was as absurd as if Socrates had banned Alcibiades from the Symposium. Always the grandiose comparison. By the same token Ginsberg saw himself as a direct heir to Whitman and knew how important it was to pay a pilgrimage visit to Céline in France and Pound in Venice. Good career move? No, the forging of a lasting link to the artistic past.

Ginsberg possessed in abundance the gift of appreciation. He was a powerful admirer and in his interviews he summons up the names of those past artists he honored and those contemporaries he championed. The reader will come across the names of Blake and Whitman but also of Pound, William Carlos Williams, Basil Bunting (who taught Pound—and Ginsberg—that poetry is the same thing as condensation), John Wieners (the great gay bard of the *Hotel Wentley* poems), Kenneth Rexroth (the elder statesman of San Francisco poetry who embraced and condemned the Beats in fits and starts), Gregory Corso, Gary Snyder, Peter Orlovsky, Lawrence Ferlinghetti, Herbert Huncke (the junky Ur-figure of the Beat movement), Kerouac, William S. Burroughs and many others. The reader will also find appreciations of Lenny Bruce, Timothy Leary, Carl Solomon and Chögyam Trungpa. Thoughts about music and photography, war protest and rock music, drugs and meditation technique—it's all here, in a profusion as generous as the spirit of Ginsberg himself.

Djuna Barnes

FOR AMERICAN WRITERS GROWING UP in the 1950s and '60s (as I did), there were few examples of the other tradition in our literature, that is, of American fiction other than the action-and-dialogue adventure realism epitomized by Hemingway. Djuna Barnes, the author of *Nightwood*—a slim novel about American expatriates in Paris, about lesbians and a male transvestite and a dubious, dolorous Austrian aristocrat—was perhaps the most prominent signpost pointing in another, more mysterious direction.

Barnes had concocted her novel out of Elizabethan poetry and Gothic props, out of a rush of imagery inspired by Synge's play *Riders to the Sea*, a vivid sense of melodrama linked to Emily Brontë and an unlikely blend of satire with tragedy. She had few antecedents in America—Hawthorne's and Melville's haunted fiction, suggestive of doom and hinting at allegory; Henry James's "supersubtle fry" maneuvering dangerously in Italian or English salons—and in the twentieth century she could look towards only Gertrude Stein, who'd broken with realism in a far more radical way, and the poets Pound and Eliot, who like Barnes had left America for Europe, not as skirt-chasers fleeing Prohibition but as genuine students of world culture.

In our day American fiction has become monosyllabic, regional and catatonic (the final dumbed-down version of the bluff realistic tradition and a style in synch with contemporary American isolationism and self-absorption), but Djuna Barnes remains as a reminder of the road not yet taken—international, devious, perverse, verbally abundant, psychologically subtle.

For two centuries Americans have been undecided whether their destiny is to inherit the European (or African or Asian) past or to invent a uniquely American future. Pound decided to take that multicultural past and "Make it New" according to the abrupt, gnomic strategies of streamlined American modernism. Djuna Barnes, like Melville, had no sense of historic or cultural restrictions and just as in *Moby-Dick* Shakespearian language is joined to a Yankee plot and Christian symbols are invoked but not embraced, in the same way in *Nightwood* an artificial, elevated language is put in the mouths of contemporary American women who are pursuing a tragic destiny. In her own way Barnes is as syncretic as Pound.

Perhaps Barnes's work gave permission to Jane Bowles to write *Two Serious Ladies,* which may be less high-flown but which is every bit as original and spooky as *Nightwood;* Barnes's writing also cleared a space for Edward Dahlberg's beautiful, touching and utterly improbable memoir, *Because I Was Flesh,* a recasting of his family story (his mother was a barber in St. Louis) in the terms of Greek mythology. Today the poetic and visionary novelist Carole Maso reads as though she'd been enabled by Barnes's example. In fact, one could make a case that American lesbians have written some of the most exalted books of the twentieth century— Nathalie Barney (who wrote in French), Gertrude Stein, Willa Cather, Djuna Barnes, Jane Bowles and Carole Maso.

Barnes, of course, was not only a superlative (and unprecedented) writer, but also a legend. According to the myth, she was supported for years by Peggy Guggenheim (to whom *Nightwood* is dedicated), edited by T. S. Eliot, befriended by James Joyce (who told her to write about the ordinary in fiction and the extraordinary in journalism). She lived on the Left Bank in Paris in the '20s and '30s before returning to Greenwich Village, where she settled in at Patchin Place (one of her neighbors was E. E. Cummings). She lived on and on but after *Nightwood* wrote just one important work, *The Antiphon,* a verse play that Dag Hammerskjöld translated and managed to have staged in 1961 at Stockholm's Royal Dramatic Theater. She became an old curmudgeon whom Daryl Pinckney worked for and describes in *High Cotton.* She created endless problems for Peter

Klappert, who wrote a magnificent poetic monologue for her character, Dr. O'Connor, in his book-length poem, *The Idiot Princess of the Last Dynasty*. Howard Moss, the poetry editor of the *New Yorker*, once told me that he had published two of her poems and then was summoned to her apartment. She complained about her poverty, resisted all his advice and, when he told her how much he admired her, she grumbled that all her problems were due to that damn Tom Eliot who'd said she had no talent (in fact T. S. Eliot had written in a blurb for *The Antiphon*: "It might be said of Miss Barnes, who is incontestably one of the most original writers of our time, that never has so much genius been combined with so little talent").

She was born into a weird bohemian ménage. Her father was a ne'er-do-well who kept changing his name and whose talents included house-building, opera-composing, wood-carving, painting and inventing (he published a pamphlet about a bicycle-driven airship). "Djuna" was another of his inventions, a corruption of a name in Eugène Sue's *The Wandering Jew;* when Shirley Walton, a friend of mine, opened a feminist bookshop near Patchin Place named Djuna Books, Barnes phoned her up hopping mad, denounced Shirley, feminism and the "theft" of her name. She even said that her father had given her such an original name because he didn't want her to be saddled with a name shared and thereby sullied by other people. Three of his sons he named Thurn, Saxon, and Shangar.

Her father's fecklessness, his espousal of free love, the many children he spawned and his energetic promiscuity (he was a sort of erotic circuit-rider and Djuna later claimed he kept a sponge tied to his saddle to mop his genitals as he rode about the country between assignations)—all these traits made the girl come to despise procreation. She later wrote a friend that "father and his bastard children and mistresses had thrown me off marriage and babies."

The evidence is shadowy but her father, apparently, either seduced Djuna when she was an adolescent or arranged for one of his cronies to do the job. In any event to her it seemed like rape and an experience so ghastly that she was still brooding about it half a century later when she wrote *The Antiphon* (published in 1958). She told the poet George Barker that "she believed her Lesbianism to have been the consequences of her father raping her when she was a very young girl" (although the theory about lesbianism sounds uncharacteristic and Barker may just have been working up an after-dinner story).

The decisive influence in Djuna's childhood was her maternal grandmother, Zadel Barnes, a woman who began to publish when she was thirteen and who supported with her pen her shiftless son and his brood (his household at one point counted thirteen members).

Zadel was a spiritualist who conducted séances in which she impersonated the dead. She was also a poet of the John Greenleaf Whittier school (typically, she writes: "Speed hither, winds, and blend in noble mirth / The many-chorded harmonies of earth..."). In 1880 *McCall's* magazine sent her as a correspondent to London, where she became friendly with Esperanza Wilde (Oscar's mother) and Karl Marx's daughter Eleanor (Zadel introduced them to each other—there's a meeting that would make a good subject for our poet Richard Howard!).

In *The Antiphon* Djuna describes the Zadel figure as an "abolitionist, free-thinker, raconteur, abstainer, known for her turbans; seizures; wit." By the time the little Djuna knew her, Zadel had come down in the world. She was ill with cancer, exhausted from a life of overwork, reduced to writing begging letters to the rich and famous people she'd known in her palmier days.

Djuna may also have been seduced by her grandmother. Djuna slept beside Zadel during her first fifteen years and named her grandmother's breasts "Redlero" and "Kedler." Zadel drew funny pictures for Djuna in letters in which one nude woman is shown lying on top of another. Zadel called breasts "Pink Tops" or "P.T.s." Not much of a dossier for an incest inquest, especially considering how passionately Djuna loved her grandmother; in 1935 she wrote a friend, "I always thought I was my grandmother, and now I am almost right." Nor do participants in incest speak so openly and cheerfully of their partners.

Certainly Djuna grew up in a strange household in which her mother (who'd been raised in a family of English gentry) had to work like a servant and failed to disguise her resentment of her husband's mistress (later his second wife). In this household Zadel read out loud from all the standard authors while her beloved son was scoring an opera, writing a verse drama or seducing a neighbor—and the children ran wild. Barnes received only the most rudimentary education and after her mother separated from her father and moved to the Bronx (in 1912 when Barnes was twenty), the gifted young woman became the main support of her mother and brothers by working as a journalist for the *Brooklyn Eagle*.

By 1915 Djuna had left her mother's house and moved to Greenwich Village (first to 42 Washington Square South, then to 220 West 14th Street, finally to 86 Greenwich Avenue). She had a number of adventures with men, one common-law marriage and a two-year live-in love affair with Courtenay Lemon, alcoholic, drama critic and reader of manuscripts for the Theatre Guild. In 1917 she wondered out loud in print why "there existed no man, young or old, who could draw the slightest, faintest word of interest from me apart from my drawing or some abstract thing connected with themselves." She attended art school, met the most visible Village bohemians, made her living by interviewing theater celebrities and even the evangelist Billy Sunday. She managed to publish *A Book of Repulsive Women,* which she later renounced. And she bore the crushing burden of supporting her mother and siblings.

In 1921 she was sent as a correspondent to Paris and soon afterwards met the love of her life, Thelma Wood, another American. The affair in its strongest form lasted some seven years, but afterwards Barnes was never able to escape from the obsessive thought (which she expressed in a letter): "I have had my great love, there will never be another." Barnes frequently told the over-inquisitive: "I was never a lesbian—I only loved Thelma Wood." Thelma was as heavy a drinker as Barnes; when she became really drunk Thelma would comb the Paris cafés looking for partners of either sex. Barnes demanded that Thelma report on all her infidelities, but Wood often couldn't comply, so total were her blackouts. Thelma was nearly six feet tall, wore boots, and the two women must have made quite an impression as they strode the boulevards in black capes and men's hats; Djuna said she loved Thelma because she resembled Zadel, Djuna's grandmother. Djuna persuaded Thelma to take up silverpoint, a medium in which she drew plants and animals with a modicum of success.

Eventually Thelma left Djuna for a rich woman, Henriette Metcalf, with whom she stayed for about sixteen years. The failure of Barnes's affair with Thelma was the direct inspiration of *Nightwood,* which she wrote largely at Hayford Hall, an English house Peggy Guggenheim rented in the summers of 1932 and 1933. There Barnes was encouraged by Peggy, a vague dilettante who seldom finished a sentence but who had a genuine passion for the arts, and her lover John Ferrar Holmes, a brilliant alcoholic who knew everything and did nothing. More importantly, the household included the novelist Emily Coleman, an American novelist (her book *The*

Shutter of Snow was about her stay in an insane asylum) who turned herself inside out over several years helping Djuna organize, complete and finally place her masterpiece.

The Dalkey Archive Press published a new, definitive edition of *Nightwood,* which gives the related drafts and restores many of the cuts censored from the original manuscript because they were considered too risqué at the time, either by Emily Coleman or by the editor she found, T. S. Eliot at Faber & Faber. Everything about this strange novel was problematical, starting with the title. Earlier titles included *Bow Down* (now the title of section one), *Anatomy of the Night* and so on. Although one biographer credits Eliot with coming up with *Nightwood,* in fact it was Barnes herself, who wrote Coleman on June 23, 1935: " 'Nightwood,' like that, one word, it makes it sound like night-shade, poison and night and forest, and tough, in the meaty sense, and simple yet singular...." Later Barnes discovered that the name could be a reference to Thelma—"Nigh T. Wood—low, thought of it the other day. Very odd."

According to the introduction to the Dalkey version by Cheryl J. Plumb, the novel may have been first conceived as early as 1927, the year of the first breakup with Thelma. The book was rejected by many publishers and went through three full drafts, but at no point did Barnes want to resort to what she called the "safety" of realism. What she did accept were Coleman's suggestions to simplify and unify the action. For instance, Matthew O'Connor's long disquisition about love, "Watchman, What of the Night?," the bravura center of the book, at one point was addressed not to Nora (the Barnes stand-in) who is hopelessly in love with Robin (the Thelma character) but to another woman altogether, Catherine. Coleman was responsible for the condensation of the text. It was she who convinced Eliot to give it a careful reading as well, whom she originally approached through the poet Edwin Muir.

On April 27, 1936, Eliot wrote Coleman that he thought *Nightwood* could be published if changes could be made to avoid the suppression of publication by the censor. Previous commentators have assumed that Eliot made extensive editorial changes in the manuscript, but Plumb has shown that most of the changes were suggested by Coleman: "All in all, the editorial hand was light; certainly because he anticipated potential difficulty with censors, Eliot blurred sexual, particularly homosexual, references and a few points that put religion in an unsavory light.

However, meaning was not changed substantially, though the character of the work was adjusted, the language softened." For instance, in the original text Dr. O'Connor asks, "Or is confessing bottom up (though keeping the thread in the tatting), to a priest who has the face of a butcher, and the finger of our own right hand where it best pleases?" Eliot suppressed this passage because of its sexual and anticlerical ring, but in the Dalkey edition it is restored—as are countless other details. Or when O'Connor says that he haunts the pissoirs "in search of my man," just as "I've seen the same thing work in a girl looking for her woman," Eliot suppressed the two homosexual references.

Despite these changes, *Nightwood* remained, even in its original version, an overwhelming, anarchic cry of passion (Nora's love for Robin) and an ingenious threnody about the disreputable nature of desire (take the scene where O'Connor tries to masturbate at St. Merri's church but remains impotent). The passage is worth quoting in full because it demonstrates better than any paraphrase the linguistic drama which animates every page of this edgy *cri de coeur*: "I was crying and striking my left hand against the prie-Dieu, and all the while Tiny O'Toole was lying in a swoon. I said, 'I have tried to seek, and I only find.' I said, 'It is I, my Lord, who know there's beauty in any permanent mistake like me. Haven't I said it so? But,' I says, 'I'm not able to stay permanent unless you help me, oh Book of Concealment! C'est le plaisir qui me boulverse! The roaring lion goes forth, seeking his own fury! So tell me, what is permanent of me, me or him?' And there I was in the empty, almost empty church, all the people's troubles flickering in little lights all over the place. And I said, 'This would be a fine world, Lord, if you could get everybody out of it.' And there I was holding Tiny, bending over and crying, asking the question until I forgot, and went on crying, and I put Tiny away then, like a ruined bird, and went out of the place and walked looking at the stars that were twinkling and I said, 'Have I been simple like an animal, God, or have I been thinking?'"

Nightwood is in fact haunted by animals, which provide most of the defining metaphors or similes for the human characters. Jenny Petherbridge, for instance, races like a squirrel in her cage, whereas when Robin Vote is first introduced it's at a circus and a lioness crouches in its cage before her and appears to weep. In the last scene, Robin even couples with a dog. But this fierce animality is matched by a loneliness, a yearning, that seems tragically human. One could say that the characters in *Nightwood* are like those Egyptian beings which combine human and animal characteristics to produce deities.

Marjorie Garber

ISEXUALITY MAKES EVERYONE UNEASY. In the 1980s bisexual men were demonized as the agents who might sneak AIDS into the marriage bed. Gay people themselves usually dismiss bisexuals as closeted queers. The category of people bisexuality defines sounds omnivorous and interstitial and above all mysterious. A magazine for bisexuals called *Anything That Moves* only reinforces the notion of the bisexual as an ever-ready skirt-and-pants chaser. Conversely, the idea of a monogamous bisexual seldom occurs to the non-initiated.

If I mention "interstitial" I do so because I remember once hearing a theory that many cultures forbid (or sanctify) animals or forms of behavior that appear to fall between two stools; for example a creature such as a lobster that lives in the sea but walks on legs is interstitial (and forbidden as food under kosher law). Incest is interstitial because it confounds the realm of the family and that of amorous choice; accordingly the Egyptians forbade incest to everyone but their rulers and gods. Bisexuality, by potentially eroticizing every aspect of everyday life, unnerves people: everyone seems to be fair game to the bisexual. Anything that moves. The world is no longer divided up into those who can be lovers and those who can only be friends (as women are just friends for gay men or other men are for straight men, for instance). No, the bisexual is the universal Don Juan or Donna Juanna, always on the prowl, plotting to seduce everyone.

Whereas technically most people could be labelled heterosexual, few heterosexuals, I imagine, actually think their sexual orientation says anything important about them, no more than a "Caucasian" in America dwells on his or her whiteness; for members of the majority to glory in their status seems just a bit fatuous. As Jonathan Katz pointed out in his study, *The Invention of Heterosexuality*, the very word *heterosexual* originally referred to an excessive interest in the opposite sex and assumed its present meaning only fairly recently—almost as an afterthought, in counterdistinction to homosexual (itself a term coined only in the nineteenth century). If homosexuals now prefer the word *gay* they do so because it doesn't sound medical nor place an undue emphasis on sex. Bisexuals are not well-organized enough, perhaps, to invent a new label for themselves, usually the first step in establishing a fresh force in identity politics.

The main point, however, of Marjorie Garber's *Vice Versa: Bisexuality and the Eroticism of Everyday Life* is that bisexuality is not just one more group to crowd onto a platform with other minorities but rather a destabilizing concept that calls into doubt many of our neat divisions. Bisexuality is the third term, the "excluded muddle," which undermines the certainty of gender identification and practice. Marjorie Garber, a professor at Harvard and the author of an earlier book on cross-dressing called *Vested Interests*, recounts that on television talk shows audiences exhibit more hostility towards bisexuals than towards people who label themselves clearly either as homosexuals or heterosexuals. Bisexuals are perceived as people who want to have it both ways, who are irresolute, immature, even treacherous.

I suppose many well-meaning progressive people are now willing to accept homosexuality as falling within the norms of human sexuality or at least as a harmless aberration, especially since AIDS, by associating male homosexuality with tragedy, has abolished the stigma of carefree hedonism that used to characterize big-city high-visibility gays and make them targets of envy.

The near-total acceptance among intellectuals of Freud's theory of universal bisexuality has certainly made homosexuality seem to fall well within the spectrum of normal behavior; Jean Genet once remarked rather astutely that Freud was the best friend homosexuals ever had, though in Genet's reading, bisexuality, according to Freud, meant merely that everyone could end up either as homosexual or heterosexual, not both simultaneously. Recent scientific speculation that homosexuality may be genetically coded also makes same-sex love appear to be less a perverse caprice or a symptom of decadence and more an inevitable, involuntary destiny. In the United States, especially, where so many political factions are linked to ethnic identity, homosexuals have been clever to present themselves as something very much like a racial or cultural entity. Of course the disadvantage is that a ghetto can also be easily targeted for a pogrom.

Into this tidy world of biologically determined polarities (homosexual/heterosexual) and an identity politics that defines these two categories as mutually exclusive, Garber's new look at bisexuality introduces a dissonant note. As she writes, "To add 'bisexuality' as a third category here is not in fact to refine the terms of analysis but instead to expose the radical limitations of rights-based arguments when linked to a concept of fixed identity."

Garber is not interested in working up effective answers to the Christian Right. For example she is willing to risk offending "community standards" by arguing that the teacher–student relationship is and should be erotic (if not always sexual), and that this erotic pull is often between students and teachers of the same sex, even when neither is homosexual outside the classroom. As she puts it emphatically, "Transference on a teacher is bisexual, which is to say that it does not necessarily correlate with the student's ordinary sexuality or sexual orientation. That many great teachers have been bisexual—have loved, and had love affairs with, both men and women—is a slightly, but only a slightly, different story." In the opposite direction, Garber is willing to anger gays by claiming that two of their icons, Oscar Wilde and Virginia Woolf, and many other sacred figures as well, were bisexual rather than homosexual.

Garber's position fits into several current debates. There is the already mentioned dispute between the biological determinists and those who argue that sexual identity is shaped by childhood experience. Then there is the overlapping but not congruent debate between the essentialists (those who believe homosexuality is something as historically invariable and as crucial as a biologically determined trait) and the social constructionists (those who argue that sexual identity is redefined in each culture and each epoch and is treated only by our culture and by our culture alone as a key difference among individuals). Gore Vidal famously remarked that there are homosexual acts but not homosexual people. Michel Foucault added that at least there were no homosexuals before the pseudo-scientific passion for taxonomy in the nineteenth century created the label; as Foucault puts it, "The sodomite had been a temporary aberration; the homosexual was now a species."

Despite Foucault's enormous prestige, his point of view has always been more intriguing than convincing to Americans, partly because Americans, unlike the French, believe in communitarianism rather than individualism. Perhaps our history as a haven for persecuted religious sects makes us want to defend the rights of groups rather than of that universal and rather abstract entity, the individual citizen. Moreover, Americans want their political philosophy to be crystal clear. As Mona Ozouf writes in *Les mots des femmes: essai sur la singularité française,* American feminists, unlike their (not very numerous) French counterparts, believe in unadorned and unwavering certainties rather than in the shifting playfulness of seduction and ambiguity. No wonder bisexuality makes us nervous.

Marjorie Garber, however, has found a clever way to argue Foucault's case to her compatriots by appearing initially to defend the rights of yet another minority and only later making it clear that in fact she is using bisexuality as a way of undoing all fixed sexual identities. As she puts it, "the proper and extensive realm of bisexuality" is the defiance of "easy, quick, or simplistic categorization."

In order to defy categorization she looks at everything from Calvin Klein's boxer shorts with a fly for women to Freud's and Kinsey's theories, the David Leavitt–Stephen Spender controversy and even the plots of old movies and novels (such as Allen Drury's *Advise and Consent*). Garber "unpacks" (a term she's borrowed from philosophers) the theme of the bisexual vampire. She examines bisexuality among bohemians of the past—in Bloomsbury, in Harlem and Greenwich Village, in Georgia O'Keefe's Taos. She discovers "cross-gender magnetism" adduced as an element of Hollywood chic in current celebrity biographies. Amusingly she says that a biographer's unfounded speculations about steamy bisexual alliances are written in a mode she dubs "the prurient wishful subjunctive" as in "Sexual intimacy...might well have been consistent with their mutual admiration." One of the delights of this long book is its mixture of classical erudition and pop-culture savvy; Garber switches from probing the myth of Tiresias to quoting a 1984 issue of *People* magazine: "A psychologist recently asked his 7-year-old nephew, 'Is Michael Jackson a girl or a boy?' The boy thought for a moment before replying, 'Both.' "

Garber recognizes that many lesbians and gay men consider the bisexual label to be just a cop-out, a somewhat acceptable halfway station in coming out, although she mentions that younger queer leaders place bisexuality "farther outside the 'mainstream' than gay and lesbian identity," an identity they apparently believe is more difficult to assume than simple homosexuality.

In this discussion she invokes the case of Jonathan Dollimore, the author of *Sexual Dissidence* and a professor in England at the University of Sussex, where he co-founded the department of sexual dissidence. "After many years with a male partner he is now living with a woman, and they recently had a child," Garber reports. "Some of the students who flocked to Sussex to study gay culture with him responded with anxiety." When Dollimore was asked if he were gay or bisexual, he replied that he is working "to dislodge the complacencies and the prejudice of other people, and to make visible new forms of sexuality, new forms of desire."

Since Freud popularized the theory of universal bisexuality, Garber writes extensively about him and his friendship with Wilhelm Fliess. It was Fliess—a kooky ear, nose and throat specialist in Berlin who believed that the nose was the seat of human passions and that nosebleeds were linked to menstruation cycles—who first revealed to Freud in 1897 the theory of bisexuality and his association of it with ambidexterity or left-handedness. A few months later Freud was able to write to Fliess: "I do not in the least underestimate bisexuality.... I expect it to provide all further enlightenment." In fact in essays written soon afterwards, Freud argued that the repression of a universal bisexual nature is the origin of most neuroses—a key concept that Freud had clearly borrowed from Fliess but whose author he just as clearly "forgot" to acknowledge (an act of strategic forgetting and intellectual appropriation that Freud later analyzed in his *Interpretation of Dreams*).

Garber's discussion of Freud's subsequent elaboration of the theory of bisexuality and of his troubled relationship with Fliess—a friendship that moreover was built on such erotic sentiments as seduction and jealousy—is always masterful.

The only problem is that we're never sure what Garber herself thinks of Freud's ideas. Does she believe in the nearly universal repression of a universal childhood bisexuality? At the heart of *Vice Versa* is a disquieting contradiction between form and intention. The form is fashionably postmodernist, a series of ludic excursions into hundreds of examples of the idea of bisexuality, a method that at its best makes distinctions among such salient terms as hermaphrodite and androgyne, but at its worst degenerates into the recounting of the plots of forgotten books and forgettable movies. This anthological approach is at odds with the very real, urgently felt thesis of the book, which defends the view that bisexuality is all around us and that to recognize this truth would be liberating. Freud's and Kinsey's theories are presented in great detail but only, one gathers, because both men believed (if for very different reasons) in the importance of human bisexuality. Whether their theories are true and their methodology is sound is scarcely considered.

Of course an apologist for Garber might claim that much of contemporary criticism grazes aimlessly if pleasurably through the pastures of intellectual history. Derrida in *Glas,* to take one example, writes on facing pages about Genet and Hegel, fills up the margins with lexical and semantic doodling—and leaves it to the reader to make sense of all these elements or, better yet, to give up his or her usual habits of synthesis in favor of a less coherent but more fertile openness of mind and feeling. I'm not sure Derrida's approach is as rewarding as it is confusing, but at least one never feels he has a secret set of conclusions he is concealing. Garber, by contrast, is nearly as playful and aleatory as Derrida in the organization of her book (although it is much more readable section by section), but *Vice Versa* does have a hidden agenda. In coquettish throwaways she intimates that she herself is left-handed, bisexual, amorous in the classroom, just as she slips in offhandedly that all sexuality is a matter of narration rather than essence. This guiding idea (as well as her whole personal investment in the subject) is never spelled out, unfortunately. I would have preferred a book that was shorter, less repetitious, less excursive, more rigorously argued, even polemical.

And yet I must confess that Garber's very multiplication of examples browbeat me into wondering whether I myself might not have been bisexual had I lived in another era. When I was a young man in the '60s, before the beginning of gay liberation, I was always in therapy trying to go straight. I was in love with three different women over a ten-year period and even imagined marrying two of them. After the Stonewall Uprising in

1969, however, I revised my thinking entirely; I decided I was completely gay and was only making the women in my life miserable. Following a tendency that Garber rightly criticizes, I denied the validity of my earlier heterosexual feelings in the light of my later homosexual identity. After reading *Vice Versa* I'm willing to give more credence to my earlier impulses.

While I was reading *Vice Versa,* however, I was disturbed by its seeming unawareness of the current American mood, especially the renewed hostility towards gays, gay marriage and the revocation of sodomy laws. Leo Bersani has argued in his book *Homos:* "Gay men and lesbians have nearly disappeared into their sophisticated awareness of how they have been constructed as gay men and lesbians.... If many gays now reject a homosexual identity as it has been elaborated for gays by others, the dominant heterosexual society doesn't need our belief in its own naturalness in order to continue exercising and enjoying the privileges of dominance." Bersani prizes the socially subversive power of homosexuality more than I do, but I think his point here is well taken: the Christian Right is not puzzling over the nuances of gay identity but merely trying to wipe it out.

Bruce Chatwin

B RUCE CHATWIN WAS LIKE JEAN GENET in one respect only: since they were both always on the go they were the ones who contacted their friends if at all when they arrived in town—which is an effective way, I suppose, of weeding one's social plot. I first met Chatwin in 1978 in New York. Robert Mapplethorpe had sent him over to meet me (Mapplethorpe had just hustled him for an introduction to one of his books, which was by far the best essay ever written on him, better than Susan Sontag's or mine). Maybe it was the excitement of druggy, sexy New York before AIDS or of the Mapplethorpe connection, but we were still standing seconds after he'd come into my apartment when we started fooling around with each other. We never took off all our clothes or lay down, and we certainly never repeated the act in the years that followed, but that initial intimacy established our friendship, slight as it was. For one thing, we were both exactly the same age though Bruce was far more handsome and famous and looked ten years younger, but whatever envy I might have had was eliminated by his physical generosity—a strategy I recommend to the enviable everywhere.

The one thing about him I did resent was his immense social success in New York, which I felt was based partly on his closetedness and lordly English accent. Whereas the editors of Random House or *The New York Review,* for instance, would have thought there was something innately risible about a militant homosexual writer, especially a homegrown one with a local accent, Bruce and his wife were eagerly welcomed at their dinners.

After that we saw each other mainly in Paris, where I moved in 1983. Bruce would come into town and ring me up and want to see me that very evening and so bewitched was I that I instantly dropped even long-standing engagements to dine with him. At the time I was living with a much younger American, who was not a reader, and he couldn't bear Bruce, since he detested a raconteur, no matter how brilliant. He pointed out that Bruce had told us the same anecdotes on successive evenings and that obviously his stories weren't tailor-made for us.

Of course my friend was right. Bruce was always working up his next book. Over the years I heard early, spoken versions of *The Viceroy of Ouidah, On the Black Hill, The Songlines* and *Utz*. The strange thing was that the first oral sketches of *On the Black Hill* and of *The Songlines* were pretty gay, whereas the final, written versions were dully normal. I had the distinct impression that Bruce had been frightened by the failure of his extravagant, hyperexotic *Viceroy* (after all, he lived by his pen) and rather cynically and shrewdly retreated into the Hardy-like solidity of *On the Black Hill* for his next sortie, which went down very well indeed with the English public. The initial impulse for this novel, however, had come from an anecdote Bruce told me of (what I took to be) a real couple, identical twins, who'd been lovers since adolescence. When one of the brothers "escaped" and married a woman, the other plotted feverishly until he won him back—and they then spent the rest of their long lives tranquilly together, sleeping in the same bed. Bruce visited a specialist on identical twins in Paris who claimed that "sixty per cent" of them had sex together, a statistic that obviously excited Bruce immensely. Susannah Clapp, in her *With Chatwin,* quotes John Updike, who observed that "their twinship is in fact a homosexual marriage," though by the time the story ended up in print their marriage bed had become chaste.

Bruce was never interested in other writers' work; Gregor von Rezzori's wife, Beatrice Monti, told me that Bruce would read out loud every day what he'd just been writing but he never asked a single question about Gregor's current book. I'd never much noticed this obsessiveness, since I was always so enthralled by his continuing adventures. The curious thing is that his abundance of detail, his strange upsurges of laughter, his sudden way of glazing over—all this odd matter and manner tranquillized any doubts one might otherwise have had about the truth of what he was saying. He really was a bit like the fourteenth-century John Mandeville telling stories of the fabulous monsters he'd encountered and any scepticism might have spoiled the fun.

Susannah Clapp records that when Hugh Chatwin, Bruce's younger brother by four years, entered Marlborough he overheard someone asking, "Is that Lord Chatwin's brother?" In fact Bruce's father was a solicitor who'd been in the navy during the war, but somewhere along the line Bruce had learned to bray, to laugh outright at funny strangers and to edit severely from his conversation anything that didn't answer to his strict sense of personal style—all lordly traits, at least for this American. When Bruce and I would go out to dinner in Paris he'd become so loud that in my petit-bourgeois way I'd be embarrassed; I'd switch the conversation, zanily enough, into French and Bruce was such a good mimic that he'd follow suit and instantly start to murmur, as the French do.

Clapp's book confirmed my impressions of Chatwin while greatly enriching what I knew about him. She points out in the introduction that he was "a collector who railed against the idea of owning works of art," and certainly this strange combination of connoisseurship and anti-materialism was one of the energizing contradictions behind everything he did and wrote, but I'd never focussed on it before. Clapp writes with beautiful exactitude, as in this telling observation: "His swiftness and dervish-like animation gave him the effect of gracefulness, though this was won against the odds: when he came to a halt, he was physically tense, planting himself on a chair, with his hands pressed on his splayed knees, as if sitting an examination of his own devising...."

Similarly, he could be very camp in his strange way (a manner he may have picked up from his lover Teddy Millington-Drake, whom I never knew). Clapp gives an example: "Sometimes Bruce seemed to surprise himself—to have turned up on his own doorstep: 'Hello darling, I'm in Islington' was rendered with exaggerated precision and amazement." I remember that he was capable of bugging his eyes and rolling them à propos of nothing at all and I was amused to see that he commented on his own "mad, mad eyes" in one of his notebooks.

Susannah Clapp mentions that he had certain "raps" that he'd return to again and again and work up. I remember well his "Hemingway rap."

Whenever there was a lull in the conversation he'd say, "You know we should really write an essay against all these wretched feminists in which we'd prove that Hemingway, far from being the brute they inveigh against, was actually the most refined stylist, the most delicate sensibility of the century—we could compare him to Ronald Firbank!" I mention this particular conversational gambit because if he despised Robert Louis Stevenson for being too close for comfort and half-admired Malraux for his effrontery in being a great talker, tomb-robber, charlatan and promulgator of a repellent *style ampoulé*, Hemingway he thoroughly liked for his writing, at once dandified and pared back, half Gertrude Stein and half *code civil*, as well as for his alternating bouts of heroism and cowardice. Now that Bruce is dead, curiously enough, a number of American literary critics, notably Marjorie Garber, are championing Hemingway as the great androgyne, especially in his posthumous, exquisitely written and dizzyingly bisexual *The Garden of Eden*.

With Chatwin is not a full-scale biography but rather a fresh, vivid portrait organized more or less chronologically but built up around certain key themes ("Objects," "Exotica," "Twins")—a novel and suitably unponderous way of depicting someone so mercurial. It's a very funny book about a witty crowd that included George and Diana Melly, Peter Eyre, Howard Hodgkin, Francis Wyndham and Millington-Drake. It's also full of subtle and revealing insights. For instance, I was surprised and instantly convinced by this original notion: "He had the paradoxical mysteriousness of the very definite person: he has been censured both for being elusive—for not being 'really there' even though physically present—and for being over-present, for being 'too much.' "

Some reviewers have complained that the collection of Chatwin essays, *Anatomy of Restlessness* (admittedly a pretentious title), does him a disservice by reprinting inferior pieces, but in fact it fleshes out the Susannah Clapp book very nicely since it contains among other things a portrait of the Rezzoris, an essay entitled "I Always Wanted to Go to Patagonia" and that long, troubled review of James Pope-Hennessy's biography of Robert Louis Stevenson that Clapp discusses so tellingly. Here we read: "Stevenson was profoundly self-centred and had a morbid concern for his public image. He liked to think he was free with information about himself. In fact he kept tight rein on the confessional; but, consciously or not, he was always dropping broad hints in his stories.... Stevenson was a talented story-teller but he was never first-rate." As Clapp argues convincingly, these are not only overly harsh judgments against Stevenson, they are also voicings of Chatwin's deepest self-doubts.

He needn't have worried. *In Patagonia* remains as bizarre and fresh as the day it was published with its search for Butch Cassidy or the plesiosaurus, *The Viceroy of Ouidah* is as unhealthy and bejewelled as Flaubert's *Salammbô,* and *Utz* is the ultimate, miniature tribute to that most driven of perversions, collecting art.

Edwin Denby

I N THE 1970s I USED TO RUN INTO EDWIN DENBY during the intermissions of the New York City Ballet at the State Theater; he'd always be accompanied by much younger gay men connected to the art or dance world. I was introduced to him at least ten times, though he never remembered me from one time to another. He was small, old, handsome, pale as an ivory crucifix, with a full head of white hair and a kindly smile; he almost never spoke but when he did he whispered. As Robert Cornfield has written: "After some years of devastating illness and deteriorating memory, Denby died by his own hand in the summer of 1983." He had been born in 1903 (in China—his father was an American diplomat).

Although in the 1970s Denby had neither written nor spoken publicly for several years (the last item in his collected writings is his 1966 Dance Magazine Award acceptance speech), nevertheless his sepulchral presence, his dignity and beauty and his constant attendance of almost every performance of Balanchine's company symbolized the role that that particular organization had played in New York's intellectual and cultural life during the previous two decades. The lobby of the State Theater was the one place where you could see, night after night, literary intellectuals such as Susan Sontag, the poetry critic David Kalstone, essayist Richard Poirier, the cartoonist Edward Gorey, the music and dance critic Dale Harris, the editor of Knopf, Robert Gottlieb—and hundreds of others. Kalstone used to joke that only an entirely non-verbal art could possibly appeal to so many contentious people. He also recognized that we were all enjoying a rare privilege—the unfolding of Balanchine's genius, he who had started out in Imperial Russia, reached his first apogee under Diaghilev in France and, after the 1930s, moved to the United States where he led dance to summits it had never known before. Balanchine was arguably the only genius of this range and force at work in New York in those years, the only one, in fact, comparable to two other Russians who flowered in the States: Nabokov and Stravinsky.

If Denby could understand Balanchine, it was partly because he him-self had trained as a gymnast and had danced professionally (in 1929, for instance, when he was twenty-six, he had worked as dancer, choreographer and literary consultant to the State Theater of Darmstadt). He frequently comments on the way a dancer carries her neck, spine, elbows, hands; he employs delicious adjectives ("the beautifully effaced shoulders...the arrowy ankles and feet"). Without affectation he is capable of saying about the great Russian dancer Ulanova's style, "It isn't the bird or dragonfly style of dancing, it's a kind of aspiration upward: lightness as a longing and a dream rather than as a possession." He also knows how to be elegantly dismissive about bad Soviet choreography ("a sort of super dinner-dance adagio couple style").

Just as important as his own dance training was the fact that he was a civilized man who had accumulated a wide international culture, which allowed him to understand the exact degree of silken seriousness Balanchine intended when he said he believed art should be "entertain-ment." Because he had seen so much dance, because he had studied the dead-pan cartoon style of Alex Katz's paintings (an enduring enthusiasm), because he had anticipated in his own poems the urban insouciance of Frank O'Hara, Denby was uniquely placed for capturing the exact mood and the slippery, fooling seriousness of a Balanchine masterpiece such as "Four Temperaments": "It is full of Beckmesserish dance jokes, classic steps turned inside-out and upside-down, retimed, reproportioned, rerouted, girls dancing hard and boys soft, every kind of oddity of device or accent, but never losing the connective 'logic' of classicism, never drop-ping its impetus, and developing a ferocity of drive that seems to image the subject matter of its title: internal secretions."

Denby's critical faculties were consecrated to Balanchine, and in that last acceptance speech he said: "Of course there's one man who has taught

me to see and hear more than anyone else, and you can guess who I mean—
Mr. Balanchine." The reference to "hearing" might at first seem curious,
but Denby was always aware of Balanchine's sensitivity to the scores he
was setting (Balanchine had been trained first as a composer). In a 1945
review of "Concerto Barocco," set to Bach's "Concerto for Two Violins,"
Denby writes, "In its vigorous dance rhythm, its long-linked phrases, its
consistent drive and sovereign articulation, Concerto Barocco corresponds
brilliantly to this masterpiece of baroque music." Gifted with a rare ability
to describe dance moments in non-technical language, Denby says of the
couple dancing the adagio, "Then at the culminating phrase, from her
greatest height he very slowly lowers her. You watch her body slowly
descend, her foot and leg pointing stiffly downward, till her toe reaches the
floor and she rests her full weight at last on this single sharp point and
pauses. It is the effect at that moment of a deliberate and powerful plunge
into a wound, and the emotion of it answers strangely to the musical
stress."

Over the years Denby reviewed the Ballets Russes de Monte Carlo in
its various stages of disarray. He took on the dancer-choreographer
Massine, whom he never liked. Here is his description of a bad Massine
ballet: "The Dark Lover was less conventional. He turned out to be Mr.
Petroff without a toupee, dressed in an old-fashioned black bathing suit
several sizes too small, so that he could get it up over one shoulder only.
For propriety's sake, he also was wearing long black stockings. He looked
as if he were employed at the local bathing establishment, though the program billed him as a figment of fancy. Fancy or no, he made persistent
advances to Miss Toumanova and finally succeeded in lifting her so that
she faced the audience in the air with—oddly enough—his backside on
view just below her. Cupid came back and cleared up matters."

I quote that review at length to show that Denby could be irreverent,
even harsh, certainly funny when he wasn't pleased. His admiration for
Balanchine must be read against an acerbic background (he was also, curiously, one of the first people to use the word *camp* in print, in a 1949
review of a new Ashton ballet). Denby's take on Martha Graham, for
instance, is always respectful, especially of her own performances ("She
herself never loses the ladylike elegance, the womanly look that makes
formal tragedy communicative"), but he never fully endorses her esthetic:
"I find she uses the stage space the way the realistic theater does, as an

accidental segment of a place, not the way the poetic theater uses the stage, as a space complete in itself."

Earlier I used the word *civilized* to describe Denby; certainly that was the word that most perfectly characterized his own understanding of dance. As he put it in a review of Balanchine's "Danses Concertantes," "The dance is like a conversation in Henry James, as surprising, as sensitive, as forbearing, as full of slyness and fancy. The joyousness of it is the pleasure of being civilized, of being what we really are, born into a millennial urban civilization. This is where we are and this is what the mind makes beautiful."

Fiction, with its automatic ironies, and poetry, with its predictable Romantic individualism, and contemporary film, with its alternation between violence and soap-opera melodrama, are all incapable of celebrating the beauty of city people living together. The other narrative arts see only intimacy as desirable and nature as restorative and complacently agree that civilization is immoral, corrupting, deadening. What dance brings into the world is a utopian vision of the expressive, healing power of the couple received into a coherent society—a vision that Shakespeare's comedies had defined so many centuries earlier. Edwin Denby understood better than anyone else this dimension of Balanchine's art; he merits being described in the terms Oscar Wilde invented to emphasize the true critic's independence and artistry: "The critic occupies the same relation to the work of art that he criticizes as the artist does to the visible world of form and color, or the unseen world of passion and of thought."

Of course Denby doesn't exist outside a tradition. Arlene Croce followed him and in her appreciation of Balanchine became even more adept at describing formal and technical innovation. Théophile Gautier (1811–1872) preceded Denby, but Gautier appreciated ballerinas first and foremost as torrid or spiritual women, knew little about dance technique and often failed to mention even the name of a choreographer or scenarist (in the nineteenth century one person thought up the plot and another worked out the movements). Denby admired Gautier's nonprofessional stance as a man of the world and Parisian; Denby said of him, "He illustrates the advantages the sensual approach to ballet can have for an intelligence of exceptional sensual susceptibility and for a man of large sensual complacency"—a rather ambiguous compliment, I'd hazard. Denby was not indifferent to ballerinas—his generic pronoun for a dancer is never

"he" but always "she"— and he wrote great hymns to his favorite ballerina, Alicia Markova. But he could also appreciate male dancers such as
Eglevsky, Dolin, Arthur Mitchell, and above all he saw ballet as art, not as
acrobatics or sentimental if inept storytelling. His definition of art is worth
repeating: "Art takes what in life is an accidental pleasure and tries to
repeat and prolong it." Denby's criticism prolongs for us the ghostly
images of past performances and traces out the half-century of Balanchine's
extraordinary trajectory.

Coleman Dowell

I SUPPOSE THAT SOMEONE EAGER FOR A LABEL to classify Coleman Dowell's fiction might call him an author of gay fiction or of Southern Gothic fiction or of metafiction. "Gay fiction" since there are gay (or at least homosexual) characters in such major novels as *Island People, Too Much Flesh and Jabez* and *White on Black on White*. Indeed, the "too much flesh" is a man's overly large penis that no woman and only a boy can physically accommodate. "Southern Gothic" because Dowell was from Kentucky where several of his stories in *The Houses of Children* take place as does the action of his first novel, *One of the Children Is Crying*. And "Gothic" since Dowell deals in such staples of the genre as ghosts and haunted houses as well as the uncanny interpenetration of one time zone by another. In *Island People,* for instance, a violent story from the past glows through the scrim of the present. "Metafiction" since nesting one box of narrative inside another is a frequent device in all of Dowell's major work and the reader is constantly being asked to revise his or her notion about which character is actually the "real" narrator. In *Too Much Flesh and Jabez,* for instance, we discover that the ultimate narrator is Miss Ethel, an old maid schoolteacher.

Dowell resisted all of these labels. He who was starved for critical attention and was grateful even for casual compliments about his work from friends, nevertheless could become emphatic in rejecting all classification.

Although he acknowledged influences (Faulkner, crucially, and the French philosopher Henri Bergson, for his ideas about vitalism and time), he disliked all efforts to categorize his work. At first this resistance looks like peevishness—a closeted older man's rejection of the frightening freedoms offered by gay liberation or a tortured Southerner's refusal to appear to owe anything to the region where he had suffered so much (his anxiety about his modest origins led him to make up self-aggrandizing and entirely fanciful stories about his childhood).

But I would propose that Dowell's rejection of pigeonholing owes less to his psychological quirks or shortcomings and more to the artistic demand that his reader face up to the full complexity of his fiction. On page after page Dowell asks us to sustain all the assaults he can deal out against any stable notion of the self, and he does not want us to be able to retreat behind the deflecting and discomfort-reducing shelter of a ready-made label. Viewers, for instance, squeal with delight at a Hollywood horror film because they have been forearmed with the connoisseur's idea that all this is just twists on familiar devices in another scary movie. Bradford Morrow, one of Dowell's most constant champions, has edited with Patrick McGrath an anthology of New Gothic writing, but I suspect Dowell would have resisted being included in it, not just out of the writer's usual urge to be unique and unclassifiable but out of a more serious expectation of total readerly submission to the full horror and degradation of his fiction in its systematic deconstruction of personality and even identity.

In *Island People,* for instance, the instability of the narrator and our uncertainty about which possible narrator is speaking do not make up a game (though the first section is called "The Game" and presents us with two dueling narrators firing back and forth competing short stories). The ludic element, though present, is less in evidence than the deconstructive. This emphasis on the fragmentary emerges in the celebrated and often quoted comment, "All there is, is fragments, because a man, even the loneliest of the species, is divided among several persons, animals, worlds." We might add not only is the individual divided among, but he is also constituted out of, several different persons.

Whereas the Existentialists, insistent on the human freedom to choose, placed all praise and blame and moral accountability onto the integral individual and (in the case of Beckett) presented the fundamental, frightening solitude of each person, Dowell has a far more deterministic view (more in line with Foucault's than Sartre's views) of each man or woman as a nexus of converging external forces, social and cultural. In Foucault's view a human being (or an author) does not "exist" in the sense that he is a unique and irreplaceable creature. Whereas the heroes of Sartre's *Nausea* or Camus's *The Stranger* are cut off even from love, Dowell's protagonists are consumed by passion and all its accompanying mischief—jealousy, paranoia, fear of the future and distrust of the past, humiliation and burning resentment. In Dowell's fiction the very effects of such corrosive passion disassemble the elements of the self and estrange a narrator from himself or, through a kind of spiritual mitosis, cause him to subdivide into several different narrators, all of them with a problematical ontology.

Although Dowell, to my knowledge, did not study Foucault, nevertheless we can notice a strong parallel investigation in the thinking of these two men. Surely Dowell, the supreme poet of transgression, would have recognized himself in this description from Foucault's 1969 talk, "What Is an Author?": "Texts, books, speeches began really to have authors (other than the great mythical figures, sacred and sacralizing) only at that moment when the author could be punished, that is to say at the moment when a discourse could be transgressive. A discourse in our culture (and in many others as well, surely) was not originally a product, a thing, a commodity; it was essentially an act—an act that was placed in the bipolar field of sacred and profane, legal and illicit, religious and blasphemous. It was historically a gesture loaded with risks before it became a piece of goods in a circuit of different properties." Foucault goes on to point out that precisely at the moment when an author finally became a producer of property in the usual capitalist fashion he paradoxically insisted on his independence by making his texts particularly transgressive.

In Dowell's work and life we see these elements at work. He who had written for the stage, including the musical stage, and for television in the era of quick live skits and musical entertainment, turned from this highly rewarding and tightly commodified domain to the world of literary fiction, which is both more substantial (a book exists in a permanent state in the way entertainment does not) and less lucrative or visible. Moreover, Dowell became in his novels more and more shockingly transgressive, playing with such verboten themes as homophobia and anti-Semitism (*Mrs. October Was Here*), pornography and pedophilia (*Too Much Flesh and Jabez*) and all varieties of exploitation and racism and degradation between members of the black and white races (*White on Black on White*). There is no form of "blasphemy" against the politically correct order that Dowell does not utter. His is not a form of adolescent defiance but a systematic transvaluation of all values—and a major source of his creative energy.

Coleman Dowell committed suicide in 1985. He had become a virtual recluse in his gilded cage of an apartment high above Central Park. He had never achieved the sort of fame that his early work in the theater and on television had led him to expect. His personal life, which centered on a black heterosexual criminal with whom he had corresponded while the man was in prison but who was now a living, dangerous part of Dowell's everyday existence, was careening out of control—a situation aggravated by Dowell's excessive drinking. Today we would say that Dowell was excited by "edge" sex—but alas he fell over the edge and plunged to his death.

Dowell's writing, far from appearing as a record of the anxieties and suffering that pushed him towards suicide, can be read only as a self-administered effort to treat these very problems, to contain and balance these tensions. If his fiction is violent, if it alternates a lyrical apprehension of nature with a dark assessment of human treachery, if it plays off the love of an animal (invariably a dog) against an animadversion to other human beings, if the experience of reading one of these difficult and illuminating texts is like watching successive curtains rising and dissolving to reveal ever deeper perspectives and ever changing settings, then we can only see this highly formal and endlessly disturbing work as an effort to contain the demons that eventually destroyed their creator.

For Dowell's novels to "work" on us we must approach them with no preconceived ideas, no genre assumptions, no labels. He will give us a walk on the wild side, but only if we have no smug idea about where he is leading us.

Grace Paley

GRACE PALEY, WHOM I LIKE TO THINK OF as The Mother of Us All, taught fiction for years at Sarah Lawrence. She is a poet and essayist as well as a short story writer and over the years she has become almost as well known as an antiwar activist. Her very personal essays, which constitute something close to an autobiography, were collected in 1998 under the title *Just As I Thought*. In that book she has a two-page essay about her everyday activities in Vermont called "Life in the Country: A City Friend Asks, 'Is It Boring?'" which exhausts me just to read—all the zoning meetings, water-board meetings, school meetings and food co-op meetings, the conservation meetings and the agricultural meetings, the community theater rehearsals, the affinity groups and the training sessions for civil disobedience—it sounds positively frantic and fulfilling, life in Thetford, Vermont.

I first met Grace Paley in Paris, where I was living for many years and where she'd come for a giant feminist powwow. I remember her French editor, my dear friend Gilles Barbedette, was absolutely astounded and delighted by Grace's bonhomie and straightforwardness and kindness and radiant honesty—qualities that can be pretty rare in the narcissistic and anxious world of writers and editors. I myself was so proud of her as a sterling example of everything that is good about America, even if she has devoted so much of her energy striving to correct the excesses or failures of our country.

I once heard a radio interview of Elizabeth Schwarzkopf in which she said that all it takes to be a famous opera singer is a voice that cannot be mistaken for anyone else's—and the lung-power to be really loud. By those standards Grace Paley would be as successful a singer as she is writer, since from her first story to her last she sounds the same, original tone and projects it with clarity and force.

Typically, she writes about middle-aged Jewish women in New York, but not the Woody Allen neurotic analysands whom Europeans usually conjure up but rather the daughters of poor Russian immigrants who grew up in Brooklyn or the Bronx or the Lower East Side. These women received a good education but now earn a meager living as social workers and fill their free time organizing antiwar protests. Paley's stand-in for herself is called Faith and lives with her grown-up sons Richard and Tonto and her boyfriend Jack, who sells furniture and is sceptical about her ideas but passionate about her body. Her friends, reappearing in one story after another, are called Ann, Selena, Ruth, all of them tough-talking feminists who like men, intellectuals who like babies, activists who have a polyanna belief in a rosy future.

A key story is called "A Conversation with My Father," in which the narrator's eighty-six-year-old father asks her to write a "simple story," the kind Chekhov and Maupassant wrote.

She thinks, "I would like to try to tell such a story, if he means the kind that begins: 'There was a woman...' followed by a plot, the absolute line between two points which I've always despised. Not for literary reasons, but because it takes all hope away. Everyone, real or invented, deserves the open destiny of life."

She reads her father the one-paragraph first draft of a story about a neighbor who becomes a drug addict in order to maintain her close friendship with her heroin-shooting son. One day the boy gives up drugs and, disgusted with what she's become, leaves his mother.

The father wants more detail—the woman's looks, her hair, her background. The daughter tries a second draft, which this time does come to startled, rustling life precisely because of the queer but believable details: "In order to keep him from feeling guilty (because guilt is the stony heart of nine-tenths of all clinically diagnosed cancers in America today, she said), and because she had always believed in giving bad habits room at home where one could keep an eye on them, she too became a junkie."

Perhaps because the story is now more convincing, her father falls into despair and keeps crying out that the woman is living a tragedy. The narrator, ever the optimist, objects that the woman is only forty and could easily become the receptionist in a storefront community clinic in the East Village.

And the strangest aspect of Paley's work—which deals with sordid old-age homes, unwed mothers, race warfare, the early death or disappearance of children, conflict and cruelty between the generations—is that it always has a lightheartedness pulsing along the veins, a quickening and excitement about even the most tragic situations. In general, her male characters, self-dramatizing and prone to exaggeration, are pessimists and her women, logical and alert to an unsuspected but probable happy ending, are optimists. "You fucking enemy," the narrator's boyfriend shouts at her in one story, "you always see things in a rosy light. You have a rotten rosy temperament."

Her fictional output is made up of three collections: *The Little Disturbances of Man* (1959), *Enormous Changes at the Last Minute* (1974) and *Later the Same Day* (1985). But despite the span of three decades and the changing topical references, her work remains delightfully the same; as Oscar Wilde said, "Only mediocrities develop." In the introduction to her collected fiction she dates her first success in prose to a sudden understanding of how to transcribe the Yiddish- and Russian-accented English of her childhood on the Lower East Side (her parents were Russian-Jewish immigrants, her mother a sweatshop worker while her father struggled to become a doctor). From the beginning her dialogue has the right comic ring:

"Have some more tea, my dear."
    "No, thank you, I am a samovar already."
    "Dorfmann!" he hollered like a king. "Bring this child a seltzer with fresh ice!"

Or take this line:

"How could you ask me to go with you on trains to stay in strange hotels, among Americans, not your wife? Be ashamed."

From the very earliest stories the women feel a strong solidarity with one another, even across the generations:

> "Ah, Grandma," I said, hoping to console, "they were all so grouchy, anyway. I don't miss them a bit."
>
> Grandma gave me a miserable look. "Everyone's sons are like that," she explained. "First grouchy, then gone."

Politically inspired fiction (and Paley has identified herself as a feminist and pacifist, and she often sounds like an anarchist as well) runs the risk of becoming predictable because it deals with iron rules, not fleshly exceptions. Paley's genius is that even if she plunges her characters down into a charged moment (a trip to China in the 1970s, say) she can't help letting her peripheral vision pick up all the swarming details that undermine (or at least complicate) her heralded convictions.

Take the subtle, slippery story "Zagrowsky Tells," in which Faith runs into an old Jewish pharmacist and his little black grandson, Emanuel. Years earlier Faith and other friends had picketed Zagrowsky's pharmacy because he was a racist; now he's here with a black grandson and Faith can't quell her curiosity.

But the story is still more troubling than Faith could at first imagine. The picketing had inadvertently destabilized Zagrowsky's daughter, who ended up in a clinic where she became pregnant by a black gardener. As Zagrowsky puts it: "A person looks at my Emanuel and says, Hey! he's not altogether from the white race, what's going on? I'll tell you what: life is going on. You have an opinion. I have an opinion. Life don't have no opinion."

Life in all its messiness, its failure to endorse even the soundest position, is what throbs in these stories, which often end on a note that suggests another whole episode. Paley is as clever a mimic as Philip Roth, as cheerfully zany and aleatory in her vision of New York as Christina Stead, as serendipitous as Donald Barthelme, but her unladylike gutsiness and friendliness are nonpareil.

At the end of the story significantly called "Listening," the Narrator is suddenly told off by a lesbian friend for never having written about her or her loves. The Narrator is thunderstruck by her own—well, deafness. She asks her friend why she waited so long to object. The Narrator then says, "How can you forgive me?"

The last paragraph reads:

Forgive you? She laughed. But she reached across the clutch. With her hand she turned my face to her so my eyes would look into her eyes. You are my friend, I know that, Faith, but I promise you, I won't forgive you, she said. From now on, I'll watch you like a hawk. I do not forgive you.

This menacing sense of accountability to everyone, especially to her friends, to other women, governs all these stories to an unprecedented degree. Who would have guessed that public art could be so private?

Jean Genet

JEAN GENET (1910–1986) WAS A WRITER of unusual versatility. He wrote five novels, a hefty volume of memoirs (*Prisoner of Love*), several long dramatic poems, several one-act plays, including "The Maids," which can be seen as a taut condensation of a five-act drama, three full-length plays, numerous film scripts, hundreds of letters and a few essays (including one about sculptor Alberto Giacometti that Picasso called the best art essay ever written). In addition, after 1968 Genet wrote dozens of political essays, articles and speeches. In 1950 he made an erotic silent film, twenty minutes long in black and white (*A Song of Love*). He prepared a speech for radio about delinquent boys called "The Criminal Child" (which was never broadcast because it was banned by the state). He even devised the story line for a ballet, " 'Adame Miroir," in which two sailors dance together (one is meant to be the other's reflection) until Death (or at least a menacing figure) arrives to put an end to the fun.

Few people in the English-speaking world (or even in France) ascribe to Genet this sort of versatility; until now he has been known primarily as a novelist and playwright. In France, due to contractual disputes between two of his publishers, his writings were generally available only in an expensive and austere edition of his complete works. Not until the mid-1970s was the legal conflict resolved; then for the first time his novels and plays began to appear in widely distributed paperbacks, but by then he had been lost to a whole generation of general readers.

In the United Kingdom and the United States, Genet's most popular works were already in paperback in the 1960s, but the extent and diversity of the rest of his work remained hidden longer than in France. His essays and poems either were not translated at all or were published in obscure or fugitive journals or in editions not widely available.

Even in France, approximately a quarter of Genet's extant writing is still awaiting publication. Nevertheless, his French publisher, Gallimard, is slowly bringing out volume after volume of his *Complete Works* which, despite the name, is in reality a judicious selection of Genet's total output, some of which is of uneven quality or (in the case of Genet's political statements) repetitious.

Which is not to suggest that Genet was an unconscious demiurge, a primitive who churned out both inspired and flat pages that wiser editors must now winnow. I mention this notion (in order to dismiss it) only because some critics, despite all evidence to the contrary, continue to see Genet as a self-educated diamond in the rough.

Quite the contrary. Genet may have received a formal education only until the age of twelve, but he was first in his class. He was a constant reader. In Alligny-en-Morvan, the village near Dijon in which he lived with foster parents until the age of twelve, he refused to perform manual labor of any sort. The most he would condescend to do was to watch a cow as it grazed. Genet spent his time reading books from the school library, including many nineteenth-century boys' adventure stories, action-packed tales that would have a complex influence on Genet's own novels.

By age sixteen, Genet was condemned because of a few petty thefts to an unusually harsh reform school, where the authorities specifically forbade the adolescent inmates to engage in any studies beyond the bare rudiments. The institution was supposed to prepare future laborers, field hands and soldiers, who would presumably be given ideas above their lowly station if they read novels or learned geometry. Despite these strictures, Genet discovered the Renaissance poet Ronsard, whose elevated diction and sentiments gave him a thrillingly exalted vision of the power of literature. Buried in Genet's prose are many small echoes of Ronsard's verse as well as of his poetic erotic writing.

At nineteen, Genet, in order to cut short his reform-school sentence, joined the army, and for the next six years he was a soldier with long hours to kill. Those hours he devoted to reading, especially the works of Dostoevsky, who became one of his favorite authors. Like Genet, Dostoevsky had been a prisoner and, in *The House of the Dead,* had written about incarceration. Like Genet, Dostoevsky was fascinated by religion and royalty—and by pure evil. But what Genet (who late in life wrote an essay about Dostoevsky) most admired was what he called Dostoevsky's "buffoonish" way of undermining his own moral points, his practice of creating distinct characters only to blur and distort them later or to let them drift out of focus. Genet declared that he liked only works of art which destroyed themselves, which were both player and target in an artistic shooting gallery.

Throughout the 1930s, while Genet was in his twenties, he wandered the world. As a soldier he was sent to Damascus and Morocco. Subsequently, as a vagabond, he wandered through Spain, Italy, Eastern Europe, Holland and Belgium. Those who knew him in Czechoslovakia recall that among his few belongings were manuscripts he was constantly working on. He had met the French novelist and essayist André Gide and had written him a long, confused, self-conscious letter (which, typically, ended with a request for money).

Genet may have been the thief, homosexual prostitute and beggar that he pictures himself as being in his last novel, *The Thief's Journal,* but such a self-portrait is only a partial view. At the same time he was also a voluminous reader with serious literary ambitions, a part-time tutor of French and French literature and someone hungry for information about the Paris literary scene.

The only traces we have of Genet the writer before 1940 are fragmentary—and suggest he was a stilted and affected stylist. He sent six long letters to Anne Bloch, a German-Jewish refugee living in Czechoslovakia whom he had tutored in French. These letters reveal a writer given to ready-made sentiments and stock phrases. Although Genet was a homosexual who never had sexual relations with women, in these letters he was trying to convince himself he was in love with Madame Bloch, a virtuous, married woman who would never have dreamed of granting her favors to her strange little French teacher with his dirty clothes and elegant manners. In his letters to her from Paris, he speaks of Gide, of the Decadent novelist Rachilde—and especially of Rimbaud.

There are many examples of Genet's fascination with Rimbaud. He tore out of a book the pages containing Rimbaud's long poem *The Drunken Boat* and sent them to Anne Bloch. Genet pretended he had joined the army, like Rimbaud, in order to receive an initial bonus before deserting after three days. Although Rimbaud in fact did serve just three days, Genet spent nearly six years in the army during several different engagements. Like Rimbaud, Genet had grown up nursing fantasies of artistic success in faraway Paris. Like Rimbaud, when Genet at last arrived in Paris, he terrorized the older, middle-class poets he encountered. Rimbaud bullied Verlaine, just as Genet intimidated Jean Cocteau, the versatile man-about-Paris who discovered Genet and paid for the publication of Genet's first novel. Somewhat in the manner of Rimbaud, who abandoned poetry at age nineteen, Genet wrote with great intensity during short periods and more than once renounced his craft. Already in the nineteenth century Rimbaud embodied the model of the homosexual hoodlum and self-created genius, given to extravagant behavior and revolutionary literary feats, whom Genet emulated some seventy years later.

Ronsard, Dostoevsky, Rimbaud—these are only three of the several gods in Genet's pantheon. The one Genet revered the most was Mallarmé, the hermetic, nearly abstract nineteenth-century poet.

Genet was discovered by Jean Cocteau at the beginning of 1943, and Cocteau arranged for his first novel, *Our Lady of the Flowers,* to be published a year later—sold under the counter in an expensive edition limited to some three hundred copies. When Genet encountered Cocteau he had already written several plays and scenarios as well as a long poem, *The Man Condemned to Death,* which Genet himself had paid to have printed up by a man he had met in prison. The printer, apparently, had been sentenced for having forged food-ration coupons, a grave offense during World War II. When he was released, he printed a hundred copies of the poem for Genet, who was still behind bars. It is interesting that Genet (contrary to what Sartre asserts in his massive study, *Saint Genet*) was already working in several different forms at the very beginning of his career—drama, film, poetry and fiction.

Very quickly, Genet (who was in prison off and on for petty thefts during the wartime years, when he wrote his first two novels, *Our Lady of the Flowers* and *Miracle of the Rose*) became a celebrity whom few Parisians had met and even fewer had read. His celebrity was sparked during a trial in July 1943, at which Genet, as a multiple offender, faced a heavy sentence. Cocteau got him off lightly—with just a three-month sentence—by intimidating the judge and proclaiming Genet the greatest writer of the modern period. Cocteau compared Genet to Rimbaud and sternly reminded the judge that one did not imprison a Rimbaud. Only in France, of course, would such a legal defense work (which is all to the glory of the country).

The period 1942–1947 was an extremely productive one for Genet and can be considered one of the most condensed bursts of creativity in literary history. During these years Genet wrote all his major poems, including *The Fisherman of Suquet*; all five of his novels (*Our Lady of the Flowers, Miracle of the Rose, Funeral Rites, Querelle* and *The Thief's Journal*) and several plays, including *Deathwatch* and *The Maids*.

This was a time when Genet either was actually behind bars or felt he was living in the shadow of prison. Even after 1944, when he served out his last term, Genet still had a sentence outstanding that had never caught up with him due to the confusion of the war years. He had written his first two novels in noisy cells filled with other prisoners. He had crouched in a corner and written on his knees, usually in student notebooks—once on paper intended to be made into bags by prisoners. When fifty pages were confiscated by an angry prison guard, Genet reconstructed the entire missing text from memory—this time on the proper paper. Not only did Genet work with the constant threat of prison hanging over his head, he also wrote his first two books on an empty stomach. Wartime shortages (and a deliberate Nazi policy to starve prisoners into extinction) meant that Genet was consumed by hunger during the composition of *Our Lady of the Flowers* and especially *Miracle of the Rose*. In letters to one of his early editors he repeatedly called for packages of food. Fully aware of his talent, Genet declared in these letters that he was giving France some of its most glorious pages of literature, pages that were genuinely "marvelous," in the original, overwhelming sense of the word; in return he angrily demanded a minimum of food for survival.

Genet was not overestimating the dimensions of his achievement as a writer. His style, rich with unexpected metaphors and animated by a strong poetic sensibility, is unmistakably original. No one had ever written like this before, and most of the genuine artists who read Genet were quick to recognize his genius. Cocteau passed along *Our Lady of the Flowers* in manuscript to many writers. Simone de Beauvoir and Jean-Paul Sartre announced that Genet gave them new confidence in the future of the novel; Sartre published excerpts from Genet's work in his review *Les Temps modernes,* arranged for Genet to win a prestigious literary award and agreed to write a book-length essay to introduce Genet's *Complete Works.* Sartre's *Saint Genet,* published in 1952, was a long "existential psychoanalysis" of Genet, a tracing out of the various stages the orphan Genet must have gone through in order to move from criminal to esthete, writer and saint. Some twenty years later Genet was once again the subject of another book-length investigation by a major philosopher—*Glas* by Jacques Derrida.

Genet's fiction appeals to philosophers because of the originality and density of the prose, equalled in line-by-line intelligence only by that of Marcel Proust, whose *Remembrance of Things Past* was Genet's main inspiration. One day, probably in 1941, Genet was participating in a covert exchange of books with other prisoners during an exercise period. Being the last to arrive, Genet was forced to take a dull-looking volume no one else wanted—*The Guermantes Way,* a volume in Proust's saga. As soon as Genet read the first page he closed the book because he wanted to savor its treasures slowly over the days to come. He later admitted in an interview that his reading of Proust at age thirty-one or thirty-two was the decisive stimulus that made him begin writing. Indeed, Genet can be seen as the Proust of the criminal class.

Unlike Proust—or most novelists for that matter—Genet felt no obligation to do justice to his subjects, to explain or apologize, to produce the illusion of reality, to document a milieu or to demonstrate his own moral fineness. To be sure, his writing can be sociologically accurate, as in his portrait of gay culture in Montmartre, just as it can be extremely moralistic, as it is towards the end of *The Thief's Journal.* But neither the sociological nor the moral impulse in Genet resembles that of any other author. Like Proust, Genet has a thoroughly philosophical turn of mind and gives pride of place to reflection on the meaning of events rather than a mere recounting of an anecdote.

Genet never stops reminding his reader, especially in *Our Lady of the Flowers,* that all the characters (Divine, Darling, Our Lady, Seck Gorgui) whom he is so stunningly inventing are mere fabrications of his imagination, figments he fleshes out only in order to excite himself while masturbating. Genet would like to suggest that he's the irresponsible god of his universe, creating and abandoning characters at will in a purely improvisational way.

But in fact the structures underlying Genet's fiction are ambiguous and complex. After he tells us repeatedly that his characters are masturbation fantasies, he's quite capable of saying, "When I met Divine at Fresnes Prison," or "Darling's real name is Paul Garcia." The level of reality in Genet's fiction is constantly in question.

The organization of Genet's fiction, equally original, bears a resemblance to film montage. Often Genet would be at work on two or three different novellas, which he initially conceived of as independent entities, but which eventually he would intercut in order to form one book. In *Our Lady of the Flowers* there are three different narrative strands. The "frame tale," as students of narrative put it, is about Genet in prison awaiting a trial which will determine his future as convict or free man. We are repeatedly reminded that the date of the trial is rapidly approaching. The second narrative is about Genet's puppets: the drag queen–prostitute Divine; her pimp, Darling; the handsome young thief, nicknamed Our Lady, who comes to live with them in Montmartre; and a black man named Seck Gorgui, who eventually drops Divine and takes up with Our Lady. These narratives begin (out of sequence) with Divine's funeral, when her coffin is accompanied to the cemetery by an honor guard of transvestites. It ends with Our Lady's trial, when he is condemned to death for killing an old man (Our Lady, horrified by his own impulsive words, blurts out his confession). The third narrative strand is the story of Divine's childhood as the boy Louis Culafroy. It comprises scenes loosely based on Genet's own childhood in the Morvan, a densely wooded region east of Paris. (Genet took Divine's boyhood name from Louis Cullaffroy, a boy Genet actually knew in the village in which he grew up.)

These are not only three different, almost unrelated stories, they are also quite different *sorts* of stories: a romantic confessional in which Genet speaks of his own approaching trial; a constantly interrupted and undermined picture of tacky Montmartre gay life just before the war; and a much more carefully constructed and consistent picture of a boy growing up as a sissy in a backwoods village.

Genet's relationship to the reader is problematical—and dramatic. He makes very clear, in all his novels except *Querelle*, that he is addressing a middle-class, respectable, heterosexual male reader, whom he alternately cajoles and menaces, seduces and shocks, wins over and repels. This pierce-and-parry *is* the action of Genet's novels—an uneasy and ever-changing relationship.

Although Genet presents his novels as autobiographical, they all take great liberties with the facts. Nevertheless, they do cover some of the major periods in his life. In *Our Lady of the Flowers,* he writes of his childhood in the village. In *Miracle of the Rose,* he documents with great care the reform school, Mettray, where he was detained from September 1926 to March 1929. In *Funeral Rites,* he covers his romantic, wartime friendship with a Résistant, Jean Decarnin, who died during the Liberation of Paris in August 1944. And in *The Thief's Journal,* he writes about his time in Spain (late in 1933 in real life) and his great, year-long hegira on foot from Italy to Albania, Yugoslavia, Czechoslovakia, Germany, Holland and Belgium (which actually occurred in 1936 and 1937). He is careful not to mention his years as a soldier (too normal, not glamorous enough), to make his short stay in Spain sound like a long one and to leave out all mention of his voluminous reading, literary correspondence and friendships with cultivated people.

By the time Genet finished *The Thief's Journal,* his last novel, he had exhausted all his colorful autobiographical material as a beggar, thief and prostitute and worked his way up dangerously close in time to his current celebrity as a Parisian artistic figure—a figure not at all in keeping with the "Golden Legend" he had forged for himself.

The only novel that does not fit into this series is *Querelle,* although Lieutenant Seblon's journal, contained within the novel, seems to echo many of Genet's thoughts. Genet does not figure as a first-person narrator or character under his own name, however. *Querelle* is apparently a wholly invented, made-up novel. Genet had been briefly imprisoned in the French seaport of Brest, where the action takes place, and the city's past as a place from which galley ships manned by prisoners had sailed certainly intrigued him. The decisive moment in Genet's erotic history had surely been Mettray; all the rest of his life he sought out in life and in art an all-male, hierarchical, military-style community in which male heterosexuals, being deprived of female company, are forced to have sex with one another. Their sex also serves as a game of domination and submission. The army, the navy, North Africa, the French penal colony on Devil's Island, the world of penniless male prostitutes—these were just some of the populations or situations that fired Genet's erotic fantasies about virile, occasionally sado-masochistic homosexuality. *Querelle* is an elaborate staging of these fantasies.

The Maids—which was first staged in Paris on April 19, 1947, but which had been conceived a few years earlier and had gone through several major rewrites—was Genet's decisive move away from homosexuality as a theme. As he said much later in an interview, he had decided to recast his personal concerns as a homosexual into other themes of oppression in his theater. In his plays, Genet treated the humiliation of family servants (*The Maids*), the splendors and miseries of whores (*The Balcony*) as well as the smoldering rage of colonized black Africans (*The Blacks*) and Arabs (*The Screens*). In a screenplay written in this period (*The Penal Colony*), which was never produced or published, he dealt with prison life on Devil's Island.

A seven-year period, from 1948 to 1955, elapsed between the time Genet composed his novels and the time he began to write his three full-length plays (*The Balcony, The Blacks, The Screens*). During this period, he was plunged into a nearly suicidal depression. He later blamed this depression on Sartre's *Saint Genet,* but it had been published in 1952, a good four years after the depression and creative sterility had begun. What actually triggered Genet's despair was, paradoxically, a presidential pardon that he had received. In July 1948, some of the most distinguished artistic names in Paris, everyone from Picasso to Paul Claudel, had signed a petition drafted by Jean-Paul Sartre and Jean Cocteau to the president of France, asking him to pardon Genet from the sentence that was hanging over his head with the threat of life imprisonment. A year later, on August 12, 1949, the president issued a pardon. Now Genet could no longer picture himself as an outcast and criminal; he had to recognize that, magically, through the power of his pen, he had beaten the system. Nothing is so depressing as success.

His fiction had been founded on his feeling of being singular, marginal and in an adversarial relationship with his intimidated middle-class reader. Now this particular formulation could no longer work, and Genet was plunged into a nearly vegetable-like state during which he found it difficult to shave, eat or even get out of bed.

The end of this gloomy period came when Genet made two discoveries. He met the sculptor Alberto Giacometti, and by 1955 the two men had become inseparable. Genet wrote a brilliant essay about Giacometti, a man above or beyond all vanity, who lived for his work and accepted his common humanity. Giacometti provided Genet with an image of how to grow old if not gracefully at least fiercely and with integrity. This encounter was seconded by a nearly mystical experience Genet had in a train, when he was seated opposite a repellent little man. Genet felt in a literal sense an exchange of souls back and forth between himself and this miscrable specimen—and this exchange revealed to him that he, Genet, was not a singular, extraordinary being but in fact someone much like everyone else. This realization in turn directed Genet towards the theater. Whereas fiction can induct a reader into the strange mental world of an eccentric writer, the theater reports dialogue and displays actions, devoid of all commentary, before an audience acutely aware of itself as a group. Theater is a social form of art and depends on a social conception of the individual.

In 1955, the year Genet became very friendly with Giacometti, he wrote a first draft of *The Balcony,* began *The Blacks,* tossed off a one-act play called *Elle* and worked on *The Penal Colony.* It was also the year in which he met Abdallah, a young circus performer whom Genet trained as a high-wire artist and who became his lover. Genet's essay "The High-Wire Artist" indirectly compares the aerial acrobat to the writer. Both are engaged in a performance art that involves great risk.

Genet pushed his lovers to dangerous limits and beyond. Abdallah fell twice from the high wire, drifted into depression and inactivity and finally committed suicide in the spring of 1964. This date marks the beginning of Genet's second long silence. Overcome with remorse, Genet swore he would never write again and literally refused to hold a pen in his hand. Curiously enough, during this period of personal grief, his plays were enjoying a growing international fame. A national scandal was created by the French premiere in 1966 of *The Screens.* Presented in a state-subsidized theater not long after the Algerian War, *The Screens* infuriated French soldiers who had fought to retain the colony and had lost. They disrupted performances by leaping on stage, setting off smoke bombs and interrupting the action, although not a single performance was cancelled during the run.

Genet's theatrical writing was not only scandalous, it was also genuinely revolutionary in an artistic sense. The Theater of Ritual, which became an artistic rallying cry in avant-garde performance-art circles in the United States during the 1960s, was virtually invented by Genet. *The Maids,* the opening scenes of *The Balcony* and the entire action of *The Blacks* are elaborate rituals designed to accomplish an act—a murder, the identification of a private individual with a public role, the exorcism of race hatred. Genet's plays are not didactic or even politically committed; they do not suggest a revolutionary program or a progressive course of action, and Sartre disliked them precisely because they were not sufficiently *engagé.* They do, however, manage to isolate inflammatory topics, and they have been used by oppressed people for political purposes. For instance, when *The Blacks* was performed in the United States in the early 1960s, its cold fury served to remind audiences that the civil rights era had only tapped, not expressed, the rage of black Americans.

Genet was as drawn to the cinema as he was to the theater but with fewer visible results. In 1950 he directed a twenty-minute black-and-white silent film, *A Song of Love,* using amateur actors and professional technicians. The result was a homosexual erotic film of great poetic beauty about prison life. One of the most memorable images is of two men in adjoining cells who exchange cigarette smoke through a straw inserted into a hole in the wall that separates them.

During the next thirty-five years Genet was to write several long film scripts, including *Forbidden Dreams* (on which Tony Richardson's *Mademoiselle* was based), *The Penal Colony, The Language of the Wall* (about Mettray) and *Nightfall,* a fiction film about the single day an Arab immigrant spends in Paris. None of these scripts, except the one for *Mademoiselle,* was produced, usually because Genet himself got cold feet shortly before they were to be shot and pulled out of the deal. Nevertheless, thoughts about film shaped all of Genet's writing.

In the last sixteen years of his life, from 1970 to 1986, Genet, the eternal phoenix, emerged from silence and depression to take up the causes of the Black Panthers and the Palestinians. He traveled extensively throughout the United States during the first half of 1970 to speak on behalf of the Panthers, and he subsequently spent long months living among the Palestinians in Jordanian camps. But except for occasional manifestos and interviews on behalf of his twin causes, Genet wrote nothing—certainly nothing long and ambitious. He traveled all over the world—Japan, North and South America, Morocco, Greece, England, Germany, Jordan, Syria and Lebanon—but he was afraid he would never be able to write the book he had promised to write for the Panthers and the Palestinians. Then in 1979 he learned he had throat cancer, and he became more than ever aware his time was running out. (Time is something, he had declared, in a television interview, that is "sacred" and must not be wasted.)

What finally triggered his last great creative flowering was a visit he made in September 1982 to Beirut. There he witnessed the appalling results of a massacre of Palestinian civilians in the camps of Shatila and Sabra; Genet was the first European to observe the hundreds of brutally slaughtered bodies. He broke his literary silence and wrote an essay, "Four Hours at Shatila," which was so powerful that he knew he could write a book. In 1983 he began work on it; when he died during the night of April 14, 1986, he had just finished correcting the proofs. The book came out in May, a month after his death.

Like four of his five novels, it is written in the first person, it is based on his personal experiences and observations and it is cinematically composed through the use of montage. But in most other ways *Prisoner of Love* marks a real break with Genet's earlier prose. Whereas the novels throw golden dust in the bewitched eyes of the reader, in *Prisoner of Love* Genet addresses the reader simply, sincerely. No longer is Genet systematically reversing all normal human values; now he is writing about the normal virtues of courage, tenacity, loyalty—although he continues to insist on his own status as an outsider. He tells the reader that even if he, Genet, wants to support the Palestinian cause, he has never been wholly engaged all at once, body and mind.

Prisoner of Love is an old man's book: ruminative, not very sensuous, composed in an idiosyncratic shorthand and reduced to the main points. Now Genet is more concerned with communicating than dazzling, with convincing than intimidating. The highly metaphorical style of the novels, with its constant (and shockingly ambiguous) references to the church and the aristocracy, is abandoned in favor of a conversational, repetitious style reminiscent of Céline's and built up out of little touches. The references are to anything and everything, including Mozart's *Requiem*, sex-change operations and Japanese Shinto ceremonies for the dead.

The book testifies to Genet's genuine devotion to the Palestinians and the Black Panthers, two causes that long seemed dangerous or at least quixotic to many Europeans. Genet was frank about his erotic fascination with the young black and Arab militants, but he didn't actually have relations with members of either group; in any event his sexual interest accompanied, rather than preceded, his political commitment. No, what attracted Genet was that both groups were *lost* causes, nations without a land, Davids fighting Goliaths. The Goliath in both cases was the United States, according to Genet; he ranked the enemies of the Palestinians as, first, the United States; second, the other Arab states; and only finally Israel. Genet averred that the day the Palestinians regained their lost land he would lose interest in them.

Genet was buried in Larache, a town in northern Morocco, within sight of the house of his last lover, Mohammed El Katrani. Since he was not Muslim he had to be interred in a long-since-abandoned Spanish cemetery. The grave, appropriately enough, is on a hill above the sea and close to the local prison and whorehouse. The grave diggers, Muslims themselves, unthinkingly oriented the tomb towards Mecca. When a sightseer stole the original, chiseled plaque, someone very close to Genet rewrote the inscription in black paint on the headstone. Since that person, Jacky Maglia, had been brought up by Genet, his handwriting was almost identical to Genet's. The result is that Genet seems to have signed his own grave.

This final statement—Muslim and Christian, Arab and European, sacred and profane, public and solipsistic—is consistent with Genet's contradictory and idiosyncratic enterprise. No other writer has been at once so moralistic and so immoral, so estranged from popular, middle-class wisdom yet so uncompromising in enforcing his personal code, so harsh in rejecting the good son who has stayed at home and so loving of the broken body of the prodigal.

Michel Foucault

ICHEL FOUCAULT, FRANCE'S MOST RENOWNED philosopher to emerge in the 1960s and the man who dominated French thought in the years that followed, died of AIDS on June 25, 1984, in Paris. He was only fifty-eight years old, but he left behind a large body of work that changed people's way of looking at madness, punishment, power, sexuality and government. When he died, he went out like a Roman emperor in full triumph. The second and third volume of his *History of Sexuality* had appeared to front-page reviews and almost universal acclaim just a few days before he died. The fourth and final volume has not yet been published.

Before his death (immediately afterwards such remarks would have sounded indecent and disrespectful), people were saying that the second volume, *L'Usage des plaisirs (The Use of Pleasure)*, would be the beach book of the summer. Not because it was trivial but because it was gripping and unexpectedly lucid. I certainly read it all summer on the beach in Crete. It was especially appealing to read a study of the sexual ethics of classical Greece by day while by night I was trying to piece together the complex nuances of the same "discourse" in contemporary Greece. Foucault's observations were surprisingly pertinent.

The first volume of the *History of Sexuality* dealt with Victorian morality, which Foucault, in a typical paradox, thinks did not suppress thoughts of sex but rather made them ubiquitous and an obsessive subject for scientific inquiry and religious, medical and judicial manipulation. Even the word *sexuality* was a nineteenth-century coinage. By studying sexuality, the Victorians created it.

The typical educated person living today in Europe or America thinks of his or her own "sexuality" as the deepest secret of his or her individuality, one that must be coaxed out of hiding through art or psychoanalysis or jogging or...sex. We all identify with our sexual nature. We feel it's a real thing, *the* real thing, our essence, and we feel we must discover it not only in ourselves but in our partners.

This view, which reached its most systematic expression in Freud, is really only the culmination of a very old Christian view, according to Foucault, in which desire is considered to be the truth about our being, whether we are in a state of nature or fallen from grace. Tracing the ways in which several already existing classical traditions were brought together into the Christian ethic is the task of the fourth and final (and not yet published) volume of the series, *Les Aveux de la chair.*

The Greeks had an entirely different way of regarding sexual ethics, as Foucault has demonstrated in *The Use of Pleasure,* and these differences have long been quite clear on the level of details. For instance, the early Christians believed that monogamy applied to both husband and wife, whereas the pagans insisted on only the wife's fidelity. The Christians forbade all sex outside marriage but especially condemned homosexuality, whereas the Greeks expected adult men to have extramarital sexual relations both with women and with adolescent young men.

But such details do not reveal the radically different way the Greeks had of conceptualizing sexual and amorous behavior. Whereas the Christians worked out a code of rules that applied to everyone at all times, the pagans made only philosophical suggestions and reflections on the problematical areas of sexual morality. The Greeks worked out a situational ethics of moderation, whereas the Christians devised an absolutist law of austerity. For the Greeks, desire was a natural force—if sometimes an excessive one that had to be held in check. For the Christians desire was temptation, the work of the devil, and a surrender to temptation was a reenactment of the Fall. For the Christians the result of a chaste and good life was salvation; for the Greeks the result of temperance was an exemplary life, a model of esthetic value that other people could admire and emulate. For the Greeks, learning to govern oneself was a prerequisite to ruling others.

Although Foucault shies away from drawing "lessons for today" from his analysis, nevertheless this reader, at least, was struck by his book's suggestiveness. During the 1960s and 1970s many "liberated" people went far towards scrapping conventional Christian sexual morality with its emphasis on sin and guilt and its aversion to pleasure. But the rejection of such constraints often led to problems of another sort—an extreme preoccupation with sex and a corresponding inability to integrate sexuality into a satisfying existence.

At this point, the example of the Greeks becomes useful. They did not work out a single punitive sexual law applicable to everyone; they were concerned with devising a gentler art of conduct that looked at the needs of individuals and recognized that these needs vary according to age, health, status, time of the year and so on. Thirst and hunger are natural appetites, but if overindulged they can lead to drunkenness and obesity. Similarly the sexual appetite is natural, but if given free rein it can distort the proper dynamics of the self. Just as a sane diet is the way to manage hunger, so a satisfactory sexual regimen is the way to govern desire.

The purpose of such restraint is not saintly asceticism or the mortification of the flesh but rational, admirable conduct. As Foucault puts it in his conclusion: "Now, the demand for austerity...is not presented as a universal law to which each and every person must submit, but rather as a principle of stylization of conduct for those who wish to give to their existence the most beautiful and finished form possible." Until now many people have felt that the only logical alternative to Christian morality was sexual license; the Greeks, as interpreted by Foucault, suggest that a standard of beauty can also determine decorum.

The convention of paraphrasing a book's contents in the eternal present ("Foucault thinks...Foucault argues...Foucault believes") is particularly poignant after the death of a writer who was also a friend; at the same time, the convention also points towards the immortality that I suspect Foucault will enjoy. I first met him in 1980 in New York when I was a fellow of the New York Institute for the Humanities, which invited him to conduct a seminar at New York University. Although the conference room in the university library was small and the number of seminarists was supposed to be restricted, an intense, excited and polite mob gate-crashed. Many people stood for hours while Foucault presented his thoughts in his clear, precise, rather deliberate English.

Of the few great people I've met, he was the most modest. During his last spring, for instance, although he was already very ill, he gave a large buffet dinner party in Paris for William Burroughs, and Foucault passed every dish and drink to every guest with his own hands. Despite his crushing work schedule, he served as a tireless and attentive adviser on many Ph.D. dissertations in the United States. In Paris, he taught at the Collège de France, where he was the reigning thinker, but he scrupulously refused to take on the role of guru. In private life, his influences over his circle of young friends (who include some of the most gifted writers in France) was subtle, indirect, but radiant. Like a modern Socrates, he brought out what was best in other people; he never imposed his ideas on anyone. His life was exemplary.

His personal modesty and courtesy, however, did not mitigate the ferocity with which he attacked hypocrisy and falsehood and defended the truth. His burning silences, his insistence on precision, his sharp eye for inconsistencies, his permanent scepticism, the precise definition he gave to abstract terms—all of these skills and reflexes lent his thought its rigor. But he was also flexible (another aspect of his modesty). For instance, he had originally planned his *History of Sexuality* as an examination of the relationship between political and societal power and sex. But after he had published the first volume, he rethought his assumptions. The final three volumes focus on the "techniques" by which "individuals have been led to pay attention to themselves, to decode themselves, to recognize and acknowledge themselves as subjects of desire." These "techniques of the self" tell us more about the historical development of sexuality, Foucault argues, than does his original analysis based on power and the metaphor of war and struggle.

Unlike the structuralists, Foucault recognized that social systems are not perfect, self-contained mechanisms that exist outside of time but are instead inflected by history and change in an unpredictable and sometimes chaotic way. Thus, despite the real differences between the pagan thinkers and the early Church Fathers, he argues that there are no themes in Christianity which did not already exist in Greek and Roman philosophy:

the change which occurs is simply one of accent, of emphasis, of (to use Foucault's word) "problematization." The Christians made problems out of ethical questions which had not preoccupied the Greeks; conversely, the Greeks had problematized sexual questions (for instance, the sexual relations between adult men and adolescent boys) which ceased to exist for the Christians.

Unlike the Marxists, Foucault did not see power as a conspiracy or as a class prerogative but as a universal (and often pleasurable) feature of human society which functions in even the most minute, "capillary" interactions (whenever two people meet, power is exercised). Unlike most philosophers in the English-speaking world, Foucault was not content to confine his attentions to a few niggling questions of language use and definition. He was far more a philosopher in the tradition of Nietzsche—bold, polemical, sometimes coquettish and hard to follow, always international and historical in his erudition and point of view. And like Nietzsche, Foucault was always using history, linguistics, anthropology and every other social science to take another look at our (and his own) preconceptions—as well as the preconceptions of social science itself.

In his earlier books, he was often obscure; typically, in his modest way, he once told me he'd been obscure only because he hadn't known how to be clearer. His teaching at Berkeley and Toronto, his lectures at Princeton and elsewhere in North America and his discussions with such devoted and methodologically acute scholars as Hubert Dreyfus and Paul Rabinow at Berkeley may have helped him to clarify his thoughts and their expression. Certainly in the *History of Sexuality* he arrived at a limpid style almost unparalleled in contemporary French. This clarity, however, did not suppress a queer, poetic turn of phrase that always marked his writing. For instance, in *L'Usage des plaisirs,* he writes: "Travel makes things young and the relationship with oneself old"—an observation that no one else could have come up with.

Alain Robbe-Grillet

WHEN I FIRST BECAME AWARE OF Robbe-Grillet in 1962 it was through the film *Last Year at Marienbad*. I was twenty-two and about to graduate from the University of Michigan and I saw the movie with a quizzical English professor, who was troubled because he was unable to identify the "central theme." I had been so over-whelmed by the atmosphere of the film that I looked at Dr. Blake in astonishment as we left the cinema. The theme?

I was profoundly under the spell of so much controlled, elegant passion—the long corridors, the formal gardens, the beautiful gowns, the doubts about the reality of the past, the restless, traveling camera, the obsessive repetition of "Laissez-moi, laissez-moi tranquille!" I felt ashamed because it had not occurred to me to probe the film as an enigma intended to be explored. Perhaps because I had grown up surrounded by abstract expressionist painters I had always thought the search for meaning was vulgar; much later I realized that I was for that very reason an unsatisfactory reader of Robbe-Grillet, who counted on his audience's urge to solve puzzles, even though he did not always make them solvable: there was a good reason he'd declared he was the natural descendant of Kafka.

There were other strange aspects of the film. We Americans were already so used to coffee-cup realism that we laughed at anything stylized, as if it were a mistake, and *Marienbad* was certainly artificial—Delphine

Seyrig was required to hold one arm extended in a very particular gesture. Often she and the leading man, Giorgio Albertazzi, spoke while looking out in the same direction rather than regarding one another. The off-screen narrator sometimes described things that were happening on-screen but more often than not they were events that would happen later or had already happened. Words and images appeared to be on out-of-sync Möbius strips. Black and white were fully exploited in this black-and-white film (night and day, white plumes and black plumes, black or white versions of the same room). Tiny glimpses of a white bedroom were allowed to flash on the dark screen as intimations of disaster. There were plenty of other such hints, including the horrible and primitive counting game that Seyrig's husband, Pitoëff, always wins, the formal but lethal target practice and the shocking moment when she drops a glass that shatters on the floor in front of the other guests at the spa.

For a young American in the 1960s, that most self-consciously youthful of decades, and especially for an American who was routinely radical, there were other striking aspects to the movie. For instance, the characters weren't young, at least not Hollywood-young. The Italian leading man (how bizarre to have this most French of all French texts recited with an Italian accent!) was in his thirties, perhaps. The men, in any event, neutralized or rather standardized by evening clothes, were indifferently in their thirties, forties or fifties, but all urbanely slender, clean-shaven, neatly coiffed and largely interchangeable. The women, despite their couture gowns and jewels, were similarly featureless. This was clearly the opposite of a Fellini film with its grotesque, memorable muzzles.

Nor did the characters have an earlier or peripheral life that was always being remembered or alluded to, as in a Bergman film. As Robbe-Grillet himself has written in the introduction to the published form of his (slightly different) scenario: "What do they do when they are elsewhere? One would be tempted to respond: nothing! They don't exist anywhere else."

If an American film of the '60s had shown so many bored, rich idlers at a spa it would have been to satirize them. We were used to the easy, pointed farce of the arrogant rich at the opera, but when it came to "serious" cinema we expected deep, psychological dramas to take place in spare Swedish rooms, ringing with silence and nearly empty of furniture, just as the women's Protestant faces were scrubbed clean of make-up. But here were these stylish mannequins, these expressionless *figurantes*, devoid of personal expression though moving about, perhaps, as pawns in some strange game devised by Resnais and Robbe-Grillet. The look of rebellion and artistic experiment in America was shaggy and tie-dyed, the bodies half-starved, not coiffed and costumed.

Later in the '60s I read *Jealousy,* which for me confirmed Robbe-Grillet's reputation as a cool, even cold avant-garde novelist, one who headed that most Gallic of all things, a "school." In America we had isolated experimental writers—John Barth, Donald Barthelme, Thomas Pynchon—but Barth's best-known experiment, *The Sot-Weed Factor,* had been an act of mimicry, the re-creation of an English eighteenth-century novel, whereas Barthelme had worked out a Rube Goldberg sort of prose that produced brilliant non-sequiturs, played freely over the whole keyboard of a cultured mind—and even reworked classic fairy tales (something Robert Coover also did). Pynchon, clearly the giant of the group, wrote with *Gravity's Rainbow* a home-made masterpiece in the line of *Moby-Dick* that, like Melville's book, mixed in technical information with apocalyptic visions and that, like Joyce's *Ulysses,* proceeded through pastiche and collage. Pastiche—whether of early English novels, of fairy tales or (in *Gravity's Rainbow*) of Hitler's prose; Rilke; English World War II fiction; comic strips; and bawdy songs—was obviously important to post-modernist American writing.

Jealousy, at first, seemed to owe nothing to anyone. Later Robbe-Grillet himself pointed out his affinities with the authors of mysteries and crime stories as well as with Raymond Roussel and Kafka, and indeed the controlled, sinister atmosphere as well as the stripped-down prose sounded like Raymond Chandler just as the obsessive objectivity, the pleasure of describing things with maniacal detail, sounded like Raymond Roussel. And the complete absence of metaphors and the plain prose did, upon reflection, remind the reader of the Kafka of *The Castle.*

At first glance, however, I felt I'd never read anything quite like *Jealousy,* with its out-of-sequence narrative repetitions (reminiscent of *Marienbad*), its absence of a chronology, its frequent use of the present tense, its prolonged, virtually scientific descriptions of banana trees, its lack of psychological analysis or interpretation. In fact, it was only on second reading that I finally understood that there was a nearly invisible narrator at the heart of the book, one who never says "I."

To be sure, there was another, competing French school of avant-garde writing, Oulipo, and there were certain similarities between them. Both tried to go beyond the habits of traditional fiction writing by setting up constraints and by imposing new rules on themselves. But the Oulipo writers (especially Calvino, Harry Mathews, Perec and Queneau) had a playful, even wildly comic tone at odds with the suave seriousness of the Nouveaux romanciers.

In 1965 I read the English translation of Robbe-Grillet's *For a New Novel* and I found myself irritated and challenged by its daring ideas and authoritative tone. In this collection of short, declarative essays Robbe-Grillet argued that in a world without God and without a human essence (a world that was no longer anthropocentric), things could no longer be interpreted as reflections of the human spirit. In this future universe of the novel, gestures and objects will be there before being something, he argued; with one stroke he established *chosisme* and *l'école du regard*. As part of his battle against signification and interpretation, Robbe-Grillet also made a tough, sardonic attack on anthropomorphic metaphors and the human-centered metaphysical system lurking behind them. The other day I read excerpts from these essays to my students at Princeton, who still found them stimulating, not to say maddening.

Perhaps at the time what struck me the most was how a genuine impression of newness could be brought about by really very slight modifications of fictional conventions. Banishing anthropomorphic metaphors and the cause-and-effect structure of the traditional plot doesn't seem all that revolutionary, any more than straightforward, objective descriptions of objects seem extraordinarily innovative, but the effect of these few changes was dramatic indeed. I began to think that I could achieve unusual effects by manipulating the basic parameters of the novel—which I did in *Forgetting Elena,* my first novel, written in the late '60s but published only in 1973. In that book I wrote in the present tense from the point of view of an amnesiac who is constructing himself and who attempts to convince the people around him that he remembers and understands everything. Like Robbe-Grillet I was influenced by Kafka and the tone of mystery novels. And I was inspired by Robbe-Grillet's own daring and rigorous example.

About 1971 I met Robbe-Grillet himself through his American translator, Richard Howard, and Tom Bishop, then the director of the French

Department at New York University. I was working for a middle-brow literary magazine, the *Saturday Review*. I couldn't speak to the great French writer in his own language at that time and he seemed to possess no English (perhaps, like a statesman, he preferred to pretend he needed interpreters in order to give himself time to reflect on his answers). I was struck by his youthful vigor and full head of hair, genial manner and general openness to the people around him. He was exploring 42nd Street, which was much more louche then than now, and he had lots to say about American attitudes towards pornography. In a moment of grandiosity I offered to get him a commission from *Saturday Review* to write about the subject, but the project was doomed from the start. The publication and the subject were a highly unlikely marriage. By now Robbe-Grillet and the *nouveau roman* had become a scholarly industry in the United States. As early as 1959 *Yale French Studies* had dedicated an issue to what they called "Midnight Novelists" with articles by Bernard Dort and Germaine Brée on Robbe-Grillet and the essays of other writers on Butor, Duras, Simon and Beckett. By 1973 there existed a book in English titled *Alain Robbe-Grillet: An Annotated Bibliography of Critical Studies, 1953–1972*, containing hundreds of items in several languages.

Even as Robbe-Grillet himself was moving on to other challenges, including films he was directing, the critical establishment in America and England was concentrating on a massive study of his first five novels. Even a non-academic American reader like me was aware of the debate over *Jealousy*. Was it truly an objective novel in which things predominated and human actions took on no more importance than the death of a centipede or the arrangement of banana trees—or was it, as Bruce Morrissette had claimed, despite all appearances a "bourgeois" novel about extramarital love narrated by a jealous husband?

Some French editors and novelists were even grumbling that the major push on the part of French departments in American universities, led by New York University, to sell the New Novel to the American public had been a dismal failure—and had destroyed the audience in the States for contemporary French fiction. Perhaps Camus had been the last "serious" French novelist to enjoy an enduring American success, just as Françoise Sagan had been the last "popular" novelist to become even an ephemeral bestseller. Could it be that Robbe-Grillet had put off American readers? Certainly his later erotic books, his autobiographical works, his collaborations with painters—indeed all his texts after *For a Revolution in New York*—have received less attention in America than his first novels.

Eventually I moved to Paris in 1983 and learned French. One night I watched a television program during which Jean de Berg, the author of the scandalous but elegant sadomasochistic novel *L'Image,* spoke about her literary and sexual practices. I was watching with a Parisian friend who said that "everyone" knew that the woman on screen wearing a half-veil was really Catherine Robbe-Grillet. Her novel, *The Image,* had been published in America by Grove Press in the wake of the success of Pauline Réage's *The Story of O.* Indeed the book was dedicated to Pauline Réage, who had signed the introduction as well (although some rumors had it that Robbe-Grillet himself had written the introduction and that after objections from the real Pauline Réage—the pen-name of Dominique Aury—he'd published it under just the initials P. R.).

As an American I felt excited and intimidated by these chilling, metaphysical and always refined ventures into violence penned by women. In America feminist theorists had coached men into believing that violence was something fantasized about and performed by men alone. Yet these detailed and sustained accounts in French suggested another reality altogether. And if Madame Robbe-Grillet was a sadist, what did that make her husband? Ah, I thought, remembering the title of one of his early masterpieces: *The Voyeur.*

Years went by. I wrote a biography of Jean Genet and conducted much of my research in Paris at IMEC (Institut mémoire de l'édition contemporaine). I'd heard that Robbe-Grillet had withdrawn his archives from the Bibliothèque National and conferred them on IMEC, especially after IMEC agreed to build a greenhouse to protect the writer's beloved cactuses. The cactuses and the papers were to be stored at IMEC's new center in the restored monastery of Ardennes outside Caen, not too far from the small chateau where Robbe-Grillet and Catherine lived and worked.

And then a year ago I met Catherine in New York and saw Alain again. We had all come together for a conference on Barthes who, after all, had written an important early essay on Robbe-Grillet. I was especially eager to see Catherine. In a vague way I was a bit like Mme Sazerat in Proust who wants to catch a glimpse in Venice of Mme de Villeparisis, the famous vamp who had ruined her father and reduced her family to poverty. Mme Sazerat is appalled when she sees a little old grandmother instead of the famous beauty she'd imagined, and I was astonished by Mme Robbe-Grillet's tiny size and great age, though she was still suitably beautiful and authoritative.

In 2002 at age eighty Robbe-Grillet published two new books, his first novel in years (*La Reprise*) and a collection of his selected interviews. From our perspective today his early novels appear severe but unassailably canonical. They are far from our cynical post-modern notion of art as entertainment. They are not amusing costume jewelry but big, glittering diamonds. After all, that least trendy or biddable of critics, Vladimir Nabokov, put *Jealousy* on his extremely short list of twentieth-century masterpieces. Perhaps he was attracted to its narrator who, like so many of his own, feels things so intensely he's become deranged.

Certainly the launching of the Nouveau Roman in the '50s and early '60s was the last internationally recognized avant-garde movement. An avant-garde movement cannot be simply an innovation; it must claim, as Robbe-Grillet argued in *For a New Novel,* that it will "inevitably" replace all other fiction, which is no longer suitable to our times and which has become hopelessly démodé.

Not long ago Robbe-Grillet said in an interview that the period of the New Novel was the same one during which people still believed in the revolution. "All that had an effect on literary life, of course, in which the debates were far more capacious than they are today, but also a direct effect on literature itself." Although Robbe-Grillet has always been more an anarchist than a man of the left, nevertheless he's perfectly right that if now we live in the aftermath of the idea of the avant-garde, our sense of "lateness" is partly due to our post-utopian politics.

James Merrill

ERRILL WAS FAR FROM ANYONE'S RECEIVED IDEA of a poet. He wasn't poor—in fact, he was very rich, the son of Charles Merrill, founder of the biggest Wall Street brokerage firm, Merrill Lynch. He wasn't tormented—at least he didn't have mental breakdowns or attempt suicide. He drank a lot but not famously and he eventually joined A.A. without becoming sanctimonious or losing his talent; some of his best poems were written in sobriety. He wasn't primarily a lyrical poet who burned out early; no, he was a strange blend of elements that weren't perfectly synthesized until he was well into his thirties. He wasn't experimental, at least not in the beguiling fashion of the far better known John Ashbery, who combines the exaltation of Wallace Stevens with the shrugging insouciance of Frank O'Hara in order to come up with something as expressive and as inscrutable as Reverdy's poems. If Merrill was experimental, then it was in the way Bach played with harmonics and textual interpretation in a late cantata such as "Ich glaube, lieber Herr, hilf meinem Unglauben!"—that is, through daring variations on forms considered even then long since outmoded (Merrill, for instance is the modern master of the sonnet, but his sonnets are often buried in what reads like a simple, flowing narrative—"Matinées" is a good example of narrative sonnets).

Merrill signed few books and gave even fewer interviews; the interviews, moreover, are as stagey as Nabokov's, and just as teasing and infuriating. He spoke in an accent of his own devising, a blend of his mother's Tidewater drawl and an ancient Northeast boarding school dialect; depending on the listener's predisposition, during his readings Merrill would sound either affected and bratty or elevated, even Orphic, especially when he was speaking of or for the dead. Although he was one of the most philosophical poets, someone who devised a system as complex (and, alas, as demanding) as Dante's, he could seem irritatingly frivolous, irresponsible, self-regarding in his off-the-cuff remarks. And what a cuff!, one is tempted to add, all stiff with brocade. Early on the poet and critic Richard Howard stigmatized him as a bejeweled poet, and that characterization stuck, though it suited only his earliest work.

In that way, as in so many others, Merrill was like Proust. Just as no one, after reading *Les plaisirs et les jours* or Proust's society portraits in the *Figaro,* would have predicted the depth and delirium of *À la recherche du temps perdu,* in the same way no one would have expected much more than brilliance from the author of "The Black Swan" (1946), the first poem reprinted in *Selected Poems:*

> Black on flat water past the jonquil lawns
> > Riding, the black swan draws
> A private chaos warbling in its wake,
> Assuming, like a fourth dimension, splendor
> That calls the child with white ideas of swans
> > Nearer to that green lake
> Where every paradox means wonder.

The Mallarmean subject, though more accessible than in "Le vierge, le vivace et le bel aujourd'hui," is every bit as immobilized; notice in the following lines Merrill's "always," the bell jar dropped over the paralyzed moment: "...Always/ The moment comes to gaze/ As the tall emblem pivots and rides out/ To the opposite side, always...."

By 1962, with the publication of *Water Street,* Merrill had hit his stride. Now he could find perfection, or at least significant meaning, in the broken shards of daily experience. He no longer relied on "poetic props," on swans or the antique subject of Medusa or on the improprieties of a broken bit of faience. Now he could meditate on a casual subject thrown up by daily life ("Out for a walk, after a week in bed,/ I find them tearing up part of my block...") in a language by turns casual and humorously cultural ("An old man/ Laughs and curses in her brain,/ Bringing to mind the close of *The White Goddess*"). The sight of the collapsing building allows his thoughts to cross several stepping stones of memory until he has half-recalled a moment from his own past. He thinks of a "cheap engraving of garlands" crumpled up "to stanch/ Boughs dripping, whose white gestures filled a cab,/ And thought of neither then nor since./ Also, to clasp them, the small, red-nailed hand/ Of no one I can place. Wait. No. Her name, her features/ Lie toppled underneath that year's fashions...." The recollected memory comes back not all at once but in pieces. The hand is fitted in at the end of a strangely constructed line that the words following the line break instantly negate. The next two words ("Wait. No.") suggest a sudden recovery that the following line dissolves. The decision to reject Latinate subtleties for Anglo-Saxon certainties informs the last two paragraphs. The poet swallows a sedative prescribed for "much later":

> With the result that back into my imagination
> The city glides, like cities seen from the air,
> Mere smoke and sparkle to the passenger
> Having in mind another destination
>
> Which now is not that honey-slow descent
> Of the Champs-Elysées, her hand in his,
> But the dull need to make some kind of house
> Out of the life lived, out of the love spent.

I think it's fair enough to say that the contrast between the first six lines and the last two could not have been written without Wallace Stevens's "The tomb in Palestine/ Is not the porch of spirits lingering./ It is the grave of Jesus, where he lay."

What had happened to Merrill in the intervening years was his discovery of the theater ("Wait. No.") , for in that period he had written two plays, *The Bait* and *The Immortal Husband*. The relationship of poetry to theater is spelled out convincingly in the indispensable study, Stephen Yenser's *The Consuming Myth* (Harvard, 1987), to which I owe many of my thoughts about Merrill. As Merrill said in an interview, "In 'An Urban

Convalescence' I first hit upon this sense of the self-reflexive side of the poem—that you can break up the argument in a very fruitful way. This is probably something learned from working in the theater where you write a line and you can have someone else contradict it."

He also learned, perhaps through a deeper reading of Auden and Proust, that the world can be made to yield up its secrets if you just stare at it, any patch of it, long enough. He certainly broadened his notion of what poetry can do by writing two novels and reading many more; he is perhaps the only contemporary poet who owes as much to two novelists (Proust and Nabokov) as he does to his key poets (Auden, Bishop, Stevens, Mallarmé, Valéry, Rilke and Montale—Valéry and Montale, by the way, Merrill translated, and "Lost in Translation" is built around Rilke's translation of Valéry's "Palme"). If sometimes Merrill seems American only in his eclecticism, his ambition and his submission to an exalted, home-made religion, then this internationalism can be credited to (or at least reflected in) this list of novelists and poets, which includes only two bona fide Americans. I say "bona fide," but Bishop lived in Brazil and translated from the Portuguese, and Stevens, like Joseph Cornell, dreamed constantly of a "Europe" of the imagination neither, mercifully, ever had to test by actual travel.

Just as Proust (the subject of one of Merrill's poems) can make minor, neurotic childhood events render universal truths and can turn social notes into modern mythology, in the same way Merrill starts out with the least promising materials—acrostics, the ouija board, a picture puzzle, amateur theatricals, garden parties, house-moving—and constructs them into masterful, all-embracing compositions. As his friend and admirer the critic David Kalstone once put it, "Frivolity is always a form of invocation for JM, a preparation like the dancer's at the barre. I have glimpsed him through the half-open study door, after a morning of work, playing a game of patience, waiting for it all to cohere. He used to like those acrostic puzzles in which a phalanx of unrelated words, rearranged, fall into a quotation from great or not so great authors. And then there is the jigsaw puzzle of 'Lost in Translation' slowly massing into meaning." (Kalstone, by the way, is not only a character in Merrill's epic poem, "The Changing Light at Sandover," but also the subject or dedicatee of three splendid lyric poems, "Matinées," "Investiture at Cecconi's" and "Farewell Performance.")

Imagine if Cavalcanti had been crossed with Noël Coward, for Merrill slips easily from sibylline utterance into silkiest nonsense. After all he was the person who went to a literary festival on "regional poetry" in northern Minnesota and was hissed when he expressed his disdain of the local product. As he scurried out he whispered to Richard Howard, "You see, my dear, what happens when the Great Plains meet the great fancies...." Not that Merrill was usually stinting in his encouragement of lesser (or even equal) writers; as Allan Gurganus recalls, "Was anybody ever better company? Ready as he was to laugh, making James Merrill laugh pleased us like a good week's work. And oh to be thought talented and graceful by the one person alive who was most purely both!"

Nights and Days (1966) contains three of Merrill's most memorable poems: "The Thousand and Second Night," "The Broken Home" and "Days of 1964." Merrill had started going to Greece in about 1959 and soon bought a house in Athens where he lived every winter for years. Many of his poems in this book and in later collections owe to Greece their settings, their characters and their very un-American blend of refined sensuality and an apprehension of the divine inhabiting the human, of the god breathing through the mask of the everyday. "Days of 1964," with its title from Cavafy, is an invocation to an ungendered "you." As Merrill much later acknowledged, closeted gay poetry of the pre-Stonewall era owed a lot to the "you strategy," an evasiveness which doesn't work well in most other languages, in which the adjectives applied to this "you" must be either masculine or feminine. The sexual ambiguity in this poem, however, is appropriate to its overall slipperiness, for in it the narrator again and again sets up oppositions that he instantly cancels out ("With love, or laughter, or both" or earlier, speaking of the char, Kyria Kleo, "I think now she was love. She sighed and glistened/ All day with it, or pain, or both"). Although this poem, just two pages long, starts casually enough with tepid jokiness about the steep hill across the street that can be climbed "for some literally breathtaking views," its inherent ambiguity quickly builds towards the vertigo of the closing lines in which up and down, pain and love, human weaknesses and divine attributes are all confounded, in which the cleaning woman is allegorized as love and the narrator and the "you" are transformed into stand-ins for divinities, as though Cavafy himself had synthesized his anecdotes of modern homoerotic passion with his odes to ancient Greek heroes or Byzantine kings:

Where I hid my face, your touch, quick, merciful,
Blindfolded me. A god breathed from my lips.
If that was illusion, I wanted it to last long;
To dwell, for its daily pittance, with us there,
Cleaning and watering, sighing with love or pain.
I hoped it would climb when it needed to the heights

Even of degradation, as I for one
Seemed, those days, to be always climbing
Into a world of wild
Flowers, feasting, tears—or was I falling, legs
Buckling, heights, depths,
Into a pool of each night's rain?
But you were everywhere beside me, masked,
As who was not, in laughter, pain, and love.

In later volumes Merrill continued to explore the essentially humorous contrast between the dusty provincialism of modern Greece and the glory of its past. In "Verse for Urania," for instance, which appeared in his 1976 book, *Divine Comedies,* Merrill pokes gentle fun at the members of the Greek family who live downstairs from him in Connecticut; they've become the ultimate American consumers and the poet, who's just been named their baby girl's godfather, grumpily-good-naturedly complains about his unending responsibilities towards little Urania:

Music lessons from beyond the tomb,
Doll and dentist and dowry, the 3-D
Third television we attain so far
Exclusively in dreamland, where you are....

A list, of course, that owes something to *Lolita,* in which Humbert is told by the headmistress of Beardsley School for girls that "we stress the four D's: Dramatics, Dance, Debating and Dating."

But this light satire quickly gives way to metaphysics, a discourse (suggested by the child's name) on the first human beings and their astrology, a passage, however, which is never allowed to become too solemn:

Adamant nights in which our wisest apes
Met on a cracked mud terrace not yet Ur
And with presumption more than amateur
Stared the random starlight into shapes.

Here the strict meters and rhymes, the high table mixture of speculation and urbane humor (the rhyme Ur-amateur), the conversational flow
all make us think of Auden; it is a tribute to Auden's fertility and, above
all, usefulness, that he should have been the covering cherub to two such
different poets, Ashbery and Merrill, as well as to hundreds of others in
Britain and America.

The upstairs-downstairs theme of social difference, the climbing and
falling, the heights and depths of love, all first stated in "Days of 1964,"
are now refigured in "Verse for Urania" as a trope about birth and death,
about the newborn replacing her aging godfather. Again the concluding lines
synthesize these differences in a vision of balance appropriate, perhaps,
only to art:

It was late
And early. I had seen you through shut eyes.
Our bond was sacred, being secular:
In time embedded, it is in us, near, far,
Flooding both levels with the same sunrise.

Again the line (and stanza) breaks only emphasize the antinomies that
are being resolved and provide a strict form for elusive meanings.

This formula in lit. crit. jargon would be called "formal overdetermi-
nation, semantic underdetermination,"as though if only the votive candles
are arranged in the most rigid quincunx then the smoke they offer the gods
may float in the loosest arabesques. It was a contrast that Merrill admired
in poets ranging from Cavalcanti to Stevens; he himself explored it with
dazzling (and sometimes chilling) results.

Perhaps the most dazzling and chilling examples (still employing
Greek themes) are "Yannina" and "Samos." "Samos" uses a rhyme scheme
which would have strangled off a lesser poet's inventiveness, but which
Merrill masters so thoroughly that the reader at first fails to notice that the
poem, in Yenser's description, has "five stanzas of twelve pentameter lines

each, plus a coda of five lines; it also uses only five end words (and ingenious variants on them): 'water,' 'fire,' 'land,' 'light' (the angels' four elements) and 'sense' (which points to both the apprehension and the interpretation of these elements)."

"Yannina" again plays off the degraded present ("Look at those radiant young males./ Their morning-glory nature neon blue/ Wilts here on the provincial vine") against the noble past ("Where did it lead,/ The race, the radiance?"). But now the past and the present, the humorous and the exalted, the personal and the mythic are intercut with magical ease, the "scissoring and mending" of a moving barge on reflecting water. Ali Pasha, who was amorous of Byron but whom Byron considered a "father" is invoked, as are the Muslim woman who loved Ali and the Christian woman who resisted him and was drowned for her pains. Ali becomes an emblem for the poet's recently dead father, a much-married pasha of sorts whom JM loved with unusual devotion, just as the two women become two versions of the Feminine ("One virginal and tense, brief as a bubble,/ One flesh and bone—gone up no less in smoke....").

It seems now, in retrospect, that Merrill's mission was to find the noumenal in the phenomenal. His phenomena were often the people and events of his own life, transfigured. As early as in "The Broken Home" Merrill was reworking the story of his parents' divorce into allegory ("Father Time and Mother Earth,/ A marriage on the rocks"). This autobiography mythologized, so Proustian, became the great subject of his epic.

Merrill was a sort of Jungian but with this proviso, that the collective unconscious is language and that puns are the means by which we can tap its wisdom. And Merrill had both the magical inventiveness of Ariel and the even-handedness of Prospero. Of all languages English is the wittiest, since it not only permits but craves sudden shifts in tone, the downshifting from the hieratic into the demotic, and in English imps always dance attendance on Solemnity. Pomposity is anathema to the spirit of English; abstraction is not only numbing but difficult to sustain in English; poetic prose—or even poetic poetry—makes English-speakers giggle. Merrill knows how to defuse English irreverence, pin down his speculations with glinting details, dazzle the reader out of his suspicions. But if his work is always unpredictable, ironic and quick to take the piss out of itself, it is also the most sustained vision of beauty, goodness and immortality that we are likely to have.

He was my hero because he responded with insolent wit to the world's lethargy and tedium and with clear-eyed compassion to the suffering all around him. He was kind without ever losing his edge, tart without ever being cruel. His poetry was as funny as Byron's, as elusive and personal as Montale's, as magisterial as Wallace Stevens's, as intelligent as Pope's. He knew better than anyone else how to make a word skip across the surface of the mind and sink deep where it landed. Like Herbert he never wrote a bad line; in fact, I can't think of another poet's work that has such a high finish as well as such a density of thought. His tone may have been light and sociable, but his vision was universal, his intellect sovereign. Pedants can't grasp his wit, just as killjoys can't see past his frivolity to his deep humanity.

Even his ordinary conversation was always erupting into jokes and puns and seemed animated by the power of meter. Through the grapevine I heard that when he was on the phone with his friend Stephen Yenser for a last conversation he was so short of breath that he said, "I don't have the strength to speak in pentameter; I suppose I'll have to switch to dimeter." And he quoted ten lines in French—in perfect dimeter.

Christopher Isherwood

ONE DAY I WAS TALKING TO A FRIEND on the telephone and I kept saying, "Very good, very good," even though what he was telling me wasn't good at all. At last he got a bit angry and asked me what I meant. I realized I was impersonating Christopher Isherwood, who had exactly that comforting, tuck-in-the-children manner of saying, "Very good." I was impersonating him because I missed him. He had died not long before.

Christopher Isherwood, like the American poet James Merrill, was the eternal young man—jaunty, bright, the juvenile wielding the racket and never needing to ask, "Tennis, anyone?" since he knew that if he was asking it would surely be tennis everyone. If, by the time I met him, he was already up in his seventies, he wore all those years as though they were nothing more than a stiff neck and a rumpled blazer earned from passing out on someone's cold, dewy lawn after an endless garden party.

Not that he was frivolous or decorative in his manner. Unlike Merrill he was interested in politics, especially gay politics, and he was not a snob in any way. Nor did he like word games. And yet he liked being young. He worried about getting old. When his guru asked him if he wanted eternal youth, he had to admit guiltily that he did. But in his case I don't think the desire was the usual vanity: I think he didn't know how to approach other people except as the puer aeternus, as the youngest boy at the party. That was his role, and one he played beautifully.

At the same time he was the closest thing to a saint I've ever met, and if this image contrasts strangely with the image of the boyish partygoer, that's because it turns out a saint must start out somewhere and must present himself in some guise or other, and virtually any mask is preferable to that of the robed, pale holy man. As the Isherwood character says of the Gerald Heard character in *Down There on a Visit,* "I don't trust these sweet child-like little wide-eyed saints. Augustus is absolutely sophisticated and absolutely aware of the impression he makes. And that reassures me. He's humanly vain, and he's no fool, and at the same time he really believes."

Certainly as a writer, one of Isherwood's main problems—one could even say "technical problems" —was how to show saintliness in a secular world. That was the very subject of a little essay he once wrote, "The Problem of the Religious Novel." As he put it:

> How am I to prove that X is not merely insane when he turns his back on the whole scheme of pleasures, rewards, and satisfactions which are accepted by the Joneses, the Smiths, and the Browns, and goes in search of super-conscious, extra-phenomenal experience? The only way I can see how to do this is with the help of the Joneses themselves. I must show that the average men and women of this world are searching, however unconsciously, for that same fundamental reality of which X has already had a glimpse.

When Isherwood, not following his own advice, attempted to show saintliness full face, he wrote his worst book, *A Meeting by the River.* But *A Single Man,* his best book, succeeds so brilliantly because it portrays someone who suffers from the total absence of the spiritual element in his life. Isherwood once called this character a stoic "who bases his entire defence on sheer agnostic courage, without the support of religious belief."

George is a professor who appreciates the spiritual only in its secondary manifestations—in art, sex, romantic love, and friendship. Evidently he has a spiritual appetite, but it's never been awakened. A believer would say he's looked at the reflections of divinity but never contemplated God. But if George represents an absence, a void, the narrative itself is replete with religious awareness. The Buddha taught that one crucial step towards salvation, towards extinction, is the recognition that the self, this seeming unity, this apparent agent, is really nothing but a ragbag of unrelated elements. *A Single Man* begins with a passage that shows George awakening and reveals how his disparate systems blink on one by one to create the illusion of ego:

> Waking up begins with saying am and now, That which has awoken then lies for a while staring up at the ceiling and down into itself until it has recognized I, and therefrom deduced I am, I am now. Here comes next, and is at least negatively reassuring; because here, this morning, is where it had expected to find itself; what's called at home.

Similarly, the book ends with George's death, which is analyzed as the dispersal of functions that never had any good reason to cling together in the first place. The dissolution is described with scientific accuracy: "And, one by one, on the roughened surface of the smooth endothelium, ions of calcium, carried by the bloodstream begin to be deposited…"

The curious thing is that Isherwood, who should have seen individuals as nothing but automata, in fact clung to their singularity, their specificity. Luckily for him and for us, since he was a novelist; a superstitious faith in human uniqueness is a great help to any novelist. Typically, when certain other devotees worried that Swami Prabhavananda was becoming the object of a personality cult, Isherwood refused to be distressed by the phenomenon. As he put it, "I flatter myself that I can discriminate—bowing down to the Eternal which is sometimes manifest to me in Swami, yet feeling perfectly at ease with him, most of the time, on an ordinary human basis. My religion is almost entirely what I glimpse of Swami's spiritual experience."

An awareness of the universal in the particular is a comic awareness, one which richly imbued Isherwood's art and life. In the last section of *Down There on a Visit* he is fully alive to the humor of two attractive gay men living in Los Angeles trying to abstain from sex and to practice meditation. Recently I was reminded of this passage when a French friend of mine went with me on a shopping spree in Paris. This man was once a concert pianist, a dandy and, as they say, the darling of Paris society. Now he's a monk and he's about to become a hermit in a small house dependent on a convent in the foothills of the Pyrenees. My friend was in Paris to buy himself warm clothes for the hermitage, since the only heat in his cabin will come from a wood stove he will stoke every morning. Should he buy the lovely blue down vest, or was it too attractive? And should he prefer the ugly wool stockings to the flashing ones, as a sort of penance? He laughed—and this laughter over his predicament reminded me of the humor of Santa Monica.

I remember once calling Isherwood in Santa Monica from Key West, where I was spending part of the winter. At that time Key West was still a sleepy Southern town and I'd been ransacking the public library out of nearly wild boredom (James Merrill had lent me his library card). Finally I'd gotten down to Chateaubriand's *Memoirs from Beyond the Tomb,* a sweetly grave, musical book in which one man's life intersects history almost by accident. In places, I suppose, the prose can be a bit pompous, but I was so swept up by its melodramatic grandeur that when I read the closing pages, in which the aged Chateaubriand declares that, now that he's ready for death, he will slowly descend into the tomb, cross in hand, I burst into tears. I called Chris. (He loved telephone calls and was quite the chatty Kathy. Anything rather than write a letter. In fact, I think the only person he wrote to was his friend Edward Upward.) Over the phone, I read Chris the great solemn passage about descending into the tombeau. He whinnied and gasped with suppressed laughter, then let it out in a tremendous hemorrhage of hilarity.

I was offended, of course—until I thought that, well, Isherwood, like Auden, never could bear the French. And Isherwood, unlike Auden, had always despised Christian camp. And—by this time we had hung up— after all, Chris was closer to the usual grave-descending age than I and if he chose to find it all so damn funny, he surely had the right. Then I remembered the play he and Don Bachardy had written based on Chris's novel *A Meeting by the River.* In that play, the Hindu monks were always laughing and joking; as Yeats observed in his poem "Lapis Lazuli," "Old monks laugh and are gay, just as Hamlet and Lear are gay."

It must be a strange experience to pick the self apart through meditation and then, in that state of exalted disarray, to go about in the world, take tea, teach creative writing classes, grant interviews. Isherwood led his life down here on earth with roaring good humor. He was a splendid drinker, an expert talker and an even better listener, interested in everyone and everything. He'd answer each new person's old questions ("Who was the real Sally Bowles? The real director in *Prater Violet?*") with generosity, even zest, and with the good actor's gift for making a familiar line ring new. The gift lies in actively making it new, imagining it anew, and that was what Isherwood did. He was very likeable.

He was small and with age his neck had stiffened and his head had retracted into his body. His clothes were a combination of Cambridge tweedy and California casual. His eyebrows had grown very long and performed disconcerting leaps and swoops. He had a trick of listening with a petrified, illegible smile and then breaking into a response that was always unpredictable, somehow unrelated to the smile and uttered in his high, irritating, upper-class voice, complete with stammer. Or he quaked and exploded with laughter. He suffered from terrible back pains in his last years, but he always seemed very merry, surely a triumph of the will.

Don Bachardy and he had started out as one of the most shocking couples imaginable—Don a teenage Californian beach bunny and Isherwood the famous English author nearly fifty years old—but during the thirty-odd years they were together their personalities merged. Don is gray-haired, a distinguished artist, and he's picked up the same high-pitched voice and well-bred stammer. Neither Don nor Chris ever seemed the least bit jaded (though Isherwood's Hollywood journals sometimes do make him sound callous and disabused, but diaries usually distort the personality: we seldom record happy thoughts).

When Chris would get confused in his last years, Don wouldn't humiliate him by rescuing him. I remember a tight moment when Chris, after a third try, still couldn't remember the four drink orders he was supposed to be filling. But Don wouldn't help out and somehow the drinks got made. While we were standing around the kitchen, I noticed a photo of Chris and Joan Crawford and Don with Marilyn Monroe. "Yes," Chris said, "they were our dates. Miss Crawford was very professional. Her secretary sent me a note the next day saying how very sincerely she'd enjoyed the evening. She was like that—she ran a very tight ship."

Isherwood's saintliness, as you can see, was ironic. He was able to harpoon his own lapses into vanity, pique, smugness and hypocrisy. I'm suggesting his saintliness was an active, discriminating force that was the opposite of the softly glowing nimbus. His voice as a writer is pure and clear, as engaging as a gossip's but more charitable and much more nourishing.

Long before any other writer, Isherwood was openly campaigning for gay rights. *A Single Man,* published in 1964, five years before the

Stonewall Uprising, is still the most rounded, unembarrassed portrait of a gay man we have. And he was the first one to sketch out the gay sensibility and one of the first (along with Edwin Denby) to mention camp in print. As he wrote in *The World in the Evening*:

> You see, true High Camp always has an underlying seriousness. You can't camp about something you don't take seriously. You're not making fun of it; you're making fun out of it. You're expressing what's basically serious to you in terms of fun and artifice and elegance. Baroque art is largely camp about religion. The Ballet is camp about love.

And all this a decade before Susan Sontag's essay "Notes on Camp," in which she spoke of camp as an effort to rescue failed glamour.

There were many reasons Isherwood's gay spirit was more evolved than anyone else's. He'd always been a rebel—against the family, the Church of England, Cambridge, war. Then he provided a link with the first gay movement, the one led by Magnus Hirschfield and crushed by the Nazis. The Auden–Isherwood years in Berlin were between October 1928, when a twenty-one-year-old Auden arrived in the German capital, and early in 1933, when the Nazis came to power and Isherwood left the city and returned to England. This was a period which corresponded to the beginning of the international economic depression, to a pitched battle, often in the streets of Berlin, between Nazis and Communists, to a marked increase in the visibility of homosexuality in Berlin—and to an efflorescence of the arts, including painting, musical theater, literature and film. 1929, for instance, was the year of Marlene Dietrich's first film, *The Blue Angel*—the most expensive film made up to that point in Germany.

I have long contended—or rather, speculated— that if Isherwood was able to write with *A Single Man* in 1964 the first truly liberated gay novel in English, one which gives no etiology of the main character's homosexuality, which shows him as functioning normally or at least not miserably and in an integrated world of straight and gay friends—if Isherwood was able to make this leap forward in consciousness, we must attribute it to three things: his residence in a California beach community just after World War II, his class confidence and the liberal atmosphere of his circle during his Oxford years, and finally his contacts in the late '20s and early '30s with the first gay liberation movement in Berlin.

In *Christopher and His Kind* Isherwood wrote succinctly, "Berlin meant boys." And elsewhere he has said: "Wasn't Berlin's famous 'decadence' largely a commercial 'line' which the Berliners had instinctively developed in their competition with Paris? Paris had long since cornered the straight-girl market, so what was left for Berlin to offer its visitors but a masquerade of perversions?"

Auden and Isherwood both made pilgrimages to Magnus Hirschfeld's Sex Institute—which made them giggle initially with its displays of high-heeled boots for fetishists, its lace panties for big-crotched Prussian officers, its garter belts and whips, its lower trouser legs cut off at the knee and suspended from elastic bands so that flashers could throw open their raincoats and expose their naked genitalia and buttocks in a split second.... Nevertheless Isherwood manfully admitted he felt "a kinship with these freakish fellow tribesmen and their distasteful customs." Eventually Isherwood even lived in a building belonging to the Sex Institute.

Magnus Hirschfeld was a Jew born in 1868 in Kolberg. After studying medicine and traveling in the United States and North Africa, he set up a practice in Berlin in the Charlottenburg district. When one of his homosexual patients committed suicide the night before he was supposed to marry, Hirschfeld decided to study sexuality. He formulated the notion that homosexuals constituted a third sex, that a male homosexual was "the soul of a woman imprisoned in a man's body." Hirschfeld published his first book, *Sappho and Socrates,* in 1896 and eventually followed it with some thirty other volumes. The most important was *Homosexuality in Men and Women,* published in 1914, in which he discerned a whole spectrum of sexual variation extending from hermaphroditism to other, less marked degrees of intersexuality. Hirschfeld himself was homosexual.

Hirschfeld was not content with writing about homosexuality. He also started the first homosexual liberation movement, founded in 1897, the WhK or Wissenschaftlich-humanitares Komitee (Humanitarian Scientific Committee). Hirschfeld attempted to get the law criminalizing homosexuality, article 175 in the Prussian legal code, revoked, and in order to do so he obtained the signatures of 600 prestigious persons, including Einstein; the sexologist Krafft-Ebing; the writers Hesse, Thomas Mann, Rilke and Stefan Zweig; the philosopher Karl Jaspers; the painter Georg Grosz; and such foreign writers as Tolstoy and Zola. Hirschfield even conducted a poll of the Berlin public; by using his questionnaire he discovered that 5 percent of the male population defined itself as homosexual or bisexual. This was obviously all heady stuff for the young Isherwood. No wonder that for the rest of his life he was a fearless advocate of gay rights. He didn't like my early, arty novels but he gave me a blurb for *States of Desire: Travels in Gay America* because he considered it an important defense of homosexuality.

Magnus Hirschfield, yes, but perhaps Vedanta is the real clue to Isherwood's objectivity about sex. His swami regarded all sex, heterosexual or homosexual, as something that interferes with the acquisition of wisdom, but he wasn't opposed to one kind of sex more than another. Moreover, the Bhagavad-Gita, the sacred text Isherwood translated with Prabhavananda, teaches that virtue consists in being true to one's particular stage of spiritual development. The Swami was happy to receive Chris and Don as a couple once he realized that Chris was not at the stage to become a monk.

Like so many other gay men of my generation, I first read Isherwood with excitement. André Gide's journals and Isherwood's novels were the only serious, non-pornographic accounts of gay experience I came across back then. Of course there were other books, including Vidal's *The City and the Pillar* and the novels of John Horne Burns, but I hadn't heard of them. Even Isherwood's novelistic allusions to affairs with people who were assigned nothing but initials and whose sex was carefully concealed turned me on. Later, Isherwood's prestige gave American gay and lesbian writers in the '70s a lot of encouragement. He who'd known and been published by Virginia Woolf, this man with a legendary past, who'd written so many beautiful books about freedom—that he should be on our side made us take ourselves more seriously.

Ned Rorem

ROLAND BARTHES IS RIGHT (in his essay on Chateaubriand's *Life of Rancé*):

> ...old age is no longer a literary age; the old man is very rarely a novelistic hero; today it is the child who moves us, the adolescent who seduces, who disturbs; there is no longer any image of the old, no longer a philosophy of old age, perhaps because the old man is undesirable.

All the more reason to be grateful to Ned Rorem for his diary *Lies*, in which (among a thousand other things) he shows us old age, sickness and death, the three inevitable and edifying truths about life, according to the Buddha, and the three great subjects Americans avoid—and even consider shameful.

The last third of this diary is the most harrowing (and the most convincing) account of AIDS that I know of. Rorem's lover, the much younger Jim Holmes (JH in the book), becomes ill and dies. As it turns out, there is no better form than the diary for showing the dull, repetitious, demoralizing despair of watching a beloved die from AIDS. The relationship between Rorem and Holmes is marked by sudden gusts of brutality (when Rorem asks coyly which qualities he, Rorem, inherited from which parent,

Holmes says the worst from each). At one point Rorem wonders why JH never mentions his love, but towards the end of his life when Holmes does say, "I love you," he then immediately wonders out loud what the love of a dying man is worth. Contained in these thoughts and exchanges is at least half the tragedy of AIDS—the inability of men to speak of their affection for one another, and their shame in accepting they're ill and dying.

Around AIDS a whole literature of devotion has grown up, writing marked by noble—noble and sustained—sentiments. In these often lachrymose accounts, the dying man achieves wisdom, declares love, suffers courageously, and his helpmeet stays cheerful, declares love and kisses the shrunken, blemished but still handsome face. This is Tragedy Lite, American-style.

What actually happens is closer to the picture Rorem paints. The dying man withdraws from his lover or lashes out at him (after all, the partner has not yet received a death sentence), all the while becoming more and more pitifully dependent on him. He contemplates suicide but doesn't act on it. He goes on bizarre, rebellious sprees of self-destruction and defiance (we see Holmes lolling in the tub, the window wide open in freezing weather, smoking cigarettes, listening to Mahler—or Rorem—through headphones). He throws himself into his work when he's well enough—and even when he's suffering; he's racing against the clock. Little things anger him greatly—and he immediately feels bad about his foul temper. The healthy partner, in turn, believes that he is always in the wrong: "I feel impotent, but not useless. If his silences for hours on end, while driving to Hyannis for instance, are sinister, at least he has me to be silent with."

He has me to be silent with—that might well be the title of a book about accompanying someone with AIDS to the grave. The diary is best equipped of all literary forms to show the way the tragic mingles with the quotidian, the way that drama is always partial, botched and freely adulterated by the ludicrous and ignoble.

Racine was wrong: tragedy doesn't befall us swiftly, there are no unities of time, place and situation, our language is never pure; we have no sustained monologues; and we are never permitted a crisis, a revelation or a dénouement. Instead, AIDS goes on for a very long time, mixing hope with despair, silence and curse words with elevated diction, and the end is so debilitating, so disintegrating, that there is no wisdom, little tenderness, scarcely any coherence. Whereas Phaedra may be mad, she's not suffering from dementia.

Despite all the horrors of the disease, Rorem does manage to capture the very real heroism Jim Holmes was capable of—his quiet determination to make shipshape their house in Nantucket, as if to fulfill a marriage vow "to hold" if no longer "to have" his partner; and his professionalism in rehearsing and conducting his church choir up to a month before his death; even his patience in taking care of the dog. Obviously Rorem credits himself with no heroism at all, but the reader can only admire his courage in going on with his composing, however fitfully, his voracious reading (even if he complains he "never" reads and watches too much TV)—and the writing of this very book, an enormous undertaking that would have proved daunting to anyone else.

Reading this book plunges one into quick, contrasting reactions: irritation with Rorem's mechanical inversions of normal values and familiar sayings; delight in his unexpected pairing of names (Susan Sontag vs. Harold Brodkey on illness, or Debussy's *La Mer* compared to Ravel's *Daphnis et Chloe*, or the contrast between two German-speaking contemporaries, Kurt Weill and Alban Berg); curiosity about his enthusiasms (I, for one, want to read more by British novelist James Hamilton-Patterson, the one writer he praises the most consistently, and I plan to listen to Messaien's *End of Time*); impatience with his blind spots and his silliness in defending them ("Emerson dates," he tells us, absurdly, and the Sistine Chapel is less impressive as a whole than in its parts, *To the Lighthouse* is "a humorless bore," the six Bartok string quartets aren't all they're cracked up to be, etc., etc.); and, finally, deep sadness as he traces the decline of his beloved Jim.

What most impressed me was the enormous cultural appetite of these two men, Rorem and Holmes, of a sort the world will not see again, probably, but which was once common enough. Rorem remembers little things his patron and muse, Marie-Laure de Noailles, told him; he refers back to—and constantly quotes—his inspiration, Jean Cocteau. His France of the 1950s is still very much present in his mind, as are his parents ("Mother" and "Father," as he calls them in the High Prissy style). He dismisses *Angels in America,* flying in the face of public opinion; has views about the Heaven's Gate suicide cult; obsesses about his bête noire, Elliott Carter, whom he clearly envies; and expresses his abiding hate for the

dodecaphonal composers, whom he calls the "serial killers." He continues
his lifelong comparison of what is German and what is French (telling
jokes is French, explaining jokes is German, for instance). He reads
Updike, Cheever, Auden and updates his evaluations of their work. He discusses the great musical performers he's known and admired or deplored.
He gives us a list of the food (usually quiche) he served on every occasion.
He hands out marks to his composition students.

Into this assemblage of details and aperçus creep the first warning signals of JH's illness. On Friday, February 17, 1995, Rorem writes:

> At noon I returned to find JH in the recovery room, less trauma-
> tized than I'd feared, but what he told me was less than Jaffin
> [Barry Jaffin, JH's doctor] told me a few minutes later in the wait-
> ing room. The Crohn's Disease is, for the moment, minor, but
> there's one huge ulcer (and smaller ulcers) which may be a malig-
> nant tumor, he won't know until the biopsies are analyzed next
> Thursday.
> "And the blood test?" I asked.
> "Positive," said he.
> "You mean HIV positive?"
> "Yes." He looked at me quizzically and walked off.
> Thus began the strange thirty minutes in the near-empty
> waiting room. One's focus on everything is changed forever. Did
> JH know? Why him and not me, he's only 55, while I could prepare
> to die now without too much bile. This sounds unselfish; in fact,
> it's pure ego: I want him to take care of me in my old age. What
> isn't selfish, since all I care about is his comfort?... On leaving the
> hospital we walked a few sunshiney blocks down Fifth Avenue. JH
> has known he's HIV positive for some months, but didn't tell me
> because I'm "obsessive."

This passage, unassuming and unannotated as it may be, nevertheless
conveys the truth about the *pudeur* that reigns between lovers, the huge
realm of the *non-dit* between the positive and the negative (French expressions seem best adapted to this sort of discretion). I can remember the
comedy of errors that surrounded the diagnosis and death of a famous
philosopher in France. The doctors didn't say the dreaded letters HIV

because they felt their celebrated patient must already know the name of his disease. The philosopher never told his lover his diagnosis because, at first, he wasn't sure of it himself and then, later, because he didn't want to cast the younger man into despair. Only towards the end did it occur to the philosopher that he might have passed the disease on to his lover—a horrible realization, indeed. Here, in the psychological fencing between JH and Rorem, we see a similar series of feints and well-meant concealments.

Of course this diary is Rorem's fourteenth published book, and behind it lie many other efforts at self-presentation. Ned Rorem started off as a gorgeous idiot and has ended up as a somber, suspicious genius. But even as a young man, as his *Paris Diary* (which covers the years 1951–55) reveals, he was already an *idiot savant*, since he kept such good company, was so ambitious and as inquisitive as he was vain and spoiled. While he was in his twenties in Paris and at the height of his "beauty" (such a period word requires quotation marks), he was kept by the brilliant hostess Marie-Laure de Noailles; introduced to Picasso; courted by handsome Frenchmen; bedded by sexy Arabs; advised by Virgil Thomson, Francis Poulenc and Nadia Boulanger; photographed by Carl Van Vechten, Man Ray and Henri Cartier-Bresson.

He could often be fatuous: "Two years ago I wrote my parents who were worried about how much money to send: 'You have given birth to an exceptional child; you must therefore expect exceptional behavior from him.' I, in turn, was given an exceptional family who have always made every effort to understand and help." He had an eye for the grotesque and blithely tells us that Moroccan cemeteries stink "because Moslems are buried upright, and at night hyenas come to gnaw their skulls." He mentions that a mouse has just died in his piano, killed "by the hammer strokes." He makes lots of references to his high calling as an artist and accordingly scorns a lady who imagines the beauty of Marrakesh might have inspired him ("If I have written better it's because I've turned my back on the view. It's hard for people to realize that the artist's inspiration is always present and all he needs to express it is concentration; beautiful surroundings are disconcerting").

A Quaker boy from Chicago with indulgent, progressive parents (his father was one of the architects of Blue Cross and his mother a dedicated pacifist), Rorem took to the decadent high life of Paris with embarrassing ease: "A cool and languid lobster lunch at Marie Laure's with Poulenc who is witty and bright and religious and knows it and you know he knows it and say so and it's a bit spoiled." Gosh....

But all teasing aside (Howard Moss did the funniest satire of the *Paris Diary* in the *New Yorker* years ago), one has to be impressed by Rorem's industry between epic drunks as well as by his culture, even by his decision to keep a diary for publication, not exactly an American endeavor. He's a wonderfully companionable writer because we explore the brand new Old World with him, and for a moment he allows us to see what it would be like to be universally adored: "The writer Miserocchi told me too that when we met at Bestigui's in Venice '51 he'd left a note at the Danieli saying that since his young friend's suicide I was the only one who could give him the *goût de vivre*. I never answered and had forgotten. If we are good to all who love us, what is there left for ourselves? Rome, Rome. Each one says selfishly: 'No one has loved you as I do.' "

If he's silly it's in imitating much older people who were brought up to integrate social charm with erudition, an awareness of rank with an esthetic acuity. Also, as he has remarked himself, "silliness is germane to the diary-as-genre." Unfortunately, he also learned to imitate his elder's cruelty, as in this unforgivable passage from *The New York Diary:* "I don't like cripples (including especially the blind), or the aged, or children (their self-conscious vanity), or the Chinese, or the irritating and noisy confusion of women's purses, and elbows and voices." Only Rorem would know how to temper the intolerable with the insufferable.

His ultimate tribute to the demigods of his youth (when he himself was a full-fledged god of beauty) can be found in his 1994 memoirs, *Knowing When to Stop*. Now that he is in his seventies he is less concerned by how many hearts he's breaking and more by the fine differences among all those hearts he'd collected. Rorem himself might say, "Whereas youth is narcissistic, age is curious." (The epigrammatic style is infectious.) "Youth is personal, whereas age is social. Keats is a young man's poet; Jane Austen is an old man's novelist." By that token an old man's journal is less *interessé* if the old man himself is interesting and has known enough success to become disillusioned but not bitter. Rorem fits the formula perfectly and brings a generosity (always nuanced, of course) to a reexamination of his past. If in his book from the late 1970s, *An Absolute Gift,* he gave us a professional musician's assessment of Ravel and Poulenc, in *Knowing When to Stop* he takes the human measure of Marie-Laure de Noailles (whom James Lord has also portrayed in his *Six Exceptional Women*). Such a figure—known only for her taste and her conversation, a faculty and an activity as *insaissisable* as charm—is always particularly difficult to capture in hindsight and through the static rendering of a literary portrait, but Rorem succeeds admirably in catching her on the iridescent wing.

He presents us with a woman fabulously rich, surrounded by Goyas in her *hôtel particulier* on the Place des Etats-Unis, the sumptuous interior decorated by Jean-Michel Franck before the war with white calf leather on the walls. Here she entertained mainly artists, including the painter Balthus and the sculptor Giacometti as well as Man Ray, Leonor Fini and Dora Maar. Her mother, a descendant of the Marquis de Sade and of Petrarch's Laura, had been one of the two models for Proust's character the Duchesse de Guermantes. Marie-Laure's husband, the Vîcomte Charles de Noailles, was largely an absent figure, even though she loved him and even revered him. As Rorem depicts her, she was a strange combination of haughty dignity and a puerile impulse to shock.

When Rorem would one-up her in conversation she would call him by the pet name she'd given him, "Miss Sly" (which she pronounced Meeze-Lye). She was a compulsive reader and she alone could compare the use of dialogue in Henry James's plays, of all things, and Diderot's novels. She read constantly—as did Rorem, if his diary of the period is to be trusted. Thursday it was Eliot's *The Cocktail Party,* Saturday *The Autobiography of Alice B. Toklas,* Sunday a Sartre play, Tuesday Ronald Firbank and Hawthorne, Wednesday Gogol's "The Nose."

The studious days were followed by bibulous, riotous nights. During one of these sodden dinners, according to Rorem, Marie-Laure said, "'Ned is America's gift to France. We all want to bugger Ned. Even Henri.' She alludes to the maître d'hôtel who, pouring more blanc-des-blancs, interpolates without changing expression: 'It's an interesting notion, but I'm sure Monsieur Rorem would object. And I'm not made that way.'"

Rorem's portrait of Virgil Thomson is no less indelible than his picture of Marie-Laure, although naturally a chapter on a composer will necessarily be more technical than one on a woman of the world. When he tells us that Virgil always spoke (even to kids) in "French-style generalities, which are always anathema to literal-minded American children," he's hit the rusty nail on its dull head. When he explains to the reader that teaching composition is as useless as creative writing courses, he adds, with indisputable authority, "But there is a craft if not an art, the lineaments of which can be imparted, even from one untalented person to another, and that is the craft of orchestration. Instrumentation is physical fact, not theoretical idea. That is what Virgil intended to show me." He presents us with Virgil at work in a clean, pressed pair of Lanvin pajamas sitting in bed and running the whole New York musical scene over the phone. He gives us a Virgil who is deliciously indiscreet except with regard to his own homosexuality; when Ned brings out his scandalous *New York Diary*, Virgil removes all reference to the confessed pederast in his own forthcoming book. When Virgil's lover the painter Maurice Grosser tells Rorem to help out by setting the table, Virgil announces, "Ned doesn't have to work, Ned's a beauty."

When I met Rorem in the 1970s I had been awed in advance by his legend, that long peacock tail of memories—heavy, encumbering, iridescent—that accompanies him wherever he goes. Perhaps because he started publishing his memoirs at age forty and had by then written so many volumes of them, he held no more secrets for me—or rather, Rorem was for me an open book but a closed life. To commandeer one of W. M. Spackman's titles, he was *A Presence with Secrets*. An author one has known only through his writings may seem miraculously approachable, a professional charmer, an idealized version of oneself with his vade mecum smile, but the flesh-and-bone man can have a strange accent, be haughtily impatient, tuned to his own past and its denizens like a bird dog to a pheasant but blind to the present—and to one's own humble, arrogant needs and expectations.

Rorem was not indifferent. He had a harsh way of treating himself and of discounting compliments, but I supposed this was an aging beauty's way of coping with the deceptions of flattery. Or perhaps he was displaying that famous French "realism" I'd heard so much about. But with me he was attentive and observant, which was flattering, and wary, which was even more flattering, especially since I had published only one slim volume at the time and even now would not intimidate a fly. I kept thinking he was like a woman who's just had a face-lift and isn't sure what the effect is and whether those complimenting her are admiring or compassionate.

I suppose what he liked about me was that I was someone younger who still cared about his world—the world of Cocteau, Poulenc and Virgil Thomson. I recognized the names of the painters who graced his walls (he had a sketch of himself by Cocteau and a painting—was it of boatmen in a clear afternoon light?—by the neo-Romantic Eugene Berman). I was responsive to his idea of conversation—which was serious, cultured, questioning. Any banality I might utter he'd immediately subject to the interferon treatment of his paradoxes, qualifications, second thoughts. Americans (especially midwesterners like him and me) are routinely more fond of sunny unanimity and easygoing optimism than anything more controversial, but Ned would arch an eyebrow and with an uneasy smile start bombarding any momentary truce with his testing questions. He'd tease and probe, talking with his Donald Duck lisp. He seemed teleprompted by his Parisian ghosts, for surely no American left to his own devices would ever want to break up the first tentative tone of concord (perhaps we treasure peace because so much potential violence is always just under the surface, whereas the French cultivate saucy sallies since under their surface is the all-too-tedious predictability of cultural uniformity).

Once at his apartment I met Janet Flanner and "Darlinghissima." They were both old ladies and Ned was very courtly, though still provocative, which I now see he considered to be a social grace. Every soft, furry phrase he uttered had a sting in its tail.

And yet he was a wonderfully gentle, kind man, so different from the moody, childish, Bacchic boor of the early diaries. The source of the difference, I learned, was drink; he'd stopped drinking thirty years ago and after that his suicidal moroseness, his mood swings, his belligerence had all vanished. Even to this day if I meet someone who doesn't like Ned Rorem, I say, "You must have known him before he stopped." Which is invariably the case.

He represents a vanishing breed, alas. In the States intellectuals are usually dowdy professors on provincial campuses, whereas socialites are power-mad philistines. In France, however, there are still a few of those salons where rich and titled people like to mix with artists. Just the other night I was at such a dinner; one of the other guests was an American billionaire stockbroker who, puzzled and offended, asked his bewildered French hostess the next day, "Why did you have all those artists to dinner when you could have had a power dinner—there are lots of makers and shakers in Paris at the moment?" Ned is the sort of artist who had his manners and wits shaped in a salon that never witnessed a "power dinner." Now that Paris is no longer in the same league as London, Berlin and New York, it must be contented with the appreciation of the art of the past. If America is the country of great writers and lousy readers, France today is the land of great readers and bad writers.

In his recent collection of essays and reviews, entitled *Other Entertainment,* Rorem has lost none of the confidence that his milieu conferred on him ("Duras is a first-class second-rater," he announces). In discussing Peter Feibleman's *Lilly,* his biography of Lillian Hellman, Rorem writes: "Theirs was unequivocally a mother–son relationship, in which Peter was the mother, Lillian the son." In page after page, Rorem delivers himself of acute, informed judgments; like his beloved Marie-Laure, he is equally at home in the French- and the English-language traditions: "Like Cocteau, Auden was an aphorist who monopolized conversation with quips that brooked no argument. Cocteau too, vastly 'official' in his waning years, had been spurned by the very generations whose style he had shaped, and he died, successful and sad, in a mist of self-quotation. When Auden had become a monument he welcomed the interviewers he had shunned for years, but spoke to them solely in epigrammatic non sequiturs." With the same international ease he can tell us that Sarah Orne Jewett did for Maine what Knut Hamsun did for Norway, Louis Hémon for Canada and Jean Giono for France.

Whenever the subject turns to music, Rorem makes the sort of canny observation only a composer is capable of. He tells us that Libby Holman was the first female pop singer "to exploit the husky purple depths of her vocal register rather than (like Helen Morgan or Ruth Etting) the squeakily poignant top." Or he can toss off a wonderfully illuminating comparison of Billy Holiday and Ella Fitzgerald: "Ella, with her nimbler vocal cords, came through as optimistic even in her plaintive songs; Billie, with her more limited tessitura, came through as plaintive even in her optimistic songs." I wouldn't agree (since Billy always sounds to my ears as though she's suppressing a laugh when she complains) but I admire the kind of observation that Rorem makes and the confidence with which he delivers his opinions. He returns for a ride on some of his hobby horses. His dis-missiveness of Beethoven is absurd—and when he tells us that Poulenc's song "La Carpe" is worth all of *Fidelio* we can only cringe. He loves to scorn the remarks about music made by most non-musicians (although he should concede that the passionate confusion of a Proust, say, is preferable to the total indifference of most contemporary writers); he takes a swipe at Kazuo Ishiguro's novel *The Unconsoled,* which is about a concert pianist. And yet how can one resist a reviewer who starts his article with a reminder of Joan Crawford's dialogue in *Humoresque:* "The music I like? Some symphonies, all concertos"? Or who remembers that when someone once complained to Jane Bowles: "The odds are against me: I'm Jewish, homosexual, alcoholic, and a communist," Jane retorted: "I'm Jewish, homosexual, alcoholic, a communist—and I'm a cripple!"

Or he recycles once more his notion that if there is a gay sensibility, then some bona fide heterosexuals possess it—James Salter, here as in the past, is the example he invariably gives. (Gay sensibility, perhaps, I can't help but grumble, but no sensitivity to gays. I remember hurling across the room a Salter novel, written in the 1970s, in which one heterosexual man amuses his wife and a straight couple with a mincing, lisping imitation of homosexuals overheard in a bookshop: "Oh, Sartre was right. Genet is an absolute saint" or something of that sort.)

Rorem likes to correct his favorite authors. In a passage of bravura erudition, he tracks down Cocteau's borrowings in his play *Monstres Sacrés* and finds the sources of the various characters' dialogue: " 'Happiness is a long patience,' comes from Balzac, not Florent"; " 'All my life I've heard, 'Wait 'til you're older, you'll see,' and now I'm fifty, I've seen nothing,' comes from Satie, not Esther"; and " 'I don't seek, I find,' is Picasso, not Liane." Typically, spanning three cultures and two centuries, Rorem is able to compare *The Sorrows of Young Werther* with *Les Enfants terribles* and *Catcher in the Rye.*

He tells us in several places that he is "morbidity incarnate" and that he's less in fashion now than previously. I hope my few darts haven't inflamed his morbidity, since he is among the handful of living writers whom I write for and love to read—one of the few, in other words, who counts for me. If he is less in fashion (which I'm not at all sure is the case—his concerts and readings are always packed out) the decline presages our fall, not his; in any civilized society his views and his art would be essential.

Rorem is a born diarist who feels compelled to comment on—well, not on everything that happens around him, for he is selective, but on the bits of tinsel that catch his eye or rhyme with some earlier preoccupation. We write about those things we know how to render. Isherwood once said that writers are notoriously unobservant, but that when an event enters the range of their talent and interests, their eyes suddenly focus and take a little snapshot. If so, then Rorem's perceptions are hair-triggered; he must use up a lot of film. And he never takes a bad picture.

James Baldwin

O F ALL THE WELL-KNOWN NOVELISTS of the day, James Baldwin in middle age was among the warmest, the most companionable, the least ironic. So many contemporary writers seem incapable of presenting loyalty, innocence or happiness, especially family happiness, but Baldwin inhabits these feelings with great naturalness and intensity. He can show, as he does more than once in *Just Above My Head*, parents and children exchanging gifts at Christmas or during a reunion. The family members have tears in their eyes, not of regret but of anticipation, not of loneliness but of love. Looked at merely as a literary fashion (and it is, of course, much, much more), the direct depiction of such ardor is unique today; one has to go back to Dickens to find a similar impulse in a major writer, though in Dickens the happy moments are all too often bathetic, whereas in Baldwin they glow with the steadiness and clarity of a flame within a glass globe.

Walter Benjamin, the German-Jewish writer, once remarked, "Death is the sanction of everything that the storyteller can tell." He meant, I think, that only in death does someone's life take shape, gain authority, turn into a tale. Acknowledging this truth, Baldwin begins his novel with the death of his hero, Arthur Montana, a celebrated gospel singer. The rest of the long book is a delving into Arthur's life by his devoted older brother, Hall, the narrator.

The most remarkable character, however, is Julia, whom we first encounter at age nine as a child preacher. Julia is a hypocrite, an eerily controlled monster of vanity and manipulation bent on destroying her mother and seducing her father. Of such stuff melodramas are made, and Baldwin drains every bit of juice from this juiciest of material. True melodrama, however, with its demand for villains and heroes, is a failure of compassion, and Baldwin is above all a wise and compassionate writer. Accordingly, once Julia achieves her monstrous goals (her mother dies, her father becomes her lover, at once pitiless and pitiful), she turns in terror from her victory, loses her faith, renounces her ministry—and, after years of self-degradation, grows into a woman of formidable dignity and understanding.

The central figure, Arthur, is another test for Baldwin's delicacy of sentiment, for his powers as a diplomat of the emotions, because Arthur is both black and homosexual. To present a homosexual character in the round and with sympathy is still, I suppose, a challenge even to a white writer, but granting acceptance to male homosexuality in the black community is a still greater problem, historically and politically. The prevailing theory is that because the black man was degraded so long by the dominant society, he must be restored to a position of pride as the head of the family (this theory has been challenged in a controversial book, *Black Macho and the Myth of the Superwoman,* by Michele Wallace). Nonetheless, among many black thinkers the idea of machismo has become an article of faith, a precondition for autonomy, self-respect and family decency; male homosexuality, mistakenly equated with effeminacy and white decadence, has been rejected strenuously by many black spokesmen ("faggot" has often served as a catchword for the white enemy). So much for rhetoric. In practice, by contrast, black writers have shown gay women and men with more straightforwardness than have their white counterparts. This acceptance seems to be especially true in the black church and in the entertainment business.

In *Just Above My Head* Baldwin has successfully placed the black male homosexual back into the context of black society. Baldwin is not, it seems, arguing for gay liberation (which black leaders have generally seen as a distracting side issue that has begun to replace justice for blacks as a fashionable "media event"). No, the attitude embodied in this novel is one of tolerance and acceptance of all forms of sexuality so that the crusaders for black rights can march forward, united.

When Arthur is a teenager and still a member of a gospel quartet, The Trumpets of Zion, he falls in love with Crunch, another member of the group. The scenes in which they discover their love for each other are the best written in the book—hushed, concentrated, immaculately detailed. Later, when he has become an adult and a well-known soloist, Arthur has two other affairs, one with a white man in France and another with Julia's younger brother Jimmy. The Arthur–Jimmy affair is balanced by a relationship between Julia and Arthur's brother Hall, a double fusion of family love and erotic love. Again and again homosexual alliances are paralleled by those which are heterosexual until the reader begins to respond to the emotions and experiences of individuals, regardless of their affectional preferences. As a young man Baldwin wrote *Giovanni's Room*, a homosexual love story in which the characters are white. He has before and since written many books about blacks who happen to be heterosexual (*Just Above My Head* is his nineteenth published work). His decision to bring homosexuality and blackness together is courageous, given the tense political situation; that he has done so with such tact is a sign of his decency and artistry.

But this novel is not merely about a character's exploration of his homosexuality. Arthur—and Julia and Hall and all the other characters—must also come to terms with their blackness. Arthur does so in Paris, where he meets an ancient black American singing blues in a nightclub, surrounded by black Africans and white Europeans. Color, no longer perceived through "the optic of power and guilt," resolves into many individual shades.

But color is a shorthand for power in America, and the integration struggles of the 1960s in the South are swiftly and dramatically related at the heart of the novel. For young people to whom those days are nothing but a dry chapter in history, this book will serve to put human flesh on schematic bones. Never has the story of the heroic civil rights movement been more powerfully rendered.

Just Above My Head is not a perfect novel; fiction that is politically engaged is always less elegant than reactionary fiction, which lavishes on form the attention a progressive literature must also devote to content. Arthur—and especially Arthur's death—are disappointingly shadowy. Too much of "Book One" is carelessly written. Too many scenes occur in bars and restaurants as anecdotes exchanged over dinner and drinks, as though

Baldwin is so eager to tell stories that he forgets to show actions. No matter. In whole long sections the style is imbued with Baldwin's peculiarly indirect vision, his idiosyncratic way of catching the imprecision, the blurriness, of experience. And, despite the clinking of forks and cocktail glasses, the tale does move forward on coiled muscles—this is the work of a born storyteller at the height of his powers, a man who, now that he is older and more mature, has truly come into his own. As the most celebrated black American novelist, Baldwin has given his readers a comprehensive and comprehending examination of race and sexuality and suggested some of the ways in which the politics of color can shape the transactions of love.

Vladimir Nabokov

NABOKOV IS THE MOST PASSIONATE novelist of the twentieth century, the high priest of sensuality and desire, the magus who knows everything about what is at once the most solemn and elusive of all our painful joys—the stab of erotic pleasure, that emblem of transitory happiness on earth. As Proust observed, ardor is the only form of possession in which the possessor possesses nothing.

But if passion is the treasure (that is, the absence) that lies at the heart of the great pyramid of Nabokov's art, he has been careful to protect it from the vulgar, the prying, the coarse, the smug—against whoever might seek to despoil him of his fragile hoard; he has surrounded his secret riches with a maze of false corridors, of precariously balanced, easily triggered and quite lethal megaliths. These are the notorious traps, the crushing menhirs of Nabokov's wit, his scorn, his savage satire. Nonetheless I'd insist that passion, not brilliance or cruelty or erudition or the arrogant perfection of his craft—that passion is his master motif. All of his intelligence is at the service of the emotions.

In a superb story, perhaps his best, "Spring in Fialta," first written in Russian and published in 1938, the love between the narrator and the heroine, Nina, is considered with—I'm tempted to say safeguarded by—the contempt directed at her husband, Ferdinand. Nina is an impulsive, generous but negligent woman who has often given herself to the narrator (and to many other men along the way); just as suddenly and often she has forgotten the gift she's conferred on them. The narrator first meets Nina in Russia "around 1917," as he says with an eerie casualness, and they exchange their first embrace outdoors in winter:

> Windows light up and stretch their luminous lengths upon the dark billowy snow, making room for the reflection of the fan-shaped light above the front door between them. Each of the two sidepillars is huffily fringed with white, which rather spoils the lines of what might have been a perfect *ex libris* for the book of our two lives. I cannot recall why we had all wandered out of the sonorous hall into the still darkness, peopled only with firs, snow-swollen to twice their size; did the watchmen invite us to look at a sullen red glow in the sky, portent of nearing arson? Possibly. Did we go to admire an equestrian statue of ice sculptured near the pond by the Swiss tutor of my cousins? Quite as likely. My memory revives only on the way back to the brightly symmetrical mansion towards which we tramped in single file along a narrow furrow between snowbanks, with that crunch-crunch-crunch which is the only comment that a taciturn winter night makes upon humans. I walked last; three singing steps ahead of me walked a small bent shape; the firs gravely showed their burdened paws. I slipped and dropped the dead flashlight someone had forced upon me; it was devilishly hard to retrieve; and instantly attracted by my curses, with an eager, low laugh in anticipation of fun, Nina dimly veered toward me. I call her Nina, but I could hardly have known her name yet, hardly could we have had time, she and I, for any preliminary; "Who's that?" she asked with interest—and I was already kissing her neck, smooth and quite fiery hot from the long fox fur of her coat collar, which kept getting into my way until she clasped my shoulder, and with the candor so peculiar to her gently fitted her generous, dutiful lips to mine.

When the narrator sees Nina indoors a minute later, he is astonished "not so much by her inattention to me after that warmth in the snow as by the innocent naturalness of that inattention...."

This passage is a microcosm of Nabokov's art. His perfect visual memory turns instantly into perfect visual invention when the lit doorway nearly becomes an *ex libris*. The seemingly innocent description soon enough resolves itself into an emblem—"out of books," indeed, since the scene that follows is reminiscent of Chekhov's "The Kiss"—the same mansion, a similar party, the same passionate kiss between strangers. Moreover, the quality of the narrator's and Nina's intermittent affair is always novelistic and the language used to recount it is invariably the language of literature: "Again and again she hurriedly appeared in the margins of my life, without influencing in the least its basic text."

If this marginal romance—lusty, a bit sentimental, not quite honest, genuinely moving but also tinged with *poshlust*—is related by a narrator who is a writer *manqué*, then the ghastly Ferdinand, Nina's husband, is nothing but a writer—cold, diabolic, coldly technical. In fact, he is one of those many grotesque versions of himself Nabokov planted throughout his fiction, a sort of signature not unlike Hitchcock's fleeting appearances in his own films. This particular double is particularly unappetizing, driven as he is with a "fierce relish" for ugly things and woebegone people: "Like some autocrat who surrounds himself with hunchbacks and dwarfs, he would become attached to this or that hideous object; this infatuation might last from five minutes to several days or even longer if the thing happened to be animate."

In "Spring in Fialta," which is just twenty-one pages long, Nabokov manages to generate as dense a sense of duration, of lived-through time, as can be found in most novels. He achieves this narrative density by two means: a complex but rigorous time scheme; and the juxtaposition of highly contrasting moods. The story progresses on two planes: connected episodes at Fialta in the present which alternate with memories of past trysts with Nina in many cities over the years. Both the present and the past are told sequentially and the last flashback to be presented is the narrator's most recent memory of Nina. In other words these two systems of time converge to produce the final scene, in which Nina is killed when her car crashes into a traveling circus company, whose arrival has been heralded throughout the tale by dozens of tiny details, as at sea the approach of land is promised by a quickening flux of grass, twigs and land birds. The convergence of the two time schemes and the disclosure of the promise extended by the hints of the approaching circus conspire to produce a strong effect of closure.

The satisfying *thickness* of this story, its feeling of duration, derives not only from the time scheme but also from the juxtaposition of highly contrasted scenes, a technique of tessellation perfected by Tolstoy. These scenes fall into two groups—the satirical and the romantic. Some of the romantic scenes are not scenes at all but instead beautifully rendered telescopings of time:

Once I was shown her photograph in a fashion magazine full of autumn leaves and gloves and windswept golf links. On a certain Christmas she sent me a picture post card with snow and stars. On a Riviera beach she almost escaped my notice behind her dark glasses and terra cotta tan. Another day, having dropped in on an ill-timed errand at the house of some strangers where a party was in progress, I saw her scarf and fur coat among alien scarecrows on a coat rack. In a bookshop she nodded to me from a page of one of her husband's stories....

The tone of these passages is elegiac, tender and sensual: it is Nabokov's genius (as one might speak of the genius of a place or of a language) to have kept alive almost single-handedly in our century a tradition of tender sensuality. In most contemporary fiction tenderness is a sexless family feeling and sensuality either violent or impersonal or both. By contrast, Nabokov is a Pascin of romantic carnality. He writes in "Spring in Fialta": "Occasionally in the middle of a conversation her name would be mentioned, and she would run down the steps of a chance sentence, without turning her head." Only a man who loved women as much as he desired them could write such a passage.

What makes the narrator of this tale a writer *manqué* is his uncritical—one might say his uninjured—ease in the world of the sentiments. There is no bite, no obliqueness, no discomfort in his responses and, though he is in no danger of becoming vulgar, he is close to that other Nabokovian sin, philistinism. No wonder he is repelled by the real writer, Ferdinand, the focus of the satirical scenes, passages which send up the culture industry, the whole fatiguing milieu of art groupies. Ferdinand sounds a bit like a combination of the sardonic Nabokov and, improbably, a naïve Western European devotee of Russian Communism. But let's not focus on Ferdinand's bad politics. Let's concentrate instead on his peculiarities as a writer:

Having mastered the art of verbal invention to perfection, he particularly prided himself on being a weaver of words, a title he valued higher than that of a writer; personally, I never could understand what was the good of thinking up books, of penning things that had not really happened in some way or another; and I remember once saying to him as I braved the mockery of his encouraging nods that, were I a writer, I should allow only my heart to have imagination, and for the rest rely upon memory, that long drawn sunset shadow of one's personal truth. I had known his books before I knew him; a faint disgust was already replacing the aesthetic pleasure which I had suffered his first novel to give me. At the beginning of his career, it had been possible perhaps to distinguish some human landscape, some gold garden, some dream-familiar disposition of trees through the stained-glass of his prodigious prose...but with every new book the tints grew still more dense, the gales and purpure still more ominous; and today one can no longer see anything at all through that blazoned, ghastly rich glass, and it seems that were one to break it, nothing but a perfectly black void would face one's shivering soul.

In this remarkable—and remarkably sly—passage, the narrator's relationship to the reader (and to the writer Nabokov) becomes intricate. We know that Nabokov's own great art is decidedly not autobiographical in the simple photographic sense, and we resist the narrator's bland assumptions about the sufficiency of memory to art. The narrator sounds too sincere, too Slavic, to our ears, although his objections to Ferdinand are phrased with all the suavity and eloquent conviction at Nabokov's command. Since we, the readers, know that a figure much like the diabolical Ferdinand has written even this argument for sincerity, our relationship to the text is deliciously slippery. The irony, the hard brilliance of such passages contrasts with the tenderness of the alternating sections to give a high relief, an almost *topographical* sense of traveling through time.

Many writers proceed by creating characters who are parodies of themselves or near misses or fun-house distortions, or they distribute their own characteristics across a cast of characters and they especially like to dramatize their conflicts and indecisions by assigning them to different personages. One thinks of Proust, who gave his dilettantism to Swann, his homosexuality to Charlus, his love of his family to the narrator and his hatred of his family to Mlle Vinteuil, his hypochondria to Aunt Leonie, his genius to Elstir and Bergotte, his snobbism to the Guermantes, his Frenchness to Françoise. In this sense (but this strict sense only) every novel, including Nabokov's, is autobiographical. Indeed the notion of a parallel life which does, impossibly, converge with one's own may have suggested the concept of two worlds and two histories slightly out of sync—the moiré pattern of Terra and anti-Terra woven by *Ada*.

But it was Nabokov's particular delight to invent sinister or insane or talentless versions of himself, characters who are at least in part mocking anticipations of naïve readers' suspicions about the real Nabokov. For all those innocents who imagined that the author of *Lolita* was himself a nympholept, Nabokov prepared a hilarious response in *Look at the Harlequins!*, in which the narrator's biography is composed from nothing but such crude suppositions: "As late as the start of the 1954–55 school year, with Bel nearing her thirteenth birthday, I was still deliriously happy, still seeing nothing wrong or dangerous, or absurd or downright cretinous, in the relationship between my daughter and me. Save for a few insignificant lapses—a few hot drops of overflowing tenderness, a gasp masked by a cough and that sort of stuff—my relations with her remained essentially innocent...." Essentially innocent—that's the kind of essence that lubricates our villainous society.

Nabokov's model for inventing such characters, the author's disabled twin or feebler cousin, mad brother or vulgar uncle, was surely Pushkin, among others, for it was Pushkin, following Byron's lead in *Don Juan*, who fashioned a distorted portrait of himself in Eugene Onegin, the young man of fashion whose attitudes and deeds sometimes draw a crude outline of the poet's own silhouette and just as often diverge completely. Of course Pushkin scrupulously disowns the resemblance (I use Nabokov's translation):

> I'm always glad to mark the difference
> between Onegin and myself,
> lest an ironic reader
> or else some publisher
> of complicated calumny,
> collating here my traits,

repeat thereafter shamelessly
that I have scrawled my portrait
like Byron, the poet of pride....

Before Pushkin establishes their differences he points out the similarities. He tells us that he likes Onegin's "sharp, chilled mind" and explains
their friendship by saying, "I was embittered, he was sullen...."

Wit, scorn and the parody of romance can be a way of rescuing
romance. Just as Schoenberg remarked that only the extreme recourse of
his twelve-tone system was able to provide German romantic music with
another fifty years of life, so Nabokov might have asserted that only by
casting *Lolita* into the extreme terms of a Krafft-Ebing case study, the tale
of a European nympholept and his gum-snapping, wisecracking, gray-eyed
teenage enchantress—that only by making such a radical modulation could
he endow the romantic novel with a glorious new vitality.

That vitality is attributable to obsession, the virtue which is shared by
vice and art. As Adorno observes in the *Minima Moralia*: "The universality
of beauty can communicate itself to the subject in no other way than in an
obsession with the particular." The lover, like the artist, loathes the general, the vague, the wise and lives only for the luminous singularity of the
beloved or the glowing page. Everything else is insipid.

Lolita, as all the world knows, is full of parodies—parodies of literary
essays, of scholarly lists of sources, of scientific treatises, of psychiatric
reports and especially of the confession and the legal defense. It is also a
compendium of sometimes serious, but usually jocular allusions to key
works of nineteenth-century romanticism, especially French fiction and
verse (Humbert's first language is French, of course, and *Lolita* is more
Gallic than American or Russian, at least in its explicit references and
models). But the function of this brilliant panoply of literary allusions is
not to disown romanticism but to recapture it. As Thomas R. Frosch
remarks in "Parody and Authenticity in *Lolita,*" as essay published in the
recent collection *Nabokov's Fifth Arc:*

In relation to romance, parody acts in *Lolita* in a defensive and
proleptic way. It doesn't criticize the romance mode, although it
criticizes Humbert; it renders romance acceptable by anticipating
our mockery and beating us to the draw. It is what Empson calls

"pseudo-parody to disarm criticism." I am suggesting, then, that *Lolita* can only be a love story through being a parody of love stories.

To be sure, the entire history of romantic verse and fiction has been self-consciously literary. One could go further and insist that romantic passion itself is literary; as La Rochefoucauld said, no one would ever have fallen in love unless he had first read about it. Humbert and Lolita's mother, Charlotte Haze, represent two quite distinct romantic traditions, the courtly versus the bourgeois. For the courtly lover, love is useless, painful, unfulfilled, obsessive, destructive and his very allegiance to this peculiar, seemingly unnatural ideal is proof of his superiority to ordinary mortals. As Frederick Goldin has remarked about the origins of courtly love in the Middle Ages:

> Ordinary men cannot love unless they get something in return—something they can get hold of, not just a smile. If they do not get it, they soon stop loving, or, if the girl is from one of the lower orders, they take it by force. But usually, since ordinary men love ordinary women, they get what they want; and then, their mutual lust expended, they go their separate ways, or else, if they are restrained by some vulgar decency, they mate and settle down. In this wilderness of carnality and domesticity, nobility declines; there is no reason, and no change, for the longing, exaltation and selfdiscipline of true courtliness. This is one of the basic creeds of courtly love.

One of the most amusing paradoxes of *Lolita* is that the satyr Humbert Humbert becomes the minnesinger of courtly love for the twentieth century. To be sure, before he can fully exemplify the "longing, exaltation and self-discipline of true courtliness," Humbert must lose Lolita and kill his double, Quilty. If Humbert and Quilty have mirrored one another in the first half of the book, in the second half they turn into opposites, as Humbert becomes leaner, older, more fragile, more quixotic and Quilty grows grosser, drunker, fatter and more corrupt; the murder of Quilty expiates Humbert of everything base.

If Humbert embodies courtly love, Charlotte comes out of a different, more recent tradition—the ideal of bourgeois companionate marriage.

A tribute to Nabokov's compassion is his gentle treatment of the ridiculous Charlotte, who in spite of her constant smoking, her bad French, her humorlessness, her middle-brow cultural aspirations and her actual cruelty to her daughter is nonetheless shown as a lonely, touching, decent women: "To break Charlotte's will I would have to break her heart. If I broke her heart, her image of me would break too. If I said: 'Either I have my way with Lolita, and you help one to keep the matter quiet, or we part at once,' she would have turned as pale as a woman of clouded glass and slowly replied: 'All right, whatever you add or subtract, this is the end.' " Even the grudging Humbert must testify to Charlotte's perfect moral pitch and characterize her, poetically, as a creature of "clouded glass," a description that denotes nothing but connotes beauty.

Charlotte has been shaped by her reading—the reading of women's magazines and home-decoration manuals and popular novels. Her pious expectations of the monogamous and "totally fulfilling" marriage in which sex, sentiment and even religious faith coincide is at odds with Humbert's stronger emotions and more desperate aspirations. The best Humbert can do by way of a domestic fantasy is to imagine marrying Lolita, fathering a daughter and living long enough to indulge in incest not only with that child but *her* daughter as well: "bizarre, tender, salivating Dr Humbert, practicing on supremely lovely Lolita the Third the art of being a granddad." Even when he attempts for a moment to abandon his own brand of romantic literature, the script of his courtly and obsessive passion, for Charlotte's kind of pulp, the attempt fails: "I did my best; I read and reread a book with the unintentionally biblical title *Know Your Own Daughter....*"

Nabokov wrote in *The Gift* that "the spirit of parody always goes along with genuine poetry." If "genuine poetry" is taken to mean romantic literature about passion, one can only concur, since passion is parody. Critics keep trying to find some Ur-text that all later romantic fiction is commenting on, but that search has turned into an infinite regress. *Don Quixote* is a parody of tales of knightly adventure; in Dante the lovers Francesca and Paolo discover their mutual passion when they read "of Lancelot, how love constrained him." The pump of Emma Bovary's ardor has been primed by her reading of cheap romantic magazine stories. In *Eugene Onegin*, Tatiana is besotted by romantic fiction:

With what attention she now
reads a delicious novel,
with what vivid enchantment
drinks the seductive fiction!

But her reading, alas, is different from Onegin's, for Tatiana reads
Rousseau's fiction and Goethe's *Sorrows of Young Werther* (as Nabokov
comments in his notes, "Werther weeps on every occasion, likes to romp
with small children, and is passionately in love with Charlotte. They read
Ossian together in a storm of tears"). Immersed in her own brand of
Lachrymose Lit, Tatiana

sighs, and having made her own
another's ecstasy, another's melancholy,
she whispers in a trance, by heart, a letter
to the amiable hero.

That letter sounds weirdly like Charlotte Haze's avowal. Charlotte writes:

I am nothing to you. Right? Right. Nothing to you whatever. *But*
if, after reading my "confession" you decided, in your dark
romantic-European way, that I am attractive enough for you to
take advantage of my letter and make a pass at me, then you
would be a criminal—worse than a kidnapper who rapes a child.
You see, cheri. *If* you decided to stay, *if* I found you at home....

And so on. Surely this letter is a parody of Tatiana's infinitely more
touching but no less fervent appeal:

My fate
henceforth I place into your hands,
before you I shed tears,
for your defense I plead....
I'm waiting for you: with a single look
revive my heart's hopes;
or interrupt the heavy dream,
alas, with a deserved rebuke.

Humbert may fake an acceptance of Charlotte's avowal, but Onegin rejects Tatiana in rolling Byronic phrases:

But I'm not made for bliss;
my soul is strange to it;
in vain are your perfections:
I'm not worthy of them.

This misunderstanding, fatal to the future happiness of both characters, is not so much due to intrinsic character differences as to different reading lists. Whereas Tatiana has read of lovers given to sacrifice, duty and devotion, Onegin has been coached by Byron's egotistical and disabused *Don Juan*:

My days of love are over; me no more
The charms of maid, wife...
Can make the fool...
The credulous hope of mutual minds is o'er.

Years go by, Tatiana suffers, becomes stoic, and then one day is drawn to Onegin's deserted country house. She enters his library, reads the books he once read, and in a stunning passage she wonders whether Onegin might not be "a glossary of other people's megrims,/ a complete lexicon of words in vogue?... Might he not be, in fact, a parody?" Just as Charlotte recognizes Humbert's criminal passions for Lolita once she reads his diary, so Tatiana understands Onegin is a fraud once she peruses his books.

The Byronic hero could, in his most degraded form, become coldly indifferent to women and with men murderously touchy on points of honor. If the calculating seduction is the way the Byronic monster approaches women, his characteristic exchange with other men is the duel. Here again Humbert executes a grotesque parody of the duel in his stalking down of Quilty; this is the final sorry end to the already shoddy, senseless business of the Lenski–Onegin duel.

My point, then, seems to be that we should not be surprised if *Lolita* is a parody of earlier works of romantic literature, including not only *Onegin* but much more obviously a whole succession of French novels devoted to the anatomy of the passions—that line that runs from the *Princesse de*

Cleves through *Les Liaisons dangereuses, Adolphe, Atala* and *René* and on to *Mademoiselle Maupin, Carmen* and *Madame Bovary*—a tradition, moreover, that Humbert specifically alludes to again and again. His mind is also well-stocked with French poetry from Ronsard to Rimbaud. Whereas some Russian Formalists (I'm thinking of Tynyanov's *Dostoevski and Gogol: Remarks on the Theory of Parody*) argued that parody is a way of disowning the past in an act of literary warfare, in Nabokov's case we see that parody can be the fondest tribute, the deepest embrace, the invention of a tradition against which one's own originality can be discerned, a payment of past debts in order to accrue future capital.

I may also seem to be saying that if *Lolita*, the supreme novel of love in the twentieth century, is a parody of earlier love novels, we should not be surprised, since love itself—the very love you and I experience in real life—is also a parody of earlier love novels. I have even intimated that conflicts in love, whether they are those between Onegin and Tatiana or Humbert and Charlotte or you and me, are attributable to different reading lists—that amorous dispute is really always a battle of books.

If I made such an assertion, or if I attributed it to Nabokov, I would be subscribing to the approach to literature and art advanced by Roland Barthes in *S/Z*, though later disowned by him in *A Lover's Discourse*. In *S/Z*, that detailed, elusive, dense, patient analysis of a story by Balzac, Barthes proposes that the literature of the bourgeoisie is nothing but an interweaving of cultural codes. Various strategies are employed by the writer (one might say via the writer, since he is scarcely conscious of what he is doing) to provide the illusion of reality, to hoodwink the reader into believing that "love" and all its rituals (the declaration, the tryst, the impediments to happiness, the vow, the discovery, the catastrophe)—that "love" is something natural and not cultural. In exploding the convention of realism, the illusion of the naturalness of love, Barthes destroys every term in the literary equation. In this extreme view, there is no reader, no text and no writer. No reader, because as Barthes puts it: "This 'I' which approaches the text is already itself a plurality of other texts." No text, because the text is merely a mathematical point traversed by the codes, a braid in the interweaving of voices. And finally no writer because he is merely a stenographer taking down dictation from the culture around him. In this absence we have, alas, "literature," that is, the ceaseless read-out of the well-stocked computer as it jabbers to itself. It would be foolish to attribute such views to Nabokov. Everything in his proud and lonely nature would have been opposed to such an automatism. As a critic, after all, he is the great spokesman for the genius and the masterpiece; he had no tolerance for schools, movements, minor works, influences. As an artist he was a convinced believer in inspiration; if he was taking dictation, it was not from the culture around him but from the angels.

For Nabokov true literature—the literature of genius—is not self-enclosed but transcendent, not reductive but inductive. Although he was exuberantly, even boisterously alert to the conventional, parody was his method of quarantining it and even curing it. If he acknowledged the nauseating repetitiveness of all past love stories, he did so in order to write one that was utterly new, just-born, perfect. As he said in the postscript to *Lolita*: "For me a work of fiction exists only in so far as it affords me what I shall bluntly call aesthetic bliss, that is a sense of being somehow, somewhere, connected with other states of being where art (curiosity, tenderness, kindness, ecstasy) is the norm."

This curiosity includes a close scrutiny of nature. Nabokov is our freshest landscape painter in words, and not surprisingly he was an admirer of other gifted writers of description. In his book on Gogol he argues that Gogol was the first Russian writer to free himself from the rigid conventional color schemes of the eighteenth-century French school of literature. As Nabokov writes:

> ...the development of the art of description throughout the centuries may be profitably treated in terms of visions, the faceted eye becoming a unified and prodigiously complex organ and the dead dim "accepted colors" (in the sense of "*idées reçues*") yielding gradually their subtle shades and allowing new wonders of application. I doubt whether any writer, and certainly not in Russia, had ever noted before [Gogol], to give the most striking instance, the moving pattern of light and shade on the ground under trees or the tricks of color played by sunlight with leaves.

For Nabokov, such observations constitute news; one might even say they figure as scientific discovery. One sometimes feels that Nabokov the lepidopterist is not unlike Chekhov the doctor, and that like Chekhov Nabokov might have declared: "My familiarity with the natural sciences and the scientific method has always kept me on my guard; I have tried wherever possible to take scientific data into account, and where it has not been possible I have preferred not writing at all." To be sure, Nabokov once remarked that fiction began with fairy tales, but again one is reminded that, as Howard Moss has observed, "Chekhov's stories tread the finest line between a newspaper account and a fairy tale."

With Chekhov and Nabokov, observation constitutes an importation of something brand new, something unprecedented into the realm of discourse. To all those critics who consider literature to be an entirely self-referential system, a grand tautology, I would submit that if their assertion is being made on an epistemological plane about the possibility of communication of any sort, then literature is certainly no *more* disabled than any other form of language (including criticism). But if the assertion is being made about literature in particular as distinct from language in general, then the assertion seems to me, quite simply, wrong, for surely literature, at least as practiced by Nabokov, is both descriptive and expressive, a new compilation of exact statements about the natural world and the self arranged into large fictional structures (mystery, suspense, plot) that re-create in the reader the very emotions which are being felt by the characters. In fact, the very old claim that fiction is a privileged form of communication because it falls between the disembodied or at least undramatized abstractions of philosophy and the random circumstantiality of history seems to me still true, not because fiction is a mirror to reality, a flawless reflection of it, but because the same convergence of pattern-making and sensation that creates perception functions in the writing and reading of fiction in much the same way as it functions in our experience of the real world. To be less vague about it, one could argue that in *Pale Fire* Kinbote's paranoid glimpses of meaning everywhere fascinate us because we identify not with his character but with his process of gathering data and constructing and revising airtight, comprehensive theories about what's happening.

Love, like paranoia, is also an organizing obsession, an imposition of pattern on the atoms of experience. But Nabokov the realist, the scientific observer, is not content to treat the sentiments as either personal or cooperative delusions, nor does he view love as merely a literary exercise. In his treatment of love in particular, Nabokov points the way beyond parody and convention. At their best his characters act out of character, transcend their roles. The most sublime moment in *Lolita,* of course, occurs when

Humbert sees the "hugely pregnant" Lolita after searching for her for several years.

> There she was with her ruined looks and her adult, ropeveined narrow hands and her goose-flesh white arms, and her shallow ears, and her unkempt armpits, there she was (my Lolita!) hopelessly worn at seventeen, with that baby, dreaming already in her of becoming a big shot and retiring around 2020 A.D.—and I looked and looked at her, and knew as clearly as I know I am to die, that I loved her more than anything I had ever seen or imagined on earth, or hoped for anywhere else....

Here the pervert breaks through the narrow confines of his perversion, the connoisseur of *le fruit vert* looks longingly at the no-longer-ripe apple in a now vanished Eden. Passion—fastidious, tyrannical, hostile—has given way to compassionate love, a grand obsession in the mode of Racine has been supplanted by tender esteem à la Corneille. Correspondingly, Lolita shrugs off her own grudges and forgives Humbert for having taken away her youth; when Humbert asks her to leave with him, she says, "No, honey, no." In the most heartbreaking line I know, Humbert writes: "She had never called me honey before."

A similar moment when love transcends passion, when sentiment exceeds sexuality, occurs in *Pale Fire*. The exclusively homosexual Kinbote, who had always treated his wife with "friendly indifference and bleak respect" while drooling after "Eton-collared, sweet-voiced minions"— Kinbote begins to *dream* of Disa, his Queen, with throbbing tenderness:

> He dreamed of her more often, and with incomparably more poignancy, than his surface-like feelings for her warranted; these dreams occurred when he least thought of her, and worries in no way connected with her assumed her image in the subliminal world as a battle or a reform becomes a bird of wonder in a tale for children. These heartrending dreams transformed the drab prose of his feelings for her into strong and strange poetry.

The transcendent virtue of love is seen again in *Ada* when the aged rake Van Veen is reunited after many years with his now plump and no

longer appealing Ada: "He loved her much too tenderly, much too irrevocably, to be unduly depressed by sexual misgivings." This from the great
sensual purist! Of course this very passage, in which love goes beyond its
conventional limits, is, paradoxically, itself a parody of the end of *War and
Peace* and the marriage of Natasha and Pierre.

Andrew Field writes, "All of his novels, Nabokov told me once, have
an air—*not quite of this world, don't you think?*" Field didn't take the
remark seriously; he thought it was just more leg-pulling. But I think the
hint that his novels are "not quite of this world" should be taken seriously.
After boyhood Nabokov was not conventionally religious, although the
poetry of his early twenties continued to rely occasionally on religious
imagery. Nevertheless, he retained within his pages a quick, visceral sense
of disturbing spiritual presences. His is a haunted world, and to prove it W.
W. Rowe has just published an entire volume to that effect: *Nabokov's
Spectral Dimension.* Inspiration itself is such a specter of course; in *The
Gift* when Fyodor begins to write, he is conscious of "a pulsating mist that
suddenly began to speak with a human voice." Vera Nabokov, the writer's
wife, editor, mentor and the dedicatee of virtually every book from his pen,
has said that a main theme in all of Nabokov's writing is "the hereafter."
Of Fyodor's father, the boy thinks: "It was as if this genuine, very genuine
man possessed an aura of something still unknown but which was perhaps
the most genuine of all."

The luminous unknown, this aura of the ghostly genuine, is always
bordering the picture Nabokov presents to his reader. The narrator of his
last novel, *Look at the Harlequins!*, is afflicted with recurrent bouts of
madness. His perception of space is so personal and so harrowing that at
one point he becomes paralyzed. "Yet I have known madness not only in
the guise of an evil shadow," he tells us. "I have seen it also as a flash of
delight so rich and shattering that the very absence of an immediate object
on which it might settle was to me a form of escape."

It is in those flashes of delight, which illuminate almost every passage,
that Nabokov's glimpses of another world can be detected. Lolita's smile,
for instance, "was never directed at the stranger in the room but hung in its
own remote flowered void, so to speak, or wandered with myopic softness
over chance objects." In *The Gift*, the hero imagines returning to his ances-
tral home in Russia: "One after another the telegraph poles will hum at my
approach. A crow will settle on a boulder—settle and straighten a wing

that has folded wrong." That straightened wing—the precision of an *imagined imaginary* detail—is worthy of a Zen master. In "Spring in Fialta," we encounter "that life-quickening atmosphere of a big railway station where everything is something trembling on the brink of something else"—a phrase that might well serve as Nabokov's artistic credo (and that recalls Quine's notion that a verbal investigation of language is akin to building a boat while sailing in it).

In Nabokov's fiction the strong, even melodramatic lines of the plot are subverted by the fluent language, phrases so joyful and highly colored that they transform tales of dimwits, freaks and madmen into ecstatic tributes to youth, glamour and the exhilaration of genius. When Humbert is about to seduce Lolita for the first time (as it turns out, she seduces him), he pulls his car into the parking lot of a country hotel called The Enchanted Hunters. Everything in this passage is cast in mythic terms, the language of the Circe episode of *The Odyssey*. The car approaches by "falling under the smooth spell of a nicely graded curve," the "pale palace" materialized under "spectral trees." "A row of parked cars, like pigs at a trough, seemed at first sight to forbid access; but then, by magic," a space is provided. "A hunchbacked and hoary Negro in a uniform of sorts took our bags." At the desk they are registered by a "porcine old man." And so on. Again, when Humbert shoots Quilty, the scene is set as in a fairy tale with echoes of Browning's "Childe Roland to the Dark Tower Came."

The function of mythology in Nabokov is not (as it is in Joyce's *Ulysses*) to limit the neural *sprawl* of a stream of consciousness. Nor is it to provide a ready-made plot (as in the neoclassical drama of Anouilh and Giraudoux). Nor is it to lend false dignity to an otherwise dreary tale, as in the plays of Archibald MacLeish or Eugene O'Neill. In Nabokov the vocabulary of religion, fairy tales and myths is the only one adequate to his sense of the beauty and mystery of the sensual, of love, of childhood, of nature, of art, of people when they are noble. It is this language which metamorphoses the comic bedroom scene in *Lolita* into a glimpse of paradise. Once they're in the hotel room, Lolita

> walked up to the open suitcase as if stalking it from afar, in a kind of slowmotion walk, peering at that distant treasure box on the luggage support. (Was there something wrong, I wondered, with those great gray eyes of hers, or were we both plunged in the same

enchanted mist?) She stepped up to it, lifting her rather high-heeled feet rather high, and bending her beautiful boyknees while she walked through dilating space with the lentor of one walking under water or in a flight dream.

Nabokov's novels are not of this world, but of a better one. He has kept the romantic novel alive by introducing into it a new tension—the struggle between obsessive or demented characters and a seraphic rhetoric. Given his inspired style, no wonder Nabokov chose to write about not the species nor the variety but the mutant individual. Only such a subject gives his radiant language something to do, to overcome—a job to perform. In fact, there is only one story, "Lance," in which Nabokov relaxed this tension and indulged in his verbal splendors with chilling abandon. In that story the young hero, Lance Boke, ascends into the heavens as his old parents watch through field glasses: "The brave old Bokes think they can distinguish Lance scaling, on crampons, the verglassed rock of the sky or silently breaking trail through the soft snows of nebulae." I like to think of Nabokov himself, the supreme alpinist of art, ascending those new heights.

He must be ranked, finally, not with other writers but with a composer and a choreographer, Stravinsky and Balanchine. All three men were of the same generation, all three were Russians who were clarified by passing through the sieve of French culture but were brought to the boiling point only by the breezy short-order cook of American informality. All three experimented boldly with form, but none produced "avant-garde trash," as Nabokov called it, for all three were too keen on recuperating tradition. In a work such as the *Pulcinella* ballet score, the Baroque mannerisms of Pergolesi are aped, even insisted upon, but Baroque squares are turned into modernist rhomboids and scalenes and mechanical Baroque transitions, the yard goods of that style, are eliminated in favor of a crisp collage built up out of radical juxtapositions. Everything is fresh, new, heartless—and paradoxically all the more moving for the renovation. Similarly, Balanchine eliminated mime, a fussy *port de bras,* story and décor to make plotless ballets that distil the essence of the Petipa tradition. As parodists, all three artists loved the art they parodied and made it modern by placing old gems in new settings.

Most important, all three men had a vision of art as entertainment, not, to be sure, as a vulgar courting of debased popular taste but as a wooing of shrewder, more restless though always robust sensibilities. Sartre once attacked Nabokov for his lack of political content, but one could reply to that charge without hesitation that the paradise Balanchine, Stravinsky and Nabokov have made visible to us is one of the few images of happiness we have, that very happiness utopian politics is working to secure, the promise of harmony, beauty, rapture.

In "Fame," a poem he wrote in Russian in 1942, Nabokov bitterly echoed the 1836 poem *Exegi monumentum* of Pushkin, which in turn echoed the poem by Horace and many another earlier poet. Whereas Horace and Pushkin could well consider their verse a monument they had raised to their own eternal glory, Nabokov, writing in exile for a tiny Russian-speaking audience which would soon be dying out, could only imagine a fantastic, garrulous visitor:

"Your poor books," he breezily said, "will finish
by hopelessly fading in exile. Alas,
those two thousand leaves of frivolous fiction
will be scattered...."

As we know now, and know with gratitude, the prophecy was not fulfilled. More glorious and surprising in his metamorphosis than any butterfly he ever stalked, Nabokov, the Russian master, turned himself into a writer in English, the best of the century. He raised a monument to himself after all.

ARTS

Marcel Duchamp

IN RETROSPECT THE TWENTIETH CENTURY seems a crazy century. Its most influential artist, Marcel Duchamp (1887–1968), did only a few dozen works, none of them very well painted, some of them just "ready-mades," i.e. bottle racks or urinals or snow shovels that he declared to be sculptures, his sculptures. He abandoned art altogether to play chess for fifteen years and, during the last twenty years of his life, to work secretly on an obscene peepshow.

Of course if you asked most muscum goers who is the greatest artist of the last century they'd name Picasso or Matisse. If Duchamp is declared to be the most influential, that's only because since the 1960s he seems to have anticipated every movement, from Pop Art to Performance Art to Conceptualism to post-modern Appropriations. And also because his playful, paradoxical mind, as expressed in Pierre Cabanne's book-length interview, *Dialogues with Marcel Duchamp* (1967), has intrigued a whole generation of art theorists.

Typically, Duchamp's most imposing work, *The Bride Stripped Bare by Her Bachelors, Even* (also called *The Large Glass*) was shattered in storage and later painfully reassembled by the artist, who professed to find the cracks, as elements introduced by chance, to be highly attractive additions. The subject of the huge glass panel (which no one would ever divine on his or her own without the aid of Duchamp's copious notes) is the machinery of sexual desire, a sort of whimsical hydraulics of marital deflowering. "The Bride is basically a motor," Duchamp asserts—a statement coherent with his early experience as a Dadaist and, later, Surrealist sympathizer.

If theories about the meaning of *The Large Glass* have varied, Duchamp welcomed the squabbling since, as his biographer Calvin Tomkins puts it, "One of his pet theories was that the artist performed only one part of the creative process and it was up to the viewer to complete that process by interpreting the work and assessing its permanent value. The viewer, in other words, is as important as the artist...." Conceptual art, obviously, is indebted to such a notion, and indeed Duchamp was, posthumously and inadvertently, the founding father of that movement, both through *The Large Glass* and its accompanying notes as well as through his "ready-mades."

Duchamp, who was to become one of the most celebrated womanizers of his day, grew up detesting his mother, whom he described as "placid and indifferent" (make of that what you will). His parents were solid bourgeois citizens in a provincial town near Rouen. His two older brothers became celebrated artists in their own right, the sculptor Raymond Duchamp-Villon (who died in the Great War) and the painter Jacques Villon. From an early age Marcel expressed his scorn for the "religion of art" and for what he called, dismissively, "retinal painting," i.e. art that appeals to the eye alone rather than to the mind (in French there was an expression at the time, *Bête comme un peintre*, "dumb as a dauber").

As a young man in Paris, Duchamp became friendly with Juan Gris (but steered clear of Picasso), showed at the Salon d'Automne (and sold a nude on a couch to Isadora Duncan) and was seduced by many women, though he scrupulously avoided all lasting attachments ("I avoid material commitments," he announced). He and his brothers were all Cubists at this time, but already Duchamp seemed unusually fascinated by words; as he said, "I always gave an important role to the title, which I added and treated like an invisible color." Eventually his comments on art—his own and everyone else's—would overshadow his meager output.

Who were his influences, the people who would help him become one of the most iconoclastic figures in contemporary culture? In 1911 he met the rich, free-wheeling, opium-smoking painter Francis Picabia, child of a Cuban father and French mother; Picabia took nothing seriously and embodied the spirit of contradiction and derisive nihilism. The philosophers Nietzsche and Henri Bergson influenced Duchamp through their writing since they both "recognize the primacy of change in life," as he put it. His epoch-making painting, *Nude Descending a Staircase,* was inspired by photographic studies of motion as well as by a recollection of big production numbers in musical comedies.

By 1912 Duchamp was already working on *The Bride Stripped Bare by Her Bachelors, Even;* at the time he said he wanted "to grasp things with the mind the way the penis is grasped by the vagina." This enigmatic work on glass was deeply influenced by the writing of the proto-Surrealist author Raymond Roussel, whose novels and plays depend on elaborate wordplay and go in for long, seemingly objective descriptions of utterly fanciful machines. Late in life, Duchamp declared, "After ten years of painting I was bored with it—in fact I was always bored with it when I did paint, except at the very beginning when there was that feeling of opening the eyes to something new.... Anyway, from 1912 on I decided to stop being a painter in the professional sense." By 1913 Duchamp had determined that *The Bride...* would be a work on glass ("Every image in the glass is there for a purpose and nothing is put in to fill a blank space or to please the eye"). At the same time he designated his first objects to be ready-mades and asked Brancusi at an aviation show: "Who can do anything better than this propeller? Can you?"

Duchamp sat out the war in New York where he quickly encountered two of the greatest patrons of modern art, John Quinn (a corporate lawyer) and Walter Arensberg, the arty son of a steel manufacturer. Arensberg began buying Duchamps during the war and by the time he died half a century later he'd amassed almost his entire oeuvre (today in its own wing of the Philadelphia Museum). Duchamp embraced the New World with flattering enthusiasm ("Look at the skyscrapers! Has Europe anything to show more beautiful than these?"). His personal and sexual magnetism must have been considerable if it could persuade his puritanical hosts to set aside the work ethic and to accept his repeated statement, "I'm lazy, don't forget that." By 1918 he'd executed his last painting, *Tu m',* which probably is short for *Tu m'emmerdes,* a coarse way of saying, "You bore me."

Essentially Duchamp was a dandy who liked to flex his muscles (disguised by his iron caprices) and to level distinctions between big and little, hand-crafted and industrial, beautiful and banal, grandiose and casual.

Like the much later Warhol, he enjoyed confusing categories, creating "multiples" and appropriating the work of other people (Duchamp wanted to "sign" the Woolworth Building, then the world's tallest skyscraper). He was even something of a gender bender; he dressed in drag and called his feminine alter ego Rrose Sélavy ("C'est la vie," get it?). Because he spent most of his life in the States, Duchamp was essentially forgotten in France until after his death (only one of his works can be found in a French museum even now). But Duchamp chose his new land cleverly, since America offered bold collectors who were willing to finance his indolent, meditative, chess-playing existence, since it had built the first museums of modern art anywhere in the world and since it responded to his mandarin pursuits with awestruck reverence.

Not working, of course, intrigues people, just as much as not making love attracts them (Warhol declared, "Frigid people make it"). Although Duchamp was out of step with the heroic spontaneity of the Abstract Expressionists and was nearly forgotten in the 1940s and '50s, by the 1960s he was back in favor. Jasper Johns did a loose version of *The Large Glass* as a set for Merce Cunningham's dancers. Richard Hamilton, the perpetrator of English Pop Art, literally and painstakingly re-created the glass, everything but the cracks. Henri Roché, the author of *Jules and Jim*, started a novel about Duchamp called *Victor* in which he recalled their frequent three-ways in the 1920s with a long series of women (Roché's death cut short the completion of the book). Duchamp himself puttered around, replacing old ready-mades that had been lost or damaged. At age 66, after a life of bachelorhood, he even married Pierre Matisse's ex-wife "Teeny," thereby surprising everyone; even more shockingly, the marriage was wonderfully harmonious.

Duchamp had always said that he had luck on his side. Unlike his brother Villon who was poor all his life and recognized only very late (he once said, "The first fifty years are the hardest"), Marcel moved from one rich woman to another and even collected legacies from deceased ex-girlfriends. His material wants were few; like Quentin Crisp, for years he lived in a single room in Manhattan and watched the dust gather. He supported himself giving French lessons to attractive women. By the time he was an old man he was hugely respected in the art world. A whole critical industry had sprung up around him. One book studied just the year 1912 in his production; several others took up, apropos of nothing in particular, the theme of alchemy. Yet another thinker related his work to Gnosticism, the occult religions of Egypt, the Orphic mysteries of Greece, the cabalistic studies of the Jews, Tantric Buddhism and God alone knows what else.

Lucky Marcel even managed to die happy in Paris. Teeny had just served a pheasant to him and several friends, including his oldest pal, Man Ray. After the guests left Duchamp read aloud to Teeny from a new humorous book by Alphonse Allais, one of his favorite writers. When he didn't emerge from the bathroom, where he was preparing to go to bed, Teeny rushed in and discovered him on the floor, fully dressed. "He had the most calm, pleased expression on his face," she later recalled—an expression only fitting for the man who'd once painted a moustache and goatee on the *Mona Lisa*.

Andy Warhol

"I STARTED OUT AS A COMMERCIAL ARTIST and I want to end up as a business artist," Andy Warhol once wrote. Although he seemed frozen by shyness and about as lively as Three Mile Island, he managed to achieve his goal by turning our very notion of what art means upside down, and this transformation set the tone for the '80s.

Warhol shrewdly (and candidly) recognized that a painter sells because he's convinced a few rich people to collect his work. Painting requires a smaller number of consumers than does fiction or film, for instance—a hundred collectors rather than a hundred thousand readers or a million moviegoers. In *The Andy Warhol Diaries* he comments, "Look. Here's how it all works: You meet rich people and you hang around with them and one night they've had a few drinks and they say, 'I'll buy it!' Then they tell their friends, 'You must have his work, darling,' and that's all you need."

But Warhol also understood that if rich people buy a contemporary, it's because his fame assures them that he must be a genius and his works will only increase in value. As the son of poor immigrants, Warhol, dazzled by the American dream, was unusually sensitive to the mechanisms for promoting celebrity. He knew that he should always resemble himself and not tamper too much with his Image, his Product Visibility. In his diary, after seeing a new Tab Hunter movie, he exclaims: "He was literally trying to act! He tried to be Clint Eastwood when all he should have done was be Tab Hunter." He applies the same rigorous logic to himself and remarks, "I think I finally look like people want Andy Warhol to look...." Celebs who refuse their destiny provoke his disdain: "I don't understand why Jackie-O thinks she's so grand that she doesn't owe it to the public to have another great marriage to somebody big. You'd think she'd want to scheme and connive to get into history again."

Such a frank (and frankly professional) concern with the media runs counter to all earlier notions of the artist. In earlier days the myth of the Great Artist was that he went Unrecognized in his own day and was appreciated only a Hundred Years Later. The delay in recognition was due to his Integrity and his being Ahead of His Times. His work Endured, however, because it was Original, Unique and Visionary.

Warhol reversed all these dictums. He made no distinction between high and popular art ("An artist is anybody who does something well," he said, "like if you cook well"). His canvases reproduce do-it-yourself paint-by-numbers kits, photomat snapshots and advertisements. In his recycling of Marilyn and Liz, green stamps, a Campbell soup can and the dollar bill, he banished at one stroke the linked ideas of the depth, singularity, authenticity and transcendence of painting. He drew an inevitable conclusion about the status of fine arts in the age of mechanical reproduction: he invented multiples.

Whereas older Abstract Expressionists in the late 1950s or early 1960s were getting nervous about the high prices they were commanding and the celebrity they were winning, Warhol turned things around and made virtues out of money and glitz. He didn't want to be a Starving Artist in a Garret; he was a Business Artist with his own Factory.

Back then people laughed at his impertinence, but in the '80s his outrages became self-evident truths. Now no distinction holds between celebrity and notoriety (between Jonas Salk and Claus von Bulow) or between market value and spiritual value (winning bids at Sotheby's and the ultimate hierarchy on Parnassus). Warhol desacralized art and replaced immortality with shelf *life*. He even dropped the romantic idea of originality (in *POPism* he wrote that he "was never embarrassed about asking someone, literally, 'What should I paint?' because Pop comes from the outside and how is asking someone for ideas any different from looking for them in a magazine?").

But he himself wasn't fooled. As he degenerated into doing portraits of Imelda Marcos or creaking out sleazy commissions, his dandified, deadpan irony slipped and his real discontent emerged: "I'm doing the Last Supper for Iolas. For Lucio Amelio I'm doing the Volcanoes. So I guess I'm a commercial artist. I guess that's the score." His naïve and genuine admiration for the more gifted or accomplished painters of his generation was one of his many winning qualities. One entry in his journal reads: "Decided to go up to see the Roy Lichtenstein show at the Whitney.... Saw the show and it was great. I was so jealous."

As long as he was working against the grain of the '60s, dismantling the mysticism that had accumulated around art over the centuries, his canvases had a bite, a flat, somber grandeur (the electric chairs or the disaster paintings, for instance). But when the age caught up with him and outdid him in cynicism, he seemed to lose direction, to founder, to go slack. He once said, tellingly, "Frigid people make it." Without a doubt his own coolness and at least apparent indifference, raised to the level of frigidity, made him both the prophet and exemplar of our cold epoch.

Gilbert and George

G ILBERT AND GEORGE CAN ONLY BE DEFINED through a series of paradoxes. They have made shocking visual disclosures by photographing and exhibiting their shit and their arses, not to mention their Bung Holes, yet no one knows much about them and the least effort to probe their lives sends them into an alarm-ringing panic. Does anyone even know their family names? (Gilbert Proesch and George Pasmore.) How many people know that Gilbert is Italian, born in the Dolomites as a speaker of Ladino? Or that George grew up fatherless in Plymouth? That the two men met at St. Martin's art school at a time when Anthony Caro was a teacher there and Barry Flanagan a fellow student? That George was once married and has children? A few years back, when gay activists were "outing" closeted gays, an enterprising journalist decided to "in" George and imply that he lived in the suburbs with a normal family.

And yet G&G could be thought of as Britain's (or the art world's) most famous gay couple (or artistic couple of any sexual stripe), the equivalent to the earlier musical duo Peter Pears and Benjamin Britten, but they rigorously resist all efforts by the gay community to assimilate them. When Daniel Farson, their biographer, asked them for details of their sex life, George became vehement: "That's part of a different story. Not part of the G&G story!..." And Gilbert added, "It would take all the magic away—it would be boring. We believe we deal with sex in the gentle way we want to in our pictures. If sexual confession was a way of changing society we'd do it, but we believe in doing it through our pictures." Their pictures, of course, are anything but gentle; they are instead shockingly confrontational, even if they are also very cool in a deadpan Warhol way. Warhol could deal with any subject matter, from movie stars to dollar bills, from the hammer and sickle to electric chairs, so long as he could present them in his bland, photographic-silkscreen manner, one that eliminated any sense of decision-making, of perilous painterly choices—of personality. In the same way Gilbert and George must bring their vast range of subject matter under the domination of their technique which, like Warhol's, has erased every trace of the artist's *patte*, of the temperament of an artist that guides a process. In G&G there is no hint of process, just as there is none in Warhol. If Warhol made multiples in order to mock one of the classic criteria of the fine arts (the fashioning of a unique and unrepeatable object), G&G represent a critique of a different criterion (the cult of the genius) by being not one person but two—a team. Romantic geniuses do not engage in teamwork.

To continue analyzing the paradoxes, G&G could be seen as master publicists, who made precedent-setting trips to the USSR (in 1990) and China (in 1993) in the full glare of international press coverage, yet their gallery shows in Moscow and Peking offered not a single work for sale. Moreover, their pictures are too large and too unpalatable (too "strong" in artspeak) to be hung in anyone's house; like Frank Stella's late sculptures, say, they are suitable only for museums, and most museums already have one.

Finally, they are "artists" of some sort, but they first became celebrated in 1969 for covering their faces and hands with metallic paint and posing, uninvited, as Living Sculptures at the London installation of a travelling international exhibit called "When Attitudes Become Form." Soon they were performing in museums and galleries all over the world as The Singing Sculpture, moving stiffly while holding a stick and glove and singing along to a gramophone record of an old music-hall team, Flanagan and Allen, belting out "Underneath the Arches." With enormous stamina and discipline, G&G were capable of performing the same song in exactly the same way for eight hours on end (even when seemingly no one was watching, according to concealed spy George Melly). They are, in fact, credited with being among those who created performance art. As an extension of these roles, when Gilbert and George visited New York in 1971 for the first time, the American critic Carter Ratcliff and his wife and friends took the pair on a walking tour of the city. Gilbert and George responded with pat phrases to everything on the tour—much like members of the royal family, one might point out:

> "That's the 52nd Street pier."
> "Marvellous."
> "Super."
> "Would you like anything to drink?"
> "How terribly kind."
> "It's a nice day, isn't it?"
> "Oh, yes, absolutely splendid."

All of life, apparently, could become a performance piece, as when Duchamp had made a decision to stay in the Green Hotel in Pasadena in 1963, an act which was seen as an allusion to his much earlier "Green Box," a miniature portfolio of his principal works, or as when Vito Acconci followed strangers and recorded their movements—or masturbated under a ramp in New York's Sonnabend Gallery and imagined the people walking overhead (*Seedbed*, in 1972).

Like many other performance artists, Gilbert and George began to produce marketable objects in the late 1970s and today they are best known for their huge "pictures," as they call these works of usually sixteen or eighteen or twenty-one square panels, often as big as a snooker table, which are almost always brightly colored, though the colors seldom correspond to those found in nature (e.g., a black man is assigned pink skin, Gilbert and George are themselves given red faces, etc.). The images are composites of photos of all sizes, the sizes seldom reflecting true relative dimensions in the real world (e.g., a flower is shown as bigger than a human face, or a turd bigger than a body, or a man the size of a microscopic slide of his *Blood Tears Spunk Piss,* to cite another title). Nor are all the elements oriented in the same perspective; figures of Gilbert and George, for instance, will radiate out from the center of a picture or be arranged head to foot like the figures on a playing card.

The result of such displacements (of relative size, color and orientation) is to reduce the documentary or anecdotal nature of photography and to play up the pattern-making aspect, as if these giant works were paper doll patterns or *images d'Epinal*. If Warhol leached out the force of an image of Marilyn or Liz by endlessly reproducing it in slightly varying formats and colors, G&G recycle their own portraits and vary them dramatically from one work to another. They are more obviously industrious and inventive than Warhol, who would have disdained G&G's hard work and obvious ambition.

Whereas Roland Barthes speaks of the human detail in a photograph that always catches our interest or sympathy, these pictures have no such puncta. Even though we are shown G&G's buttocks and penises and turds, not to mention their naked middle-aged male bodies, in reality they are no more exposed in these pictures than they are when they pose with metallicized faces. They are impersonal. In fact they present in clear, focussed detail every anatomical, even "shameful" detail, without ever arousing our interest, much less our disgust—or desire. Barthes argued that the photographic portrait always leads to thoughts of death, through an awareness of the touching mortality of its subject, but G&G's pictures defuse this buried content by making it manifest. So often their pictures are explicitly about death; *Dead Heads* or *Death Over Life* or *Down to Earth*, just to choose three 1989 works. *Down to Earth,* for example, shows G&G's small, yellow-suited bodies rising out of a row of graves in order to poke their heads into their own mouths in much larger blow-ups of their faces; they look like resurrected if damned souls being swallowed by devils who are their twins.

Curiously, these pictures never seem transgressive, even though the male nude, when viewed outside the classical or mythological optique, usually remains one of the few disturbing subjects of the modern age. As George, who'd obviously been reading his Linda Nochlin, told Farson, "'The male nude is still shocking.... Nudes have always been women because men have the money; look at advertising. If a woman artist painted women, her work would not be described as lesbian.'" Whereas men who paint men have long been thought of as dodgy.

The male nude remains hot subject matter, though G&G have somehow managed to cool it off. We cannot make up real-life stories about these naked men, Gilbert and George, because they are shadowless, stripped of context and never guilty of an unguarded, unconscious moment. They are not caught unawares in a snapshot doing something without cognizance of the camera. Nor are they pictured in dreamy, erotic repose. No, they are posing in the studio in highly stylized actions (walking in synchrony, hands over their eyes, or standing side by side, George's head on Gilbert's shoulder). Nothing can be deciphered, nothing interpreted and added, because everything is already fully intended as a sign, totally saturated with meaning. Their terribly average nakedness, in which no detail is either monstrous or enticing, functions, paradoxically, as a depersonalizing uniform as efficiently as their suits, always cut to the same mold, all three buttons invariably buttoned. A short film about them, directed by David Zilkha and shown at Edinburgh in 1996, was appropriately titled *Normal Conservative Rebels*. That G&G are both photographers and principal subjects works, as in Cindy Sherman's pictures, against any sense of exploitation, so often an aspect of experiencing photos.

As Farson reveals, after G&G first started earning big money in the late 1960s they became heavy, angry, quarrelsome drinkers, but so potent is G&G's personal and professional style (where draw the distinction?) that they were able to turn these dark days into subject matter, too. As Farsen has them singing out:

GILBERT: "Reality is much more complex."
GEORGE: "Than anything they can imagine."

From 1971 to 1980, as Gilbert told the critic Wolf Jahn: "We went through this big destructive period of the drunken scenery, exploring ourselves, exploring our dark side, going out, getting drunk, all those destructive elements, mucking about, being totally unhappy. We felt it all had to do with us, we were always looking inside ourselves. And that's why we never even looked for another person to be in our work. We felt we didn't need it. Like *Dead Boards* (1976), it all had to do with us."

Joe Brainard

WHEN JOE BRAINARD DIED in New York City on May 26, 1994, he had been nearly forgotten, except by his legion of friends. Tibor de Nagy Gallery has since then presented two major one-man shows, large exhibitions containing samples of a huge body of work, including paintings, drawings, collages and assemblages. The first show established that, early on, Brainard shared Warhol's love of product labels and that he enjoyed doing parodies of all sorts of artistic styles and movements long before visual appropriation became fashionable. As Robert Rosenblum puts it in the exhibition catalogue, "Brainard gives us a preview of the nostalgic regressions of so many recent artists, from Duncan Hannah to Mike Kelley." Rosenblum also suggests that "on a totally different wave-length, Damien Hirst's artistic recycling of crushed cigarette butts might look déjà vu after we've seen what Joe Brainard quietly did at home with the same theme back in the 1970s."

In his fairly short life (he was just 62 when he died of AIDS), Brainard worked with remarkable intensity and enviable fluency—and then abruptly stopped and devoted the last twenty years of his life to reading. Before the reading set in (it was something like a disease, the equivalent to Marcel Duchamp's chess-playing), Brainard had managed to do *thousands* of collages, as well as sets and costumes for the Joffrey Ballet Company and art-and-text collaborations with many New York School poets, including

Frank O'Hara, Kenward Elmslie, Kenneth Koch, James Schuyler, Edwin
Denby and John Ashbery. He also designed the covers for numerous
magazines and books of poetry.

Most important, he wrote a completely original book called *I Remember*,
which was reprinted by Penguin in 1996 but which was first launched
twenty-five years earlier in a shorter small-press version. Brainard had discovered a simple but irresistible form. In a text which eventually ran to
more than 130 pages, he started each short paragraph with the words, "I
remember," and then recalled an isolated, highly personal memory or an
interlocking set of recollections or just the existence of a product or a fad
from his youth.

> I remember having a crush on a boy in my Spanish class who had a
> pair of olive green suede shoes with brass buckles just like a pair I
> had ("Flagg Brothers"). I never said one word to him the entire year.
> I remember sweaters thrown over shoulders and sunglasses
> propped on heads.
> I remember fishnet.
> I remember board and brick book shelves.
> I remember driving in cars and doing landscape paintings in
> my head. (I still do that).

The form of *I Remember* was so delightful and infectious that soon
everyone started imitating it. As Brainard's childhood friend the poet Ron
Padgett writes in his afterword for the 1995 edition: "It is one of the few
literary forms that even non-literary people can use." In the early 1970s
Kenneth Koch was teaching poetry to children and he found that the
"I Remember" format was a natural for kids. Classroom creative-writing
textbooks soon took up the idea and by now thousands of teachers have
used the device across the country, but few people are even aware of its
inventor.

Padgett recalls that Brainard was reading Gertrude Stein in the
summer of 1969 when he first started writing *I Remember*, and there is
something of her shrewd naïveté in Brainard's wry declarations. Most of
the entries he came up with he rejected; the full manuscript runs to over
600 pages. With his usual directness he wrote to a friend at the time he was
composing the book that *I Remember* is "very honest. And accurate.

Honesty (for me) is very hard because I suppose I don't really believe there is such a thing, but somehow I think I have managed to do it." He went on to say that he had "practically no memory and so remembering is like pulling teeth. Every now and then, though, when I really get into it, floods of stuff just pour out and shock the you-know-what out of me. But it pours out very crystal clear and orderly."

Paul Auster, the author of *The New York Trilogy,* seemed to agree when he blurbed the Penguin edition years later: "One by one, the so-called important books of our time will be forgotten, but Joe Brainard's modest little gem will endure." Harry Mathews, the American novelist and poet who has lived in France since the 1950s, told the Paris-based avant-garde writer Georges Perec (*Life: A User's Manual*) about Joe's book, and soon Perec had produced his own *Je me souviens.* When Perec died, Mathews wrote an obituary for *Le Monde* titled "Je me souviens Georges Perec" and now Mathews's wife, the French novelist Marie Chaix, has translated Joe's *I Remember* into French. The form is so reassuring—with its openness, the mixing of big things with little, the option of lumping memories or leaving them discrete—that I found myself turning to it quite naturally when my French lover, the illustrator Hubert Sorin, died of AIDS three years ago. I was so terrified of forgetting something about him (his quirks, his tastes, his mannerisms, his opinions) that I started an "I Remember" list of my own.

Joe Brainard had been a panhandler for a few years after he arrived in New York in 1960 at the age of 18, fresh from Tulsa, but by the time I met him in the mid-'70s he seemed to be swimming in cash (he was rumored to have a very rich lover from a famous family). This combination of early poverty and more recent wealth meant that he was weirdly naïve about money. I remember that he had a big drawer in his nearly empty SoHo loft which was stuffed with thousands of dollars. He loved to invite everyone to dinner in a restaurant, and when he'd set out for the evening he'd fish out of the drawer enough money for ten dinners. "Do you think this is enough?" he'd ask, anxiously. He'd tip the waiter 50 percent, usually, and if one objected that it was too much he'd stutter, "Oh-oh-oh, but he was so nice."

Joe Brainard was both a collector and an antimaterialist. He loved beautiful objects and bought them, but he loved emptiness more and was always giving away his collections and restoring his loft to its primordial spareness. As one of his closest friends told me, "He was like a teenager.

It was difficult for him to live in the real world. He'd get rid of everything. His loft was Spartan—too much so. I remember at the end, when he was so ill, the nurse would have to kneel next to his mattress on the floor—it broke my heart."

He loved to give away his work: he must have been the despair of his gallery. He gave me a wonderful collage of a young man in sexy white underpants floating against a blue sky. The man's mouth and the tip of his nose are just visible but his eyes are obscured; he is inscribed inside a bold oval. There is something of Saint Sebastian (that classic gay icon) about him, something of a Bellini madonna (the ethereal figure floating against a cerulean blue) and something of a Leonardo da Vinci anatomical study (the geometry imposed on the body). I used the picture as the cover of the British paperback edition of my novel *The Beautiful Room Is Empty*.

When I met Joe he had already begun his great reading binge. He had a single bed, that mattress on the floor, and a radio tuned to a country-and-western station twenty-four hours a day. He'd lie on his bed all night and read, he'd finish *Great Expectations* at 3 A.M. and pick up *Middlemarch*. When he went out he would dress up in his beautiful Armani suits. He'd leave his impeccable, starched white shirts open to his waist and he almost never wore an overcoat, not even in the coldest weather, since someone had once told him he had a great chest. In fact, he was self-conscious about how skinny he was and was always beginning bulking-up schemes which he would quickly abandon.

Joe Brainard was born in Arkansas but was brought up in Tulsa. "I remember," he wrote, "that for my fifth birthday all I wanted was an off-one-shoulder black satin evening gown. I got it. And I wore it to my birthday party." "I remember when I got a five-year pin for not missing a single morning of Sunday School for five years. (Methodist)."

As a teenager in the 1950s he was already friendly with the poets Ron Padgett, Dick Gallup and Ted Berrigan, who were about his age, and with Pat Mitchell, who later became Ron's wife. "I remember giant discussions with Pat and Ron Padgett, and Ted Berrigan, after seeing *La Dolce Vita* about what all the symbolism meant." Even in high school Ron was publishing a little magazine, *The White Dove Review,* for which Joe was the art editor (LeRoi Jones and Allen Ginsberg sent them poems). Joe was considered the best artist in school. "I remember when

I worked for a department store doing fashion drawings for newspaper ads." Joe's father, who worked on an oil rig, enjoyed drawing as a hobby, and both of Joe's brothers became artists, and his sister now works in a Denver art gallery.

Pat Padgett recalls that when Joe moved to New York he lived in a storefront on the Lower East Side which he later shared with Ted Berrigan. He had friends and patrons back in Tulsa who occasionally sent him twenty or thirty dollars. He sold blood from time to time and worked in a junk-antique store. One day he received a notice for his army physical. "I remember when I got drafted and had to go way downtown to take my physical," Brainard writes. "It was early in the morning. I had an egg for breakfast and I could feel it sitting there in my stomach. After roll call a man looked at me and ordered me to a different line than most of the boys were lined up at. (I had very long hair which was more unusual then than it is now.) The line I was sent to turned out to be the line to see the head doctor. (I was going to ask to see him anyway.) The doctor asked me if I was queer and I said yes. Then he asked me what homosexual experiences I had had and I said none. (It was the truth.) And he believed me. I didn't even have to take my clothes off."

As Pat Padgett recalls, "In high school he had had crushes on boys and girls. But in his family no one ever spoke about personal things. And I certainly didn't think about things like homosexuality. I guess he told Ron and me as soon as it became apparent to him. After[ward] he became close with Joe LeSueur, Frank O'Hara and Kenward Elmslie."

Although everyone agrees that Joe felt bad about his scanty education, they all speak of his intelligence and superb instincts. John Ashbery had just come back from years of living in Paris where he'd been the art critic for the *Herald-Tribune,* and he was very impressed by Joe's artistic judgment, by "an intelligence disguised by a surface naiveté." Kenward Elmslie, who became Joe's best friend and with whom he spent summers in Calais, Vermont, once said that Joe had the finest intuition of anyone he'd ever known. Joe LeSueur agrees that Brainard had a perfect eye and ear. As LeSueur puts it, "I met him when he was nineteen and he already knew everything. He was a true master of collage. He'd do five a day—and he couldn't wait to get on to the next one. He wasn't influenced by anyone. I bought his painting *7-Up* for fourteen dollars—but Joe gave up Pop Art of that sort as soon as he saw Warhol's work later."

In his first show at the Alan Gallery in 1965 Brainard did big Puerto Rican–style altarpieces. Soon afterwards he wrote to James Schuyler that he had had no specific religious intention in mind when he constructed his shrines. "On the other hand, a lot of people said I was making fun of religion which would be even worse. I'd almost rather be religious."

Except for the annual summer pilgrimages to Vermont, Joe was faithful to New York, although he once lived briefly in Boston ("I remember when I lived in Boston reading all of Dostoevsky's novels one right after the other") and in Dayton ("I remember when I won a scholarship to the Dayton, Ohio, Art Institute and I didn't like it but I didn't want to hurt their feelings by just quitting so I told them my father was dying of cancer").

Whereas Pop artists took an adversarial position against everyday images, Joe liked everything, and was himself immensely likeable as a man and as a painter. In a catalogue essay for the recent show, John Ashbery writes: "Joe Brainard was one of the nicest artists I have ever known. Nice as a person, and nice as an artist. This may present a problem…. One can sincerely admire the chic and the implicit nastiness of a Warhol soup can without ever wanting to cozy up to it, and perhaps that is as it should be, art being art, a rather distant thing. In the case of Joe one wants to embrace the pansy, so to speak. Make it feel better about being itself, all alone, a silly kind of expression on its face, forced to bear the brunt of its name eternally."

Joe drew a coffee cup with a 1930s illustrator's abstract smartness, or turned out an Ingres-like pencil portrait of Pat as a young woman, or composed a breakfast still life in the comfortable, life-enhancing, *pleasurable* mode of Fairfield Porter (one of his idols). He did a huge gouache-collage of hundreds of flowers arranged in a *Garden*, or he painted a sumptuous, four-foot-tall gouache of a *Madonna with Daffodils*. He crammed cigarette butts into small, intricate patterns. Sleek athletes in underpants (often with parts of their bodies replaced by bits of blue sky) recall the innocence of physique magazines of the 1950s: "I remember how many other magazines I had to buy in order to buy one physique magazine," he wrote.

One series of small oils was devoted to Kenward Elmslie's dog Whippoorwill. In one canvas, just nine inches by twelve, painted in 1975, the lean white dog is shown crouched on very green grass before a small white clapboard house; it's called *Whippoorwill's World* as a funny allusion to Wyeth's painting, but the humor is gentle, not sarcastic, and it does nothing to detract from the sheer beauty of the image.

Brainard often alluded to other artists (in his 1968 cover for an *ARTnews* annual, the head of the comic-strip character Nancy is shown in turn collaged onto Goya's *Nude Maja,* Manet's *Olympia,* Duchamp's *Nude Descending a Staircase* and De Kooning's *Woman,* and she cavorts through a Mondrian abstraction, a Johns Target and a series of Donald Judd boxes). But his own style has no antecedents and only one real parallel— Donald Evans. Like the art of Evans, whose oeuvre consisted of several thousand meticulously painted postage stamps of fictive nations, each of which corresponded, as Bruce Chatwin observed, "to a phase, a friendship, a mood, or a preoccupation," Joe's work was also often miniature, gently parodic *and* personal. Brainard's brother John told me that Joe and Evans were friends and exchanged letters and that Evans, who died in 1977, signed and gave a stamp to Joe as well as a book about his work.

The one event in Brainard's life which puzzles everyone is why he quit painting. When I mentioned the parallel with Duchamp's virtual "silence" as a painter from the 1920s to his death in the 1960s, Pat Padgett laughed and said, "Yeah, but Duchamp was not a very good painter. He may have been a brilliant thinker but he had little talent. Whereas, Joe had a good hand and could do *anything.* And yet Joe thought he wasn't good enough to do great easel painting, which for him was the ultimate form. I think Joe felt that no one after the Abstract Expressionists had come up to their level and that disparity tormented him."

Joe LeSueur added, "I think that at first he was excited by fame and was thrilled by all the attention he got. But then he saw that success doesn't bring much happiness. After all, he knew the most famous poets of the day—Ashbery, Kenneth Koch, Frank O'Hara—and his friendship with them convinced him that success isn't such a big deal. Then he came off speed; he'd been on amphetamines for years and during those years his hands couldn't work fast enough. He must have seen he couldn't go on like that." Another friend told me that Joe had freaked out when he saw little men and after the mid-1970s he'd never done speed again. "Anyway," LeSueur concluded, "he'd already created a huge, totally original body of work. Maybe he felt satisfied with his achievement."

Ron Padgett believes Brainard was too hard on himself. "Towards the end of his painting days he wanted to do lace as well as Velázquez, a gentleman's waistcoat as vividly as Raeburn, a horse as solidly as Stubbs, a cherry as convincingly as Manet. When he couldn't always reach those impossible heights he just stopped." Everyone agrees that the fact he'd had a considerable fortune settled on him *permitted* him to stop painting; in that sense the money was bad for him. Curiously, he didn't seem to miss the creative act.

The poet Bill Berkson said, "Joe had a difficult time coming off speed. There were times when he seemed nervous, laughing bizarrely at some private joke. Ted Berrigan would tease him and ask, 'Why don't you want to be great like De Kooning?' Joe would demur, but he probably did mean to be great in his own sweet way, like Joseph Cornell. He liked to show people doing dumb, everydayish things—that's why he liked Sluggo and Nancy. And in that way his art was a lot like John Ashbery's poems."

Actor Keith McDermott, whom Brainard fell in love with in 1979 and remained close to, remembers that Joe was surprised by his positive HIV status. "I thought he'd commit suicide, but no, he became very docile and just did whatever the doctors said." John Brainard was with his brother constantly from December 1993 till Joe's death the following May. "He stayed from December to March in the hospital, then he lived in my apartment. He was very accepting of illness and death. Only in September 1993 did he tell me he had AIDS, but at that time he said it was okay with him, he knew much younger people who were dying or who had died. He felt he had had enough time. Though he went through a lot of pain, he suffered it very bravely." At his memorial ceremony several speakers called him "saintly."

I myself always mentally compared him to Dostoevsky's Prince Myshkin—he was that unworldly and Christlike. Joe was the only person I've ever known whom I'd try to talk and act like when I was with him. My imitations were embarrassing and never successful, but the urge to delete all phoniness and really *look* at the surrounding world with a fresh eye and to shower everyone with generosity was so compelling that by the end of an evening with Joe I was even unconsciously imitating his stutter. Joe's personal style was certainly hypnotic.

Steve Wolfe

S TEVE WOLFE MAKES OBJECTS that are so original they are hard to describe—they could be called "hand-made ready-mades." Whereas Duchamp startled the world a century ago offering industrial bottle racks and urinals as artistic works of his own, Wolfe re-creates existing mass-produced articles (mostly books and records from the '60s and '70s) in other materials (oil, screenprint, modeling paste, canvasboard, wood, paper) and in such a way that the originals and the copies are indistinguishable one from another (unless they are actually put side by side). When compared closely the discerning eye will of course pick out differences, say, between machine-stamped LPs and hand-painted grooves. The re-creations take months to make, sometimes years, and involve typesetting, bronze-casting, lacquering, various distressing and discoloring processes, etc.

The objects that Wolfe so painstakingly fashions in different media are not selected arbitrarily. They are the music and books about painting and the novels that constituted his own formation as a sensibility; they provide a record of his talismanic influences. Given the fact that he was born in 1955 and was a teenager in the late 1960s, his interest in the cultural icons of that decade might seem precocious. But he had a flair for these books and records, as if he divined that Nabokov and Colette, Beckett and Isherwood would later transport him to a world of culture he could use.

Wolfe's method of translating his books and records into new (often more durable) media is a way of "rescuing" them from oblivion, of sacralizing them as fetishes and thus separating them from the myriad competing artifacts of the period, of raising them in status by dint of the hundreds or even thousands of hours devoted to each re-creation. To be sure, Wolfe has also selected for representation books that are either influences on him or significant forebears—Duchamp is the subject of one book and another is devoted to the nineteenth century *trompe-l'oeil* American artist John F. Peto, for instance. (Wolfe's *Peto* is one of that artist's paintings of a candle, an inkwell, a quill pen and—appropriately enough—three battered books.) Other art books are dedicated to Magritte and Joseph Cornell, as if in acknowledgment of the international diaspora of Surrealism. Wolfe's selection of records and books is not arbitrary, and it is certainly not always dictated by admiration for the cover art, which is sometimes almost comically "period." No, he has obviously selected the music and words which he admires and which define a sensibility that is more French than German (Raymond Queneau but no Thomas Mann, Colette but no Brecht, Satie but no Hindemith), which is often high modernist (Mondrian, Picasso, Stein, Beckett) and which can even succumb to the rather shopworn charm of Cocteau, even as a draftsman.

For someone who came of age in the 1960s in the United States, there was a sudden, liberating mix of high and low culture—in fact, an erasure of this distinction. Books by Beckett and Sartre were shelved with those of Raymond Chandler, just as records of Satie were placed in the same cartons as those of the Beatles. In the same box of books were placed novels by Céline and Tom Swift boys' books, a biography of Montgomery Clift and *Lolita*. Gone was the notion that beauty should be difficult, that high art required a strenuous effort to be understood.

Wolfe, in his monklike way, has lavished endless patience and remarkable ingenuity on re-creating those cardboard grocery cartons and their precious, heterogeneous contents. For the typical poor grad student of the period (or the beginning artist), these cartons of records and books were his or her only significant belongings, a declaration of identity and a lien on the spiritual and intellectual world which was often far away, in Paris, say, or New York. The books on one's shelves were seen as badges of one's aspirations and affinities, and when eggheads of the period went out on a first date they examined each other's bookshelves early on to discover exactly what kind of person they were dealing with. A Marxist might say that one reason artists since the Romantic era have suffered so much is that they have had the earnings of the lumpen proletariat and the cultural allegiances of the aristocracy. These bohemians and dandies, who first emerged early in the nineteenth century at the same time as the mechanical reproduction of works of art, have always perpetuated their fragile sense of identity by clinging to their key books and (starting in the twentieth century) their favorite records.

The urban, heterodox mix of high and low, French and American, traditional and modern is as much on display in Wolfe's re-created artifacts as it is, say, in a poem by Frank O'Hara (Wolfe has done a sculpture based on his *Lunch Poems* and *Collected Poems*), who can refer in the same stanza to Tolstoy and Warner Baxter in *Vogues of 1938*. Just as O'Hara can salute in one of his lunch poems Billie Holiday and in another the poet Pierre Reverdy, and treat both with the same queer combination of proprietary familiarity and solemn respect, in the same way Wolfe parades us past his personal icons clothed in book jackets covered with cigarette burns, tears and creases, all the signs of constant use— and a use that in the originals has literally left its individualizing stamp on mass-produced objects. These "flaws" are the endearingly personal signs of individual and daily wear and tear, of reading, reshelving, of moving and moving again. To be sure, some of Wolfe's objects look fresh and well-cared for.

The book enjoys a strange ontological status. It is a mass-produced object, yet even the first Guttenberg Bibles were hand-ornamented in red, in order to make them resemble something more valuable, i.e., a genuine individually copied and illuminated manuscript. In China some of the first examples of printing were Buddhist prayers carved into woodblocks and stamped thousands of times on paper with ink in order to proliferate their holy efficacy. Each prayer was stamped at a slightly different angle and with more or less ink. But we need not reach so far back into history to discover the individuality of books and printing. Even copies of modern books have pedigrees, they are given or sold by one person to another, inscribed with names and dates, pasted over with book plates. They have been deaccessioned by public libraries, key passages are underlined, corners are turned down. Blank pages in the back are covered with lists that have nothing to do with this book. Well-loved books with a bit of history on them reveal their past, just as the colophon of a Chinese painting attests to the enthusiasm—or just the random thoughts—of its successive owners.

To be sure, a book isn't a unique work of art like a painting or sculpture. But it isn't exactly like a print of a photograph either, since a photo (ideally at least) doesn't pick up signs of wear and tear. Books are left out in the rain or dropped in the tub or are invaded by silverfish (Wolfe's Proust volumes have been bleached by sunlight), whereas valuable photos are framed and protected from direct sunlight. The mechanical reproduction of works of art, Walter Benjamin has said, changes their status from cult objects to instruments of entertainment (Benjamin had in mind the difference between the connoisseur's appreciation of a statue and the public's enjoyment of a movie). But a book—not a glossy book in the shop window but a battered book in someone's home library—may be a source of entertainment or instruction, depending on its contents, but to the collector it is something very much like a cult object, a "portable altar" (in the sense of *The Portable Whitman*). Or it is like a friend, or at least a letter from a friend.

If the book itself is neither an interchangeable mass-produced item nor a unique work of art, what can we say about Wolfe's "books"? Or his "records," based on the old vinyl LPs that had a limited life and were scratched or worn down with each playing? Wolfe has transformed these objects into the uniqueness of the painting or the sculpture, stripped them of their ambiguous status between individual possession and standardized product and elevated them into the heaven of high art, where each star is a solitaire. Warhol might have painted Campbell soup cans, but he was making two-dimensional portraits of mass-produced objects in three dimensions (except in rare instances such as the Brillo boxes) which could never be confused with their original subjects. Wolfe has understood Warhol's philosophical playfulness but has raised the stakes by making objects which are all but identical to their humble, much-thumbed, well-traveled originals. This remarkable feat of *trompe-l'oeil* conceals from the profane, casual viewer Wolfe's heroic accomplishment.

I suppose Wolfe is a bit like Pierre Menard, the hero of the Borges story ("Pierre Menard, Author of the Quixote") who devotes his whole life to reconstructing a few pages of *Don Quixote,* word for word, pages he read years ago and of which he possesses only the dimmest memory, though he knows Cervantes's other works and has studied all the influences that bore upon Cervantes at the time. The pages now, however, are by an early twentieth-century Symbolist from Nîmes and not by a sixteenth-century tax collector in Granada. Now the work must be read as an entirely different set of intentions. Thus when Cervantes writes, "Truth, whose mother is history," he is just indulging in a bit of rhetorical flourish typical of his period, whereas when Menard, the contemporary of William James, writes, "Truth, the mother of history," he is making an "astounding" statement. He is defining truth not as an inquiry into history but as its origin.

Of course Borges was spoofing a bit but he also was arguing that when a work is re-created—even if the re-creation is impeccable—it no longer has the same impact or the same meaning as the original. The copy has been inscribed into a new world of values and signifiers and it has become an oeuvre of the new artist. When we see the abstract shapes on the covers of the Beckett trilogy we may smile at the tastes of another period, but Wolfe's tributes to those books function in an entirely different way, not as pastiche much less satire and certainly not as blind endorsement but as a consecration of the books, their role in his own formation and in the evolution of our culture. He is also saluting the '50s, when the paperbacks were published, and possibly the '60s, the period when writers from all over the world polled by the *New York Herald* ranked Beckett as the greatest living writer.

Wolfe's is not coldly calculated conceptual art. It requires the organizational skills and artistic resourcefulness of a (successful) rocket launch. And it is never heartless, purely cerebral or ironic at someone else's expense. In comparison to some of his contemporaries, Wolfe is more self-effacing, less self-dramatizing—and far more playful. Wolfe's re-creations are delivered to the viewer sometimes reverentially but more often in a bemused, noncommittal way. Whereas other artists shout out their sardonic comments, Wolfe never raises his voice.

In a famous essay, "Unpacking My Library," Walter Benjamin talks of the joys of opening crates of books that were long held in storage—the excitement of unpacking old friends, of greeting them one after another and arranging them tenderly on new shelves. If the Romans said, "Books have their fates," Benjamin, speaking as a collector, insists that copies of books also have their destinies. "I am not exaggerating," Benjamin writes, "when I say that to a true collector the acquisition of an old book is a rebirth." Nor are the books in a collection necessarily those which one has read—in fact, Benjamin insists, the nonreading of books is much more characteristic of collectors. For the true collector each book has a personality and one that can only be fully realized in his collection. "One of the finest memories of a collector is the moment when he rescued a book to which he might never have given a thought, much less a wishful look, because he found it lonely and abandoned in the marketplace and bought it to give it its freedom—the way the prince bought a beautiful slave girl in the *Thousand and One Nights*. To a book collector, you see, the true freedom of all books is somewhere on his shelves."

This attitude is of course very different from that of the obsessed reader, who cares not at all about the material object but only about the intellectual content. After all, what copyright lawyers protect is not the book-as-object but the so-called "intellectual property." Nevertheless the lawyer is the first to admit that intellectual content that has not been written down is indefensible. It must be "captured" in print or in a typescript before it exists, at least in the eyes of the law. It cannot just be a book outlined in conversation or a folk story repeated at bedtime. But for the genuine reader, however, this written down form of the book is merely a convenience, an instance, and the true reader quickly loses all sense of the art director's and bookbinder's presentation and immerses himself or herself in the vivid and continuous dream evoked by the novel as story.

The collector, by contrast, doesn't read his books, though he intends to do so some day. He cherishes a particular edition and will collect books designed by Chip Kidd, say, without really noticing which particular books they might happen to be. Or the grad school reader does read his books, but he would take it as a personal assault if someone stole the particular volume he read in a Russian lit course oh so many years ago, a volume punctuated with alarming frequency with big question marks and bigger exclamation points in the margin.

Steve Wolfe is someone who "likes things" (which is how Andy Warhol once described himself). He has taught himself a whole array of arcane techniques but not out of vanity about his craftsmanship but rather out of a love of his collections. We are used to writers who have been inspired by paintings; ekphrasis, or the verbal evocation of a painting or sculpture, is a device that goes back to Homer's description of the Shield of Achilles and has been brilliantly deployed in the twentieth century by such poets as

Auden, Richard Howard and John Hollander. The opposite process, the celebration in visual art of books (their material envelope if not their invisible content), is a device that has inspired many artists in recent years and there have been several important shows dedicated to this very subject. To be sure, books themselves are often illustrated or illuminated; the painter Archimboldo composed human heads out of books; statues of saints and especially doctors of the church are often given books to hold; and erudites such as Voltaire are characteristically shown in portraits reading or writing books. Decorators give expensive and uniform bindings to books of no importance to lend distinction to a "library"; such volumes are referred to in the trade as "book furniture." There are many hollowed out books designed to conceal a pistol or a flask of whiskey or money. But Wolfe is the first sculptor I know of to undertake such an elaborate practice of simulating known books.

One of my favorite Wolfe sculptures is his version of Nabokov's *Speak, Memory*. The memoir is an elusive text heavy on atmosphere and sensuous detail and lean on information or even feelings. No matter how much it might frustrate the nosy contemporary reader, it remains one of the most "artistic" of all twentieth-century autobiographies. Its very silences are characteristic of Nabokov at his most elegantly reticent.

Wolfe has captured this book as if it appears to be falling from its picture-level perch and heading for the floor. The cover is flung open in full precipitation to reveal the signature butterfly and a map printed on facing fly leaves. It is labeled "Sketch map of the Nabokov lands in the St. Petersburg region" and shows everything from the length of a verst to the path of the Warsaw railway, a blue Oredezh River and red roads south to Luga and north to St. Petersburg. The all-print cover with, on the back, a photo of its cravatted and bespectacled author in a sports coat has fallen faster than the volume itself. The cover (re-created of course in lithography and oil paints on paper that has been sanded and treated to look sufficiently glossy) is covertly attached to the wall and floor with a removable adhesive in such a way that a passerby will cause it to flutter ever so slightly. If God is in the details, then Steve Wolfe's sculptures are certifiably divine.

Rebecca Horn

EVERYTHING IN THE WORK OF REBECCA HORN is intimate, yet nothing is personal. A sculptor who makes fantastic machines, a filmmaker who realizes her wildest dreams, a writer who concocts wry texts to accompany her museum and gallery installations, this red-haired German-Swiss artist (with a pure profile worthy of a cameo) never stops telling her secrets—only they're ended, as in dreams.

Horn's sculpture runs an extraordinarily broad gamut. A blue electric charge sizzles and glows between fourteen pairs of brass rods suspended from the ceiling; paint splatters down on high-heeled shoes fixed on rods to the gallery wall; gray feathers, stuck to a wheel, turn in a circle, spreading open, then suddenly snapping shut, shuddering off balance. Waves gently undulate over the surface of a black pool; piles of black and yellow pigment slowly build up on the floor; liquid drips into open cones; an electric-powered rod revolves like a geometer's compass. These machines sometimes seem like martian animals (one of Horn's titles is *An Art Circus*) and sometimes like the whimsical pseudoscientific mechanical actions that Marcel Duchamp dreamed up—the rotating chocolate grinders and the rising humidity of lust, for instance. In his monumental work *Bride Stripped Bare by Her Bachelors, Even* Horn is quick to admit that the purring, cerebral Duchamp is her spiritual mentor.

"Photographers are usually disappointed with me," Horn tells me with a smile in her pristine Berlin studio, all vast spaces and white marble floors, the sort of place where every piece of furniture counts as a statement. "They think if I'm a sculptor then I should be covered with marble dust or up to my elbows in mud, but in fact, all I do is think out my pieces, which are realized by a team of technicians." Indeed, the only signs of her work when I visited were photos scattered on the floor, of the inner dome of the Guggenheim [Museum] on which she was superimposing various forms.

Rebecca Horn is quick, funny, and *sympathique*, but her easygoing ways in no sense diminish her integrity and her fidelity to an extremely private vision—one that sometimes, paradoxically, produces public outrage. She is a genuinely international artist. She teaches in Berlin but usually spends just two weeks of every five there. She has a studio near Heidelberg, and the rest of the time she's in Paris; perhaps due to her years in New York and Paris, she is free of the Pina Bausch–style angst that characterizes most German artists today. If she's tormented, she doesn't show it. In Paris she lives in the upscale bohemian area of the Bastille, where she occupies the top floor of an old public bathhouse; her rooms are the former massage parlors. There she has nine windows that look out onto trees growing in the roof gardens below ("It's like suddenly being in the country," she observes). But more often she's on a plane or living out of a suitcase in Los Angeles or New York, Barcelona or Amsterdam.

She was a New Yorker from 1972 to 1981. When she arrived from Germany she was a penniless student, and her first year she camped out in one studio after another as friends went on vacation. "That was a great time to be in New York," she tells me in her fluent but heavily accented English. "In the eighties the New York art scene became too vain, is that the word? And much too expensive. The prices for fledgling painters tripled within a year—whereas those of a Marcel Duchamp remained the same. Unfortunately an economic crisis was needed to restore normal values. Now I like New York again."

All of Horn's work involves a personal sense of geography, of the spirit of places, and proceeds through a dialogue—sometimes between cities (East Berlin and Barcelona, for instance) and sometimes between two or more places in the same city. When I spoke to her she was looking for a cellar or a warehouse in lower Manhattan where she could stage a second installation, as an adjunct to the upscale Fifth Avenue show at the Guggenheim.

Sometimes the dialogue takes place in time, contrasting a superficially tranquil present with a turbulent past. In 1987 the German town of Münster invited her to create an installation wherever she liked (other artists were doing similar pieces). With her unerring instinct, Horn chose a tower that had long been condemned as "unsafe," often a strategy used in postwar Germany to efface or bury the unpleasant past. The festival organizers refused the space. She threatened to make a fuss in the press, and eventually she got her tower but at a price: not one local would work with her, as she explained, and she was forced to bring in assistants from Holland.

When she researched the history of the building, she found it had been used by the Gestapo during the war to execute Russian and Polish prisoners; four at a time were hanged in the central tower. She summoned up this past (but did not illustrate it) in an installation of forty mechanized hammers placed throughout the building. In an irregular rhythm they would knock on the walls—the sound of prisoners trying to get out or perhaps the violence of guards striking their victims. In the years the tower had been neglected, airborne seeds had drifted into it and sprouted there; Horn carefully preserved these tokens of the renewal of life. She added countless muted red lights—an allusion to the votive candles in the churches of Catholic Münster. From the top of the tower, a drop of water fell at regular intervals into a black pool below—a sort of water torture.

"But still there wasn't enough life in the tower. So I brought in two serpents from Amsterdam and put them in a heated, lighted transparent box and fed them a mouse from Münster every day. That drove the locals wild! They tried to stop me, accused me of inhuman cruelty—this in a town where no one had objected to the Gestapo."

Horn smiles, delighted to be a provocateur in a country where events have shown that fascism has never been completely eliminated. Her formally pure and cerebral pieces are anything but agitprop, nor are they "committed" or "politically correct." But in their playful, nearly abstract way they can lance a festering social boil.

Sometimes her pieces are more difficult to decipher. Recently she took over seven rooms in a seedy hotel in the old red-light district of Barcelona. She had been invited by the city to do an installation to coincide with the

Olympics—a work for which she won the city's most prestigious art award, never before granted to a foreigner.

Without fully working out in advance her meaning or choices, Horn selected the Hotel Peninsular, which she later discovered had been not just a hotel but also a bordello and a convent.

In the first room, *Earth*, a bed was half-retracted into the wall. Flashes of light briefly shattered the gloom, and a pair of shoes constantly trembled in the middle of the floor. In the second room, *Water*, tears dripped from the ceiling into waiting funnels. In *Circle*, a pole emerging from a bed rotated a long needle that repeatedly scratched fine marks onto the walls of the room. In *Lovers*, nine violins played all by themselves, like the sorcerer's apprentices. In the next room two pistols, aimed at each other, kept firing. In the sixth room, *Tenderness*, two small machines, decked out in the plumage of pink flamingos, spread their tails and caressed each other. In the last room, *Light*, bolts of brilliant illumination shot up glass tubes that ran out the windows towards the sky.

Nothing in these rooms, except the emotion-soaked atmosphere, would give a direct clue that the installation was based on a real story, or rather several. Barcelona was the city where Horn had had a passionate love affair. In art school in Germany, her teacher had told her that rather than studying traditional sculpture techniques, she should simply read thoroughly Jean Genet's *The Thief's Journal,* an autobiographical novel that records Genet's experience in Barcelona as a beggar, thief and prostitute of the Barrio Chino. The book quickly became her principal fetish. While Horn was still in art school, her father invited her for her birthday to Barcelona and a surprise boat trip to Tangier, where he'd arranged for her to be serenaded by an old violinist whom she had known and idolized since childhood. Soon after this trip her father died, and Horn never went back to Barcelona until the city commissioned her to do her installation. The work draws on memories of her affair, of Genet's humiliations, of her old violinist, and her grief over her father's death. That the work is elliptical, not anecdotal, in no ways robs it of its force.

The need to document her ephemeral performance pieces was what first prompted her interest in films. Her first film, made in 1971, was a twelve-minute documentary of a young woman dressed as a unicorn crossing the countryside. Several other short documentaries followed. Then in 1978 she made *Der Eintänzer,* a fictional film she herself scripted; the star was David Warrilow, the great English actor for whom Samuel Beckett had written a number of short plays.

Her real love in the movies, Buster Keaton, became the subject of her longest (and most expensive) film to date: *Buster's Bedroom,* which she worked on in 1989 and 1990 and which was budgeted at $3 million. "I first discovered Keaton's films in New York in 1974 during a marathon screening at the old Elgin cinema. He reminded me of me; like me he can't get along in the normal world and must resort to private fantasies. That's why the Surrealists loved him, of course. And then, like me, he constructs absurd machines. Even his way of making films he created, acted in, and edited is my ideal." The resulting 112-minute film, shot by Ingmar Berman's cameraman, Sven Nykvist, and starring such actors as Geraldine Chaplin, Donald Sutherland and David Warrilow, recounts the story of a young woman, obsessed by the long-dead Keaton, who travels to California to find an asylum where Keaton had once been treated for alcoholism. At the sanatorium she meets a group of weird characters, undergoes some zany adventures—and encounters strange machines designed by Rebecca Horn.

But Horn is not just a Surrealist mechanic, she's also a mystic. When she asked David Warrilow to play a blind man in *Der Eintänzer,* he was shocked since, unbeknownst to everyone, he had just had serious problems with his vision. Horn found the coincidence completely natural. She also readily accepted a revelation given to her in Barcelona when someone told her she'd been murdered there in a previous life, during the sixteenth century.

When she began to plan an original work for her Guggenheim show, she discovered that the wife and daughter of the museum's architect, Frank Lloyd Wright, had been students of the Russian-born esoteric philosopher Gurdjieff. She also realized that the fountain designed for the ground floor resembles the Turkish charm against evil in the form of an eye. As a result she decided to have a milky liquid drip from the dome into the pool far below, at once an allusion to the tears of the spiritual eye and a reference to the relationship between the paradise of the dome and the netherworld below—a relationship that would be underscored by lightning machines that Horn calls Jacob's ladders.

But such heavenly hydraulics are never purely abstract; she links the Guggenheim piece to a potent personal experience. When her parents died, Horn was still in her twenties. The only surviving member of her family was an old aunt who had lived her whole life in luxury, although she was quickly becoming penniless. Horn worked hard over the years to support the aunt in the luxurious style she'd always known. And when the aunt became very weak and ill, Horn promised to sit by her bedside until the moment of death—and beyond.

Horn in fact sat holding on to her body eight full hours after the doctor had pronounced her dead. Although Horn is reluctant to discuss her experience and sketches it only very lightly, she'd once been haunted by someone dear whose ghost had not been properly laid to rest. This time she was determined to accompany her aunt all the way into death. At a certain moment she felt the process had come to an end. Her aunt's face at last relaxed, pretty as the face of a young girl. Horn released her, and she felt the freed energy rise.

This is the energy Horn believes she is tapping in her wry inventions and cabalistic installations, her mystical time and motion studies, her machines with a human heart.

Cy Twombly

C Y TWOMBLY'S PERSONALITY IS AS ELUSIVE as his paintings. He speaks in half-sentences, full of what he calls "reference"—tentative allusions to high and low culture, both European and American, recent and ancient—just as his paintings, with their penciled-in quotations from poets or their scrawled or scratched names, invoke worlds varying from the lyric purity of Sappho to the bloodiest pages of Roman history.

He's tall, with a big Founding Father nose and a hazy elegance of sketched-in gesture. He has a sloppy, shuffling way of walking. He dresses in high-WASP thrift-store chic (shapeless old white linen trousers, a moth-eaten blue pullover). And he speaks with a mouth full of corn pone, for he was brought up in Lexington, Virginia, by an African-American nanny to whom he remains fiercely attached. When I interviewed him, he was planning to take her to the opening of his Museum of Modern Art retrospective in New York in September 1994, though he was afraid she might shock the other guests with her outspokenness. I had been warned about Twombly's imperious aloofness, his neurotic skittishness and his lordly ways, but I was surprised to discover how down-home he could be; when I asked him where he was from, he said in a good-ol' boy drawl, "Me? Hell, I'm just from Chitlin' Switch," his way of saying he's nobody from nowhere.

Could be, but at the same time he has lived in Italy since the 1950s, he has been married to an Italian aristocrat for thirty-five years, and he possesses a formidable mastery of past and present culture (not to mention a vast Borgia palazzo in Rome). In the course of the two days we spent together, his conversation skipped all over the map and through the ages. He referred to the turn-of-the-century French travel writer Pierre Loti, the Greek Alexandrian poet C. P. Cavafy (whose verse Twombly has quoted in his work), the provocative French painter Balthus and the iconoclastic American novelist Gore Vidal—just to mention four names out of a hundred.

Like Loti, Twombly is a tireless traveler; I first met him in the mid-1980s on Crete, and later ran into him again in Luxor, where he was impressed less by the temples than by the desert and the traces of everyday domestic and agricultural life in ancient paintings and tomb objects. Travel books make up an essential part of his reading, in which one work leads thematically to the next. Currently, on his worktable, he had a pile of four related texts: George Gissing's *By the Ionian Sea*, which had inspired the next under it, Norman Douglas's *Old Calabria*, which was written at the same time as *Moving Along,* by Norman Douglas's friend Giuseppe Orioli. The last book in the pile was *Capri: Island of Pleasure,* a look at the decadent history of that millenarian resort, where Douglas held court for twenty years.

Like Cavafy, Twombly lives at the juncture of several cultures and epochs and has struggled to plunder the classical past of its passion and force. Like Balthus, a hermit who resided in a castle and had assumed a noble title, Twombly is the absolute deity of a closed guild made up of his family and a few friends. He flees casual celebrity as assiduously as he cultivates artistic perfection. Finally, like Gore Vidal, Twombly is an American who has long lived in Italy in arrogant, splendid solitude, although both men have vigilantly scrutinized the States from a safe distance and staged raids on it at unexpected moments.

Twombly has a very light touch when he juggles his references: "I've never much liked the Byzantine or medieval worlds—they're too closed-in for my taste. But Gore Vidal's *Julian* [about the late Roman emperor and apostate] did explain many of the backgrounds to Cavafy's poems for me, especially the intricacies of the city of Antioch. Of course, I love E. M. Forster on Cavafy. But the real question is: where did Cavafy himself *learn* all that?"

It's a stumper, and such a question could be intimidating, except that in this situation the listener is just a twig caught up in the flood of Twombly's conversation. Imagine a pond overflowing to engulf fields, ruins and roads and you'll get an idea of the range and rush of the man's interests.

For all of the time he has spent in Italy, he speaks the language very approximately, and usually replies in English to questions asked in Italian. He bristles when the word "expatriate" is mentioned. "Art is international in this century! It's true, though," he drawls, "I prefer Rome to Chicago, but the whole idea of an expatriate is dated. I never think about that; I just go to the place I want to.... What's the difference whether you live in Italy or Houston? Of course, Americans don't like it if you live abroad too long—they think you're getting uppity. Have you noticed how America is becoming more and more...*proletariat?* The other day I posed for an American photographer wearing a tie and shirt, and the photographer acted as though I were putting on airs."

Of course, you can't trust everything Twombly says. When I asked him what his parents did, he said that they were Sicilian ceramists, and that he'd sold their pots in Ogunquit, Maine. When I asked him how many paintings would be in his MoMA show, he said, without a blink, "Forty thousand." He will tackle a subject at an angle, crablike, then quickly abandon it. He often breaks into a radiant, gap-toothed smile that gives a raffish splendor to a face deeply creased with unexpectedly *vertical* lines. And he can sit for hours in a hard metal chair, then burst into urgent, pointless activity. In his judgments of his contemporaries, he takes away with one hand what he gives with the other ("Balthus is rather haughty in the French way, but he's a cultured and deeply interesting man"). And he enjoys puncturing pretension, with darts that seem small and harmless ("Gore Vidal once told one that the only one of his novels that compares with Joyce's *Ulysses* is *Julian*").

Sometimes Twombly seems to live more in the past than in the present. He drew a total blank when our conversation turned to the intricacies of Italian politics, but he warmed up considerably when we started discussing Peter the Great: "There was such a contrast between the *refinement* of Peter's palace in Petersburg and his barbaric cruelty. He cut off his wife's lover's head and put it by her bed for six weeks! But she never cracked or showed the least sign of emotion."

On the other hand, he talks about Picasso's bad character as though the tyrannical master were still living: "He was so unpleasant with his children that they're still *discussing* him. I suppose that's the way to make sure you're remembered. Nice dads are quickly forgotten." In this respect Twombly resembles his vision of the Irish, who he says go on about remote events as though they happened just yesterday. "People down South are a bit like that, too," he adds.

Twombly was born in Lexington, Virginia, on April 25, 1928, in a hospital that occupied the site of Stonewall Jackson's old house ("You can't get much more Southern than *that!*" he exclaims). Although his mother was born in Bar Harbor, Maine, he calls her "Dixie Bell." His father was a professional baseball player from Maine and later an athletics instructor in the South. "He could still do a backflip at age forty," the sedentary Twombly recalls with some amazement. Named Edwin Parker Twombly Jr., the boy was always called by his father's nickname. Even today, when he returns to Lexington, the women call him "Cy Junior" and the men "Little Cy."

In Lexington he was taught by a Spanish artist, Pierre Daura, who had lived for years in Paris. The first painting Twombly recalls doing was a copy of Picasso's portrait of Marie-Therese Walter. In the course of interviewing Twombly, I saw a Picasso-ish portrait—perhaps the same one on the dining-room wall in the house of his closest friend. "Oh, have you seen Cy's Picasso?" he asked.

Twombly studied art at the School of the Museum of Fine Arts in Boston, the Art Students League in New York and Black Mountain College in North Carolina, but the decisive experience in his formation was seeing the work of such Abstract Expressionists as Willem De Kooning, Jackson Pollock and Franz Kline. Twombly was immediately influenced by them, and to this day he defends the importance of the process. " 'Influence' is not a dirty word," he declares. "I'm influenced by everything I see—a painting but also a rush of sky. The more character you have, the more influence you can take on. In the 1980s a lot of painters became intoxicated with their own image and saw everything as reflections of themselves. Of course, it's harder to be a painter now. People treat painters today the way they used to treat movie stars, which is absurd. Why make a hero out of a *painter,* of all things? A painter needs a sense of humor to resist that sort of idolatry. In the 1950s everyone ignored painters. Museums were temples to the Muses then; now they're cattle cars."

If not an influence on, at least a catalyst in, the explosion of Twombly's talent was his early encounter with Robert Rauschenberg, a fellow student at the Art Students League and the first person he'd met of his own age who shared the same interests.

Twombly first traveled to Italy and Morocco with Rauschenberg, in 1952. Even before the trip, Twombly had begun to incorporate into his painting elements drawn from so-called primitive art and from the layered, textured canvases of the contemporary French painter Jean Dubuffet. During the trip he intensified this vision. In Rome he filled notebooks with sketches of tribal artifacts from Abyssinia and sub-Saharan Africa that he saw in an ethnographic museum. In Morocco he worked on a dig of ancient Roman ruins.

After he returned to New York, he and Rauschenberg had a show in May 1953 at the Stable Gallery. Some of Twombly's canvases—*Tiznit* and *Quarzazat*—were named after Moroccan cities. Abstract, black-and-white, they owed something to the monumentality of Robert Motherwell's *Elegies to the Spanish Republic* (Motherwell had been Twombly's enthusiastic and admiring teacher at Black Mountain), yet the forms were defaced with a scratchy, seemingly random irritability, as though an archaeologist had damaged a Latin inscription by brushing aside the covering sand too violently. Twombly had by then perfected his technique of drawing with pencil and Conté crayon directly on wet white paint.

One critic, writing for the *Herald Tribune,* ranked it as one of the two worst shows of the season. Already people were complaining of the "infantilism" of Twombly's doodles and scrawls. Curiously, over the years the hostile responses to his work have veered between accusations that it is too elegant and that it is too childish, painfully overcultivated and insultingly messy. Twombly is apparently both a Paleface and a Redskin, to use politically suspect terms once invoked to describe the extremes of the tricky American sensibility.

The artist has learned to be philosophical, funny, even scatological about his defeats. As he says, "You name it and I've been through it." He recalls that as recently as 1979 his big retrospective at the Whitney "went over about as well as a turd in a punch bowl." Public scorn or indifference has never bothered him. Until the 1980s he was much less well-known than his contemporaries Rauschenberg and Jasper Johns. "But I always had a few people who believed in me," he hastens to add, "like the German art critic Heiner Bastian and various European collectors. Of course, I was never miserable, not like van Gogh or Pollock." Suddenly

I realize he's using the word *"misérable"* as the French and Italians use it, to mean destitute (as in *Les Misérables*). "In any event, the whole art market has became absurdly inflated in our day—so many mediocrities playing with their talent as though they were in the stock market. I was happy when the art market collapsed after the 1980s." He looks at me with a new interest and a glimmer of compassion. "It's pitiful how little writers are paid. I suggested to the Whitney that Roland Barthes write the essay for the catalogue for my retrospective. I insisted that he be paid $5,000—after all, he was one of the most famous writers in the world! The Whitney tried to renege and lower the fee to $2,000, but I held out for the full sum. Barthes was very touched. It was the most he'd ever earned—can you *imagine?*"

His 1953 defeat preceded, perhaps precipitated, the most important step ahead Twombly was ever to take. Drafted into the army that fall, he was stationed at a camp near Augusta, Georgia. He rented a room in town for a studio, and during weekend leaves he drew at night in the dark—a deliberate strategy to defeat the natural eloquence of his eye and hand. This systematic undoing of his skill as a draftsman, Twombly said later, set "the direction everything would take from then on."

In this regard, as in so many others, Twombly is a pure product of the 1950s. The suspicion of anything merely decorative or "ingratiating" (a taboo word), the conviction that the unconscious can guide the hand better than the awakened mind, even the action-painting credo that painting does not *mean* but *is,* does not refer to an external object but rather records the painter's choices, finally the belief that "primitive" art is closer to this contemporary process than is the "high" art of the European past—all these are the *idées reçues* of the period. In 1957, Twombly dutifully wrote, "Every line is thus the actual experience with its unique story. It does not illustrate; it is the perception of its own realization."

Twombly, Johns and Rauschenberg were not, however, just abject disciples of Pollock, Kline and De Kooning. They were broader and more heterodox in their reach than their masters and often more outrageous. Johns incorporated numbers and a real broom and plaster casts of faces into his canvases, while Rauschenberg included growing grass and a real bed into his. Twombly began to scrawl words and names and phrases, sometimes illegible or half erased, onto his huge paintings. As Roberta Smith, art critic for the *New York Times,* has written, "Like Johns's and

Rauschenberg's, these paintings talked back to the viewer in a new way and helped establish the preoccupation with meaning that has been central to the art of the second half of this century."

In 1957, Twombly traveled to Italy in what turned out to be a permanent move. When I mentioned to him that one critic had hazarded that he'd been attracted there by the remaining traces of ancient Roman graffiti, Twombly sputtered, "How sick would you have to be to cross the water just to see some dirty words written on a toilet wall?"

Twombly insists he was drawn to Italy by its stimulating and beguiling modern atmosphere: "I came to Rome for the life." He spent the summer of 1957, however, not in Rome but on the island of Procida, near Naples. "I had a two-domed house with a terrace, an iron bedstead in one room and a window that looked out towards Capri," he recalls fondly. "There were wonderful sounds then that have since disappeared—the heehawing of a donkey, for instance. That summer I met Dylan Thomas's widow, Caitlin, who was sleeping with all the fishermen. Arshile Gorky's widow was also there, as was Iris Tree, who had a role in *La Dolce Vita*."

Soon after this second arrival in Italy, Twombly was introduced to two members of the Franchetti family. Giorgio Franchetti, who shared Twombly's taste for old houses and new paintings, would become an important collector and eventually a close friend. Giorgio's timid, high-strung sister, Tatiana ("Tatia"), would become Twombly's wife in 1959 (the marriage took place in New York) and the mother of his son, Cyrus Alessandro.

Twombly loves to talk about the Franchettis, whose history obsesses him. Sometimes he is mildly contemptuous of them, but one senses that the contempt is proof of his privileged access to these people he admires so much. He will say, "No, the Franchettis don't like *building*. They like fixing things up. Giorgio's grandfather was the one who restored the Ca' d'Oro in Venice. He did lots of the repair work himself, and his son would stitch away, mending some old piece of Venetian embroidery. Giorgio is always restoring things. He restored my house in Bassano. But when he designs something from scratch, it's too...." He doesn't finish the sentence.

The family, which came from Venice, had become vastly wealthy in the early nineteenth century, when the Austrian emperor confided the postal service to its care. The money allowed the descendants to indulge their taste for acquisitions and eccentricity. Twombly recounts their lives in his scattershot, breathless, impressionistic way. One of Tatia's uncles, Alberto Franchetti, wrote an opera about Christopher Columbus. "Half Wagner and half Puccini," Twombly says, "and with so many set changes the Fenice [opera house in Venice] couldn't afford to put it on, and he had to pay for it himself: There are all these sailors in the crow's nest singing, 'Terra! Terra!'"

Another uncle was an explorer, who gave his children unusual names—Afdera, for example, after an African volcano, and Nanuck, in honor of an expedition he made to the North Pole. Afdera became the fourth wife of the actor Henry Fonda. Yet another relative was a dashing lesbian who won Liane de Pougy, the most celebrated French courtesan of the turn of the century, away from the American writer Natalie Barney, known as "the Amazon of Letters." "One of Tatia's relatives," Twombly says, "was a French Rothschild—in fact, only one of the recent Franchettis was actually an Italian. This Rothschild girl received two marriage offers, one from an Englishman and one from a Franchetti. She and her mother waited a week in vain to cross the stormy English Channel. Exasperated, the mother finally announced, 'Let's go try the Italian.'"

Twombly bought a seventeenth-century Roman palazzo on the Via di Monserrato in the early 1960s. Stimulated rather than burdened by a tradition that was not, after all, his own, he then began to produce paintings that strike me as his best—canvases with such titles as *The Italians, The First Part of the Return from Parnassus, The Empire of Flora* and the five-part "Ferragosto" series, named after a mid-August Italian holiday that dates back to ancient times. Vivid, even festive, these large works look like the aftermath of a bull's tormented passage through a pastry shop.

Twombly's work has been appreciated in Europe for decades, perhaps because it represents a marriage of the slashing American style of action painting with an august European cultural heritage—as though a jazz riff and a strict Bach canon had been united.

He has, in fact, inspired significant European painters of the recent past, a sign of the continuing relevance of his vision. Anselm Kiefer, the German painter who became prominent in the late 1970s for his homages to such philosophers as Hegel, learned to enshrine on his canvases a few key names and words in order to invoke, at least for the cultured few, a whole long filiation of ideas and personalities. Francesco Clemente—who shuttles from India to New York to his native Italy and back again—has derived from Twombly not only a sense of invigorating internationalism but also the power to appropriate erotic and naïve imagery from other cultural traditions.

In America the acceptance has been much slower in coming. When, in March 1964, Twombly presented an ensemble of nine paintings called *Discourse on Commodus* at an early show at the Leo Castelli Gallery in New York, the exhibition was widely labeled a fiasco. As Kirk Varnedoe, the director of painting and sculpture at MoMA, puts it in the catalogue for the 1994 retrospective, "The same painter who had been criticized in the late 1950s for insulting high art with his lack of aesthetic organization was now accused of being over-refined and arty in a damningly old-world, European way."

Twombly is *both* primitive and over-refined, even in his manner. Insulated from the grubby realities of the art marketplace by his expatriate status, by the wealth and power of the Franchettis and by his own indolent indifference, he is free to explore his fraught sensibility which despite (or because of) his remoteness is wonderfully sensitive to the world around him.

He has an extraordinary gift for creating beautiful environments in which to live and work. I visited his house in Gaeta, up the coast from Naples. It looks down on a blue bay and the mountains beyond. "This town was named after Aeneas's wet nurse," Twombly confides, "who died here as soon as he and his followers landed. Cicero had a villa here, as did Hadrian and Catullus—I'm sure Gaeta was an *artists' colony* in ancient times." From the outside his house, which towers above an imposing nineteenth-century church, resembles a military outpost ("I call it Fort Laramie," Twombly jokes). He flies an Italian flag, though typically Twombly sees no political—only artistic—significance in that: "It's one of the most beautiful of all flags, and here, seen against the bay, it looks like a Manet. Anyway, we're in Italy. What should I fly, the Puerto Rican flag?"

The seven or eight rooms in the house are all on slightly different levels. The floors are covered with a mixture of old tiles, some of which Twombly found in trash heaps after the big Naples earthquake a few years back destroyed many structures. The external walls of the house are unpainted and unplastered. In the inner courtyard, the wood lattices supporting grapevines are raw and unfinished. Palm trees, a trickling fountain, cement turbans crowning columns copied from the finials atop the church next door, tree trunks in the upper garden painted white to repel ants—

these are the elements with which he pieces together his daydreams. The sparse furniture inside the home was picked up at flea markets—blue-and-white Delft china, a silver sword, curvaceous imitation Louis XVI chairs around a long dinner table, a genuine Louis XVI canopied bed, a velvet screen from Portugal. On the walls are two photos of the old Matisse by Henri Cartier-Bresson. In Twombly's study are stacks of catalogues from his shows. It is the sort of treasure a connoisseur would swoon over and a thief would leave untouched, disgusted, convinced there was nothing of value in it. Of course, the three paintings in progress in Twombly's high-ceilinged studio are worth, literally, millions. He hurries me through that room, saying, "I don't want you to see my work in that unfinished state."

Twombly stammers slightly. He is by turns paranoid and innocent and open. He has trouble writing, even something as familiar as his address in Rome, and he keeps looking at his letters as though he'd just learned how to hold a pen. This mild aphasia or dyslexia throws a curious light on the painter celebrated for incorporating words into his canvases. He mumbles the conclusions of phrases into his hand, often the qualifying, tart little truths that come at the end of otherwise blandly conventional sentences.

When he comes to life is when he conjures images in clipped phrases—all improvisational, entirely pointillistic. "Have you ever been in Arcadia?" he'll ask, lighting up. "You must make the trip from Olympia to Epidaurus. The landscape is extraordinary—springs gushing out from the base of plane trees. In a village, I saw a young woman weeping. She'd stop crying, then start again. Her knees would buckle; she'd have to be held up by the other villagers. She'd just lost her husband, who'd died a few days after their marriage in a car crash. She would never find another husband, since she was no longer a virgin. Her whole life had already become tragic."

If he grows enthusiastic while talking about his pet subjects ("My favorite arts are landscaping, architecture and painting—I don't care for music anymore, though it was once necessary to my work"), he becomes shy and even cagey if you ask him a direct question about his personal life. His son, Alessandro (whom he has nicknamed "Goon Baby"), is now a handsome painter in his mid-thirties; Twombly admires Alessandro's paintings of wild irises but scoots away from any speculation about his son by saying, "I wouldn't know about that. We have a very formal relationship. He went to an English-language school in Switzerland, and lives part time in New York, so his English is impeccable, but even so he's 120 percent

Italian and a true Franchetti." He is similarly evasive about his wife, Tatia, though friends say that she is the first person to whom he shows a new painting. One could even say that Twombly's delicate, allusive painting style is the exact analogue to his conversational evasiveness and mercurial personality.

Classical mythology is an important aspect of his oeuvre, but he is quick to say his form is not classical. "I think of myself as a Romantic symbolist. My painting is not fixed. I show things in flux: I respond to the Greek love of metamorphosis. The Greeks had a very strong love of nature and a religion based on the change of seasons."

In the last decade Twombly has slowed down. "I don't go to the studio every day. I have to be in a certain mood to work, and I only work when I feel a real need to paint. Of course, I've always worked in spurts, and often do sets of eight or ten all in a rush. Not to say I'm less active, I'm just not like those assembly-line painters who have studio assistants and who churn out a canvas a day. I have lots of paintings I've been working on for fifteen years and many others I've finished but not yet shown."

Twombly is casting an inquisitive glance at the fate of old painters. "Matisse and Titian both took motifs from their earlier work and rethought them in a freer fashion." Much as he may despise the market, the public seems to have a growing respect for him. A Twombly fetched $5.5 million in 1992. In Houston, a $3.5 million Cy Twombly Pavilion is being built to house some thirty-five paintings, sculptures and drawings done by the artist from 1954 to the present.

Despite this attention and the consecration of the MoMA retrospective, there are still sharply dissenting voices. A year ago, *60 Minutes* presented a segment entitled "Yes…but is it Art?" in which reporter Morley Safer, who is a Sunday painter, attacked the hype used to promote "worthless" contemporary art. A prime target was Twombly. Describing a 1950s painting auctioned at Sotheby's, Safer said, "This one, a canvas of scrawls done with the wrong end of a paintbrush, bears the imaginative title of *Untitled*. It is by Cy Twombly, and was sold for $2,145,440. And that's dollars, not Twomblys."

Such philistine murmurs don't even reach the god's ears on Olympus. Or on Parnassus West, for he spends more and more time every year in his native Lexington, Virginia, where he is insulated from insults by the adoration of neighbors, friends and professors at Washington and Lee

University. His 1920s brick house there has four bedrooms, four baths and lots of light on each side. "Everyone in Lexington is a retired general out walking a fussy little dog," Twombly says approvingly. "One of my neighbors, whose wife is a great cook, brought me the new Fagles translation of the *Iliad*. I have lots of charming acquaintances—better than *friends* who always turn on you. I love the architecture. There are more *columns* between Lexington and Charlottesville than in all ancient Rome and Greece."

I dined with some of his Lexington neighbors who were passing through Gaeta—a classics professor, a professor of ancient history and the wife of the one and the sister of the other, intelligent, good-humored people with impeccable manners and conversation that veered from lightly worn erudition to mild teasing. One of the women said, "Well, Cy Junior, how can you give up Italy and move back to Lexington?"

"You see, ma'am, I'm like an old dog who's gone home to die."

"I declare, don't say it like that."

Social smiles, a small tightening around the eyes to register the truth behind the banter, an easy flow of optimistic chat—these are the graces which this most enigmatic and elusive of all modern artists likes to surround himself with. They are the soft cotton batting around the hard, angular gem of his edgy genius.

Jasper Johns

H E USED TO LOOK LIKE WILLIAM S. HART, the poker-faced cowboy. Now Jasper Johns resembles a Zen Buddhist abbot, not only physically with his snowy, circumflex eyebrows, his lidless, penetrating gaze, his expressionless mouth and his basset-hound cheeks—but also in his manner, which is mysterious, taciturn, given to riddles and evasiveness. Even his way of exploding into laughter at a joke he's made, and only he understands, has the feeling of a Zen koan, as though the sound of one hand clapping were his convulsive, off-the-wall laugh.

The Zen comparison keeps cropping up. Michael Crichton, the author of *Jurassic Park* as well as of the most ambitious study of Johns, juxtaposes two quotations:

Time does not pass
Words pass.
—JASPER JOHNS

It is believed by most that time passes;
in actual fact, it stays where it is.
—DÔGEN, A ZEN MASTER

Johns was stationed six months in Japan when he was in the army, and he has gone back twice since. One rumor goes that he had a major love affair with a Japanese woman. When I asked Johns about the circles, squares and triangles in *The Seasons,* his series of four paintings from the mid-1980s, he said, "A nineteenth-century Japanese Zen artist, Sengai Gibbon, used these same three shapes, though his style was so cursive one scarcely recognizes them. The circle, square and triangle are the elements that make up the whole world—*and* they form the basis of Cézanne's art."

Johns's Buddhist calm has been subjected to a few trials recently, though only of the exalted sort befitting America's most famous painter—and one of the two or three highest paid artists in the world. (In 1988 his *False Start* sold for $17 million to publishing magnate S. I. Newhouse, a record for a living artist and an anomaly, according to Johns's longtime dealer, Leo Castelli, when the "going price at the time was just eight or nine million.") These trials, as in a medieval legend, are three in number—an exhibition, a house and a book.

Johns was the subject of a major retrospective in October, 1996, at the Museum of Modern Art, and he finds nothing positive in such an ordeal. He says half-jokingly, "I've never had the experience of learning anything from a show. It will be interesting, of course, to see if my work looks dilapidated. Some paintings I haven't seen in decades. My idea of a retrospective would be to hang everything. *Everything.* I'd like to see my development—anyone's—painting by painting."

Johns is also critical of his own work. "I use too many things from past paintings. Of course, you have to paint something, but repetition-and-variation as a method seems very limited." He has admitted that he doesn't really know how to draw from life, and he has laughed at his new practice of tracing elements from other people's paintings. And, in his dandified way, he complains that he never works enough and that as a child he never acquired proper working habits. One close friend, however, says that he is a workaholic, and if he sometimes turns out no more than four paintings a year, that doesn't mean he isn't constantly struggling.

Perhaps the worst part of having a show, for Johns, is giving interviews. As one friend put it, "He's terrified he might let slip something personal." Johns said, "I find it hard to recapture the feelings of the past. Painters are constantly being asked about the past. I say the same old thing or make up something. But you'd like to say something different each time."

Talking about the difference between a painter's and a writer's need for publicity, he said, "A writer needs to be on television, because he must sell a lot of books, but if a painter has ten collectors, that's a lot. The people who are going to buy my work already know who I am." When I asked him which aspect of the current art scene dismayed him the most, he replied, "The crowds."

"Your sense of privacy is very different from Robert Rauschenberg's, isn't it?" I asked, naming the artist with whom he was the most intimate when they were both young (the art historian Jonathan Katz claims in "The Art of Code: Jasper Johns and Robert Rauschenberg" that they were lovers). According to Leo Castelli, "When they are with each other, they are amiable, but there's not much left for them to share. Originally, Rauschenberg was the older man, more experienced. And, of course, Bob is so ebullient. Whereas for Jasper, every stroke he paints is an effort." I remember once saying to Johns that he and Rauschenberg struck me as so different, and Johns exclaimed, "Thank God!"

"What's it like to have been famous for so long—forty years now?" I asked.

"I'm known only to a very small community," he said modestly, although his name has been the answer to a question on *Jeopardy* more than once. "Marcel Duchamp used to say you're famous only when a cabdriver recognizes you. Once, a U.S. immigration official asked me to sign his autograph book. At first I was taken aback, but then"—huge laugh, the kind that turns his face red and makes his interlocutor smile queasily—"I thought that immigration people could put together a very good autograph collection."

For everyone, moving into a new house is an important step, but for a painter it can be especially wrenching, since the question is whether he or she will be able to create in it. For Johns, the adjustment to the pleasures and vicissitudes of his new domain has been alternately inspiring and vexatious. It's a 100-acre estate in Connecticut, two hours north of New York, dominated by a fifteen-bedroom mansion built at the turn of the century. Johns-watchers call it "Brideshead." At one end of the estate is a simple country lane, at the other a large pond in a valley.

Bill Katz, the designer, who has known Johns for years and who helped him hang his prizewinning show at the Venice Biennale in 1988, is renovating all the buildings on the property. Katz started with a three-bedroom guesthouse, where Johns lived for a few months. The style might be described as "rich Quaker," the sort of extreme simplicity that only money can buy. In each bedroom, a bed, a lamp, a table and a straight-backed wood chair are posed on a shiny wood floor. There's nothing more, except, of course, works by Barnett Newman, Philip Guston and Marcel Duchamp.

In fact, wherever I looked, I kept having a feeling of déjà vu, since Johns lives surrounded by the very works he has been "sampling" in recent years: those I just mentioned, as well as images by Odilon Redon, a Barry Moser illustration for *Moby-Dick,* and a photo of a vase by George E. Ohr, the flamboyant American ceramist of the turn of the century.

In just one of Johns's painting, *Ventriloquist* (1983), for instance, one finds the Barnett Newman print *Untitled* (1961), reversed; two of Johns's signature American flags (one with forty-eight stars and the other with fifty), stacked and colored black, green and yellow; seven pieces of Ohr ceramics; and the shape of the whale in the Moser illustration. On the wall are hinges and a nail casting a shadow, allusions to John Frederick Peto (1854–1907), an American master of *trompe l'oeil* still life whom Johns has admired since discovering him in the early '60s.

Typical of Johns's work of the '80s and '90s, *Ventriloquist* brings together these citations from other artists and artisans (including a white shape, used in perceptual tests, which can be seen either as facing profiles or as a vase) and combines them, with recycled images from his own reper-toire (the flags in these bizarre colors were first used in a poster for the Whitney Museum of American Art). In this painting he has also drawn on elements from his former house, in Stony Point, New York—a wicker hamper and bathtub faucets, all meticulously rendered by someone who claims he can't draw.

The coach barn, where Johns is living now, is covered with cedar shin-gles. A trellis shelters the porch outside the kitchen door. Inside, on the ground floor, is a studio (the biggest Johns has ever had) and storage space, a kitchen and a print studio. Upstairs is an office, a high-ceilinged room with bare white walls, exposed roof beams and wood floors. When I asked about all the drawers, Johns said, "I started keeping records of my work in the 1970s, a job that's usually done by the gallery. I thought I could do a better job—the gallery also thought so. Now I'm stuck with it." Upstairs there are also a bedroom and a living room. The fanlight and windowed barn doors at one end open to reveal a metal balcony and, in the distance, "Brideshead" itself.

Johns avoided showing me Brideshead, which obviously troubles him. Katz thinks that the house won't be finished for some time and that this delay makes Johns extremely unhappy. Katz, who has built a house for the Italian painter Francesco Clemente in the New Mexico desert, is used to artists' quirks. "My problem," he said, "is that Jap [Johns's nickname] doesn't want to live grandly. He's afraid of pretension." But to me Johns said, "I had a dream last night that we just bulldozed the whole thing. I felt terribly relieved."

While I was visiting Johns, he discovered that Katz had placed an Ohr vase on reserve for him at an antique dealer's. "I think he seriously overestimates my financial resources," Johns grumbled. Which may sound unreal, coming from a man whose paintings sell for millions. But Johns, a child during the Depression, constantly worries about money. As one friend said, "If Johns has a choice at the market between damaged tomatoes that are on sale and good ones that are more expensive, he'll always choose the cheaper ones." Yet, as another friend pointed out, he always picks up the tab in a restaurant. And cheap tomatoes don't keep him from being one of the best cooks around; he prepares exquisite dinners for his friends, who include Barbara Rose, the art historian and critic, and Leo Castelli and his wife.

Katz has finished work on the gatehouse, and Johns has lodged his full-time printmaker and his family in it. His secretary has just moved Johns's whole office to the country from Manhattan; she's rented a house in the neighborhood, as Johns's full-time studio assistant has for himself and his family. Sometimes one gets the impression that Johns is preparing for some kind of spiritual Armageddon or is creating a feudal village to rule.

It is perhaps not the healthiest tendency for a man who is already if not a hermit at least a part-time misanthrope. He's a very difficult conversationalist. As someone said recently, "With Jap, the ball is always in your court." Even Castelli, who says he has "a deep friendship" with Johns, admits that many people find the painter tough sledding. "For me, I'm not aware of the long silences—or at least let's say when we're together we don't need to talk. Of course, he's a very impressive personality—people are afraid of him. I know he'd like it if his relationships with other people were easier."

Johns is capable of staring at you unsmilingly and simply not responding with any of the gurgles and little expressions that ordinary discourse depends on. He once collaborated with Samuel Beckett, and they had in common—aside from a habit of recycling their own work and of making that work self-referential—a vision of life so bleak as to be funny. When Beckett saw the endpapers Johns had designed for the book, titled *Foirades/Fizzles,* he said he hoped that Johns would place his familiar cross-hatching design at the front of the book and his flagstones at the back. When Johns asked him why; he said, "Here you try all these different directions, but no matter which way you turn you always come up against a stone wall."

The house Johns owned previously, in Stony Point, was very modest. Now he spends most of his time either at the new place, or at his town house on the Upper East Side of Manhattan or at his house on St. Martin, in the Caribbean. "It seems to me I'm very social—that is, there are lots of events I'm obliged to attend," he told me. "I see a lot of people, although I don't like parties and I freak out in crowds."

Where he truly opens up is before a work of art, preferably by someone else. When I interviewed him in 1977, at the time of his last major New York retrospective, the warmest and most interesting moment we spent together was looking at a copy of *La Celestina,* the classic Spanish text, in an edition illustrated by Picasso. This time he showed me *Cézanne: The Bathers,* a book of the artist's nudes published by Harry N. Abrams and the Museum of Fine Arts in Basel. "Nothing could be stranger than Cézanne's enormous reputation, given how inept he was," Johns said. "It's a miracle that he was recognized as soon as he was. I keep saying to myself, since the work seems so alive and contemporary to me now, What must it have seemed like to people ninety years ago?"

"You've said *you* can't draw. Are you inept in the same way?"

"Well, for one thing, Cézanne worked much harder than I do. He worked in museums copying paintings, whereas I'm relatively lazy."

I told him that every single morning Françoise Gilot had had to talk Picasso out of a depression and convince him that he was talented. Johns roared, "She must have been very good at it!"

If we talked little about Marcel Duchamp, it was because Johns has so thoroughly assimilated Duchamp's Dada influence over the years that he has nothing more to say about him. "I never saw that much of Duchamp—just ten or twelve times. I didn't want to bother him. One remark he made keeps puzzling me. He said, 'I like Picasso except when he repeats himself.' Now, I keep wondering, *When* did Picasso repeat himself?"

In the last two decades Johns has recycled bits of Munch and Picasso. ("He's always been involved with Picasso," Castelli told me, "more than with any other painter.") After doing paintings for years with brightly colored chevrons of cross-hatching, Johns discovered that Munch had used a nearly identical pattern for a bedspread in a late self-portrait called *Between the Clock and the Bed* (1940–42). Forty years later, Johns did several nonfigurative, cross-hatched paintings as variations on Munch's theme—I say nonfigurative, but Johns's 1981 *Between the Clock and the Bed* in encaustic on canvas comprises three panels of cross-hatching, and seen *through* the chevrons are the clock (left panel), the bed (right panel) and Munch himself (middle panel).

The main image by Picasso that has haunted Johns is the 1936 *Straw Hat with Blue Leaf* (sometimes called *Woman in Straw Hat*), an extremely distorted face whose features are rearranged and pushed to its perimeter. Johns has done many paintings and drawings since the mid-'80s using these redistributed features, sometimes on a Veronica's veil that is "nailed" to a wall—or even to a sky.

One of the key questions posed by the current retrospective at the Museum of Modern Art is how people will evaluate the three main periods in Johns's production. As Leo Castelli puts it, "Johns is always ahead of the public. At first, people resisted the cross-hatchings, though now everyone seems to like them. Of course, they'd prefer it if he'd stick with flags and targets, but he'll never go back to that." Johns denies that there have been radical changes and says, "It only appears that way now, but later people will perceive more of a unity." But despite his fidelity throughout his career to encaustic (wax that is heated, colored and applied to the canvas with a brush, then heated again on the canvas) and to images such as recycled flags and numbers, three distinct periods are perfectly obvious.

From the mid-'50s to the late '60s Johns, in his most influential and celebrated style, signaled a return from Abstract Expressionism to the figurative, but employing cool, banal objects. "The American flag took care of a great deal for me, because I didn't have to design it. So I went on to similar things like the targets—things the mind already knows. That gave me room to work on other levels." One of the other levels was beauty of finish—his exquisite, painterly touch. In that way, he represented a bridge between the painterliness of abstract masters such as Willem De Kooning and the use of mass-produced, man-made images (dollar bills, Campbell's soup cans) by Pop artists such as Andy Warhol.

Beginning in 1972, however, Johns took up abstraction, or rather, he began to reproduce over and over the cross-hatching pattern he'd glimpsed on a moving car and the flagstone pattern he'd seen painted on the side of a building in Harlem. He eliminated direct references to the figurative. The mathematical possibilities of alternating colors and lines became themes that he explored obsessively.

As Johns entered his third period, in the late '70s and early '80s, the figurative made its reappearance, first in conjunction with cross-hatching—handprints on cross-hatching in *Céline* (1978), marginal drawings of a cicada and a skull and crossbones below a panel of cross-hatching in *Cicada* (1979).

From the very beginning Johns took a Surrealist's delight in combining ill-sorted images (a bull's-eye and parts of the human face, for instance), and, like his masters Duchamp and the American composer John Cage, he enjoyed taking advantage of elements that chance presented him with. But only in his paintings of the last fifteen years has he concocted such strange visual bouillabaisses—out of tracings from the early-sixteenth-century *Isenheim Altarpiece,* by Mathias Grünewald; a photo of Leo Castelli; a reproduction of the *Mona Lisa;* psychological perception tests; Ohr vases; references to Picasso, Cézanne and even his autobiography (in one recent painting, for instance, he re-created from memory the floor plan of his grandfather's house, where he grew up).

There are younger painters such as Clemente who prefer Johns's most recent work, because it's more personal. There are others who think it's just silly—the worst sort of intellectual Easter-egg hunt (I hide the symbol and you find it). When I told Johns that I found his new work "playful," he roared with one of those horror-movie laughs of his and said, "I prefer 'playful' to 'silly,' which is what one critic called it recently." I asked him if he thought he was following in the footsteps of Picasso, who repainted the old masters in his late period, but Johns just drew a noncommittal (perhaps self-effacing) blank.

And here I come back to the book I mentioned at the beginning, Johns's greatest trial of the moment, Jill Johnston's soon-to-be-published *Jasper*

Johns: Privileged Information. Johnston, whom Johns has known since the early 1960s (he gave her a work, ink on plastic, in the late 1980s), was once the dance critic for *The Village Voice* and made a spectacular coming out as a lesbian in its pages in 1968 and 1969. She never much liked Johns's targets and numbers; what intrigues her most is his latest work, although she reads it in a way that makes Johns so uncomfortable that he has forbidden her publisher, Thames and Hudson, to reproduce his paintings—a damaging omission in a book that is so much about deciphering specific works.

What apparently irritates Johns is that Johnston sees him as a "*secret autobiographer,*" as she calls him in the preface, and considers his recent work to be full of coded references to his childhood and to a family he has never discussed, as well as to his same-sex relationships. Johnston traveled to Allendale, South Carolina, and learned that when Johns was a child his father was a bad binge drinker, whose wife divorced him and remarried but did nothing to become permanently reunited with their child. Jasper was raised by his paternal grandfather and his second wife, Montez, who used to play the piano and sing "Red Sails in the Sunset." The Veronica's veils in several of Johns's paintings may be references to that song.

As for Johns's homosexuality, it is far from a biographical certainly. David Sylvester, the English critic, told me that I should write an article called "Jasper Johns the Great Heterosexual," since he has had affairs with several well-known women. When I mentioned that to Johns, he said, "Tell David to write his own damn articles!" Johnston has written a chapter about his homosexuality and has interviewed the man she claims was one of the great loves of his life, Jim Self, who used to be a dancer in Merce Cunningham's company (for which Johns did a number of sets) and who now teaches dance at Cornell University.

Johns railed against Johnston, telling me, "I've known her for more than thirty years. She used to call me up in the middle of the night in a panic and I'd comfort her. Once she was so drunk I put her to bed. I'm shocked that she's decided to write this book. She came to see me. I told her I wasn't going to cooperate. She became furious and started marching around the room, swearing that I couldn't sue her. I think she has a complex about me. You see, she announced she was going to write a book about her mother, herself and her father. Well, she wrote [about] the first two, but couldn't make any headway with the third, since she's so full of rage against her father. At that point she started writing this 'critical biography' of me, which is full of the hostility she feels towards her father."

When I confronted Johnston with Johns's interpretation, she swore she'd never mentioned anything about anyone suing anyone, but as to his interpretation that she'd made some sort of father transference onto him, at first she said, "That's ridiculous. I'm older than he is." But then, after reflecting a moment, she said that his theory was intriguing. "He's intelligent, Jasper," she said.

He certainly is.

Herbert List

HERBERT LIST'S PHOTOGRAPHS of young men seem, at the beginning of the twenty-first century, still uncannily contemporary. Nothing about them, except maybe the cut of the swimsuits, reveals that the pictures weren't taken yesterday. Compared even with photos that were snapped in the '50s and '60s—especially the oiled, spear-wielding commercial Hollywood studio shots of guys in posing straps published by the Grecian Guild or the American Models Guild—List's pictures look more natural, unassuming, intimate.

If the subjects are sometimes placed against Greek ruins or the fragments of Greek statues, they—the living men—are not draped in togas or crowned with fig leaves or posed on tiger-skin carpets, as in the troubling Sicilian photos of another German, Wilhelm von Gloeden. Having discovered Sicily in 1880, von Gloeden continued to take pictures there for the next fifty years. His young men, with their farmer tans and peasant feet, their dirty fingernails, stiffly posed bodies and all-too-mature penises, look intensely uncomfortable in their Attic drag—and very far indeed from the ancient ideal of the Greek eromenos. They have obviously been hired because of their compliance, their big endowments—and their neediness.

Indeed, what Roland Barthes called their "worn out and dirty feet," as well as their bellies swollen from hunger and their scratched and scarred legs and hands, reveal that out of their obvious need for a square meal they've agreed to cooperate with the fantasies of the rich German "amateur." Their bodies are those of manual laborers, not of Athenian athletes. Though they are given flutes to play, white ribbons to tie around their dirty hair and elegant verandas overlooking the Bay of Naples and the distant Vesuvius on which to expose their buttocks, we can only guess that the next day they'll be summarily ferried home to their village on the nearby island of Procida and dumped back into a subsistence level of existence.

What makes us cringe the most—after the kitsch taste of the photographer and the grotesqueness of the "classical" props he's placed in the grubby hands of bewildered farmers—are his stage directions. He's obviously instructed his boys to leer at each other lustfully or to gaze soulfully at one another's ripe genitalia and glossy axial hair or to touch one another in poses at once "artistic" and provocative. We are far from the world of the hairless, modest, small-sexed, proud ephebe; the "Greek alibi" has never been invoked more carelessly, more grossly, we might say.

Above all, everything is static, thick; it won't pour. We feel the suffocating heat of the Mediterranean and the lethargy induced by humiliation. The poses are not those the young men themselves would ever have chosen; every gesture has been imposed on them, following the dictates of a lurid and strangely barren imagination. Gloeden has contrived neither *tableaux vivants* nor *natures mortes*, but something like *tableaux morts*.

How different are the photos of Herbert List. He, too, may have responded to the appeal of the Classical World and, like so many other Germans, made the trip south. He had read the Greek classics, especially Pindar and Homer, though he responded to them sensually, not as an intellectual, which he never claimed to be. He, too, could not resist echoing the poses of classical or Renaissance sculpture; one picture taken in Italy in 1936 shows a young man half submerged in water, a hand resting on a crooked knee, his head turned in profile—the whole recalling Neptune in Cellini's salt cellar.

According to his friend Max Scheler, List was deeply impressed by what he saw in the classical visual arts, both in pottery painting and sculpture; he appreciated the ideal of muscled youths formed by physical education in the gymnasiums. And he responded to the ideal of intergenerational homosexual love in ancient Greece—an ideal that has since been revised by Michel Foucault's *History of Sexuality* and by K. J. Dover's *Greek Homosexuality*—but that before their revisions was generally regarded as a thoroughly happy and unproblematical reciprocity. List subscribed to this older, sunny vision of a love between the older man (the erastes) and the younger (the eromenos) that was both physical and educational.

List succumbed to the seduction of the Mediterranean and followed in the footsteps of Johann Joachim Winckelmann, the eighteenth-century art historian who invented Neoclassicism and whom his friend Casanova discovered in the arms of a boy, or of the nineteenth-century gay poet August von Platen or of Platen's twentieth-century admirer Thomas Mann, whose *Death in Venice* was inspired by Platen, perhaps even by his most celebrated lines: "The man who contemplates beauty with his own eyes/ Has already come under the sway of death." But List does not strike us as a Romantic pining after transcendence or oblivion nor as an "historical" artist in need of a Roman or Greek alibi for his homosexuality.

List may have photographed men in Greece in the 1930s, but not before he had already taken similar pictures in Hamburg or on the Elbe River or the Rhine or the Baltic Sea or the North Sea. When he was in his late twenties and early thirties he began to photograph his friends on the weekends or whenever he could get away from the family business in Hamburg. Stephen Spender, who met List in Hamburg in 1929 when he was a student of twenty and List a coffee wholesaler of twenty-six, recalled half a century later:

> Herbert, a coffee merchant, a brilliant young business man, while proud of his business ability, nevertheless thought that his "real life" only began when he had left his office: at midday when he went, together with his good-looking amiable blond friend Willy Lassen, to the Schwimmbad, or, in the evening, together with friends, to bars frequented by sailors, in the Red Light Sankt Pauli district near the harbor. Sometimes he gave parties for his friends at his penthouse studio.... He and his friends represented to me all that was freest, most open minded, most consciously new about the New Germany. They were the Children of the Sun. To them, far more than politics, business, self promotion, was "life." "Life" consisted of friendship, free love, the cultivation of their own bodies, nature, and the sun. At the beach or the swimming baths, the aristocrats among those beautiful people were those with the brownest bodies. Naked, or almost so, they were a classless society....

This "classlessness," this nature worship, these casual exchanges of friendship are all apparent in List's seaside pictures. No longer is von Gloeden, the aristocratic sexual tourist, paying second-world peasants to stage his fantasies. Now List is silhouetting his friends against the sky as they fish or lean on a bicycle or splash each other or play leap frog. Or he looks down on them as they nap together like lion cubs in a promiscuous pride or stretch out on a promontory to take the sun. Here the subjects forget the photographer (who in any event is only ten years older than they are) or they look at each other. They are smiling. They have stylish haircuts, good teeth, athletic but not overly muscular bodies. They are wearing swimsuits—not because they are afraid to expose their genitals or hips to the camera, but because for the photographer being partially clothed is "cooler" (more sophisticated, but also less steamy). It's a difficult point to make without sounding prudish, but just as in fiction all the words for the sexual organs sound either clinical ("penis") or like little-boy dirty words ("weenie") or like heavy-breathing grown-up pornography ("cock"), in the same way total nudity in photography solicits a prurient response or at the very least so hypnotizes the viewer's eye that all other details of the picture are upstaged.

Roland Barthes has dismissed, perhaps definitively, the idea that one can look at a photograph as an abstraction or as a strictly formal composition. There is always something human or unusual or shocking (at least in the best pictures) that catches the eye. Resorting to Latin rhetorical terms, Barthes called this point of curiosity and fixation the punctum, the arresting detail, the accident (the "small hole" or "little spot") that "punctuates" the deliberately chosen and studied theme of the picture, the studium, which has been selected with a general investment of creative energy but without any particular acuity.

Now List obviously didn't want genitals to become the punctum; perhaps only seasoned nudists can ignore them, and then only in a nature colony after a week-long visit. In a photograph the penis will always attract notice and thus be the punctum and invite desire, comparisons, disgust, pity, envy, shock and outrage, certainly curiosity. Is the penis small because the subject just came out of the North Sea? Or is it large because it's semi-erect and someone has been "fluffing" it? Such pornographic obsessiveness was not List's subject. As Max Scheler, List's long-time friend and heir, told me recently, "List was more attracted to the eyes of his subjects. He was interested in projecting an atmosphere of innocence and purity, even Romanticism."

Perhaps "romanticism" shouldn't be capitalized, for there is nothing heavy here or dated, nothing that suggests remote countries or epochs or fantasy; there isn't anything sulfurous or even energized by yearning. Here, in this seaside world, all desires seem reciprocal, casual, even interchangeable. In *The Temple,* the novel that Spender wrote about Germany in 1929 but did not publish for over fifty years, List is called "Joachim." The young English narrator (called "Paul") admires Joachim's photos, especially of boys, but Joachim says:

> I don't want to be a professional photographer. Doing that means pretending to everyone that you are an artist, but I do not think photography is an art. It is a skill, and having a good eye, like shooting, which is what it is quite rightly called. It is a technique only. A good photographer is not like an artist who transforms what he sees, he is like a hunter who is in search of some particular animal which he happens to see more clearly than other hunters, at some particular moment, his particular vision. But the animal, however special to him, does not come out of his particular soul. It is given to him by the world outside, on which he is totally dependent for it.

Today, of course, in the era of "appropriations" and "multiples," not to mention plagiarism, no photographer or painter would feel so confident (nor so scrupulous) about distinguishing between the artist who transforms and the technician who documents, and even Spender came to downplay this passage. But what is relevant about these sentences is that, despite the somewhat sinister image of the "hunter," it is clear that List is concerned to capture something unique about the subject, something that the subject gives off, even if unwittingly.

This respect for the subject is reflected in *The Temple,* where Joachim is described picking up guys on the beach or at the lokal, the small harborfront bar. His technique is easy, joking, affectionate, not too demanding, often focussed on some external distraction. In fact, Paul writes his friend Ernst to explain that what he most admires in the relationship between Joachim and Willy is that it "is directed towards things outside themselves which they share, as though these things—their outdoor life—the sun—their own bodies—were passionate intermediaries between them. They are friends without tormenting each other with consciousness of what each thinks about the deepest nature of the other."

(I should mention here that Max Scheler disagrees with my interpretation, insists on List's Romanticism with a capital *R* and would like me to add: "Except for some occasional encounters, most of the young men had accompanied List for a number of years.... The boys were like adopted sons. Some of them weren't homosexual, but when after some time another young man showed up in List's life, they still shared a lasting friendship with him. Most of them traveled with List extensively...").

If I emphasize the relationship between the photographer and his subject, I do so because this topic also haunts the rapport between photographer and viewer—and much contemporary gay esthetic discourse. Essex Hemphill, the late gay African-American poet, attacked Robert Mapplethorpe for occasionally cropping his pictures of black men to block off their heads or even torsos and leaving nothing visible but an erect or semi-erect penis ("Man in a Polyester Suit," which shows a giant penis protruding from an open fly of a man who is cut off at chest height, is only the most notorious example). Bruce Weber has been accused of a different sort of political incorrectness. He usually hires handsome, heterosexual males and parades them in playful, old-fashioned, all-American action poses before the abashed, self-hating but hungry gaze of his excited but ashamed gay customers. Of course Weber might say that he doesn't know the sexual orientation of his subjects or of his viewers, but in fact he often shoots fashion or photographic models, members of a profession that looks askance at real or perceived homosexuality. Weber's other specialty is filming or photographing very young ranch-hands or small-town kids, necking with their girlfriends in pick-up trucks or playing Frisbee on the beach with the fellows.

This is not to single out either Mapplethorpe or Weber for criticism; I have even gone to great lengths elsewhere to defend Mapplethorpe in print, and as the critic Vicky Goldberg has argued, when Weber sought for a precedent for his art of the male nude as something more serious than beefcake, he found it in the work of Herbert List. But what I do want to point out is that List does not fetishize body parts nor invite our eye to do so, nor does he present the tormented gay voyeur with straight men in all their self-confident, unconscious grandeur. No, List is showing us a tribe of teens, his friends, who are never models and are often his lovers.

Nor are these pictures carefully haloed studio shots, often of naked, thick-thighed dancers, such as those we find in the portfolio of List's contemporary George Platt Lynes. Perhaps Lynes is a greater photographer than List, but the atmosphere of his work is tormented, dramatic, unhealthy. A famous man (Christopher Isherwood, for instance) is shown, formally dressed in coat and tie, beside a naked youth. Or the white British choreographer Frederick Ashton, carefully groomed, wearing a silk rep tie and a dark suit tailored with extremely wide lapels, stands beside three crouching naked black male dancers—the whole scene smacks of paternalism, the master with his elegant pets.

Other series by Lynes show black and white men together in amorous embrace or picture a small-sexed masochist bound and strung up. Many of the pictures are shot with surrealistic trick photography ("Sleepwalker," in which the legs of one man support, for instance, a plank on which another man is lying on his side, curled up) or are extravagant nude dance scenes—sometimes drawn from real ballets, such as Balanchine's *Orpheus,* in which the dancers are costumed. The point is that Lynes works only in the studio, builds sets, carefully stages scenes, plays on the contrast between fully clothed celebrities and anonymous nudes, isolates body parts and, at other times, puts together fantastic scenes of what he called "mythologies."

To be sure, in the 1930s List, too, occasionally played with mirrors or masks or empty window frames projecting into space above a brick wall or covered the heads of real men with plaster so that they would appear to be statues; or he shot statues so that they would seem, at first glance, to be human; or List would use the effect of a double exposure of a young man's masked face. But these pictures (which were influenced by the American surrealist photographer Man Ray and by the Italian metaphysical painter Giorgio de Chirico) are exceptions in the gallery of List's pictures of young men; his most manipulated images, those that earned him the reputation of having invented la fotografia metafisica, are still lifes (conch shells, tailor dummies, sun glasses on a table in front of a seascape).

Nor are these pictures ever a camp and stylish recycling of Surrealism as in Cecil Beaton's photo of a naked black Moroccan on a round white rooftop trailing a twenty-foot-long piece of pale gauze. List's models are regular guys, not the affected, "allegorical" weirdos seen in Cocteau's postwar films or drawings with their Pierrot getups and their theatrical, "meaningful" stares.

List's pictures of young men are most often a cross between a snapshot, with its intention to record a particular moment on a memorable day with a friend, and an ideal, timeless, utopian vision of male friendship. Yes, these are relaxed pictures, but the moments that have been selected out of the flowing stream of time and sight are those that reinforce List's distinct concept of masculine society—young, carnal but cool. As List once wrote, "Works of visual art are visions made visible."

To my taste, one of the most "visionary" of List's photos is of three adolescents standing in the water (shot at Ammersee, Germany, in 1950). The camera is looking up at the nearest young man, who is up to his knees in the rippling water, which disperses his reflection in a liquid pointillism. Behind him and to his left is another guy, in almost the same pose and wearing the same clinging white swimsuit. Farthest away and even more to the left is yet another young man in a white swimsuit, his profile turned to us, a fish or shell, possibly, in his hand. And behind him is the narrow, gray band of land along the horizon. All three figures are photographed *contrejour*, which turns the face of the largest, nearest figure into a smiling but partially effaced mask. All three silhouettes are sharply delineated, as though cut out of metal, against the cloudless but light-suffused sky, emphasizing the coltish knobbiness of shoulders and elbows, the thinness of the neck, the negative space between the arm of each figure and his body. In a sense they are the same figure, seen in a time lapse.

Their skinny, underdeveloped bodies contrast with the imposing way they're seen from below, like the statues on a bridge (Bernini's leading to the Castel Sant' Angelo in Rome, say, or the black and gold statues lining the St. Charles bridge in Prague). These boys are at once fragile, negligible beings and looming presences. At every point, however, no matter how shadowy they become, they retain their uniqueness, their identifiability. They are recognizable people (Willy or Hans or Ulrich) unlike the carefully lit and posed studio abstractions by, for instance, Horst, a German-born photographer (who eventually settled in the United States) working with the male nude in the 1950s. Horst may take a photo of the celebrated painter Tchelitchew, but no one except an intimate could identify him. He and the other Horst models seem like machine parts or green peppers—like the female nudes of Edward Weston, for instance.

When I mentioned that List looks at his young men *contre-jour* and often from below, as though they were statues on a bridge or above a stadium, I'm inevitably courting a comparison with the glorification of heroism in Nazi art. Hitler's film-maker, Leni Riefenstahl, took a picture of a slender young Greek at Pyrgos in 1936, another in the same year of a running javelin-thrower wearing nothing but a cache-sexe, and still another of a discus-thrower (1936, almost completely naked) in the pose known to everyone from classical sculpture. These are stills from the film *Olympia* and are from sequences that show the metamorphosis of a Greek sculpture such as the discus-thrower into a living male model. In all three cases the camera is looking up with admiration at these god-like athletes— what could be called "the master-race pose" except that Riefenstahl shot Nuba warriors in Africa in the same pose well after the war.

But the poses also recall the fascist sculptures in Mussolini's Foro Italico outside Rome or those by Arno Breker, the official Nazi artist, the student of Maillol who stiffened his teacher's supple females into heroic males. Of course it would be absurd to confuse List with his Nazi enemies; as someone who was a quarter Jew, List fled Germany in the mid-1930s, lived in penury in Paris as a photographer then moved on to Athens where at last, in 1941, the Germans caught up with him after they had conquered Greece. List was brought back to Germany and eventually sent off to Norway to work as a map-maker for the army. He was profoundly indifferent to politics and to the degree he thought about it at all he was hostile to Hitler. According to Spender, List once said to him in the late 1920s "that there existed somewhere in Bavaria a man who was a magician with words and who, as long as he was talking, could completely convince an audience of the truth of what he was saying. But the moment the meeting was over every single member of the crowd, when he had returned home, realized that what he had been hearing was nonsense, utter nonsense. The man's name was Hitler."

What is true, however, was that List was of course influenced by the prevailing esthetic in Germany in the 1920s and '30s. Just as List's photos of classical ruins were preceded by similar pictures by Aenne Biermann (Pantheon, 1928) or Walter Hege (Acropolis, 1928/29), in the same way List's beautiful, subtle pictures of young men beside the sea resemble the much clumsier pictures by Kurt Reichert and were preceded in the first two decades of the twentieth century by stiffly posed or ridiculously frolicsome gay male nudes in nature from *Der Eigene,* the first gay male journal in the world.

By the time List came along, in the late 1920s, a homophile movement within the Jugendbewegung (the "youth movement") had evolved into an anti-bourgeois, nonconformist grouping of young people who worshipped the sun with pagan fervor and longed to travel. They were not exclusively or even primarily gay, but in their shadowy sentiments, however, there was little difference between this movement and the Wandervogel movement at the turn of the century as well as the more strictly homosexual one represented by *Der Eigene*. Someday the history of the idea of "youth" in pre-1945 Germany will be written, but already one can see that the movement lasted half a century and was a sort of *terrain vague* delimited by Hellenism, nudism, anti-authoritarianism and a yearning for generational solidarity. For gays it was a rejection of the medical, scientific justification of homosexuality advanced by Dr. Magnus Hirschfeld and an ecstatic affirmation of homosexuality as a form of German romantic friendship. The tone of *Der Eigene* sometimes sounds dangerously close to the eugenics theories of the Nazis—and no wonder, since as Harry Oosterhuis, the Dutch scholar, has argued in *Homosexuality and Male Bonding in Pre-Nazi Germany*, Hitler's rejection of homosexuality came late in the day and primarily as a cynical strategy for eliminating a political rival, Ernst Röhm, who happened to be gay.

Most serious painters, writers and photographers rejected Nazism (that was why the endorsement of the movement by Knut Hamsun, the Norwegian Nobel Prize–winning novelist, was so scandalous, since he was virtually alone in his enthusiasm). As art historian Rolf Sachsee has written recently, the photographers who worked for the National Socialists "were born between 1895 and 1910 and in various interviews they later mentioned their more or less strong links with the German Youth Movement— whatever the respective individual may have understood by that term. The majority of the Youth Movement associations and clubs pursued a common aim: a basically apolitical return to a harmony with nature— nature being regarded as given and immutable. For this the groups required binding links such as a nature mysticism, nutrition strategies and a body culture."

As Sachsee argues, a vacuum was created in Germany once all Jewish and progressive photographers were killed or driven out of the country or imprisoned. in the 1930s. As for the Nazi photographers, they fell back on their "Youth Movement repertory of leisure and nature activities, body culture and community ideals. Not only was this timely, it also enabled them to regard themselves as heralds of future generations."

Of course there can be no question either of List endorsing Nazi ideals (quite the contrary) or of his own pictures of boys and young men influencing Nazi photography, since he never published them in his own lifetime. Herbert List was unquestionably influenced by the Jugendbewegung, but he was too much of an individualist to be closely associated with any of its constituent groups. Some of the ideals of the Jugendbewegung were cleverly co-opted by the Nazis, but eventually all of its groups were outlawed and many of their leading representatives were put into concentration camps or even killed.

All I'm suggesting is that if List's work sometimes reminds us of Riefenstahl's, it's because they had a common source in the German Youth Movement, a very general and vaguely defined moment of Romantic paganism that, for instance, touched even Walter Benjamin, the Jewish Marxist thinker, who attended the country boarding school Haubinda, with its devotion to hiking, farming and philosophy and its emphasis on "youth." There was always a rowdy, violent, irrational, resentful side to National Socialism, but in its early days it also drew on the general impulse toward anti-authoritarianism and male bonding.

As Harry Oosterhuis has written, supporters of the Third Reich

> ...regarded male friendship as the germ cell of the German nation, referring to the experience at the front during the First World War and to traditions which went back to the 18th century or even to the Germans of former ages and the ancient Greeks. Thus the Nazi lawyer R. Klare stated that the severe penalties he proposed for homosexuality should not become a hindrance to spiritual love for members of one's own sex on the basis of the ancient Greek love of youths. In the pseudo-scientific *völkische Germanenkunde* which the Nazis promoted, the *Männerbund* was a central theme. The myth of primordial male bonding served the purpose of establishing a continuity in German history, of which the Nazis were supposedly the heirs.

Of course the fact that List dared not show his photos meant that he knew the Nazis would be able to see the difference between his sensuality, his brand of individualism, his subversiveness and the "virile" poses of Nazi athletes, who almost never have a face, a name, a personality, who never touch and are most often seen in groups. Symptomatically, Nazi pictures of handsome young men are never portraits, never show them up close, never expose the vulnerability of a body. Their photos present nothing but idealized types of virility.

What we must never forget is that List's pictures were explosive. Herbert List was so frightened that they would be discovered that he kept them hidden in his mother's house in a sack called his "poison bag." Many times after the war he contemplated publishing them but never could work up the nerve to do so. Similarly, George Platt Lynes published only a few of his male nudes in his lifetime and then only under two pseudonyms (Roberto Rolf and Robert Orville) in the Swiss gay magazine *Der Kreis*. What may be more significant is that Lynes destroyed all his commercial photography at the end of his life and left behind only his portraits, his nudes, his "mythologies" and his dance photos—precisely the pictures he'd previously suppressed. These photos he sold to Alfred Kinsey, the sex researcher.

The male nude, of course, has had a troubled history in modern times. Whereas female nudes are the great staple of nineteenth- and twentieth-century art, replacing in importance the aristocratic portrait and the religious theme of earlier epochs, male nudes (which had been the great subject of classical sculpture, after all) were virtually ignored in nineteenth-century painting, except in scenes of the death of Christ or in those drawn from history or mythology. In fact, it is easy to make a short list of the exceptions to this rule—Géricault's *Raft of the Medusa* (1819), Gustave Courbet's *The Wrestlers* (1853), Gustave Caillebotte's *Man at Bath* (1884) and especially Frédéric Bazille's *Fisherman with a Net* (1868) and his *Summer Scene* (1869). No modern painting exhibition has focussed on the male nude except the Cézanne Bathers show in Basel in 1988, and many male nudes painted in the nineteenth century either were never shown until the twentieth century (Renoir's disturbingly androgynous *Boy with a Cat* [1868–69] is a good example), or if they were shown they created a scandal. The Bazille paintings, for instance, were especially controversial, perhaps because they do not have a classical or allegorical subject and are so obviously sexual and realistic; *Fisherman with a Net,* for instance, was rejected by the Salon jury of 1869 precisely because it was so shockingly modern and veristic.

In the United States Thomas Eakins, generally conceded to be the greatest of all nineteenth-century American painters, lost his job as a painting teacher at the Philadelphia Academy of the Fine Arts in part because of the controversy aroused by his *Swimming* (generally known as *The Swimming Hole*), which pictured six males who were not only nude but were also people whom Eakins counted among his friends and students—identifiable men. In fact Eakins's painting of the mid-1880s was distressing because it showed men and boys at a swimming hole, not in an ancient or exotic locale, and its poses and portraiture were also troubling precisely because they were based on photographic studies that Eakins had himself undertaken (including photographic studies of motion, based on similar studies by Eadweard Muybridge, the author and photographer of *Animal Locomotion,* a work that influenced Francis Bacon much later).

What is significant is that Bazille and Eakins are often discussed today as homosexual painters, although there is little extra-artistic evidence of a homosexual orientation. Whereas viewers of female nudes (whether painted or photographed by men or women) do not automatically begin to speculate about the sexual orientation of the artist, male nudes are so unusual and still so taboo that viewers and critics, even today, assume the male artists are homosexual and that the female artists are somehow indecent or morbid or "obsessed."

Photographs are more disturbing than paintings because whereas the viewer can always suppose that a painting is a composite of sketches of several models, or a pure invention of the imagination, or an idealization, a photograph does not benefit from this immunity. We are instantly curious about the real-life identity of the subject, we wonder if he is dead now or very old, we wonder what happened to him, we even spin theories about his psychology, his social position, his sexual orientation. We speculate about the encounter between the photographer and his or her subject. A photograph comes to us trailing clues, whereas a painting truly does what its apologists have always asserted it does—it elevates its subject and the viewer's perceptions. Many photographs of male nudes before the present era were never exhibited openly; they were usually reserved for the initiated. Those that weren't cloaked in secrecy, such as the male studies by A. Calavas or G. Marconi, were of painters' models in conventional poses.

Because at the end of the twentieth century we enjoy the privilege of seeing the male nudes of List, Lynes, Hoyningen-Huene and other photographers of the 1930s, we are in danger of rewriting art history and of giving a false "naturalness" to these amazing photos, which were seen by their contemporaries only in private and then furtively. Today we contemplate these extraordinary photographs—these men!—with all the pleasure and equanimity that List, at least, invariably communicates even if it was a joy he did not always permit himself to experience much less to share.

Robert Mapplethorpe

PARADOXICALLY, ROBERT MAPPLETHORPE is both a link in a long photographic tradition and someone who was startlingly original, without precursors. And his place on the artistic map was entirely something conscious and chosen; although he was not a reader, his visual culture was probably deeper than that of any other contemporary photographer, due to his own interests and those of his companion of two decades, Sam Wagstaff, one of the most ambitious private collectors of photographs of our time. Mapplethorpe, moreover, imposed his personal visual style on every element in his environment, from his simple, sturdy, virile Stickley furniture to his collections of glass and pottery to his own clothes, his saturnine leathers, which, when I knew him in the late 1970s and early 1980s, were never stiff, shapeless, clunky jackets out of a Brando film but rather supple, form-fitting Dutch black leathers elegantly seamed in blue.

In those days Robert lived in a loft on Bond Street just a few blocks away from me in the no-man's-land between the West Village and the East Village and north of SoHo. The exact historical and cultural moment of the late 1970s in gay New York is hard to re-create, partly because it was overshadowed after 1981 by the dark and ever-growing anxiety generated by AIDS, which not only cast a pall over an earlier exuberance but also changed values so radically that we can scarcely understand that vanished era.

Mapplethorpe was conspicuously apolitical and obsessed with his own career, with a degree of self-absorption friends might have called anarchic individualism and enemies might have labeled narcissism.

Even he, though, was inevitably influenced by contemporary political events, if for no other reason than that his stated ambition to raise gay male pornography to the level of high art plunged him into the turbulent and quickly changing moral values of the epoch.

In its first decade gay liberation (which began in 1969 in New York during the Stonewall Uprising) was all about sexual freedom. In preceding years, gays had been afraid to assemble lest their bars be raided and their names printed in the paper—a common practice, and one that usually resulted in losing jobs and apartments, not to mention friends and the sympathy of family members. What impelled lesbians and gay men to get together was sexual urgency, and these sexual encounters were what the police and psychiatrists were intent on stopping. For Mapplethorpe, gay life began and ended with sexual opportunity, always of the most urgent importance to him. As he explained in 1988 without a trace of irony, referring to the late 1970s: "I had many affairs during that period, but I was never into quickie sex. I've only slept with maybe a thousand men." Even today older gays have trouble understanding what "gay culture" means and what "gay identity" might represent, since for them gayness was only a matter of sexual necessity best forgotten once desire was sated.

But by 1969, the year Mapplethorpe moved to Manhattan, the mood was changing in response to a general social ferment. As Michael Bronski, one of the founders of the Gay Liberation Front, has written: "The Stonewall riots and the Gay Liberation Front would not have happened in 1969 had it not been for the enormous social vitality of the times. If it were not for the presence of the Black Power movement, the second wave of feminism, the youth culture, the civil rights movement, the drug culture, the hippies, the yippies, and rock and roll, the raid on the Stonewall Inn would have been petty police harassment against one more mob-owned drinking hole that housed another dozen queens."

Indifferent as Mapplethorpe might have been to sloganeering, his work became celebrated because it flourished precisely during this period of heady freedom—from censorship and from received ideas about gender, race and sexual orientation. As he later said, "My life began in the summer of 1969. Before that I didn't exist." If he was later able to investigate perversion; to take self-portraits of himself as man and as woman; to picture a black man and white woman embracing naked; to coolly observe self-mutilation; to mix pictures of flowers, society women, and fist-fucking, this visual daring and promiscuity was endorsed and even empowered by the epoch. Ezra Pound once wrote that "the age demanded an image of its accelerated grimace," and Mapplethorpe provided his age with the very image it required.

In its first decade, 1969 to 1979, the one that formed Mapplethorpe's art and sensibility, the battle for gay liberation was still a violent one. For instance, on October 1, 1971, Connecticut became only the second state, after Illinois, to decriminalize homosexuality between consenting adults. In some states sodomy was still a capital offense. Early in 1972 the New York City Council vetoed a gay rights ordinance that would have prohibited discrimination against lesbians and gay men in employment, housing and public accommodations. In 1973 the Supreme Court decided that communities could censor works of art that might offend local standards of morality—which led, for instance, to a raid in New Jersey on six allegedly obscene movies, including Warhol's *Flesh* and *Lonesome Cowboys*. The continuing closetedness this persecution brought about even in the gay artistic community in New York had a direct effect on Mapplethorpe's career. Dealers in the early 1970s might have been enthusiastic about Robert's explicitly homosexual art, but they all shrugged and said they couldn't sell it. Patti Smith, Robert's girlfriend, would show his work to gay dealers who'd reject it; as she recalled, "Several of them told me, 'I think the work is really interesting, but how can I exhibit it without making a statement about who I am?' Robert was really hurt by that."

As Michael Bronski points out, the original impetus behind gay liberation was the fight for the right to behave homosexually—to commit homosexual acts. This is no longer the case. Now in response to the pressures of the religious right, the anxiety and stigma associated with AIDS and the ambitions of lesbian and gay assimilationist political leaders, the goal has shifted from sexual liberation to identity politics. We are no longer defending our right to behave homosexually but rather our right to *identify* as homosexuals. The army's "Don't ask/don't tell" policy reflects this shift, alas; gay sexuality is still illegal, although the right to identify as homosexual is now permitted; yet even there, the assimilationists argue, the question of identity should ideally be kept a private matter of self-identification in silence.

Although Mapplethorpe set out to incorporate explicit gay imagery into high art, he was reluctant to be identified "simply" as a gay artist. In the 1970s and '80s (and in many gay circles today), the term "gay artist" was considered a restriction, not just commercially but also esthetically, although it could be pointed out that a presumed membership in a dominant culture ("white writer," say, or "heterosexual painter") does not strike anyone as a limitation. But whether Mapplethorpe wanted to be considered gay or not, retrospectively he has been thrust into this role. The unfortunate shift today away from an emphasis on sexual freedom to gay identity has made the explicit sexual content of Mapplethorpe's photos look sleazy, politically incorrect, even racist.

Gay history evolves so quickly that the particular moment Mapplethorpe so fully inhabited and indeed helped to shape is in danger of being lost. What should not be forgotten is that when his photos became famous in the late 1970s, the gay community was one of the few entities in which white racism and black separatism were not yet in full control; in fact, back then the gay organization of Black and White Men Together seemed to hold out at least the faint possibility of healing the schisms of race through love. Of course, this trend was a minor one. Many white-dominated gay bars barred black customers from entering by asking for five pieces of identification at the door. Even in the gay pornographic press there were very few pictures of black men. I can remember that when I was interviewing black gay men in Atlanta in 1978 several told me that Mapplethorpe was virtually the only photographer who was giving them exciting and beautiful images of their race, a fact I mentioned in my 1980 book, *States of Desire: Travels in Gay America*.

Today, of course, all that is changed. Gay assimilationists want to play down the troubling question of sexuality altogether. The prevalence of identity politics rules that only blacks can photograph blacks; for whites to do so is considered invasive at best, exploitive at worst. A talented black gay poet, Essex Hemphill, attacked Mapplethorpe (after his death) in 1990 by singling out his famous photograph *Man in Polyester Suit*, in which the subject's head is not shown although his immense penis protrudes from his fly. He writes: "What is insulting and endangering to Black men is Mapplethorpe's *conscious* determination that the faces, the heads, and by extension, the minds and experiences of some of his Black subjects are not as important as close-up shots of their cocks." Quite rightly he adds a paragraph later: "It has not fully dawned on white gay men that racist conditioning has rendered many of them no different from their heterosexual brothers in the eyes of Black gays and lesbians. Coming out of the closet to confront sexual oppression has not necessarily given white males the motivation or insight to transcend their racist conditioning."

At the time I tried to argue back in print that the subject was Mapplethorpe's lover Milton Moore, who forbade the photographer to show his body and face together; he was afraid family members would see the pictures and figure out he was gay. He gave Mapplethorpe permission to photograph his body alone, without the head, or the head alone without a nude body.

Of course, I realize this is just an anecdote, but I think it's a telling one. The subject dictates the very terms of the photo, an unusual situation except, perhaps, in the portraits of royals, corporate executives and movie stars. Yet Mapplethorpe's remarkable acquiescence in this matter reflects his more general attitude towards photography. His portraits were almost always shot in the studio under controlled conditions and with the full cooperation and even complicity of the sitter; not for him the shadow-stealing of the unauthorized snapshot. If I underline this point I do so because he has sometimes been compared to the white ethnographic photographer of the last century, the very symbol of exploitation.

One glance at his pictures, of course, belies this absurd accusation; his models are not people caught unawares at their folkloric habitual activities. Rather, they are carefully lit and posed bodies, sometimes placed against backdrops or sculptures Mapplethorpe designed. Sometimes their bodies are also oiled, although Mapplethorpe himself disliked this look, believing it to be reminiscent of corny physique photography of the 1950s, and shot oiled bodies only when the subjects insisted. Moreover, Mapplethorpe was an adept of the cult of beauty and rejected the freakish photo à la Diane Arbus or the unmasked-celebrity photo à la Avedon.

Of course, one could say that he was "objectifying" these bodies, but I would contend that photography by its very nature objectifies (the French word for "lens" is *objectif*). A photograph is always one person's glance at another, and the model never speaks or in any other way expresses his or her opinion about the results. It strikes me as not coincidental that so many of the general debates about exploitation that have wracked America have involved photography—women against pornography and the Native American critiques of early ethnographic photographers are but two examples. Photography is by its very nature an invasion and, to the degree that a portrait suggests an insight into another person, a definitive likeness, a revelation of character. It is an imposition of one person's vision on another person's identity.

If objectification is at the heart of photography, the visual arts in general conceal precisely in their very formal categories certain built-in prejudices and conservative social agendas. Take the genre distinction between "nudes" and "portraits," as old as sculpture and painting in the West. I would contend that this very distinction, one that Mapplethorpe observed and perpetuated in his work, is inherently insulting, as though only notables merit a careful, respectful depiction of their personalities and faces, whereas less important if usually more beautiful men and women are to be prized for their bodies alone. An emperor poses for his (admittedly idealized) portrait bust; he chooses the sculptor. A sculptor, however, chooses a woman to represent a muse, say, or an abstraction such as Justice, and if he accomplishes his purpose the actual identity of his model will not be recognizable from the nude statue. As Marina Warner has pointed out in *Monuments and Maidens,* one reason sculptors in the nineteenth century used a woman to represent Justice was because in so doing there was no danger that the woman would resemble any actual judge. A good portrait is an unforgettable likeness, whereas nude figures—naiads or bathers, for instance—are generic figures, virtually interchangeable. Most nudes invite the viewer's desire; as feminist critics have shown, even seemingly consecrated images such as the Polynesian bare-breasted women Gauguin painted are actually soft-core porn. Since Gauguin's figures are women, the traditional and conventionally "formal" subject of figure painting, we do not even register the erotic element invoked by the round fruits they hold beneath their breasts (although this strategy became more obvious when art critic Linda Nochlin created analogue paintings of men with large penises holding trays of bananas).

I enter into these genre distinctions and the class prejudices and sexual politics behind them because some critics have questioned why Mapplethorpe so often gives us portraits of white society women, for example, and impersonal-nude studies of black men. The question, I would concede, is a legitimate one, but I'd also argue that the supposedly demeaning attitudes expressed by Mapplethorpe are linked to desire. He desires black men and studies their bodies; he is fascinated by women "only" as personalities and therefore makes portraits of them. If Mapplethorpe is inherently racist (in this sense alone), he is certainly not sexist. He "exploits" men's bodies in nude photos and renders women the full (if finally hollow) honors of portraiture. Interestingly, when his sensibility was truly engaged by either a man or a woman (Bob Love or Lisa Lyon, for instance), the distinction between nude and portrait breaks down; his figures may be naked, but the subjects' personalities are intensely rendered. Nevertheless, it remains disconcerting that in the National Portrait Gallery show in London, *Mapplethorpe Portraits,* only ten of the seventy-one images in the catalogue were of black men or women, whereas in a corresponding book of nudes more than half the photos would have been of black men.

In some ways photographs are like music—likely to awaken strong but not very specific emotions. Most people respond with intense feelings to a Mozart piano concerto, but if a roomful of people were asked to write descriptions of what they feel while listening to a largo, no two descriptions would be the same. Similarly, images in general and photographs in particular evoke strong reactions, but seldom the same ones. The written word, by contrast, conjures up much more precisely defined feelings, but usually those feelings are somewhat milder and slower to be evoked. The French novelist Jean Genet, for instance, never had any problem with the law until his fourth novel, *Querelle,* was given sexy illustrations by Jean Cocteau; perhaps censors prefer glancing at disturbing images to reading long books. Or, to give another example, hundreds of books can be bought in the United States that are far more sexual or even more sadomasochistic than the most extreme images produced by Mapplethorpe, but none has awakened the rage elicited by his photographs.

Why?

Not only can a photograph be quickly apprehended, but it can also be seen inadvertently and by anyone who happens to glance at it; seeing it does not depend on a decision by the viewer, whereas reading a text is a project that must be voluntarily embarked on. Of course, one could argue that this problem is eliminated when these potentially disturbing images are restricted to a book or an exhibition one must pay to see, or when the most extreme images are relegated to a particular part of the exhibit or to a sealed book available only to adults.

But the problem does not end there. Whereas words are symbols that evoke visual images provided by the reader's own imagination (and presumably no two readers' images are the same), a photograph provides the viewer with a ready-made image of a specific individual; no participation on the part of the spectator other than looking is required.

Moreover, that photographed individual has a history, a scar, an age, a name (Mapplethorpe usually gives us his subject's names, or at least, depending on the model's preference, his first name). If one man is photographed urinating in another's mouth, that picture gives the participants' names, a date on which the event occurred and the name of the site (Sausalito in this case). We are not dealing with a fantasy invented by a writer or a painter but with a real event staged for the camera. In the case of Mapplethorpe's sadomasochistic pictures, real people are presumably being shown practicing their real vices: they have been recruited because they are already adepts of, say, bondage or water sports. No matter that these pictures are rather cold, formal, even static and, at least for this viewer, decidedly unexciting and therefore nonpornographic; some of them make one think less of enslavement and possession than of the banal pride of the deep-sea fisherman posing beside the day's stupendous catch.

When we look at a photo, we're always aware of time; for that reason we speak of "old photos" and even "old movies" but never "old paintings" or "old novels." When we look at Thomas Eakins's paintings of boys jumping into a swimming hole, we never stop to ask questions about the models, whereas when we look at the photos he worked from we say, "I wonder what his name was?" or "How old would he be if he were still alive?" or "I wonder if Eakins made it with him?" Roland Barthes said that photography is always about death; because we're confronted with a living person, we wonder about when he died in the past or will die in the future. In this sense, as Marina Warner has argued, photos are descendants of wax death masks, and even their glossiness reminds us of the shininess of wax itself.

But if photos arouse ideas of death, of real individuals, and consequently awaken feelings of outrage that writing does not usually evoke, by the same token their instantaneous availability means that they can elicit an enthusiasm denied to literature. Mapplethorpe became much more famous and rich, for instance, than any gay writer of the same epoch. To read Larry Kramer's *Faggots,* for example, involves a week-long immersion in a very specific ghetto life, one that the reader must re-create in his own mind, drawing upon his own supply of memories, psychological knowledge and visual experience; the book must enter into the very fiber of its reader, whereas the photograph can be glanced at without being assimilated. The photo, of course, also has an inherent value as a precious object. And it can travel faster, farther, easier than a text; in that way it is like music. No need to translate it. Patti Smith's records are known the world over, whereas her poetry is read by only a cult, just as everyone knows Gauguin's paintings but not his book, *Noa Noa.*

Mapplethorpe's most disturbing images, those of bondage, sadism, humiliation, scarification, are somehow appropriate both to his particular moment as a gay man and to a more general, less time-bound American sensibility. When I speak of that American sensibility, what I have in mind is a puritanical hatred of pleasure. Sex cannot be esteemed by Americans as an art, a form of dalliance, an expression of affection; no, it must stand for a transcendent search, a quest for self-revelation or self-perfection. The early Christian martyrs excoriated the flesh in the name of the spirit; the modern American puritan unites the flesh and the spirit and excoriates both. Pain is a guarantee of spiritual mission; self-destruction is a form of martyrdom.

The particular gay moment of the 1970s I referred to was one of virilization; as gay men rejected other people's definitions, they embraced a new vision of themselves as hypermasculine—the famous "clone" look. Soldier, cop, construction worker—these were the new gay images, rather than dancer or decorator or ribbon clerk. A new tribalism replaced the isolation of the self-hating queer individual; a kind of body fascism came into vogue, as muscular bulk took precedence over boyish slimness, as the weathered thirty-five-year-old man instead of the hairless ephebe became the *beau idéal.*

The very success of this revolution brought its own problem: conformity. Whatever its shortcomings might have been, at least preliberation homosexuality had been guaranteed to be irrevocably marginal, transgressive, scandalous. What Mapplethorpe (and Pasolini) found in sadism and scatology was a practice, a world, so revolting that even (or especially) other homosexuals were horrified by it. Like every good Catholic, both Pasolini and Mapplethorpe were attracted to Satanism (indeed Mapplethorpe reportedly would whisper into his lovers' ears, "Do it for Satan"); the torture Mapplethorpe documented in his photos and Pasolini in *Salò* will smell eternally of brimstone. In the gay movement the two verboten subgroups are still sadists and pedophiles; it is no accident that Mapplethorpe alluded to both.

Of course, for Mapplethorpe there were precedents for homosexual photography—F. Holland Day, von Gloeden, Herbert List—just as there were influential homosexual painters of an earlier period, including Paul Cadmus, Jean Cocteau and Pavel Tchelitchew. Mapplethorpe also had important photographers as contemporaries, including George Dureau, Arthur Tress, Bruce Weber and Duane Michals. But the most relevant to an appraisal of Mapplethorpe seems to me to be George Platt Lynes.

Born in 1907 in New Jersey, Lynes traveled to France when he was just eighteen, where he met Cocteau and Tchelitchew as well as Gertrude Stein. From the age of twenty until his early death in 1955 at age forty-eight, Lynes worked as a photographer. He did fashion work, celebrity portraits—and homoerotic photography. He took pictures of erect penises, of black and white male couples, of a suffering man in bondage; he paired nude men with classical sculpture. In all these ways Lynes set an important precedent for Mapplethorpe. Lynes, too, isolated body parts and fetishized sexual organs. He, too, photographed other gay men, usually dancers or artists; in this way Lynes and Mapplethorpe differ from photographers such as Bruce Weber, whose subjects (cowboys, greasers, professional athletes, fashion models) are usually homophobic. They may awaken gay desire, but the desire is not reciprocated. Quite a contrast with Mapplethorpe, who often had sex with his subjects on the same night he photographed them. In fact his usual procedure was to pick up someone or other for sex and then only later ask if they'd pose for him (he'd always give them two prints as payment, which as the years went by and his prices rose astronomically turned out to be very handsome recompense indeed). Mapplethorpe was always frank about and even proud of his own sexual involvement with his models. As he told *American Photographer* in 1988, "Let's face it, most photographers are living their lives vicariously by taking pictures. When they get into sex or pornography it's often a sort of cover-up for their own sexual inactivity or inadequacy. They'd rather do it through the camera and sublimate their desires in order to take pictures."

In Mapplethorpe's case his sexual encounters with models preceded taking their picture.

If Mapplethorpe was linked to earlier photographers and painters, he was also genuinely original, especially in his simplicity, his directness, his unapologetic curiosity, the unwavering force of his regard. As any look at gay art, whether literary or plastic, reveals, nothing is so difficult, so recent, so evolved as the simplicity of unmediated vision. Early gay fiction, for instance, is set in ancient Greece or in another country or occurs between innocent schoolboys or touches on the subject of forbidden sexuality only on the last page or takes place between an aristocrat and a peasant on a a fog-swept island or involves a doomed couple living far from other gay people. Madness or suicide or accidental death is usually the conclusion. (But Michael Bronski's *Pulp Friction* collection contests this general view and sees gay fiction of the 1940s and 1950s as more nuanced and cheerful than I do.) Similarly, the alibi of early gay photography is the classical world of ballet or mythology or "scientific" studies of motion or degeneration. Sleeping boys or the dead Christ or the martyred Saint Sebastian or mud-larks fishing coins out of the Thames or naked wrestlers or exotic Arab dancing boys dressed as girls—these are just a few of the pretexts for earlier gay photography.

What is extraordinary about Mapplethorpe is his abandonment of all these contexts, this window dressing for, if you will, the naked fact of sexual curiosity and erotic intensity.

Mapplethorpe once said that all his photographs were altars. When he first started to work, this adulation of the body was still staged in Catholic terms; only later did he eliminate the element of Catholic kitsch, although what remained was a sense of ceremony, of mystical transformation. He liked to say that S&M stood for "sex and magic," and certainly the first and last article in his faith became sex, and the principal mystery in his cult that of the magical transubstantiation of the naked into the nude, the fallible body into the perfection of flesh.

"I guess you could say I have a certain Catholic aesthetic," he confided to his biographer, Patricia Morrisroe, to whose book I am indebted for some of the information in this essay.

He was born in Hollis, Queens, on November 4, 1946, the third child in a pious middle-class family. As a boy he attended the local church, Our Lady of the Snows, and did Cubist portraits of the Madonna. Later, as an adult, he told Ingrid Sischy, the editor of *Artforum,* "A church has a certain magic and mystery for a child. It still shows in how I arrange things. It's always little altars. It's always been this way—whenever I'd put something together I'd notice it was symmetrical."

He attended art school in Brooklyn at the Pratt Institute. In 1967, when he was twenty, he met Patti Smith, with whom he lived for years and with whom he shared an intense period of creative discovery. They each worked part-time, and for a while Patti was earning enough money selling books at Scribner's to be able to support Robert entirely, liberating him to work nonstop on his art. He did not become a photographer right away, although from almost the beginning he used sexy gay photos he found in magazines as collage elements.

He and Patti both read Rimbaud's poetry and Genet's novels, the work of two writers who resorted to Catholic imagery, usually for profane purposes. Genet was the first writer to break with the earlier evasiveness regarding homosexuality and to present himself under his own name as a gay protagonist and narrator living not in some never-never land but, in the case of *Our Lady of the Flowers,* in the gay ghetto of Montmartre itself. In Genet's novels there are no medical or psychological or genetic explanations of the origins of homosexuality. Unlike most middle-class writers of his day, he did not present homosexuality as a malady calling for compassion from the reader; no, Genet always presented homosexuality as a sin and a crime.

Mapplethorpe, like Genet, would invert Catholicism and would emphasize the satanic side of homosexuality. His self-portraits would become the equivalent to Genet's various first-person narrators, always named Genet. And Genet's erotic fascination with violence and torture would find an echo in Mapplethorpe's hard look at physical brutality.

When Mapplethorpe would work beside Patti Smith in the early 1970s, he would wear a monk's robe; as he said, "When I work, and in my art, I hold hands with God." In their room Mapplethorpe set up an altar that included his own drawing of a pentagram, a black cloth draped over a table, statues of the Virgin purchased at a Puerto Rican bodega, bronze figures of the devil, and the skull of a monkey he had named Scratch (one of the devil's names) and later decapitated and boiled down.

During these early years he would devise collage pieces from gay pornography, and on November 4, 1970, he opened his first one-man show of twelve "freak collages," as he called them. But the religious theme was never far from his mind. He referred to his collages as "altarpieces from some bizarre religion." In 1969 he tacked a tie rack onto a found lithograph of the Virgin. At home he put together an altarpiece by covering a nightstand with Patti's wolf skin, a magic talisman for both Robert and her. On the table he placed a statue of the Sacred Heart with black tape covering the eyes. He bought a conventional Advent calendar but replaced all the holy images with pictures of Patti. He created two Cornell boxes in which he placed a statue of the Sacred Heart, a crucifix and a skull.

This religious theme was paralleled by—and sometimes even mixed in with—pornographic images, some of them self-portraits. He appeared in a thirty-three-minute movie called *Robert Having His Nipple Pierced.* Among the first photos he took were the 1972 black-and-white Polaroids he shot of David Croland, which he later photostatted and hand-colored. They show Croland crouching naked under a net, his back to us, or again lying down, face up, under the same wide-mesh net. He did a nude self-portrait in 1971 which he placed behind a piece of wire mesh, the whole affixed to paper bag. The bag may suggest disposable garbage, but the Saint Sebastian pose alludes to martyrdom, whereas the wire mesh evokes the screen in a confessional. Some of these works, as well as four nude self-portraits in which the body is juxtaposed against classical sculpture, were shown in his earliest shows (his first photography show was held in January 1973).

Mapplethorpe learned from the men he attached himself to. Through his intense friendship with Metropolitan curator John McKendry, Mapplethorpe was introduced to Thomas Eakins's photographs of naked boys and Alfred Stieglitz's photos of Georgia O'Keeffe nude. Since Stieglitz and O'Keeffe were married, this encounter may have suggested to Mapplethorpe the idea of photographing Patti Smith nude. Thanks to Sam Wagstaff, Mapplethorpe first saw the nudes of von Gloeden (which Wagstaff collected) as well as the magisterial portraits of nineteenth-century artists and writers photographed by Nadar.

By the late 1970s Mapplethorpe had become a mature artist. He had entirely eliminated the last tacky bit of collage or Catholic kitsch, although his early orientation towards creating unique pieces led him sometimes to fashion elaborate frames out of silk panels and wood and even to make stylized crosses out of white shag carpet and wood or of frosted mirror in a shaped frame. As his taste became purer he eschewed anything juvenile or ironic or sacrilegious, but his urge to adore and his sense of reverence are still transparent in his awe-inspired portrait of say, Bob Love, the enthroned African deity, the Ur-principal of fertility. Even his flowers, far from being an escape into the natural or the decorative, are meticulously posed organs—"New York flowers," as Mapplethorpe called them. As he once remarked, "Sex is magic. If you channel it right, there's more energy in sex than there is in art." He made the two so interchangeable, and mingled them both so intimately with his life, that in the end neither he nor we need to choose between them.

PERSONALITIES

Yves Saint Laurent

F OR AT LEAST TEN YEARS Yves Saint Laurent has been rumored to be *le grand malade* of French fashion. People have whispered about drugs, drink, disease, car accidents and disastrous public appearances. For instance, one English fashion editor told me that five or six years back he came out on the runway looking puffy, disoriented and reeling. He kissed one of the models drunkenly on the mouth and then proceeded to smear her scarlet lipstick on each of the other girls he pecked at haphazardly on the neck or forehead. In the end, it looked as though everyone had been shot and was suffering from a serious head wound.

Another year he kissed the girls and then just stood there on the runway, silent, frozen and befuddled. Finally, one of the models led him off, as though she were a nurse in an absurdly chic mental hospital.

"Sometimes," a leading fashion journalist told me, "I think we were just applauding the fact that he was still standing up."

And yet Saint Laurent has emerged triumphant once again, as I was able to see for myself in a long interview he granted me, during which he spoke with surprising frankness, particularly about his drug problem. "I was a crazy little guy," he told me. In a subsequent conversation with Pierre Bergé, almost scorching in its candor, I caught a glimpse of the admiration and frustration that powers their highly dynamic relationship.

Grunge is out, glamour back in, and many of the top young American designers are apparently leafing through YSL's old backlist and drawing inspiration from his vintage inventions. One of these *hommages,* by an older, highly established American designer, came too close for comfort. Last spring YSL won a court action against Ralph Lauren for having copied his famous tuxedo dress (the French judge, a woman, had ordered two models to come to the courtroom wearing the rival—and all too similar—dresses).

A month ago Saint Laurent, smiling and confident, paid his first visit to New York in a decade to launch his new perfume Champagne (in another court case a vintners' association had won a court order forbidding YSL to use the name in France). In New York these squabbles were forgotten. As Suzy Menkes, fashion critic for the *Herald Tribune,* told me, "The party was extremely glamorous. Boats brought the crowd out to the Statue of Liberty—the first time a party had been given there that I know of. There were Grucci fireworks and of course champagne and 20,000 white candles marking the path. Perhaps the only problem was that the beautiful people couldn't quite see each other in the dim candlelight. But it's undeniable that Saint Laurent can provide a true sense of a party."

Most important, his haute couture winter collection shown to journalists and buyers last summer was his best in many a season. After several years in which he seemed simply to be recycling tried-and-true ideas during stately but tepid semi-annual rituals before an aging audience, Saint Laurent was suddenly back again, bristling with ideas, as vital and ingenious as ever. Even Menkes, not an automatic YLS fan, admitted that it was a very fine collection. It may have lacked "the ebullience of his early work," as she confided, "but it had a clear point of view and showed an astonishing virtuosity in the use of color and fabric."

When I asked Saint Laurent himself the reason for the latest comeback, he said, "It's because what I did was truly haute couture, done in the great tradition of the métier with all the necessary attention to detail." Perhaps that's a way of saying that it was a very hands-on collection, i.e., his hands and eyes were involved in every tiny decision. When speaking to *Women's Wear Daily,* he added, "I wasn't surprised by its success. When I went back to look at it on video, I realized what a beautiful collection it was."

Shyness and grandiosity, weakness and strength, timidity and egotism—these are the extremes that characterize this enigmatic man who was once dubbed *le petit prince* of fashion but who now seems more like its Last Emperor, by turns feeble and febrile, concealed and cosseted in the heart of the Forbidden City of his sumptuous houses, limousines and town house offices.

When I asked Catherine Deneuve about him, she said that she's known him a long time, ever since he dressed her for *Belle de Jour* in 1967. "But I don't see him that often. He hates the telephone and he's too shy to see people much, but he does write me, very beautiful letters."

"He writes you when you're both in Paris?" I asked.

"Yes," she said. "I know that everyone says for the last ten years he's been in very bad shape, and of course he's extraordinarily delicate and sensitive, but I also think he's terribly strong. Have you ever looked at his shadow? You'd be shocked to notice that he's not at all willowy—no, he's very tall and strong."

Before I pondered Saint Laurent's personality and almost routine *crises de nerfs*, however, I wanted to know what he'd really accomplished. Fashion journalism is often so coded, so abstract or flowery that one can scarcely discern the real achievement of a particular designer. For that reason I looked up Susan Train, who has been in the offices of American *Vogue* for decades and is remarkably lucid and knowledgeable.

She said: "Saint Laurent was first of all a media genius. After Dior died in 1957, the leading couturiers were Givenchy, Balenciaga and Saint Laurent. But Givenchy and Balenciaga detested the press. Balenciaga would never give interviews. Both he and Givenchy were annoyed that their collections were so widely photographed and instantly ripped off in cheap copies, so they decided to ban all journalists from their collections and show their designs a month later to the press. For ten years they kept that up—which left the field wide open to Saint Laurent. He took charge and for the next twenty-five years he ruled as the absolute monarch of world fashion. He always showed his work on the last night of the collections and we all waited breathlessly to see what direction he'd take—fancy, simple, hems up, hems down.

"His second major achievement was that he was the first to figure out that haute couture and ready-to-wear were entirely different. Towards the end of the 1950s a few designers started to do ready-to-wear, but their collections were just watered down, cheaper, simpler versions of what they'd already created for couture. Later other designers, such as Sonia Rykiel and Kenzo, did nothing but ready-to-wear. YSL was the first and foremost designer to do separate collections and to dominate both fields.

"Finally, in his ready-to-wear line Saint Laurent understood that a woman's wardrobe should be as comfortable and above all as basic as a man's." (He once declared, "I design classic clothes for women so that they can feel as comfortable in their clothes as men do in their suits.") "He saw no reason why women should have to throw away all their clothes every season. On the contrary; he wanted women to have certain unvarying separates—raincoats, sweaters, trousers—to which they'd add a few terrifically fashionable items each season. Basically, even Dior had realized that even in an haute couture collection one-third of the clothes should be classics, one-third the successes of the previous season slightly updated and only one-third should be brand new experiments. Saint Laurent, who of course was trained by Dior, has only elaborated this fundamental idea."

The house of Yves Saint Laurent has existed for thirty-four years and been celebrated for so long that it's sometimes hard to remember that he himself is only fifty-eight years old. He once said that what he most regretted was his youth, since he'd had to work too much too soon and never had a chance to enjoy the insouciance of being young. Of course Saint Laurent also enjoys his martyrdom. His partner, Pierre Bergé, claims that he was born with a nervous breakdown and Saint Laurent enjoys repeating this remark. Another couturier of his generation, Marc Bohan, the man who took over Dior after Saint Laurent was drafted into the army, not long ago observed that designing clothes is not exactly torture, especially since one has such a large team to help out. But Saint Laurent obviously subscribes to the doctrine of Romantic Agony, the suffering of the sensitive spirit who has one layer less of skin, and in 1983 he quoted with approval a passage from Proust, his favorite writer and fellow neurasthenic: "The magnificent and pitiful family of the hypersensitive is the salt of the earth. It is they not the others who have founded religions and produced masterpieces." Saint Laurent went on to comment: "That family is my second family, and whatever I have achieved that might approach a masterpiece I owe to that affiliation.... At the time of my early suffering I did not perceive mental suffering as a gift...but now I know it is."

Yves Henri Donat Saint Laurent was born on August 1, 1936, in Oran, a city in the then French colony of Algeria. His parents were well-off, very sociable, amusing and tolerant. His father managed a chain of cinemas in North Africa; his mother loved to entertain, was a demon canasta player, regularly ordered cases of champagne for the house and doted on her son. Summers were spent in Normandy in the coastal town of Trouville.

At an early age little Yves was already drawing queens and princesses and in art class he astonished everyone by adding a bit of silver to his white paint. At home he devoured copies of *Vogue* and presented plays in a little theater of his own devising. According to his biographer, Laurence Benaim, he once dressed his little sister up as a duchess and seated her in the drawing room, then called his mother in and pretended they had a very distinguished visitor indeed.

At home and in his intimate circle he may have been adored, but at school he was tortured by the other boys, who would push him into the lavatory and lock him up in the dark. Often Yves would rush to chapel for refuge between classes or beg to stay in the classroom during exercise period.

When he was thirteen he was already designing dresses for his mother and sister, patterns that the local dressmaker would run up for him. He designed costumes for a play (the theater would remain one of his governing passions). The next year he did illustrations for *Madame Bovary*. By the time he was seventeen he had received third prize in Paris from the Wool Secretariat for dress design.

Yves came to Paris and showed his fashion drawings to Michel de Brunhoff, the director of *Vogue,* who was impressed but recommended that Yves return to Oran to finish his studies. Although the adolescent followed this advice, in 1953, when he was eighteen, he was back in Paris enrolled in a fashion institute. He hated the drudgery of the classes but apparently benefited from them, since that year he won the first prize (for a black cocktail dress) from the Wool Secretariat. The twenty-one-year-old Karl Lagerfeld won first prize in the same contest for the best overcoat.

Soon after, Saint Laurent showed fifty new sketches to Michel de Brunhoff, who realized that several of them were nearly identical to the latest top-secret "A-line" designs of his close friend, Christian Dior, which the young man could not possibly have seen. On the recommendation of the *Vogue* editor, Saint Laurent was engaged by the master couturier. Dior had complete confidence in his young assistant and it was Saint Laurent who designed the famous evening dress that the model Dovima wore as she posed with two elephants for the even more celebrated Avedon photo in 1955.

Two years later, in October 1957, Dior was dead from a heart attack at Montecatini in Italy, where he was undergoing a cure for obesity. The next month Saint Laurent was named his successor; at twenty-one he was the world's youngest couturier. He immediately justified the confidence the house of Dior had placed in him by designing the "Trapeze" line of dresses, which won him the Nieman Marcus Award.

In 1960 Saint Laurent was drafted into the army and promptly had a nervous breakdown. Pierre Bergé, six years older, an arts impresario who had already discovered and promoted the vulgar but popular painter Bernard Buffet, visited Laurent almost daily in the hospital (Buffet had deserted Bergé for a woman, whom he subsequently married).

By January 1961 Saint Laurent was out of the hospital and the army and living with Bergé. Dior refused to take the fragile young designer back; Bergé successfully sued the house for breach of contract and with the settlement money set Saint Laurent up in business for himself. The two partners rented a two-room atelier in the seventh arrondissement and started working with three former colleagues from Dior, including Gabrielle Buchaert, who is still their *attachée de presse*.

During these decisive years Saint Laurent was forming his taste, which is after all the primary tool in a trade that the poet Paul Valéry once called one of the "delirious professions" in which everything is based on one's opinion of oneself. Valéry even asserted that as one draws closer to Paris one can feel the heat thrown off by so many egos chafing against one another and exclaiming, "I am the only one!" Like so many Parisians of his generation, Saint Laurent was influenced by Cocteau's fluency and his fidelity to Diaghilev's original injunction, "Astonish me!" Saint Laurent was specially taken by the visual style of Christian ("Bébé") Bérard, a bearded, perfumed painter and set designer (he did the costumes for Cocteau's film *Beauty and the Beast* in which the Beast rather resembled Bébé himself).

Bérard's effortless transition between high art and decorative art soon became a hallmark of YSL's own style. In 1965 Saint Laurent presented a winter collection based on the paintings of Mondrian, one of the first times dressmaking and painting were united. *Women's Wear Daily*, the bible of the rag trade, declared YSL to be the king of Paris, an opinion echoed by the *New York Times;* these newspapers are the two most important determinants of world fashion sales. In later years YSL would build on this tendency by showing Picasso ballet costumes, pop art dresses, Van Gogh sunflower prints and Matisse textiles.

In 1966 Saint Laurent concocted his first tuxedo dresses, the "smoking" that signaled the sexual ambiguity that would haunt fashion in the next decade (Saint Laurent claimed that he'd been inspired by a photo of Marlene Dietrich in trousers). From the very beginning, however, Saint Laurent had played with gender bending; in his first collection in 1962 he had already dressed his models in his elegant versions of sailor suits (he shared Cocteau's fascination with the navy). If such experiments seemed decadent at the time, Saint Laurent was quick to agree. He announced: "Decadence attracts me. It signals a new world, and for me the struggle of a society caught between life and death is absolutely magnificent to watch."

Exoticism, the subject of a recent museum show of Saint Laurent's work, became another source of his ideas. The Sahara safari jacket of 1969, the "Chinese" embroidered satin slacks and tunics of 1970, the astonishing "Ballet Russes" collection of 1976, the sensual Spain of Carmen in 1977, the fairy tale atmosphere of the Raj in 1982 and various versions of saris, harem pants, beaded ethnic halters and leopard-skin sarongs have borne witness to his constant preoccupation with other cultures.

Other cultures have returned the favor. He was the subject of the first show ever devoted to a living designer presented by the Metropolitan Museum of Art in New York in 1983, an exhibition organized by the Empress of Fashion herself, Diana Vreeland (the show attracted a million visitors). Shows in Peking and at the Sezon Museum of Art in Tokyo awakened a lasting Asian interest in his work.

Although most of the press attention continued to be focused on his couture collections, the big money (accounting for two-thirds of the company's profits) came from its perfumes (especially Opium) and cosmetics. The rest of the earnings were made by the YSL Rive Gauche boutiques and ready-to-wear clothes. Haute couture is a bit of expensive window dressing—so expensive that Bergé enraged the other leading designers when he suggested that couture will soon go the way of the dinosaurs.

When I met Yves Saint Laurent I scarcely knew what to expect—a zombie or an alert genius, a holy relic or a dynamic creator. I was led into his little office with its rock crystal chandelier, its Louis XIV armchairs and its sleek 1930s fireplace by Jean-Michel Frank, the apostle of art deco expensive simplicity. I drank a cup of coffee while sitting on the couch, but then Saint Laurent hurried me over to his desk, as though he needed its imposing formal presence between us. He explained that the Louis XV desk was the very one on which an ancestor of his had signed the wedding contract between Napoleon and Joséphine. When Napoleon became emperor he ennobled the magistrate. A large portrait of the noble ancestor as a hunter, posing with his beagle, painted by David, hung on the wall.

Saint Laurent looked a bit like Rodin's *The Thinker* with a few pounds, years and worries added on. He was certainly lucid and had no trouble recalling names and dates, but he seemed heavily tranquilized or perhaps just depressed; enormous silences crept into our conversation. All too often I'd lose my nerve waiting for him to respond and I'd start babbling.

It was a bit like a psychoanalytic session in which the patient was on lithium and the shrink on speed. Only when I listened to the tape at home did I realize how ill at ease YSL was and how quickly (and with what disarming politeness) he echoed my words, as though simple agreement would spare him the agony of communication. Several times I thought of a description I once read of a visit to Samuel Beckett, during which the perky interlocutor kept posing leading questions; the great man would simply bury his face in his hands and wait for the tides of melancholy and nausea to go out. More than once Saint Laurent let his head slump onto his chest; I was certain he'd dozed off, but no, a second later he was heroically returning to the problem of responding.

Again and again he would utter the words *marvelous, interesting* and *beautiful,* the spare change of enthusiasm handed out liberally with a hope that it might do instead of the real currency of thought and evaluation I was hoping for: in an ordinary conversation at a party, for instance, it would have worked perfectly.

I wanted him to feel that I had shared many of his problems and I mentioned my own fears of aging, of undertaking creative work, of gaining weight and of losing inspiration; if I mention these fears now I do so in order not to seem indifferent to Saint Laurent's anguish. I despise journalistic invulnerability, the code by which an atmosphere of camaraderie is created and then only one-half of the conversation is reported.

When I asked him which great couturiers of the past he admired, he said there were only two, Schiaparelli and "Mademoiselle" Chanel. "She wanted to meet me and told Pierre Bergé to bring me by, but I was too afraid of her."

Cocteau? "A prodigious man. I met him at Saint-Jean-Cap-Ferrat at the house of Mme Weisweiller, Santo Sospir. It was a joy to hear him talk. He never stopped talking." A laugh at the recollection of Cocteau's ceaseless eloquence, then the sage summary: "an enormous personality."

Andy Warhol? "We were both very timid and communication was difficult. But I so admired what he did. We had a great friendship and whenever he came to Paris there were lots of parties. He's a man who changed fashion and our times." Long silence. When I suggested that Warhol's use of silk-screening to create "multiples" was a bit like YSL's use of ready-to-wear, he said with a strong combination of enthusiasm and exhaustion, "That's it" (*"Mais c'est ça..."*). I remembered that years ago when Warhol had done a portrait of the American dress designer Halston, Saint Laurent had thrown a fit and threatened to burn his own Warhol portrait, but that moment of pique was now long since spent and the portrait was in the hallway just outside his office. He added, "Warhol's last painting was of my dog Moujik. After he did it he died."

Pierre Bergé? "A marvelous man—an intimate friend. We started the house together. He's very artistic, he reads everything—he has a universal culture, he's a universal man. Poor thing, he became a businessman for my sake. We like each other so much. But we don't live together anymore. The business is an eagle with two heads." For a moment Saint Laurent drifted away into a brown study, then came out to whisper, "Even dead an eagle would frighten me. I'm terrified of predators."

His future as a couturier? "But if I quit, what would I do with myself? I'd like to be a writer, but I haven't quite decided to sit down at my desk and write. I've written lots of things, but of course they're all in drawers, not for anyone to see. Ten years ago, at the time of my Russian collection [YSL's single biggest success] I was so miserable that I wrote something, a piece of prose, that you'd have to call a *cri du cœur*. I suppose it was a bit like Lautreamont's *Songs of Maldoror*." Pause. Little smile. "Perhaps I'll stop designing and become a writer. Nathalie Sarraute saw two letters I wrote to François-Marie Banier and called me up to say that it was a pity I hadn't been a writer. She said that if I'd written I'd be much more famous."

When I asked him if he preferred success or failure, he stumbled and said, "Of course I prefer failure—I mean success."

Catherine Deneuve? "She's one of my great inspirations. She's always impeccable. That's what I admire. She doesn't let herself go. I dressed her for *Belle de Jour* and she was delighted by my work. Later she married David Bailey and it was he who brought her here to be dressed. Now she's the figurehead of the house. She's very protective of me—like a big sister. We seldom talk on the telephone. I don't like the phone. No, we go out to the cinema and take tea together."

Later, when Deneuve told me that she seldom saw Saint Laurent and didn't really know him very well, I realized how deep his isolation must be; his dearest friendship was her chance acquaintance—no, I'm exaggerating, but that was the disparity I felt. Almost as though their friendship was something he elaborated more in his fantasies than pursued in reality.

When we discussed his working methods he was at his most detailed and clearheaded. He told me that in the past he had drawn a great deal but that now he liked to work by draping fabric directly on a model. "Suddenly I'll look in the mirror and see something I like and we'll take a Polaroid. Then I'll work up drawings based on the photo. I'm often inspired by the fabrics I work with. They're all done by Gustav Zumsteg of Zurich, who has started up seven workshops in Lyons, the old capital of the silk industry. There's a bit of synthetics in his fabrics, just to lend them versatility. They're all made by hand, and there's nothing like them in the world today. They're museum pieces."

I told him that Balanchine had choreographed by working directly on a particular ballerina and that, aside from a thorough knowledge of the music, he had had few ideas in advance of an actual session with the dancers. "I'm a bit like that," he said. "My ready-to-wear collection is just a few weeks away and I still haven't started on it, but I'm hoping that my upcoming trip to New York will open my imagination. It's a city that has always thrilled me, though it's not as interesting now that Diana Vreeland is no longer there."

I was embarrassed to bring up the subject of his addictions and told him that I'd been a drunk until I stopped drinking altogether in 1983. But he was very matter-of-fact about the problem. "I'm cured. All that's finished.

I stopped cocaine and alcohol. Four years ago I did a cure of disintoxication. I felt horrible emotions during the cure that frightened me. When you're young and you drink, your work takes off like a rocket. But when you don't drink anymore you have to work much harder." A long laugh. Then, with a devilish glint of his eye, the world's most famous designer murmured, "I was a crazy little guy" (*"J'étais un petit fou"*).

If Saint Laurent is shy, Pierre Bergé is brassy; even his voice rings out with a metallic resonance that the French consider aristocratic. If Saint Laurent's office is cozy and small, Bergé's is large and imposing (though he himself is a short if feisty man). I'm such a timid and overly polite journalist that I couldn't think how to ask Pierre Bergé all the tough questions I thought I should pose, so I hit on the stratagem of showing him a hard-hitting paragraph from the English press about him, his business dealings and his relationship with Saint Laurent. The article, by Georgina Pulianowsky, appeared in the *Evening Standard* on July 12, 1993, and the first paragraph reads: "Fashionable Paris is poised with bated breath in anticipation of Yves Saint Laurent's latest couture collection next week. It's the make or break moment in the great man's career after nearly drowning in a sea of troubles. He was said to be stricken with illnesses varying from suicidal depression to AIDS; he has been investigated for insider trading of his own shares on a large scale; he was rumoured to be ready to give up couture altogether, depressed since his lifetime companion and partner Pierre Bergé moved out of their shared Paris townhouse to live with a twenty-eight-year-old fashion assistant on whom he has spent lavishly...."

Bergé read the article with a small frozen smile, put it aside, drew a breath and began, "First of all neither of us is seropositive. We could have been but by chance we're not. As you may know, I'm very active with money and leadership in the struggle against AIDS. We've lost many, many friends, including employees we loved. Everyone knows Yves had a problem with alcohol and drugs but he was completely cured five years ago. I locked him up against his will, but after a day or two he entered into the cure with his full cooperation. He still has psychological problems and takes antidepressants. Mind you, none of these problems has ever slowed him down in his work. They have never kept him from having one success after another. He has the power of great recovery. Other designers may excite everyone for a season or two but they all fade. The truth always comes out, and Yves represents the truth of his métier. His designs are profoundly classic, he understands the real construction of a garment and he is a master tailor. Many of the designers are, as it were, writing trash, whereas Yves is Flaubert. Again and again he has set trends—the see-through dress, the military look, pop art, the Russian look, *le smoking*— but these fantasies are always executed with a perfect respect for the syntax of his trade. Or you could say he's like Jean Genet, who wrote outrageous things in the purest possible French. All the other designers are"—and here Bergé used a word in English, a language he speaks with evident relish if little skill—"one shot."

"As for our relationship, we met in 1958, it was a *coup de foudre,* we own three houses together, in August we spent ten days together in our house in Deauville, there's not a single decision we make without discussing it with the other. We telephone each other three times a day. There's an umbilical cord attaching us. Of course I've had other affairs. Robert Merloz, the new young designer I'm sponsoring, of course we had an affair. So?"

When I suggested that Saint Laurent was a very solitary person Bergé thundered, "Yes, but not for the reasons you think. He's not afraid of people. He's simply terribly egocentric. He's supremely indifferent to people. When he'll give a dinner party at his apartment, I'll phone him the next morning to find out how it went. 'A nightmare!' It's always a nightmare. Why? Not because the food was bad or the company disagreeable (he only sees his oldest and dearest friends). No, it was a nightmare because he had to make an effort. He had to show an interest in other people, ask them questions about their lives. He doesn't care about other people. I'm the only person he can dine with three times a week. That's because we've known each other nearly thirty-seven years!

"He'd like to see me even more often, but I'm not always available. He doesn't have to make an effort with me. He adored our vacation together this summer and told me it was the best time he'd had with anyone in years. Why? Because he feels comfortable with me. We'd eat a little supper together in Honfleur, then I'd let him go to bed by 9:30. No demands. When I suggested he read a book for once, just guess what he started rereading? Proust of all things, for the hundredth time. No, he's a man who lives entirely in the past. The present and the future are reserved exclusively for his work. He never goes to the cinema, he never watches television, all he'll do is watch again and again the same movies at home— Visconti's *The Damned* for the fiftieth time or Maria Casarès in *Les Dames du Bois de Boulogne.*"

I questioned Bergé about his recent business dealings. In the last days of the socialist rule in the spring of 1993, Bergé sold YSL to the state-owned conglomerate Elf-Sanofi. Sanofi owns 100 percent of the YSL perfume business and 90 percent of the fashion sector. Saint Laurent and Bergé own the remaining 10 percent, but have total artistic control until the year 2001 over fashion as well as the right of veto over cosmetics and perfume. For this deal Bergé and Saint Laurent netted more than fifty million pounds each.

Because of an earlier operation, which took place in July 1992, Bergé is now being accused of insider trading. A watchdog organization for the stock market claims that when Bergé offered stocks for sale at that time he already knew that YSL earnings for the first semester of 1992 had fallen dramatically. A secondary question is whether the anonymous Swiss purchaser of the stocks might not have been none other than Bergé and Saint Laurent themselves, hiding behind the front of a Swiss bank. In that case the charge would not be insider trading but tax evasion.

Bergé responds to all these accusations with equanimity. "Usually insider trading affects buyers; people who've received a hot tip buy cheap. I was selling and I sold cheap because I needed cash to pay off a big bank loan. I had already announced that the results for the first semester of 1992 would be disappointing. Moreover, the foreign investors who bought the stocks have never complained. Apparently they are satisfied and bought the stocks as a long-term investment. In any event I don't want anyone to group my case with the other financial scandals affecting France right now. Unlike some others I could mention, I've not dipped my hands into party funds, for instance."

While Bergé—with all his feistiness and flare and tactical intelligence— surveys the collapse of French business and political ethics and tries to counter the serious charges brought against him, in a twilight world of fantasy and luxury his lonely colleague Saint Laurent dozes and dreams his way into yet another stunning collection, the airy fabric on which this mammoth empire is built. I was struck by the sweetness and sadness of Saint Laurent and the burning vitriol poured on him by Bergé, but I thought,

Gee, after all it's a marriage, isn't it? Yet I couldn't help remembering how Saint Laurent had said he and Bergé were the two heads of a double-headed eagle—and then Saint Laurent had shuddered and said, "I'm terrified of predators."

Catherine Deneuve

THE FRENCH ARE DIFFERENT FROM YOU AND ME. They're more discreet. One of Catherine Deneuve's women friends told me Deneuve wouldn't give me anything intimate about herself. "Oh, and I admire her so much for that!" the friend exclaimed. A well-known Parisian photographer, who doesn't especially even like Deneuve, said, "Of course she never lets journalists into her home—she's got to protect herself, after all." Even Deneuve herself is quick to admit that she has a rule about never talking to a journalist about her love life, her family, her children, her homes, her friends—in fact, almost everything American stars systematically divulge if they hope to be good copy. One of her young male friends who vacations with her told me his lips were sealed.

I'd lived in Paris for sixteen years, and I've come to accept, or at least anticipate, French standards of discretion. In addition, the French press is gagged by such strict laws about the invasion of privacy that the potentially injured party can get an injunction against an article or book just because he or she doesn't like it.

Now I live in New York, where people systematically reveal everything about their parents' Alzheimer's, office battles and romances with their personal trainers, and where the press serves up the tiniest, nastiest morsels about the celebrated. Of course American movie stars don't really reveal all that much, but they know how to keep the press excited through acts of selective disclosure. But this endless confessing and tattling is not at all Gallic. And I knew in advance that Catherine Deneuve—whose face has graced everything from the classic Luis Bunuel film *Belle de Jour* (made in 1966) to ads for Yves Saint Laurent—would treat me with suspicion. After all, she is the last of the old-fashioned screen goddesses, and her secrecy only adds to the mysterious, even ethereal feeling her name invokes. Deneuve is almost like a movie star of the silent era.

But I also knew that she was clever (as I learned from reading a long interview in the forbiddingly intellectual *Cahiers du Cinéma*), very sociable (as I knew from mutual friends), always late for appointments, still beautiful but obsessed with ageing (at least that was a safe bet—which actress isn't?). And, of course, not all the reports on her are favorable. One of her friends told me she was engaged in a terrible rivalry with her daughter, film actress Chiara Mastroiani (daughter of the late Marcello)—although I found that hard to believe, since Deneuve told me she longs to write a film script for her daughter. And she'd just invited her daughter and son (stage actor Christian Vadim) to Las Vegas for a week of gambling and sun. And Susan Sarandon, who knows Deneuve well, told me that even when Chiara was little her mother knew that someday the daughter would put some distance between them: "It's a natural thing that kids go their own way."

Roger Vadim himself—he who started off with Brigitte Bardot, went on to be the seventeen-year-old Deneuve's first love and ended up with Jane Fonda—writes of Deneuve and the period just after the birth of their son, "When I met her, Catherine had two secret ambitions: to be a mother and to become an actress. Now that she was fulfilled in both domains, her true nature began to emerge; she was made to dominate. She had a very precise view of life to which she expected people and events to conform. Each night this attitude became more and more pronounced until, at the height of success, she proved to be a domestic tyrant. And she remained so."

He goes on to observe, "She was convinced that she alone was right and capable of making people happy as long as they obeyed her in everything. She was intelligent and lacked neither sensitivity nor humor, and it was easy to be charmed by her before realizing that one always had to say yes, or be excommunicated." Maybe this desire to dominate is the real reason she-who-must-be-obeyed likes young lovers; at least the gossip in 2002 was that her latest beau was a twenty-five-year-old technician she picked up on a film, though no one would confirm the rumor or seemed to know his name.

Susan Sarandon gives a completely different picture of Deneuve. "At the time we made *The Hunger* in the early '80s I didn't have kids yet. That was a great time to be in London and we were all partying every night till dawn. Deneuve had two small children and was leading a much saner life. She would show up every morning with every hair in place and help me put my apartment back together. But she wasn't stuffy—she had a great sense of humor and irony. I know that she's considered the symbol of France all over the world, but—this will sound crazy—I saw her more as a single working mom, a wonderful actress but also a great mother to her kids. She's a hands-on kind of person." David Bailey, the English photographer, remembers that during the three years he was married to her she was always full of fun. "She was just twenty-one or so. Not as fussy as some women. Never fanatical. Easygoing. She's smart. And she works harder than most people, much harder. She smoked a lot. Always smoking. Moody. She'd been with Vadim just before me and he was rather bourgeois and Deneuve, of course, is bourgeois, too, like all the French. Well, I don't know what I am but I'm the opposite of bourgeois and she liked that." He smiles, reflecting. "Yes, she liked that. I'm just a simple boy from the East End."

I told him that Deneuve attributes her fashion sense to him. "When I met her she was being dressed by some guy who dressed Bardot as well. I told her she should go to this new guy, Yves Saint Laurent."

In America, lesbians worship Deneuve, ever since she wore a tux for Yves Saint Laurent—and especially since she played a lesbian vampire in *The Hunger* and exchanged blood and kisses with Susan Sarandon. An American lesbian magazine named itself after Deneuve, till she sued. Unfortunately for her female admirers, there's every indication that Deneuve is 200 percent heterosexual. Sarandon told me that in the original script Deneuve was supposed to get her drunk in order to seduce her. "I asked, Why make me a victim? Shouldn't the seduction be mutual, reciprocal? In a love scene the beginning and the end are the most character-revealing moments. In the rewrite the beginning occurs when Deneuve spills something on my shirt and takes it off—that's the moment of contact, the circumstances of consent."

I waited for Deneuve in the wood-paneled, somber and stately bar in the Lutetia Hotel on the Left Bank—a hotel that had provided living quarters to Nazi officers during the Occupation but that in true Orwellian fashion now has a historic plaque out front saying that the surviving deported Jews were welcomed back to France in this very place. Hmnn.... I mentioned to the concierge that I was expecting Miss Deneuve and he whispered something to the bartender—they were all used to the routine.

At last she breezed in. She burbled an apology in English for being late, but when I switched to French she looked hugely relieved. The eyes quickened, the shoulders dropped, the smile grew more canny. She was wearing a pale brown corduroy pants suit over a powder-blue, low-scooped, well-filled-out stretch sweater, dark sunglasses, copious glossy hair, flat shoes, no handbag—the very image of a man's woman, unfussy, more cute than beautiful, entirely accessible, her body more generous than disciplined. The powder-blue made me think of a starlet of the '50s—I say "starlet" because she seemed a younger, less intimidating version of herself. The cloudy, mysterious gaze for which she is famous had been replaced by a sharp, humorous glance; even the full, slightly down-turned lips on the screen had thinned out and now wore a shrewder smile. Cute. Bright. As she relaxed she performed a subtle strip-tease. First the dark glasses came off, then the coat, finally her suit jacket. She spoke in her low voice, scarcely drew a breath and almost never repeated herself—in that way, too, she was generous, as if she'd decided to make up for her discretion by lavishing me with her ideas. She freely admitted that she and every member of her family speak at breakneck speed. With me she was never pretentious or self-important, and she frequently broke off her responses to laugh, even at herself. Although I made it clear in a remark or two that I was gay, she never lapsed into a tailored sexlessness as straight women so often do—I was always aware of her brand of sophisticated seductiveness and she started many sentences with the words, "As a woman...."

She moved us to a table away from any neighbors, ordered a decaf espresso and lit up a cigarette. She explained that she liked bars in "grand, international hotels" where you could "study travelers from other countries, where you could"—well, it was all bull, she just didn't want me in her apartment. After she'd decided she liked me and had given me her home number, she confessed that she no longer receives journalists at home because they inevitably try to read into her apartment all manner of things. "I have a very big room that divides in half with sliding screens. On one side I have the office, with hundreds of books in it; on the other side is the salon. Once a journalist visited me when I'd closed off the office and he wrote, 'There's not a book in sight.' Why don't they just ask?"

When I wondered out loud if she was ever tempted to write her autobiography, she said, "Just to clear up mistakes like that." She said that the *Guardian* in London had done a piece about her that had infuriated her, and that frequently she was presented as "cold," even "glacial," but that it had become a cliché and was just a misreading of the natural reserve she felt when she was around strangers. She is frequently dubbed "the ultimate cool blonde." When I told her I'm tired of being described as fat (or "portly" or even "matronly") in the interviews that are done of me when my books are published, she said, "They should ask you how you feel about your weight. Whether you accept it or suffer from it. But journalists speak of things without asking questions, which I find very dishonest. Poor. Pauvre."

I'd heard that she and her lawyers were such control freaks that they had sued to block certain overly revealing passages in both Vadim's autobiography and in the biography of François Truffaut, who was her lover and friend for years and who directed her in *Mississippi Mermaid* and *The Last Metro* (a huge hit, shot in 1980, in which Deneuve starred with Gérard Depardieu and for which she won a César—the French Oscar—for best actress). I can't imagine what she wanted to expunge from the Truffaut biography, except that he was so devastated when she left him that he had a nervous breakdown and had to be sent to a clinic. But perhaps she is wise to discourage all gossip about herself. In the near-void of concrete information her legend can continue to flourish. She's virtually the only movie star about whom no one has a grubby tale to tell; she enjoys a semi-official, almost mythical status in France. About fifteen years back she was voted "Marianne," the nickname for the French Republic and the symbol of France, and busts in her likeness were installed in the more than 30,000 town halls throughout France and its overseas *départments* (including Guadeloupe and Tahiti). It's a bit as if Jane Fonda had been voted "Liberty" and her face had been clapped on the Statue and incised on our dimes and her bust installed on every Main Street.

Deneuve herself seemed slightly vague about it all. She laughed out loud when I told her it confused me and she confessed that it was her mother who'd had to point out to her that her face was on the stamps. When I asked if "Marianne" is the name of the heroic, bare-breasted woman on the barricades painted by Delacroix (it is), she murmured, "I suppose." Deneuve was replaced a few years ago as Marianne by a young Corsican fashion model, Laetitia Casta, who was partially chosen, no doubt, to pacify Corsican separatists, who are always blowing up people and buildings. Then Casta moved to England to escape onerous French taxes, and everyone was furious.

Sometimes Deneuve's official status must weigh heavily on her. As she put it, "I've occasionally served as a sort of ambassador for France. In fashion and the cinema. But my relationship to fashion is mostly due to my friendship for Yves Saint Laurent. Anyway, I don't want to become an institution, I don't want too many testimonials, which starts to happen at my age. Let's say that I don't mind being put on a pedestal so long as there's a step ladder for scrambling down the other side a minute later." She laughed hard.

One of her friends said to me (off the record), "She's half a bourgeoise with her devoted dresser, coiffeur, secretary—all these terrifyingly devoted women including her sister, who's the secretary—and then she's also half a modern woman, someone who is modest and curious. I think she'd like to be someone younger, more dynamic, more in the swim, but she moves like a queen with her horrible devoted court around her." I asked her directly if she felt like a queen and told her I'd met three crowned queens and was aware of their special problems, but Deneuve sidestepped the question with a modest smile and said, "Not if I stay here in my neighborhood. People are used to me here in Saint-Germain and leave me in peace."

She may have a bourgeois streak, but I'd hazard it doesn't run too deep. When I told her about the rich man who'd kept me awake on the plane filling me in about his fortune, she said, "I don't envy the rich. They must always be worrying about how to keep their money. You and I get to read the movie reviews in the newspaper, but they have to read the stock market results. Fortunately there are a few rich people, like Pierre Bergé"— who used to run the business side of Yves Saint Laurent—"who know how to have fun in life without worrying about their money. I'm glad I'm a spendthrift. The rich are deformed by their wealth. They never think about the real worth of a project, just its profitability."

Another friend, an actor who has worked with her often, told me off the record (they're all afraid of her, or possibly of her lawyer), "The day she decides to renounce her beauty for good, then she will become a truly great actress. In any event, she's already changing. Recently she's gone from tried-and-true roles to films that are much more unconventional and to parts that correspond to something new in her personality. *Elle est un peu moins déesse, un peu plus spontanée* [she's a bit less of a goddess, a bit more spontaneous]." David Bailey, who follows her career and has made two videos with her, thinks she's already a top actress. "The French are the best movie actors in the world," he says. "They don't act, they become. Deneuve is superb at becoming."

When I asked Deneuve if she had any American films in the works, she said she could see no good reason why America, which has so many great actresses of its own, would want someone foreign with an accent. "Usually we Europeans get offered the roles that American actresses don't want. In France I'm lucky, I can do the projects that excite me. Whereas in America I'm offered all those roles that are too bourgeois or too classic, and why should I accept parts there that I wouldn't touch here? I don't want a role that's for a woman who's 'nice-looking-for-her-age' or 'glamorous' or 'sophisticated'—that's not for me."

The French are of course great believers in *auteurs*, those film-makers who function somewhat like literary novelists and who pursue from film to film their own esthetic. America, in Deneuve's opinion, has few *auteurs*, but she would be eager to work with the rare exceptions, someone like Woody Allen or Jim Jarmusch. In France she collaborated with actress-turned-director Nicole Garcia (*Place Vendôme*), a movie for which she was named best actress at the Venice Film Festival. She has an affair with her son-in-law and smokes a joint in *Belle-Maman* ("Mother-in-Law"), a box-office hit in France. She's also worked with Leos Carax (*Pola X*), Philippe Garrel (*Le Vent de la nuit* or "Night Wind") and Raoul Ruiz (*The Past Recaptured,* the Proust film in which she plays Odette and co-stars with John Malkovitch). I'd heard that she'd been unhappy on the Proust set since the male roles were all much more important than those of the women; she'd reportedly ended up refusing even to greet her fellow actors. She may be civilized, but she's not without temperament. Even her biggest admirers admit she can be moody.

I asked her about her relationships with famous directors. She scarcely mentioned Bunuel, with whom she seems to have had no personal relationship at all (nor does he say anything substantial about her in his memoir, *My Last Sigh*). In one interview she once mentioned that there had been an unbearable tension on the set of *Belle de Jour* that almost led to a major explosion. David Bailey, who was married to her at the time, confirms that she was miserable—"Bunuel was of no help to the actors. He wouldn't talk to them about their motivations. For such a great man he was shockingly ordinary." Despite—or perhaps because of—the tension, it remains her greatest role; she is utterly convincing as the bored, frigid housewife who turns to prostitution to live out her sexual fantasies and falls for a client, a young gangster with silver teeth.

No, for her the three great directors were the ones who became friends and from whom she learned her craft. The earliest one was Jacques Demy, for whom she played her first major role in *The Umbrellas of Cherbourg,* that daffy, over-the-top musical with the somber conclusion that was made in 1963. In it every last scrap of dialogue is set to music by Michel Legrand and sung, not as in an operetta or musical comedy but as in an opera— except that the dubbed voices (Deneuve doesn't sing in it) are never forced and the words remain entirely comprehensible. Although Deneuve had had bit parts in earlier films, Demy gave her her big break. She won the Golden Palm at Cannes that year—and the film made her famous all over the world. Audiences gasped at her pure, mysterious beauty, especially in three long shots when she looks directly at the camera.

"Although I made that film thirty—thirty-five!—years ago, it's the only one for which I can remember all the dialogue. Of course I didn't do the singing. I had to lip-sync it, so I had to know the words perfectly and figure out the timing down to the second. And then Jacques Demy couldn't get the financing—it took two years to get that film off the ground. So I had plenty of time to remember all the words. *The Umbrellas of Cherbourg* was timeless, and so original. I was fortunate that Demy liked me (I was just seventeen) and would talk to me off the set for hours and hours. He shared with me all his ideas about the movies. I didn't have any training as an actress, so I was lucky to meet such extraordinary directors so young."

"But weren't you from a family of actors?"

"My grandmother was the prompter at the Odéon Theatre," Deneuve recalled with a laugh. "My mother started acting when she was just five and by age seventeen, incredibly, she was the doyenne of the Odéon. My father acted—" he starred in the French stage adaptation of *The Caine Mutiny*—"and did dubbing for Paramount; he was head of dubbing for them. And of course my older sister was an actress. She and I dubbed a few films for Paramount. But we never talked about the business. We were four girls in school, our parents' life was completely separate, we were not bathed in an artistic milieu like the children of some actors I know of."

Catherine's sister, Françoise Dorléac (Dorléac is the family name—Deneuve took her mother's maiden name), was a star very young. She played Colette's Gigi on the stage when she was eighteen. Dorléac was a bit older than Deneuve, but they looked almost like twins, except Dorléac had a more comic face, a stronger chin, a more upturned nose, and she kept her hair dark, whereas Catherine became a blonde. Françoise had a brilliant international career in just a few years. She made films with directors such as Roman Polanski, François Truffaut (*La Peau douce*) and Ken Russell, and she played opposite such stars as Jean-Paul Belmondo (*The Man from Rio*), Omar Sharif, David Niven and Donald Pleasance.

The two sisters, Deneuve and Dorléac, were so close that for a long time, even after they began to make their way in the cinema, they continued to live at home and sleep in bunk beds. Although Françoise was more anguished about her looks, her career, her loves than Catherine (who had a child while she was still a teenager and who, at first, did not take the cinema very seriously), nevertheless the sisters shared a deep complicity, which is evident in the musical film they made together for Jacques Demy, *The Young Girls of Rochefort*.

And then Françoise Dorléac died in a car accident on June 26, 1967, at age twenty-five, and the loss was so violent, so sudden, that Deneuve was unable to discuss her sister until just three years ago, when she helped put together a book in her memory. During their adolescence they had often fought bitterly and Françoise had often disapproved of the men in Catherine's life; nevertheless, after her death Catherine missed her terribly—and resented other women and their sisters for their shared intimacy. David Bailey, who was with Deneuve at the time of Françoise's death, remembers that Deneuve suffered terribly. "Maybe that's why she works so hard," Bailey speculates. "Her parents weren't all that successful as actors and her sister died young. She's having a huge career for all of them."

Françoise had lived with Truffaut for a short while, and later Deneuve had an affair with him as well. "He loved to talk about his work," Deneuve told me. "He had two great passions—his work and, why not admit it, women. He was a very intense person. Early on he had figured out what interested him and he devoted himself to those two things with total intensity. He loved words, he loved to read, talk—and he explained things very well." Although Deneuve did only two films with Truffaut, she shared his life and thoughts for a much longer time—a period that she still looks back on as decisive in her development as an artist and woman.

The third major director in her life is André Téchiné, a Frenchman from a Czech family who grew up gay in the south of France, a coming-out story he tells in his lyrical film, *The Wild Reeds*. He's worked several times with Deneuve, and his best film is with her and Daniel Auteuil, *My Favorite Season*. This quietly stormy movie is about a brother and sister (Auteuil and Deneuve) who come together to deal with their ageing mother and the need to provide care for her. Their reunion reawakens the brother's lifelong passion for his sister, which borders on the erotic.

"It was odd to be in a film in a brother–sister relationship with a man like Daniel Auteuil, who would seem more likely to be cast as my lover. I liked this fraternal relationship, I who had nothing but sisters in real life. Of course it's true the relationship is more or less incestuous. It's very rare that this relationship, this closeness between brother and sister, is shown in a film, and I was thrilled by it. "

I asked Deneuve if it was true that from time to time she calls up young directors and actors she doesn't know to compliment them on their work. "Yes," she said, "that may sound audacious, but French films have such limited commercial possibilities that I thought it might be a comfort if I expressed my appreciation, even if it meant calling them out of the blue." When I asked if the people she called were ever so astonished that they doubted it was really Deneuve on the line, she said, "No, they recognize my voice. People are very used to my voice."

"Are you happy?" I asked her.

"I'm a woman who's not happy, no. Sometimes I'm happy, of course, but when people ask me that as if happiness were a permanent state of being, then no, that's impossible. Happiness depends on too many external factors—lovers, health, friends, career. You can't control it. But pleasure! Pleasure is something you can cultivate, and I cultivate it assiduously. I pursue the pleasure of seeing my friends, of gardening—I love nature! I love cooking, but only when I'm with friends. It's sad to eat alone and it's intolerable to eat with people you don't know well, but to eat with friends you love is truly, truly a pleasure. Pleasure is something you can cultivate, even if the rewards are strong but fleeting. I'm very partial to pleasure."

I knew that she lives in a vast apartment facing Saint Sulpice church and its fountain, and that she has a country house where she gardens. I asked the decorator Jacques Grange, who's been a friend of Deneuve for twenty-two years, if he'd "done" her residences, but he said he'd only given her advice and gone shopping with her at the flea market.

"Does she have good taste?" I asked.

"Well, she has her taste, which is more important. A distinctive taste of her own."

"Is she good fun?"

"Oh, yes, she loves to laugh with friends."

"And if she were sad would she phone you?"

He thought for a second. "No," he said. "She's too discreet."

I asked her how she felt about ageing.

"Any woman who says it's not a problem for her is lying," she said. "Some people know how to live with this lie, but it's even more of a problem for an actress, because the cinema is a visual medium and one is constantly confronted with a record of physical changes." She sighed and lit another cigarette. "I handle it as best I can. I try to slow the process down. But I'm aware of it in any event—I'm a mother and grandmother." (Chiara has a little boy.) "My mother is incredibly youthful, not just in the way she looks but in her energy and attitude. She's not an old woman—her voice is that of a young woman, not an old lady. She's vivacious and has a real appetite for people and things and events."

She answered her portable and realized she had to be leaving. As a parting shot she said, "In France women have the right to age, to put on a few extra pounds and curves, especially if the personality and character adapt gracefully to change. Whereas in America women must be perfect, especially in the movies. And this mania for working out in America! I can understand wanting to stay in shape so that you have the energy to do what you want to do."

She rose and shook my hand. "But working out for its own sake?" She sang a snatch of "You're So Vain." Then she added, "I'm lucky because I can sleep on the set. It's not a real sleep, just a sort of dozing until I'm needed. It's like being a guard on duty in a castle—you might doze off, but if something requires your attention, you're instantly awake."

Deneuve seems alert not only to artistic possibilities but to the slightest hint of civilized pleasure. When I asked David Bailey why he shot her in a photo for *Talk* with a bunch of naked young guys, he said, "I wanted to show she's ageless, that she's transcended age. She looks right with all those young blokes."

"Have you heard about her young lover, whether the rumor is true?"

He looked confused for a moment, then smiled and said, "You'll have to ask her about that. But if it's true, I say more power to her."

"Do you think she's aging gracefully?"

"Well, none of us likes it, do we? But it is better than the alternative."

David Geffen

KNEW THAT DAVID GEFFEN had nearly two billion dollars, had made a killing as a record mogul and had recently launched the first new movie studio in Hollywood in fifty years. What I couldn't understand was why his seaside house was so simple, especially in a town where human value is determined by overhead costs.

His secretary had given me the address on Pacific Coast Highway in Malibu. I overshot it, backtracked and had a burger in a family-style restaurant down the block. When I returned to the house, my back was to Topanga Canyon and the mountains, where recent brushfires had been smoldering for a week. I rang the bell, identified myself over the intercom and was buzzed in by Geffen himself, who was waiting with a smile in the doorway. I told him I'd just stopped down the street. "I invited you to lunch—that message didn't get through?" he asked, only very mildly annoyed. I saw right away that one of his typical responses was a shrug and a soft smile, but I wondered if such insouciance might not be an affectation designed to cool down what used to be called a Type-A personality.

As I was going up the short path to the house, I noticed the manicured garden on the left and an office on the right, where a man was working a Xerox and a secretary was filtering calls. Geffen might be a relaxed guy in jeans, T-shirt and sneakers, inhabiting a six-room, two-story little house, but this glimpse through a doorway suggested that his casualness depended on a highly organized hive.

The house itself was just polished wood floors, potted plants, a few comfortable chairs, a beeswaxed antique table, lots of books—and a glorious view of the beach, which was so narrow it seemed to be visibly eroding, although wide enough for passersby to scuff their way along through the incoming surf. I knew that Geffen had a famous art collection, but here, as he explained, he kept just a few works on paper, since the sea air was very bad for paintings. I stopped to admire a beautiful big lithograph by Richard Diebenkorn, the San Francisco artist who painted figures in the 1950s when everyone else was an Abstract Expressionist, then went abstract in the '60s when the rest of the herd thundered past towards the figurative. I thought it normal that Geffen, himself such an exception to all rules, would admire this individualist.

At the same time I never forgot Geffen's reputation for being one of the world's most powerful and enigmatic people and I was careful not to over-interpret my meager clues. As we talked together during a long afternoon, I realized he played with his cards very close to his chest. He'd been much interviewed and seemed unusually wary of being misquoted. He never let himself go and was always careful to stress which of his remarks were off the record. As a journalist I'd met everyone from the king and queen of Sweden to six Nobel Prize–winning authors, and yet I'd never been so intimidated by someone. Was I impressed by his steely self-control or just by his legendary wealth? Or did I realize that he didn't need this interview, that it would never make the slightest difference to his vast, international enterprise?

David Geffen has gone through so many California-style self-improvement programs that he radiates a take-me-or-leave-me-I-have-nothing-to-hide attitude. But if he dresses in jeans, curls up in a bare room in Malibu beside the ocean with just a telephone, a million-dollar-view and a wallful of recent memoirs and biographies, that simplicity and tranquillity don't mean that he's lost any of his New York edge. He never gropes for a name or a date and in the first five minutes I was in his presence he'd already delivered opinions on Noël Coward's diaries, Christopher Isherwood's journals, Alan Helms's memoirs of growing up gay and handsome before Stonewall and Gore Vidal's acerbic *Palimpsest*. What made the opinions all the more pointed was that Geffen knows or knew all four of the authors and what he had to say about them was strictly off the record. And all this in a city where most producers pay writers to come in and tell them a story.

Geffen may have grown up poor in Brooklyn, but now he is the only billionaire, self-made mogul in Hollywood who generates the same excitement as the legendary studio bosses of the past. In fact, Steven Spielberg, Jeffrey Katzenberg and Geffen created DreamWorks SKG, the first new major movie studio to be launched in fifty-five years.

When I asked Geffen why Hollywood was no longer making the sort of epics he most admires, films such as *Bridge Over the River Kwai, The African Queen, Lawrence of Arabia* and *All About Eve,* he said, "The directors are as good as they were in the past, the actors are just as good—it's the writers who aren't turning out well-plotted scripts and books. And it's the audiences that have been corrupted by television. The question is: would a modern audience seeing *The African Queen* for the first time today really have the patience to sit through it? And the answer is: I don't know."

I asked Geffen if he responds to current social trends in choosing properties. "Would a phenomenon like the Million Man March, for instance, make you—"

"No. Not at all," he replies before I can get my question out, so fast does his mind work. "When I'm interested in movies or plays it's usually because someone's called me or a friend of mine is involved. Often it's just a coincidence. A friend of mine named Bruce Weintraub who died from AIDS told me about the book *Interview with a Vampire.* One of his great interests was being involved with that as a movie. So when it came up for me I thought I'll do this and I donated all the money I earned from it to AIDS charities so it was sort of a double blessing that it turned out to be a hit."

Geffen, to be sure, is famous as the man who sits in an empty room with just a phone posed on a miniature chair beside his armchair as he takes the whole world's calls. It struck me as a rather passive, respond-to-the-latest-stimulus method, as opposed to a more aggressive mode of hatching schemes and assigning subjects, but his attentiveness to all these signals pouring in, combined with his unerring judgment, has made him one of America's most successful record and movie producers. And even if he is often in repose, it's the repose of a cat about to spring. He told me that he never has felt overwhelmed in his life. He always thinks he has more than enough time to do whatever he wants—and to take on even more.

Perhaps this sense of mastery comes from what Barry Diller, his friend for the last thirty years, calls his focus. "David has more focus than anyone," Diller says. "He has energy and will and total concentration on any aspect of a project. I've never met anyone more effective."

As an agent in the late 1960s Geffen managed such stars as Laura Nyro; Joni Mitchell; Crosby, Stills, Nash & Young; Janis Joplin; James Taylor; and Bob Dylan. In 1970 he formed Asylum Records and promoted the talents of Linda Ronstadt, Jackson Browne and the Eagles (the top-selling band for many years). Two years later he sold Asylum (he'd chosen that name because the artists he admired seemed like brilliant misfits) to Warner Communications for $7 million ("The biggest number I could think of").

In 1980 he started Geffen Records with a roster that included Guns n' Roses, Nirvana, Peter Gabriel and Aerosmith. When he sold Geffen Records to MCA in 1990, he received stocks that eventually, after Matsushita bought out MCA, were worth more than $700 million. He produced movies such as *Risky Business* and *Beetlejuice* and put up money for Broadway hits such as *Cats* and *Dreamgirls* and the off-Broadway smash *Little Shop of Horrors*. At the end of the twentieth century his wealth was estimated in the Forbes 400 at $1.9 billion, which makes him, in the words of *Forbes,* "Hollywood's richest guy." It also represents a meteoric rise even in the realm of mega-bucks; in 1989 he was worth "only" $490 million, according to *Forbes.*

Although Geffen dresses simply and seems happiest in his modest house by the sea, nevertheless he owns his own Lear jet and a few years back he bought the old Jack Warner mansion, which he says resembles the White House and is 16,000 square feet large. He paid $45 million for it ("I bought it in a moment of grandiosity"). It took him three years to redesign the interior and another nine months to overhaul the gardens.

The Warner mansion houses his vast art collection, which focuses on his favorite period of American painting, between 1945 and 1965. "That was the high point in American art," he says with confidence. "And I have as good a collection of Abstract Expressionist, contemporary and Pop Art paintings as any museum in the world." In his collection he has many Pollocks and De Koonings as well as works by Jasper Johns, Barnett

Newman, Arshille Gorky—he even owns Andy Warhol's seminal *Dick Tracy*. "I'm inspired by great art and it makes me want to do good work of my own. It's a great privilege to live with great works of art and collecting is one of the few reasons I can think of to have lots of money."

Geffen is quick to admit that when he first looked at similar art in 1964 at the Museum of Modern Art in New York he thought a lot of it was crap. He laughs: "Today the same stuff looks extraordinary to me. My taste has become educated." Perhaps this evolution is part and parcel of what Barry Diller calls Geffen's "enormous growth." As Diller puts it, "Geffen is a great testament to evolution and energy and willpower. Today he looks better, acts better and talks better than he did in the past. He's become a full and confident person."

While I was visiting Geffen he received a call from comic writer Fran Lebowitz thanking him for a TV he'd just sent her for her birthday. When I phoned Fran a few days later, she said, "I first saw David Geffen in the early 1970s at Max's Kansas City. He was pointed out to me as a millionaire, which made him a real martian in my world at the time. He was kind of reclusive then, just as he is now, that's why I didn't know him, because in those years I was going out all the time. It's no mystery how these guys get rich. You can't sleep till eleven and get rich."

"How often do you see him?" I asked.

"Well, we've been best friends for the last ten years and we talk to each other on the phone once or twice a week usually. He hasn't been in New York much recently and I've been in L.A. as much as I want to be, which means not lately. I'm usually sleeping when he calls, which is 8:30 A.M. for me and 5:30 for him. He's not only awake, he's perky."

"Do you ever see him in the flesh?"

"We travel together. He likes to charter boats. On our longest trip, we met our boat in Venice and travelled to Greece, then to what was still Yugoslavia, then Italy (I'm not too good at geography). But he mostly likes the Caribbean, which is way too sunny for me, but the good thing about a big yacht is that you can stay inside and you need never go to a beach. What is it with David? He lives on a beach and he is always going to a beach. Which is funny, since he doesn't swim. I think he lives on the beach mainly for sartorial reasons: he doesn't like to wear a suit. And I suppose if you just stay home all day you might as well look out the window at the ocean rather than, as in New York, at a mugger on the fire escape. But other than that, David's not even interested in cars, the universal L.A. obsession. When he bought the Warner mansion it came with three vintage cars, and I begged him to keep them, but he was totally indifferent."

"I noticed that most of his books are biographies and memoirs."

"Yes," Fran said, "he's read everything about movie moguls."

"Role models...."

"I can remember on one Caribbean cruise David and Barry Diller were fighting over the proofs of William Paley's memoirs. I said to them, 'You're both richer than he ever was. You don't have to read this any more. When you were young you read these books and learned how to do it. If Paley were still alive he'd be reading your memoirs.' "

"Does Geffen have a crazy side? Does he like to get dressed up—"

"David is the least silly man who ever lived. He does have a sense of humor (though he'd never like to be the object of it). He likes a laugh—that's why he likes the agent Sue Mengers, who's hilarious. But he doesn't have an antic side, and he isn't even entertained by antic people."

"I was just reading an article about the Disney top brass in *Vanity Fair*. Do readers really want to know all that about what is essentially a corporate non-subject?"

"It's people in L.A. who read it. It's hard for people to understand that the entertainment business for the entire world is run by just twelve people. When they quarrel out there it's a family argument. It's nothing like New York. In L.A. everyone knows everything about one another. In New York only doormen actually know everything and everyone else is pretending. And of course readers are interested in a...formerly glamorous business. If movies were the shoe business, they'd be less interested. I'm not interested in executives. I want to read about stars."

"Is Geffen a good friend? Would you take a financial problem to him?"

"Geffen is a loyal person and so am I—I'm the Mafia—and he'll always talk to you. He likes to help you. He's a fantastic rescuer, generous with his advice. He doesn't make any money from me—I don't make any money from me—but I can read him a contract over the phone and he can understand it, not just the numbers and the clauses but how relationships play into the deal. I become bored with it right away and it's my life, but he stays incredibly attentive. He knows numbers the way Beethoven heard music. Once I asked a friend, 'Do you think Geffen would understand something about publishing?' and he said, 'Geffen knows about all businesses.'

It's true, he has that kind of mind, he's the Isaiah Berlin of capitalism," she concludes, chuckling, naming the historian of ideas, best known for his books *Karl Marx* and *Russian Thinkers*.

"Are Geffen and Barry Diller close?"

"They have a lifetime bond. They're like brothers; I'm more like a cousin. David and Barry are like a family. Sometimes—" and here she laughed and said ominously—"they're like brothers in every respect. They have overlapping businesses, they speak in shorthand. As for me, I've known Calvin Klein much longer than I've known them."

Diller himself says of Geffen, "We each think the other one is impossible, but he's in my family, even if he's not the only member of the family. We've been very careful not to discuss business issues of some drama with each other. The strength of our friendship lies in our not talking about direct business issues that affect our lives."

The Velvet Mafia, as it's often called, is a loosely organized, interlocking set of pals who are gay or gay friendly and it includes not only the people mentioned but also the painter Ross Bleckner and the top Hollywood agent Sandy Gallin as well as the entirely endearing Diane von Furstenberg, Diller's wife. Not everyone—not even all gay people—admire the group. Articles about the group's bratty behavior are frequently published in glossy magazines. But my impression of Geffen, at least, is that he isn't temperamental at all. On the contrary, he seems programmed at all times for success. He makes very few unnecessary gestures, he responds to elaborate questions with one-sentence answers and he knows exactly what he feels on every subject that interests him ("Can I tell you what I think of him?" he said of a mutual acquaintance. "He's a shit. I despise him"). Oddly enough, the one subject that doesn't much interest him is himself. He's curious about what's happened to people he hasn't seen in twenty years. He has precise, up-to-date information on all his subjects, from AIDS treatment to national politics. But he has none of that excited, preening self-regard that most successful men and women lavish on themselves (for that matter, the unsuccessful are just as self-regarding, though they usually have a harder time finding a sympathetic audience).

Perhaps his indifference arises from boredom; after all, he has spent years studying himself. He admits to having been miserable as a young man: "Were you confused about sex?" "Sure." "Hated yourself?" "All of it." "Not handsome enough?" "All of it, all of it." But for twenty years he went to a Freudian and then a Jungian shrink, both of them in Los Angeles, and since then he's done Est, the Course in Miracles, Life Spring. "It's been a lot of work. I was unhappy when I was young. Everything bothered me. I feel very good that I've confronted all my demons." And now? "I'm a happy guy." He added, "Look, if all those things can improve your life even one percent, they're worth all the time you invest."

One of the "demons" he learned to ignore was the negative voice that he thinks is always rattling on in everyone's head. He told me that he'd dropped one of his friends because he felt that that person always addressed his dark side. "One lives with a dark voice in one's head. It never goes away, no matter how much therapy one has. But I've learned I'm not in my voice. It's going on but I'm not listening to it. I just don't plug into it. When I was younger I thought I was Jiminy Cricket."

One of the things he learned was to take his life one day at a time and never worry about the future. When I asked him what he imagined he'd be doing three years from now, he said, with that falling cadence that brooks no contradiction and invites no further discussion, "I don't think about three years from now."

Nor does he dwell much on the past. A *Wall Street Journal* reporter (now deceased) named Thomas R. King wrote Geffen's biography. King astonished and even dismayed his subject by discovering important events in his past that Geffen couldn't recall at all. For instance, King found out that as early as 1967 Geffen had made a lot of money buying stock in a record company, yet Geffen has no independent recollection of that.

When I asked Geffen if it had given him the creeps to have someone following him around writing his biography, he said, "To have a biography written at all is not a choice I would have made, but I was persuaded that if King didn't do it I'd get someone I'd like far less. I'd end up with a schmuck as a biographer talking about which bartender I fucked, which is the least interesting part of my life. The details of my sex life—it doesn't disturb me how much people know, but it doesn't speak to who I am."

In the past, to put off potential biographers, Geffen would say that he was writing his memoirs. But in fact he's far too discreet to take up such a project. When I told him in an aside that I don't feel an experience that has happened to me is quite real until I've told someone, he said, "I don't feel like that. I can keep a secret. It's not that I'm secretive—I'm very willing to talk about anything that's going on in my life as long as it's not exposing a third person. I remember when I read Elia Kazan's autobiography I was offended that he wrote at the beginning that he was not going to talk about people who were still living—and then he said right afterwards that he'd fucked Marilyn Monroe on the day she got engaged to Joe DiMaggio. I thought, But DiMaggio is still alive. Of course Kazan couldn't resist talking about fucking Marilyn Monroe—and who gives a damn if that would clearly hurt DiMaggio? As for me, I'll never write a book—I wouldn't want to expose secrets or breach confidences."

Geffen's sexuality certainly has provoked endless gossip, from the stories of his reputedly setting out to seduce straight men to his supposed penchant for bartenders—all the way up to that classic of urban folklore, the utterly mythical "marriage" to Keanu Reeves (whom Geffen scarcely knows).

When I tried to pin Geffen down, he was neither evasive nor particularly enlightening, though he said that he had his first gay experience when he was just eleven years old with another kid—"But it never occurred to me I was gay." For a long time after that he was dating girls, thinking about girls and wanting girls. In fact, Geffen might be described as someone who lived as a genuine bisexual for years before tipping towards homosexuality. When I asked him, very crudely, whether he'd thought of men or women when he was masturbating as a teenager, he said, instantly and without the slightest quaver of doubt, "Both."

He went on to develop a strangely culinary metaphor of his own. "You don't eat the same food every day and very often I try things I've never eaten before because I'm curious about what they'll taste like. That's been true of both food and sex. I never knew how much I'd love caviar until the first time I tried it. Before I ate it, the idea of it was offensive to me. But then Tony Perkins insisted I try it at the Russian Tea Room and after the first bite I was immediately addicted to it for the rest of my life."

The addiction, in fact, was less immediate in his sexual tastes. Until 1975, when Geffen was thirty-two, he'd lived with women and had sex with women—and only occasionally had he had adventures with men. His most famous affairs were with Cher (whom he met in 1973) and Marlo Thomas. "I lived with Cher for two years and with Marlo for two years. I was madly in love with Cher, even though I'd been living fifty percent of the time before her as a gay man. She knew everything about me because I told her. That didn't stop me from falling in love with her and being wildly sexually attracted to her and devastated when we broke up." When their love affair was over, Cher wounded him all the more by telling *Time* magazine, in response to a question about leaving Sonny for Geffen, "I traded one short ugly man for another."

In 1975 he discovered he had a tumor on his bladder and quit the entertainment business, collected art and Tiffany lamps, bought real estate—and partied a lot. Almost every night he went out clubbing. He also had lots of sex with men. "I never thought I was going to die; I really thought I might have to wear the bag. And I said to myself that if that's the case then I want to have as much sex as possible before the event." When he found out that the tumor had been misdiagnosed and was in fact benign, he went right back to work. Except that now he'd decided he'd no longer do what he thought he should do; now he was going to satisfy himself, and he had to admit that he derived more pleasure from men.

"Although very frankly," Geffen added, "once in a while I'm in a situation where I end up having sex with a woman because she wants to and I think, Try it, I can try this—and it feels good and it really is no big deal for me." He thought for a moment, then added in a louder voice, that insistent voice of people who've learned to put honesty above all else, "Having said that, I don't think—before, during or after sex with a woman—that I'm straight. These are not issues that I'm dealing with in my head."

Unlike someone who must reinvent himself everyday, Geffen relies on tried and true verbal formulas that he's learned or worked out, formulas that depend on words and expressions such as "These are not my issues," "It's the dark voice in my head," "You don't get a vote in this," "Your nature is revealed to you in time," "I can live with that," "I take it a day at a time," "I get it" and "I don't have a problem with that." He's constantly opening his hands in a revelatory gesture that suggests, "Look, my life is an open book," or perhaps, "It's really terribly simple." Strangely, it's not true, since everything he says is censored or at least veiled. For him to submit to an interview must be vaguely threatening, because Geffen is definitely a control freak and he wants to make sure he's not giving away too much. When I said, "You take care of everyone else—who takes care of you?" he didn't seem to understand the question. He thought I was wondering who was capable of telling him the truth. "I have many good friends," he said. "If I needed a reality check, there are people I can call who are very honest. I invite the truth and I offer the truth in return."

"Yeah, but," I objected, "don't you have anyone you check in with? You live alone. If you go to the dentist, say, isn't there anyone you could tell?"

He looked completely puzzled by the idea of checking in with someone. He said, "I wouldn't make a big thing out of going to the dentist."

"Yeah, but who takes care of you?"

"I take care of me."

That sounded very lonely. Of course in his own view, everything is much less complicated. "I'm not secretive, but I know how to keep a secret," is his last word on the matter.

In fact, his personality marks that awkward point where art meets business, for if art is based on sympathy (compassion and understanding and above all empathy, a readiness to plumb one's own feelings, even the vaguest, and to divine other people's sentiments, even the most transgressive), then business is, more brutally, all about knowing when to cut one's losses, when to shut down the film if it's running over budget, how to fire a friend and how to distinguish between one's own taste and one's judgment about what will sell. Typically, Geffen listens to Mozart at home but in his car plays tapes of the latest pop groups; Mozart appeals to his taste but second-guessing what new pop music will hit the charts is proof of his business acumen. When I asked him if he was ever afraid that age or isolation would cut him off from the latest trends, he said, "No. I don't feel cut off from things. I'm not twenty years old anymore but I feel I still know what young people like." He talked about the rap group Roots, which records on the Geffen label, as well as about his early signing up of the Broadway musical *Rent*, the update of Puccini's *La Bohème*.

I wondered out loud why we know the names of the women in his life, Cher and Marlo Thomas, but not those of the men. Again, with his cautious good judgment, he said, "It's not appropriate for me to mention their names if I don't know how their parents would feel about it—or their current lovers. I don't want to be capricious or cavalier with other people's lives. With Cher and Marlo I had famous relationships that have been written about and documented in photos, but my relationships with men are not nearly so celebrated. Then again, if an ex-lover wants to mention that we had an affair, I have no problem with that. Don't you think that's appropriate?"

When I asked Geffen if he felt under any obligation to make gay-themed films, he said, "I don't make movies with that in mind. I make movies because they appeal to me or because I think they're going to be successful. Movies are very expensive and I think one should enter the realm of investing other people's money with the idea they're going to get their money back."

In fact Geffen has been criticized in the gay community for not having made any gay films except *Personal Best,* which was about two lesbians, and *Interview with a Vampire,* which appealed to gay audiences (just as the book appealed to gay readers), although the "gay themes" amounted to nothing more than the promise of frozen time and eternal youth and the AIDS-related idea that an intimate act (unsafe sex, or sucking blood, as the case might be) can kill. A well-known tale about *Personal Best* has it that Geffen discovered one day that he had become the sole producer of an arty film that had originally been slated to come in at $7.5 million but that eventually cost twice that amount. "In order to do something with the movie," Geffen told an interviewer, "I went to Steve Ross and said, 'Help! I want you to buy this film from me.' He said, 'Do you think it's a hit?' I said, 'No, I don't.' He said, 'Why should I buy it from you?' I said, 'Look, if you buy this film from me and it flops, it will be just another flop picture; you have many of them. But if I don't sell this to you, it will obsess my life. I'll lose a fortune. I won't be able to work.'" Ross agreed to take the film off Geffen's hands if Geffen would sign a five-year contract setting up his own business with backing from Steve Ross's Warner Brothers Pictures. Geffen agreed—and the first film he made under the new deal was *Risky Business,* from which Warner's made a profit of more than $20 million.

But *Personal Best* remains one of the few Geffen projects that lost money, and it may have made him wary of gay movies. To be honest, gays constitute a very small part of the population, and if anything they are overrepresented as subjects in the arts and the media, probably because homosexuality still intrigues the public and serves as a way of discussing the hot topics of gender and sexuality in general. But Geffen has always held that experiments and off-beat ideas are easier to realize in musical recordings than in the cinema, since movies take so long and cost so much to make. He concludes the subject rather ferociously, "I don't have to make gay movies because I'm a gay man—nor do I think I should make ones that are heterosexually oriented because I'm a gay man. It's not an issue in my head. Because I'm a gay man I'm going to have sex with men—and nothing else can be concluded from that."

Geffen insists that he's never experienced homophobia in his own life. "There might be people who don't like me because I'm gay, but I don't know about it—and I don't care. Anyway, if people are homophobic, it doesn't affect me. People are afraid of everything—there are even people afraid of the water—but that reveals something about them, not about me. I'm not looking for anybody's approval. I approve of myself. I don't mean that in an arrogant sense. I have to approve of myself, first of all. It would be nice if you approve as well but if you don't, what can I do about it? I'm just presenting myself as I am. I've done what I wanted to do in my life. Frankly, I think a lot of gay people use this issue of homophobia as an excuse for not realizing their ambitions. I'm unwilling to say I can't do something because someone else won't let me."

Despite all this brave talk, Geffen admits that he would never have chosen to be gay. "If I could have had a vote, why would I have chosen to put myself through all this stuff?"

Nevertheless, he's happy to serve as a role model to young gay people. He receives letters from many gay youngsters, who are grateful to him for setting them an example. He was glad that young gays knew that he, Geffen, was often invited to the Clinton White House. "Since I'm a role model for young gays," Geffen says, "there are some things I'd never do in public, which is a burden, but that comes with the territory. I never go into bars or discos—it's not appropriate for me to meet people that way, it's not something I'd feel good about. After all, I'm over fifty, I'm not going to stand around a bar with my Perrier. I know exactly who I am and what I look like. I'm not everyone's cup of tea, but I get it all completely. I know that like everyone else I have my fans, but not as many fans as someone else, perhaps. The other night at a dinner I was attracted to a young guy because he was artistic and sensitive, but he made it very clear that I was much too old for him. I wasn't hurt or insulted."

I asked Geffen's friend Ross Bleckner if he'd observed Geffen on the make. He said that he'd spent time with Geffen at his house in the Pines on Fire Island, the gay resort off Long Island. "But he's a serious guy. Sure, there were boys floating in and out of the house during the day, but at night Geffen would rather curl up with a good book."

"But aren't there a lot of guys after those billions?"

"Of course, but Geffen is a very good judge of character. So am I. Aren't you? It doesn't take very long to figure out what someone is after.

Money of course is an attribute, and someone is attracted by the whole package, including wealth."

I asked Geffen whether it was hard for him to date. "It's uncomfortable for everyone," he said, "but...I date. I meet people by accident. Or at parties. Or at public functions. Sometimes I'm introduced by other friends of mine."

I asked him about his AIDS activism and fund-raising. "I've had so many friends who've died. In any case, HIV is a big fucking ten thousand pound guerilla in anyone's life. I've been fortunate, since I'm negative. But when I received the commitment for life award from the AIDS Project Los Angeles I looked out at all these people who'd suffered so much and that's when I decided to come out. I thought I can't pretend to be straight while addressing an audience like this. Of course I'd always been open with my associates and friends. But now I was saying it in public. Not that I think everyone should be outed or should bother to come out. I have a friend in a rock group who made a mistake by coming out, in my opinion."

Geffen shook his head and added, "When people I knew started dying of AIDS I couldn't bring myself to tear up their Rolodex cards, so I started saving them and I ended up with hundreds of cards with a big rubber band around them. And the last time the Quilt was on display in Washington I would walk past the panels and I'd see those of acquaintances whom I didn't even know had died—you know, you have lots of acquaintances from wherever, and here I was, coming across their panels, and it was very, very disturbing."

For many years Geffen has given money to AIDS charities, but his efforts intensified in 1990 when he sold his record company. At that point he retained control of the part of his enterprise that produced Broadway shows and movies. He decided to donate his $600,000 annual salary as well as all his stage and screen profits to his foundation. "I have enough money," he said, "and I don't need to be accumulating any more—although as it turned out I made more money anyway because money makes money." His foundation has not only lavished money on AIDS organizations; he's also contributed money to the "temporary contemporary" wing of the Museum of Contemporary Art in Los Angeles and to the city's Geffen Playhouse.

I asked him if he thought the theater might develop new writing talent—the principal ingredient he finds lacking in today's movies.

"Maybe," he said dubiously. "I think writers develop themselves. I think we're all figments of our own imagination. We invent ourselves. We have a vision of ourselves and it takes us where it will take us. There may be a normal course for doing ordinary things, but there's no normal course for doing extraordinary things. Very often your destiny is beyond your ability to imagine it. I certainly never had an idea that I'd ever be a very wealthy, successful and accomplished person. But I was very happy doing whatever I was doing. I graduated in the lowest ten percent of my high school and I never thought I'd accomplish anything—nor did anyone who knew me."

His first big break, working in the mailroom of the William Morris Agency, was an accident. He'd been a receptionist for a television show called *The Reporter* and was fired (some people say for having been too pushy). He talked to Alice Lord, the casting director on the show, and asked her what he should do. She asked him what he was good at. He said, "I don't think I'm good at anything. I don't have an education or any skills." She replied, "You should be an agent. Agents don't have to know anything." Alice Lord made Geffen an appointment at William Morris— and the rest is history. It was at the big Manhattan agency, which handled movies, plays and books, that Geffen met Barry Diller, who was also in the mailroom. Geffen lied on his application, saying he'd been graduated from UCLA. When the letter arrived from the university denying that he'd been a student, Geffen steamed it open and slipped in a forged transcript.

He listened to agents' conversations on the phone and said to himself, "I can do that." Soon he was a secretary to an agent, then an assistant— and before long he was signing on new talent.

His mother had always been his biggest fan. Although he had a brother ten years older than he (who became a lawyer in Los Angeles), it was David whom his mother referred to as "King David." She was a survivor. As Geffen puts it, "Mother went through the worst part of the twentieth century. She was born in the Ukraine. Her family sent her to Romania to get an education. While she was there the Russian Revolution broke out, she had no papers, so she literally never saw her family again. She lived as an orphan although she had nine brothers and sisters. She immigrated to Palestine, where she met my father, and together they moved to America— at the worst possible time, since it was during the Depression."

But she was an optimistic person and she was soon making corsets in their two-room apartment in Brooklyn. Little David would overhear her schmoozing and wheeling and dealing—from her he learned everything about business and people. His father was a dreamer, a great reader—and not much of a worker. The mother, however, fell into a terrible despondency when she received a letter that told her that anti-Semites in their village in the Ukraine had thrown her entire family down a well just as the Nazis were marching in. The approach of the German army released all the latent hate of the villagers.

"But during the last conversation I had with her," Geffen recalls, "she was recovering nicely from a very serious stroke. She could still talk and I asked her what she attributed her miraculous recovery to and she said, 'I recovered because I have no envy, no jealousy and no hate.' For someone to have lived through a revolution, exile, the Depression and the slaughter of her entire family and still have no hate—well, that's a remarkable thing." Shortly before she died she asked her son how much he was worth. When he mentioned the fabulous, unimaginable sum, she just laughed.

Elton John

ELTON JOHN'S HOUSE IN WINDSOR (which looks out towards the Queen's castle) is almost suffocating under the odor of tuberoses. It's a heavy, funeral parlor smell wafting up from the French scented candles that he has lit in every room even at midday. It's all part of his new class act now that he's clean and sober and has hitched up with a nice Canadian film-maker and has just spent several years and enormous expense converting his English estate, Woodside, from what he described as a typical rock 'n' roller's pad, complete with pinball machines and juke boxes, into a stately home filled with miles of parquet floors, paintings by Gainsborough and Venetian masters and lots of Meissen china, the kind your grandmother would have if she were rich and tasteful. Anyway, by all rights it should be a stately home—after all, it was built in 1066, it has two lakes, thirty-seven acres of grounds, a white garden and an Italian garden designed by the former head of the Victoria and Albert Museum. It even, reputedly, has a ghost, though Elton has never seen it. In the living room there are huge, overstuffed sofas groaning under tapestried pillows, a gas fire under fake logs, a staff of five tiptoing about including a butler with a Cockney accent wearing striped trousers but no cutaway jacket or white gloves. His name is George and he and Elton are on a first-name basis.

Elton gave me a tour of Woodside, pointing out the statues of Roman emperors, the acres of painted boyflesh in the canvases by Victorian pedophile Henry Scott Tukes, the wooden bedstead created for him by the Viscount Linley, showing me the Princess Bedroom ("This is where you'll stay, dear"), drawing my attention to photos of himself in drag ("My Audrey Hepburn look") and with the *Absolutely Fabulous* cast. He is especially proud of his paper shredder in which he inserts hate mail sent by religious bigots. From an upstairs window we can see a new artificial lake that contains three million gallons of water.

You gotta like Elton, he's so warm and well-spoken and shy and eager to please. You've even got to like his hair, every fiber of which represents a mega-investment of money, technology and will power. The other day I sat next to a Croatian woman from Los Angeles on the plane who'd been a doctor back in Sarajevo but who has now just completed a hair transplant course in Paris and even she used him as her best selling point: "We're the group that did Elton's hair," she said with triumphant modesty. Elton's hair has become a point of reference even in the Balkans, for Chrissake.

You could picture Elton as a tireless consumer, if you like. He shells out hundreds of thousands of dollars buying his clothes and glasses—so many that he has to auction them off regularly to benefit his AIDS foundation. He's the ultimate shopper—for Old Master paintings, high heels, photos. In his house he has a room the size of a small Tower Records store lined with thousands of CDs, all alphabetized with what he calls his "anal retentive" compulsiveness. Next to it is an even larger video library with shelves that glide on wheels to give access to other, hidden shelves. His book library is two stories tall and stocked with biographies and art books, all focussed around a large self-portrait by scary English expressionist Francis Bacon ("I always thought it was a picture of me, broken and small," Elton confides). In his Atlanta apartment, he has so many pictures of naked men by the world's greatest photographers, including Greg Gorman, Herb Ritz and Robert Mapplethorpe, that his mother asked him, "Do you buy these by the dozen, darling?"

"Of course," as Elton adds, "there are pictures of women as well. But I do like a nice naked man, don't you, love? That's going to be the title of my next book: I Do Like a Nice Naked Man."

You could just as easily see him as a giver. In his old cocaine-snorting days he liked to pick up boys and "Eltonize" them—that is, give them clothes, jewels, hopes and aspirations. "If you want to have a great orgasm, take cocaine," Elton declares flatly. "I'd walk into a bar and see a guy and have the wedding planned and the complete relationship worked out before we'd even said hello. That's over. I spent enough time on cocaine talking about how to save the world and please take your underpants off. If I was still taking drugs I'd be trying to get you in the hot-tub."

"How many people can you sleep in this place?" I asked.

"Fourteen, if they're couples. But we've got a room with a single bed if someone's having a spat."

He looks great—pink-cheeked, unlined, galvanized with energy, with his small, chubby hands, lop-sided smile and just a bit of shaved chest visible under his squishy-sounding black track suit trimmed in green. He has a funny, knock-kneed way of walking, almost as though he's a wind-up doll which has been overwound and sent heading for the top of the stairs—there's something reckless and unreflecting and determined about every movement he makes.

He has an AA way of talking positively about himself and about his work and though he's sent letters to everyone apologizing for his past mistakes he's "a very tomorrow kind of person" as he puts it. "No looking back." What was new for me was his way of grafting an American-style twelve-step rap onto a nice English middle-class manner, for he is well-brought up and self-mocking, always quick to take the piss out of himself. He seldom lets the conversation wander from himself, but he is interested in the people around him and does ask questions. He is at home at Woodside, but the whole place looks like an oversize stage set version of English country life—which only makes sense, since he says that the stage is "the only place I feel safe." Like so many performers he's shy but constantly daring himself to be extraverted. AA attempts to deflate the ego, but although Elton has picked up the lingo—and achieved sobriety—he's turned the whole act into just another way of grandstanding. But if he's full of himself, he's also an affectionate man, touching in his desire to please, camp in the old English way, clever and cultured and experienced.

Reginald Kenneth Dwight, the future Elton, was born in a public housing apartment belonging to his grandparents in a London suburb on March 25, 1947. His mother wanted a girl and for a while baby Reggie had all the golden curls she might have fancied and that Elton would pine after years later. His father was a flight-lieutenant in the Royal Air Force who was seldom at home and his grandfather left the rearing of the prodigy to the child's mother and grandmother. "I don't think your father liked you," Elton's mother, Sheila, declared flatly not long ago. He certainly was a prodigy—by the time he was three he could hear a piece of music and play it on the piano. When he was eleven he won a four-year scholarship to study piano at the Royal Academy of Music.

"I never had fabulous sexual interludes as a child," Elton tells me. "At all my AA meetings and when I saw my shrink in Atlanta people were always asking me if I was ever molested as a child. I told my shrink, 'I was dying to be molested,' and he said, 'No one has ever said that to me before.' " Maybe Reg was neglected by pedophiles because he was more than a mouthful. His biographer, Philip Norman, writes: "A school photograph, taken when he was about thirteen, shows a boy no longer just chubby or plump, but unequivocally fat, his hair mousy dark, his round pug face resignedly studious in half-frame glasses."

He was a quiet boy, obsessively collecting his records which he would never lend to friends—they might soil the sleeve or scratch something! He loved Little Richard and Jerry Lee Lewis because they were outrageous. "I hated classical music as a kid," Elton tells me, "since I had to have lessons, Monday to Friday, had to go to the Royal Academy of Music on Saturday. Then when I did my homework on Sunday it didn't leave me much time for socializing, did it? The only classical music I liked was what we sang in the choir at the Royal Academy."

He listened to a lot of radio, which he feels stimulated his imagination, especially radio plays with all their eerie sound effects. He spent most of his free time alone in his room cataloguing and listening to his records. His only outings for fun were to attend football matches, especially those of his local Watford team; soccer was the only interest he shared with his remote father. The word *homosexual* was never even mentioned in Britain in the 1950s; the only person he ever heard of who was gay was a radio comic, the ultra-sophisticated Kenneth Williams. "The first gay person I saw on TV was a hero of mine, Liberace. Of course Liberace never said he was gay—he didn't have to, did he, dear? Oh, my mother and I loved that glamorous side of America that we saw in the early days of TV, all those dancers and fountains on the Perry Como show and the Andy Williams show. And Liberace's glamor—my mother was enthralled! He was what every straight person wants to think gay people are like—so camp, not at all threatening.

Much later, in 1972 or so, I did the Royal Variety Show with Liberace. We shared a dressing room. I thought, God, I'd better make an effort. I had two fabulous lurex suits run up. Then he wheeled in trunk after trunk, including a suit covered with electric lightbulbs. I knew I was outclassed. How could he play the piano with all those rings on? Maybe that's why he missed some of the notes—he had fun. He said, 'Fuck you' to everyone."

Before he got to co-star with Liberace, however, Reg had to pass through a lot of stages. By the time he was fifteen he was playing the piano and singing in local pubs, mainly Ray Charles ballads. Before Reg finished high school his cousin, a famous soccer player, arranged through a pal for Reg to get a menial job with a music company. Once he was in the pop milieu, Reg was quick to join a band called Bluesology. The year was 1965 and in the post-Beatles rush it was easy for almost any English group to put together a demo and a few club dates. Though he was roly-poly and dressed in a tweed jacket and called every older man "Sir," it was little Reg who could sing and play and who, even then, had learned to kick away the piano stool and sit on the floor—anything to make an impression.

Americans knew nothing about Bluesology, whose singles were released between 1965 and 1967 in England only. Nor did we know anything about the newly renamed Elton John's first solo singles in England recorded between 1968 and 1971. He emerged here only in 1971 at the time he'd recorded his hit single "Your Song" and had come over to promote the album; his first date was at the 300-seat Troubadour in Los Angeles, a folkie venue. According to an article written at the time, "Elton's performance was one of the great opening nights in Los Angeles rock." Everytime he played a cut off the album the audience broke into applause. "They clapped at the start! I couldn't fuckin' believe it," Elton declared the next day. "That never happens in England. People over here are ridiculous."

Soon Elton was so exhilarated by his American triumph that he'd overcome his shyness and reluctance to perform live. As *Rolling Stone* reported at the time, in Santa Monica two months later, "During 'Burn Down the Mission,' Elton kicked away the piano stool, ripped off his jumpsuit and finished with a series of giant bunny kicks in purple pantyhose. The crowd, to use Elton's term, went mental."

A tune like "Your Song" struck Americans as mellow and sweet but not in the lugubrious, sedated Simon and Garfunkel style. It was distinct—nothing like Jefferson Airplane, Led Zeppelin and the Stones, who were all rockin' out. In fact he emerged in the vacuum created by the break-up of the Beatles in 1970; the introspective ballads of their vintage years obviously inspired him. What made him his own man, however, was his brilliant piano-playing, especially in "Rocket Man" in 1972 and "Goodbye Yellow Brick Road" in 1973.

His success also largely depended on an earlier event—Elton's collaboration with English lyricist Bernard Taupin, whom he had met in 1967. Whereas Elton was a composer who couldn't invent words, Taupin was a wordsmith without a tune in his head. Taupin's lyrics were individualistic and often rebellious: "You know you can't hold me forever/ I didn't sign up with you./ I'm not a present for your friends to open,/ This boy's too young to be singing the blues" ("Goodbye Yellow Brick Road"). These searching words, combined with Elton's plain looks and outrageous outfits, said to his public (even then), "I do whatever I want, and so should you."

At first Bernie and Elton were roommates. "I had a crush on Bernie," Elton confides. "He was like the brother I never had. Of course there was no sex—Bernie's straight—but he was so shy and I became very attached. In fact he was the first person I ever fell in love with. Now he's a cowboy on his own ranch in Santa Barbara, he's living with his third wife, he has two stepdaughters—and he's never been so happy. We phone each other from time to time, but he just faxes me his new lyrics."

Elton met his first lover after three years of unrequited love with Bernie. It was in August 1970 and Elton had just scored his Troubadour triumph and was playing in San Francisco when he ran into John Reid, a twenty-year-old English bloke who represented Motown in Britain. Elton was ecstatic with his recent reviews and just had to share the news with a fellow Brit. "I didn't have sex until I was twenty-three," Elton admits. "And then it didn't stop. John Reid was the first. He was in San Francisco on a Motown convention and I was on tour. We had an early dinner and I said to myself, 'If it's ever going to happen it's going to happen now.' I'd known him before in London and I thought he was very attractive. We lived together for five years, but in the end he was more unfaithful than I liked. I'm even worse now that I'm sober—very picket fence, dear. He became my manager. Almost all the people around me are men and women I've worked with for twenty years or more."

When Elton began to live with John Reid in London, Elton's mother never blinked twice. In fact after she divorced Elton's father and took up with a new man friend, "Derf" Farebrother (whom she married before long), it was Derf who decorated Elton's and John's new place and it was Sheila who received the press and posed for the photographers. She seemed to accept Reid wholeheartedly, although biographer Philip Norman mentions, "Only the closest members of Elton's circle ever detected a faint note of ambivalence in her attitude. 'For Christmas, she always used to give John an electric carving knife,' a former Rocket Records employee says. 'I used to wonder if there was any significance in that.' "

In his early glory days Elton, who'd always been a fan at heart, got a chance to meet the legendary stars of earlier generations. "I've met everybody—I had tea with Mae West twice," Elton exclaims, lighting up. "She had a fabulous Hollywood apartment with a butler, everything white—white piano, white carpet—and we ate carrot cake together. Then I met Groucho Marx when he was an old man. He had a fire going in the middle of the summer and sat there in his overcoat, freezing. We were all sweltering. He pretended he couldn't grasp my name—he was just winding me up. When he signed his autobiography for me he wrote, 'To John Elton from Marx Groucho.' " In 1976, just before Elvis died, Elton went backstage and saw the King in his dressing room, fat, disoriented, black hair dye running down his face, surrounded by Memphis Mafia. It was a chilling vision and a warning.

Elton had always been a soccer fan, and his happiest moment ever came in 1974 when he took over as the director of the Watford Football Club. "That was the team I supported as a kid," Elton says. "I used to go to matches with my father. In 1974 I had green hair and huge platform shoes and the men probably laughed behind my back, but they were nice to my face. Everyone knew I was gay anyway. People would chant, rather good-naturedly, 'Don't sit down while Elton's around or you'll get a penis up your arse.' "

In fact Elton came out as a bisexual in the pages of *Rolling Stone* in 1976, despite the warnings of John Reid (who was no longer his lover) and of his own mother. She also begged him to be less camp around the Watford team. Wasted words, since the widely reported *Rolling Stone* revelations caused rival supporters to label the Watford players "poofters" and once to chant for twenty minutes, "Elton John's a homosexual" to the tune of "John Brown's Body."

"Even so," Elton tells me, "I had a lot of success as chairman. I hired a brilliant young man, Graham Taylor, as manager and he brought us up from the fourth division to the first in just five years and qualified us for European competition. Quite a fairy tale. It was fun being a gay man and as chairman of a football team having the right to go into the changing rooms. Of course it makes it easier if you're an artist—that's acceptable in England. After all, we have a great vaudeville tradition behind us and in Christmas pantomimes all the male roles are played by women and vice versa. Just last year I played Albert Hall in a Versace gown and sang 'There is Nothing Like a Dame' and 'I'm in Love with a Wonderful Guy'—all in five-inch heels. Three days later I couldn't walk." He also posed for the London *Sunday Times Magazine* in Versace's new collection.

After he broke up with John Reid, Elton began to slide into drugs—especially marijuana and cocaine—and on tour he'd run through bag after bag in his hotel room watching porno videos. "With coke you get rid of so many inhibitions," Elton remarks, "but on stage, it's no good for performing. You have a hundred thoughts in a minute, but other people can't follow you. And then when I'd come down I'd be a complete monster."

Before 1976, Elton had produced enough hits to last a lifetime. In four years of feverish activity, he accumulated the musical capital that he's been able to draw on during his long career. But despite his artistic drive and repeated triumphs, he was beginning to take bigger and bigger risks with his talent, his mental health—and even his life. In November 1975, during "Elton John Week" in Los Angeles, he became violently depressed, despite the fact he was singing to sold-out concerts every night at Dodger Stadium and living in the old David Selznick mansion in the Hollywood Hills. In front of his relations he swallowed sixty Valiums. "I jumped into the pool in front of my mother and my seventy-five-year-old grandmother, screaming, 'I'm going to die!' I always remember that, as they pulled me out, I heard my gran say, 'I suppose we've all got to go home now.' "

Despite the sad clowning, Elton was genuinely unhappy and over the next decade he estranged everyone including his mother, who finally gave up on him in the mid-'80s and left England with Derf to live in Minorca. In the recent tell-all documentary *Tantrums and Tiaras*, Elton's mother began to weep while recalling those difficult days. Elton was addicted to cocaine for twenty years and at a certain point even began to have seizures.

He could still compose as effortlessly as ever, but as his mood darkened his sound became relentlessly vanilla and his costumes more and more outrageous as if to conceal the inner dread. He pranced around the stage in a duck suit or a Tina Turner gown or an Ali Baba turban or a Mozart wig and beauty spot. He launched into many high-profile activities. He became friendly with members of the Royal Family. He breached the Iron Curtain to become the first pop star of the West to be invited to the Soviet Union. He toured China as well and now came to seem as much an ambassador as a performer.

And he got married to his tape operator, a German woman in her late twenties named Renate Blauel. When I asked him if he'd married to quiet rumors, he pointed out that he'd already come out as a bisexual seven years earlier. "No, I got married because I was desperately unhappy. I thought my life would change. And we did have some great times together and our sex life was good, but I was just fooling myself. It's impossible to have a good relationship when you're a drug addict." Over the next three years Renate appeared less and less frequently in public and before long the divorce was announced. Although the separation was amicable and dignified, Elton still has the nagging feeling that the one person in his life to whom he has not made amends, AA-style, is Renate, but she won't communicate with him.

A sign that there was still plenty of fight left in Elton, however, came in 1988 when the singer sued England's mud-slinging tabloid paper *The Sun* for falsely claiming that he'd attended a five-day cocaine and rent-boy orgy. Although the battle got very bloody and *The Sun* paid some greedy hustlers to testify falsely against him, Elton stuck to his guns, won a million pounds (the largest libel settlement in British history)—and forced the paper to print a banner headline retracting their allegations: "SORRY ELTON."

A young American lover, Hugh Williams, convinced Elton to join him in detox, but all except one clinic turned him down because he was cross-addicted (sex, food, drugs, booze—and of course shopping!). Finally the Parkside Lutheran Hospital in Chicago took him on. Elton the Magnificent, who lives on 14 million pounds a year, was reduced to sleeping in an army-style bed, sharing a room and washing his own clothes. "They pointed out that I couldn't do anything for myself such as drive or shop for food; suddenly, during treatment, I was on my own. I had to become self-sufficient."

Now everything is looking up. Elton met the love of his life, Canadian-born David Furnish, on October 30, 1993, and he's clean and sober. Elton went public with their relationship only at the Oscars in 1995; when he and lyricist Tim Rice received an Academy Award for the song "Can You Feel the Love Tonight" from Disney's *The Lion King,* Elton kissed David and then, from the stage, thanked his lover for his support.

Elton feels that he wasted so many years with druggies and layabouts that now he and David are eager to cultivate intelligent, creative people. When I saw Elton they had just returned from Paris where they'd dined with Karl Lagerfeld, the couturier and head of Chanel. "Karl paints, takes photos, designs clothes, knows everything. Even though he's a German aristocrat he's never relied on his family. He's gone out and done things on his own." Versace was another of his great pals.

David, who is fifteen years younger, was a highly paid executive at the London office of the advertising firm of Ogilvy and Mather when he met Elton. So many of Elton's friends had died of AIDS or moved away that he no longer knew many people in London; he asked a friend to invite a few amusing guys to dinner and among them was David. The very next night they had a date and ordered in a Chinese meal—and the rest is history.

At first David, who quit his job after a year in order to spend more time with Elton, was a bit lost. "He was used to driving to work and having an identity of his own," Elton confides. "Suddenly he had too much time on his hands and felt like an accessory. But he'd always wanted to make movies—and after a couple of 16 mm shorts his very first documentary was *Tantrums and Tiaras.* My management didn't want him to do the documentary, they were afraid it would be damaging and when they saw it they had lots of trouble with it. It is outrageous, but I'm so fed up with a documentary in which everyone comes out as sweetness and light. I want one where people will say, 'She was an absolute cow.' I have to be honest now. I can't be deceitful. This is the first time I'm able to look at myself on screen without feeling uncomfortable. David followed me around for a whole year and he caught me in the midst of two terrible tantrums. In one I was in a snit over a video. I'm not very good about the way I look. You know, you always want to be slimmer, taller, younger."

In the film Elton blows up when a flunkey arrives late with outfits for his new rock video. In another scene he hyperspaces into a terminal funk when a fan begins to wave and throws off his tennis game. During the course of the documentary he admits that travelling with hundreds of items of clothing is "obscene" but he says, "I find it comforting." Over the year he travels to fifteen countries and plays before one million people. He is irresistibly bitchy; for instance, at one point he wonders how "Miss Jagger" is able to give 236 interviews a year. He uses pseudonyms in hotels to protect his anonymity, including "Sir Colin Chihuahua" and "Sir Horace Pussy." He studies the top forty record charts obsessively.

Probably the most poignant moment occurs when the couple are at a luxurious hotel near Nice and Furnish asks Elton if he would ever consider going away without his driver, valet and tennis coach. "Probably, but.... No, I wouldn't enjoy it very much." When Furnish asks him if he'd consider lying by the pool or water-skiing or driving through the country or taking a moonlight walk, Elton replies that he might consider the walk, "But the other three are absolute no-nos." Later, when Furnish, behind the camera, asks Elton how he could get more balance into his life, the singer appears cornered, slightly frustrated and then looks straight at him and whispers gently, "Sshhh." At one point Furnish discusses Elton with the star's shrink, who says that Elton buys people with his love but also with expensive gifts. Elton exclaims: "You're talking about me like some fuckin' piece of soap powder."

Elton is as busy as ever. He's still a shopping addict and is always buying new treasures for their four residences—in Windsor, in London, in Nice and in Atlanta. "I love Atlanta, people leave me alone, I guess it's out of Southern politeness. I drive around and shop just like a regular person. I have normal friends, no one in show business, all my friends have normal jobs. When I'm on tour in America or Canada I can always fly home to Atlanta and sleep in my own bed. I started off with just one apartment in Atlanta but now I have five that I ran together so that I have 18,000 square feet altogether in which I can display my huge collections of black and white photos, mostly vintage. Atlanta has great galleries, it's civilized, and of course it's a very gay city." He was initially drawn to Atlanta by an American lover, the one who got him into detox and who has remained a friend.

Considering how promiscuous Elton was in the eighties, it's a miracle he's still negative and he's the first to recognize his good luck. And even after years of sobriety he recognizes how precarious it is. "I love promiscuity—but why should I sabotage my life? Every performer has that self-destruct element somewhere inside. I'd love to have a glass of red wine, but why should I destroy my whole life just for that? My career is still there, I have a great art collection, a fabulous relationship. But if I were to go and fuck one boy and take one line of coke or one drink my whole life would be in ruins." He gives a little smile. "I know I sound like *Thoroughly Modern Millie.*"

Versions of these essays were originally published in the following:

"Writing Gay": Hopwood Lecture, University of Michigan, April 16, 2002, and published in the issue of the *Michigan Quarterly Review,* summer 2002.

"The New Historical Novel": Lecture, University of Minnesota, 2003, and published in the *Times Literary Supplement,* July 25, 2003.

"George Eliot": *Times Literary Supplement,* January 18, 2002.

"Ivan Bunin": *Los Angeles Times Book Review,* June 20, 1999.

"Knut Hamsun": *The Review of Contemporary Fiction,* fall 1996.

"Marcel Proust": Prepared for Amazon.com, fall 1999.

"André Gide": *London Review of Books,* December 10, 1998.

"Oscar Wilde": Introduction to *The Picture of Dorian Gray,* Oxford University Press, 1999.

"Joe Orton": *Sunday Times* (London), November 23, 1986.

"Paul Bowles": Introduction to *Their Heads Are Green and Their Hands Are Blue*, Ecco Press, 2003.

"Allen Ginsberg": Introduction to *Spontaneous Mind: Selected Interviews, 1958–1996,* HarperCollins, 2001.

"Djuna Barnes": *Village Voice,* November 7, 1995.

"Marjorie Garber": *New Yorker,* July 17, 1995.

"Bruce Chatwin": *Times Literary Supplement,* February 14, 1997.

"Edwin Denby": *New York Times Book Review,* November 8, 1998.

"Coleman Dowell": From the catalogue of "Swan on the Balcony," an exhibition and reading at the Fales Collection of New York University, February 2003.

"Grace Paley": Introduction to her reading, Princeton University, fall 2002.

"Jean Genet": Introduction to *The Selected Writings of Jean Genet*, Ecco Press, 1993.

"Michel Foucault": *Vogue,* November 1984.

"Alain Robbe-Grillet": *Los Angeles Times Book Review,* August 26, 2001.

"James Merrill": *Village Voice,* February 21, 1995.

"Christopher Isherwood": Presented at the symposium "Christopher Isherwood: Private Faces," Huntington Library, Pasadena, California, December 2, 2000.

"Ned Rorem": Forward to *Lies: A Diary, 1986–1999,* Counterpoint, 2000.

"James Baldwin": *Washington Post Book World,* September 23, 1979.

"Vladimir Nabokov": *New York Review of Books,* March 29, 1984.

"Andy Warhol": *Savvy Woman,* October 1989.

"Gilbert and George": *London Review of Books,* July 1, 1999.

"Joe Brainard": *Art in America,* July 1997.

"Steve Wolfe": Catalogue for an exhibit at Luhring Augustine Gallery, fall 2003.

"Rebecca Horn": *Vogue,* January 1993.

"Cy Twombly": *Vanity Fair,* September 1994.

"Jasper Johns": *Vanity Fair,* September 1996.

"Herbert List": Essay in *Herbert List: The Monograph,* Monacelli Press, 2000.

"Robert Mapplethorpe": Essay in *Altars,* Random House, 1995.

"Yves Saint Laurent": *Sunday Times Magazine* (London), October 9, 1994.

"Catherine Deneuve": *Talk,* March 2000.

"David Geffen": *US,* April 1997.

"Elton John": *Rolling Stone,* July 10–24, 1997.

About the Author

EDMUND WHITE has written seventeen books, including a trilogy of autobiographical novels—*A Boy's Own Story, The Beautiful Room Is Empty* and *The Farewell Symphony*. His most recent novel is *Fanny: A Fiction*. Other novels include *Forgetting Elena, Nocturnes for the King of Naples, Caracole* and *The Married Man*. His collection of short stories is titled *Skinned Alive*. White won the National Book Critics Circle Award for his biography of Jean Genet. He has also written a short biography of Proust. He is a member of the American Academy of Arts and Letters and is the director of the creative writing program at Princeton University. He lives in New York City. Previously he lived in Paris for many years and is the author of *The Flâneur* and *Our Paris*.